Transfer State

Transfer State

The Idea of a Guaranteed Income and the Politics of Redistribution in Modern Britain

PETER SLOMAN

OXFORD
UNIVERSITY PRESS

OXFORD
UNIVERSITY PRESS

Great Clarendon Street, Oxford, OX2 6DP,
United Kingdom

Oxford University Press is a department of the University of Oxford.
It furthers the University's objective of excellence in research, scholarship,
and education by publishing worldwide. Oxford is a registered trade mark of
Oxford University Press in the UK and in certain other countries

First Edition published in 2019

Published in the United States of America by Oxford University Press
198 Madison Avenue, New York, NY 10016, United States of America

British Library Cataloguing in Publication Data
Data available

Library of Congress Control Number: 2019941470

ISBN 978–0–19–881326–2

DOI: 10.1093/oso/9780198813262.001.0001

Preface

The origins of this book go back more than a decade, to autumn 2007, when I took José Harris and Ben Jackson's special subject on 'War and Reconstruction' as an Oxford undergraduate. Juliet Rhys-Williams's pamphlet *Something to Look Forward To* (1943) was a set text for the paper, and I was struck by the way her vision of a 'new social contract' had been obscured—among historians as well as her contemporaries—by the development of Sir William Beveridge's social insurance system. After I finished my first book on *The Liberal Party and the Economy, 1929–1964* (2015), I set out to explore the tangled history of tax and benefit reform which lay behind Universal Credit and twenty-first-century basic income proposals. This book does not attempt to offer a total history of the UK welfare state. Rather, I hope it will illuminate a neglected dimension of British social thought, and help explain the enduring appeal of what Sir Alan Peacock once called the 'social market' tradition of welfare: providing an income floor for citizens through cash transfers.

I began research for this book at New College, Oxford, and completed it in the Department of Politics and International Studies (POLIS) and Churchill College in Cambridge, so I would like to thank my colleagues for making all three institutions such lively and supportive places to teach and write. I am particularly grateful to David Runciman and Jason Sharman at POLIS for encouraging this research, to Pieter van Houten and Glen Rangwala for helping me master the idiosyncrasies of the Cambridge system, and to Dame Athene Donald and the Fellowship at large for making me so welcome at Churchill College.

Daniel Zamora came to Cambridge as a visiting scholar in Michaelmas Term 2018 to work on his own book on the intellectual history of guaranteed income, and this project has been enriched by discussions with him. I am also indebted to Tom Kelsey, Stewart Lansley, Colm Murphy, Tony Orhnial, Felix Römer, and Malcolm Torry for reading and commenting on draft chapters, and to the five anonymous reviewers for Oxford University Press, who provided constructive feedback on the initial proposal and encouraged me to draw out the contemporary implications. Those errors and omissions which remain are, of course, my own. Dominic de Cogan, Stewart Lansley, Scott Lavery, Felix Römer, Walter van Trier, and Daniel Zamora generously shared unpublished work of their own with me and have allowed me to draw on it in what follows. Parts of the argument have been presented at seminars in Cambridge and Oxford and at three conferences: the Modern British Studies conference in Birmingham in July 2015, the Political Studies Association conference in Glasgow in April 2017, and the North American Conference on British Studies in Providence, RI, in October 2018, where Hugh Pemberton, Andrew Crines, and Andrew Seaton were cogent and insightful discussants. More generally, I am grateful for the comradeship and encouragement of my fellow historians, particularly Lise Butler, Aled Davies, Catherine Flinn, Ben Jackson, Gary Love, Jan Machielsen, and Jim Tomlinson.

One of the pleasures of writing contemporary history is the opportunity to talk to politicians, civil servants, and campaigners about their life and work, and I would like to thank my interviewees for being so generous with their time, whether on or off the record. I am also grateful to Philippe van Parijs and Walter van Trier for sharing their memories of the early basic income movement, to Anna Towlson at the LSE Archives for granting me advance access to Sir Tony Atkinson's papers, and to Adam Corlett for allowing me to use the Resolution Foundation's adjusted data series for child poverty in Figure 7.3. Thanks also to Katie Bishop and her team at OUP for their help during the publishing process, and to Munizha Ahmad-Cooke for her meticulous and professional work on the bibliography.

Some of the material in Chapters 3, 5, and 9 has previously appeared in the following journal articles: 'Beveridge's Rival: Juliet Rhys-Williams and the Campaign for Basic Income, 1942–1955', *Contemporary British History* 30/2 (June 2016); '"The Pragmatist's Solution to Poverty": The Heath Government's Tax Credit Scheme and the Politics of Social Policy in the 1970s', *Twentieth Century British History* 27/2 (June 2016); and 'Universal Basic Income in British Politics, 1918–2018', *Journal of Social Policy* 47/3 (July 2018). I thank Taylor and Francis, Oxford University Press, and Cambridge University Press for allowing me to reproduce this material.

I am grateful to the following institutions and individuals for permission to quote from unpublished works in which they hold or administer the copyright: Elspeth Chowdharay-Best; Churchill Archives Centre, Cambridge; the Confederation of British Industry; the Conservative Party; Henry and Joe Harrod; the Institute of Economic Affairs; King's College, Cambridge; Cherry Lewis; the National Council for Voluntary Organisations; Ann Oakley; Lorna Parker; Chris Pond; Sir Gareth Rhys-Williams; Verena Schumacher; the Trades Union Congress; and Viscount Waverley. The Borthwick Institute for Archives at the University of York, the Hoover Institution Archives at Stanford University, the

Labour History Archive and Study Centre in Manchester, and the Special Collections at the University of Essex also granted me permission to quote from works in their possession. Crown Copyright material is reproduced under the terms of the Open Government Licence. I have made every effort to trace other copyright holders, but would be glad to rectify any omissions in future printings.

Finally, but most importantly, I thank my parents, my grandparents, my brother Ben, and friends in Cambridge and beyond for all their encouragement and support.

Cambridge
March 2019

Contents

List of Figures

List of Abbreviations

BIEN	Basic Income Earth Network (Basic Income European Network, 1986–2004)
BIRG	Basic Income Research Group
CASE	Centre for Analysis of Social Exclusion
CBIT	Citizen's Basic Income Trust
CPAG	Child Poverty Action Group
CRD	Conservative Research Department
CSJ	Centre for Social Justice
CTAs	Child Tax Allowances
CTC	Child Tax Credit
DHSS	Department of Health and Social Security
DSS	Department of Social Security
DWP	Department for Work and Pensions
EITC	Earned Income Tax Credit
FES	Family Endowment Society
FIS	Family Income Supplement
GDP	Gross Domestic Product
HMRC	HM Revenue and Customs
IEA	Institute of Economic Affairs
IFS	Institute for Fiscal Studies
ILO	International Labour Organization
IPPR	Institute for Public Policy Research
LPC	Low Pay Commission
LSE	London School of Economics
MIT	Massachusetts Institute of Technology
MPS	Mont Pèlerin Society
NAIRU	Non-Accelerating Inflation Rate of Unemployment
NCVO	National Council for Voluntary Organisations
NFCU	National Federation of Claimants Unions
NFRB	New Fabian Research Bureau
NHS	National Health Service
NIT	Negative Income Tax
NLW	National Living Wage
NMW	National Minimum Wage
OECD	Organisation for Economic Cooperation and Development
OEO	Office of Economic Opportunity

PAYE	Pay-As-You-Earn
PEP	Political and Economic Planning
RML	Redistributive Market Liberalism
RSA	Royal Society of Arts
RTI	Real-Time Information
SDP	Social Democratic Party
SNP	Scottish National Party
SSRC	Social Science Research Council
TELCO	The East London Community Organisation
TUC	Trades Union Congress
UBI	Universal Basic Income
WFTC	Working Families Tax Credit
WLF	Women's Liberal Federation
WTC	Working Tax Credit

PART I

THE POLITICS OF REDISTRIBUTION

1
Introduction

The 2008 financial crisis and the era of austerity that followed have pushed poverty and inequality to the top of the political agenda for the first time since the 1970s. Across the western world, anti-austerity movements have given voice to public concern about the power of financial elites and the growing concentration of wealth in the hands of the '1 per cent'. Within academia, Thomas Piketty's bestselling study of *Capital in the Twenty-First Century* (2014) has raised the spectre of a return to 'patrimonial capitalism'.[1] The question of how to achieve a more equal distribution of income and wealth looks set to be one of the defining policy dilemmas of our generation.

One of the most striking responses to the new politics of inequality has been the surge of interest in the idea of a Universal Basic Income (UBI)—a 'universal, unconditional, and non-withdrawable income paid to every individual'.[2] For proponents such as Philippe van Parijs, basic income offers a powerful means of reaffirming the social rights of citizenship and providing a foundation for creativity and life choices—what van Parijs calls 'real freedom for all'.[3] Others, such as the economist Guy Standing, have held up UBI as a way of strengthening workers' bargaining power in an era of rapid labour-market change and managing the disruptive impact of automation.[4] Indeed, the most radical accelerationist thinkers—such as Nick Srnicek and Alex Williams—see basic income as a cornerstone of a 'post-work world' in which capitalist exploitation gives way to a more egalitarian and ecologically sustainable future.[5]

The explosion of interest in basic income in the developed world dovetails with the growing use of cash transfers to tackle poverty in the global south. As the anthropologist James Ferguson has pointed out in *Give a Man a Fish* (2015), this trend has become increasingly visible in Latin America and

[1] Thomas Piketty, *Capital in the Twenty-First Century* (Cambridge, Mass., 2014).
[2] Malcolm Torry, *Money for Everyone: Why We Need a Citizen's Income* (Bristol, 2013), ix.
[3] Philippe van Parijs, *Real Freedom for All: What (if Anything) Can Justify Capitalism?* (Oxford, 1995).
[4] Guy Standing, *The Precariat: The New Dangerous Class* (2011).
[5] Nick Srnicek and Alex Williams, *Inventing the Future: Postcapitalism and a World without Work* (2015).

Transfer State: The Idea of a Guaranteed Income and the Politics of Redistribution in Modern Britain. Peter Sloman, Oxford University Press (2019). © Peter Sloman. DOI: 10.1093/oso/9780198813262.001.0001

southern Africa since the early 2000s.[6] For much of the twentieth century, development policy was structured by a 'productionist' paradigm which valorized paid work by male breadwinners as the main route out of poverty, but since the turn of the millennium, international organizations have become increasingly open to the possibility of empowering the poor through direct transfer payments.[7] The apparent success of the Bolsa Familia in Brazil—which pays poorer families a monthly stipend so long as their children are vaccinated and attend school—has helped spawn a 'cash transfer revolution' across the developing world, encompassing a mixture of conditional and unconditional, universal and means-tested programmes.[8] International institutions such as the World Bank have tended to promote targeted and conditional transfers on the model of Mexico's Oportunidades programme, as a way of encouraging human capital development and reinforcing work incentives.[9] For Ferguson, however, this 'new politics of distribution' also opens up the potential for more radical forms of political mobilization around universal social entitlements.

Enthusiasts for UBI frequently present it as a radical break with existing forms of social insurance and income support, and a response to the distinctive social and economic challenges of the twenty-first century. Yet the idea of a basic income dates back at least as far as the industrial revolution, and has surfaced repeatedly in British and North American policy debates since the First World War. The notion of providing citizens with a guaranteed minimum income chimes with powerful strands in Anglo-American political economy and social thought, including the long tradition of measuring poverty in income terms, the liberal commitment to personal autonomy and consumer choice, and the neoclassical vision of a flexible and self-adjusting labour market. At the same time, the relationship between UBI and other forms of guaranteed income floor—such as Milton Friedman's Negative Income Tax (NIT)—has often been blurred in public discourse. As David Purdy has put it, basic income 'is a field of debate, rather than a settled programme'.[10] Any attempt to understand the intellectual history of basic

[6] James Ferguson, *Give a Man a Fish: Reflections on the New Politics of Distribution* (Durham, NC, 2015).

[7] Ferguson, *Give a Man a Fish*, 38; Bob Deacon, *Global Social Policy in the Making: The Foundations of the Social Protection Floor* (Bristol, 2013); Moritz von Gliszczynski and Lutz Leisering, 'Constructing New Global Models of Social Security: How International Organizations Defined the Field of Social Cash Transfers in the 2000s', *Journal of Social Policy* 45/2 (2016), 325–43.

[8] Ferguson, *Give a Man a Fish*, 12–20.

[9] Jamie Peck and Nik Theodore, *Fast Policy: Experimental Statecraft at the Thresholds of Neoliberalism* (Minneapolis, 2015), 85–129.

[10] David Purdy, 'Citizenship, Basic Income and the State', *New Left Review* I/208 (1994), 30–48, at 31.

income must start by recognizing the fluidity of the idea and the ambiguity of many real-world proposals.

This book explores how the idea of a guaranteed minimum income has shaped the politics of the welfare state in Britain over the past century. It argues that the possibility of establishing a minimum income through direct cash transfers has formed an important strand of social policy debate and has been a major influence on policy-making since the inter-war years. From Juliet Rhys-Williams and Douglas Houghton to Gordon Brown and Iain Duncan Smith, a long succession of policy entrepreneurs have sought to re-engineer the tax and benefit systems in order to provide an automatic income floor for all or part of the population. For the liberal right, fiscal transfers represented a market-friendly solution to poverty which made it easier to dismantle trade union rights and collective welfare provision. For progressive liberals and social democrats, they offered a way of sidestepping debates about wage bargaining by redistributing resources directly from rich to poor. For tax-benefit reformers of all stripes, integration provided a 'holy grail' of policy rationality which would improve benefit take-up, reduce administrative costs, and impose order on a dysfunctional system.

The idea of rationalizing welfare provision through a guaranteed minimum income is not, of course, unique to the United Kingdom. Guaranteed income schemes attracted wide support in the United States during the 1960s and 1970s, as historians such as Gareth Davies and Brian Steensland have shown, and have left their mark on contemporary US social policy through the creation and expansion of the Earned Income Tax Credit (EITC).[11] The 'cash transfer revolution' of the last twenty years has been a multifaceted global phenomenon, and UBI campaigns have gained traction in a variety of social and political contexts—from India and southern Africa to Silicon Valley and Finland.[12] Nevertheless, the highly centralized and 'materialist' character of the UK welfare state has perhaps made tax-benefit integration particularly attractive in Britain. As José Harris has noted, British welfare provision has long focused on 'relief of quantitative need...by contrast with the greater priority given in many continental systems to more ambitious and complex

[11] Gareth Davies, *From Opportunity to Entitlement: The Transformation and Decline of Great Society Liberalism* (Lawrence, Kan., 1996); Brian Steensland, *The Failed Welfare Revolution: America's Struggle over Guaranteed Income Policy* (Princeton, 2008).

[12] Joseph Hanlon, Armando Barrientos, and David Hulme, *Just Give Money to the Poor: The Development Revolution from the Global South* (Sterling, Va, 2010); Philippe van Parijs and Yannick Vanderborght, *Basic Income: A Radical Proposal for a Free Society and a Sane Economy* (Cambridge, Mass., 2017).

goals of social solidarity, family cohesion, and efficient citizenship'.[13] In Gøsta Esping-Andersen's terms, the idea of a guaranteed minimum is a more natural fit for a 'liberal' welfare regime, based on means-testing and 'flat-rate universalism', than for social democratic and conservative welfare states which provide earnings-related social insurance in partnership with trade unions and employers.[14] The UK's Pay-As-You-Earn (PAYE) system of income tax collection, which adjusts tax deductions week by week on a cumulative basis, has also fostered a widespread (if misplaced) confidence in the state's ability to supplement low incomes.

Although a guaranteed minimum income for all British citizens has never been achieved, the idea of establishing an income floor through cash transfers has nevertheless left its mark on British social policy. Social security spending has ballooned since the Second World War—from 4 per cent of GDP in the late 1940s to 8 per cent in 1975 and more than 12 per cent by 2010—and the growth of transfers to working-age households has been particularly striking. The twin planks of twentieth-century social security policy—the contributory National Insurance system championed by Sir William Beveridge and the National Assistance system which emerged from the old Poor Law—have given way to a highly routinized system of means-tested support for those in and out of work, which is now being unified under the banner of Universal Credit.[15] At the same time, the decline of manufacturing employment and trade union membership since the 1970s and 1980s has helped shift the focus of British social politics from wage bargaining to cash transfers. In an era of widening earnings differentials and declining confidence in state intervention, both Conservative and New Labour governments have become increasingly reliant on transfer payments to manage the distributional consequences of neoliberalism and globalization.

In many ways, it is surprising that a book of this kind has not been written before. The relationship between tax and social security has featured prominently in British social policy debates since the 1960s, and comparative welfare scholars have long recognized the appeal of guaranteed income schemes, especially in 'liberal' welfare regimes such as Britain, Canada, and the United States.[16] John

[13] José Harris, 'From Poor Law to Welfare State? A European Perspective', in *The Political Economy of British Historical Experience, 1688–1914*, edited by Donald Winch and Patrick K. O'Brien (Oxford, 2002), 409–37, at 437.

[14] Gøsta Esping-Andersen, *The Three Worlds of Welfare Capitalism* (Cambridge, 1990).

[15] Paul Gray and Nicholas Timmins, *Reforming Working-Age Social Security: Lessons for Policy Makers* (2018).

[16] John Myles and Paul Pierson, 'Friedman's Revenge: The Reform of "Liberal" Welfare States in Canada and the United States', *Politics & Society* 25/4 (1997), 443–72, at 444.

Myles and Paul Pierson, for instance, have argued that the Negative Income Tax is 'a historically novel form of state redistribution' which 'prove[d] ideally suited to the new politics of austerity' during the 1980s and 1990s, not least because it was often cheaper than social insurance benefits.[17] There is also a growing international literature on the politics and feasibility of UBI.[18] The historiography of the British welfare state, however, has been strongly shaped by the social administration tradition established by Richard Titmuss, with its empiricist focus on welfare institutions and its distinctive set of ethical commitments—to collectivism over individualism, universalism over selectivity, and altruism over profit.[19] The idea of providing a minimum income through the tax and benefit systems cuts across these binary categories, and forces us to rethink established narratives of the rise, maturity, and crisis of Britain's 'cradle to the grave' welfare state.[20]

The ideational story: The idea of a guaranteed income

The history of guaranteed income can be approached from two different perspectives. Firstly, the emergence and reception of proposals for a minimum income floor is a classic subject in the history of ideas. UBI proponents have traced the idea back to a long series of visionaries—from Thomas Paine's plan for a universal endowment in *Agrarian Justice* (1797) through Edward Bellamy's utopian novel *Looking Backward* (1888) to Bertrand Russell's discussion of a 'vagabond's wage' in *Roads to Freedom* (1918).[21] Basic income can be conceptualized in a variety of ways—as a social right, a share in common wealth, a foundation for personal freedom, or an economic regulator—and attached to a wide range of political projects. Historians face the challenge of establishing where these ideas have come from, how they relate to each other, and why they have gained traction in particular contexts.

How, for instance, should we understand the relationship between basic income and selective income guarantee schemes such as NIT? Economists often see UBI and NIT as functionally equivalent, and point out that (under

[17] Myles and Pierson, 'Friedman's Revenge', 444.

[18] See, for instance, Richard K. Caputo, ed., *Basic Income Guarantee and Politics: International Experiences and Perspectives on the Viability of Income Guarantee* (Basingstoke, 2012).

[19] Martin Bulmer, 'The British Tradition of Social Administration: Moral Concerns at the Expense of Scientific Rigor', *Hastings Center Report* 11/2 (1981), 35–42.

[20] Daniel Wincott, 'The (Golden) Age of the Welfare State: Interrogating a Conventional Wisdom', *Public Administration* 91/4 (2013), 806–22.

[21] Van Parijs and Vanderborght, *Basic Income*, 51–94.

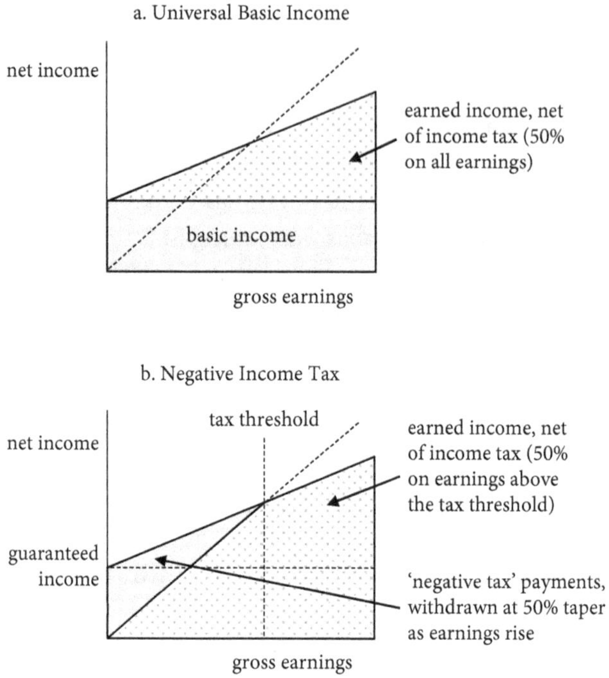

Figure 1.1. Universal Basic Income and Negative Income Tax

certain parameters) they can have the same distributional effects: an NIT or tax credit scheme simply reduces 'churn' by netting the basic income entitlement off against tax liability. Milton Friedman, for instance, argued that '[f]or any given schedule of tax rates under the negative income tax, positive and negative, there exists a subsidy [i.e. basic income] plan which would involve paying exactly the same amount of money to precisely the same amount of people'.[22] As Figure 1.1 shows, a basic income of £5,000 which is paid for by a flat-rate 50 per cent tax on all other income and an NIT supplement of £5,000 which is tapered away at 50 per cent have the same guaranteed minimum, the same marginal tax rate, and the same net cost. On the other hand, philosophers and social policy experts have pointed out that the choice between universalism and selectivity can have major implications for people's lives and for the broader politics of social citizenship.[23] UBI provides citizens with a

[22] Hoover Institution Archives, Stanford University, Friedman papers, 201.6, Milton Friedman to Joseph C. Farber, 11 Jan. 1967 (copy).

[23] Davide Tondani, 'Universal Basic Income and Negative Income Tax: Two Different Ways of Thinking Redistribution', *The Journal of Socio-Economics* 38/2 (2009), 246–55.

Box 1.1. Definitions

Guaranteed income: a level of income guaranteed to every individual or household, which may be universal or means-tested

Universal Basic Income (also known as a basic income or citizen's income): a universal, unconditional, and non-withdrawable income paid to every individual

Negative Income Tax: a scheme which supplements low incomes using the apparatus of the personal tax system

Tax credit: a lump-sum allowance which is offset against tax liability. (If the tax credit is *refundable*, any allowance which remains after tax liability is reduced to zero is paid to the individual in cash.)

Participation income: a basic income which is conditional on some form of social participation, such as paid work, care, or volunteering

stable and predictable income source on which they can build through work or investment, whereas NIT (and Universal Credit) requires the state to engage in a much more sophisticated administrative operation to assess incomes and pay out supplements to those who need them. Well-publicized implementation problems with tax credits and Universal Credit have highlighted the difficulty of responding promptly and efficiently to fluctuations in income. Selective income guarantee schemes also tend to be administered on a household rather than an individual basis and to withdraw benefits from claimants at a higher rate (often 60 or 70 per cent) than the tax rate charged on income above the tax threshold. Too often, the result has been to reinforce the social distinction between net taxpayers and net claimants and to throw the burden of administrative failure onto the poorest citizens.

Contemporary activists and policy-makers have come to distinguish sharply between UBI, selective income guarantee schemes such as NIT, and conditional schemes such as Tony Atkinson's proposal for a 'participation income'.[24] These definitions (set out in Box 1.1) are essential to clear policy analysis, and are adopted so far as possible in the chapters that follow. Nevertheless, the historian must be sensitive to the risk of reifying UBI and

[24] A. B. Atkinson, 'Beveridge, the National Minimum and its Future in a European Context', in A. B. Atkinson, *Incomes and the Welfare State: Essays on Britain and Europe* (Cambridge, 1995), 290–304.

NIT and reading contemporary distinctions back into the history of the field. For much of the past century, the terminology of tax-benefit reform has been fluid and the boundaries between different schemes highly permeable. Indeed, the term 'basic income' was not widely used in Britain until the early 1980s, when the formation of the Basic Income Research Group (BIRG)—now the Citizen's Basic Income Trust (CBIT)—helped stabilize the meaning of the idea.[25] We can only understand the history of basic income in Britain in relation to a wider nexus of cash transfer schemes.

The circulation of ideas about guaranteed income has always crossed national boundaries. Politicians pick up ideas from an eclectic variety of sources, and policy devices are 'co-constituted through the networks, and across the landscapes, through and over which they travel', as Jamie Peck and Nik Theodore have argued.[26] Several of the waves of interest in tax-benefit reform examined in this book—the vogue for NIT in the 1960s, the development of tax credits in the 1990s, and the contemporary enthusiasm for UBI—reflect the influence of transnational exchanges. At the same time, 'the field of policy transfer is itself socially and institutionally constructed': 'structured by relatively enduring policy paradigms' which mediate the reception of ideas and proposals.[27] A study of guaranteed income in Britain must thus attend to the distinctive features of the UK welfare state and the patterns of policy development which these have created.

The framing of basic income proposals in Britain has been particularly strongly shaped by local contextual factors. At different times, campaigners have characterized UBI as a 'vagabond's wage', a 'state bonus', a 'social dividend', a 'new social contract', and a 'citizen's income'—each of which evokes a rather different set of connotations. Since the 1940s, however, the dominant conception of guaranteed income among British policy-makers has been as a social security benefit, financed out of income tax receipts and designed to facilitate tax-benefit integration. This focus on the tax-benefit interface has reflected both administrative realities—such as the complex relationship between PAYE, National Insurance, and National Assistance—and distinctive strands in British social thought. For instance, the UK has a long tradition of quantitative 'poverty line' research, which stretches back to

[25] The term 'basic income' was used intermittently during the mid-twentieth century, but even in the early 1980s many British commentators still described it as a 'guaranteed minimum income', 'social wage', or 'social dividend'. 'Basisinkomen' enjoyed wide currency in the Netherlands from the late 1970s onwards, and it is possible that the term was introduced to the UK by the physicist Keith Roberts under the influence of the Dutch debate. I am grateful to Philippe van Parijs for drawing this point to my attention.

[26] Peck and Theodore, *Fast Policy*, xxiv.

[27] Peck and Theodore, *Fast Policy*, 27.

Charles Booth and Seebohm Rowntree's pioneering studies of urban poverty at the end of the nineteenth century. Neoclassical market economics has also been relatively influential in the UK and other English-speaking countries, fostering scepticism about the possibility of tackling poverty through minimum wage laws or other forms of direct state intervention. As Alice O'Connor has shown in the post-war United States, the conjunction of 'poverty line' research with neoclassical policy analysis techniques pushed policy-makers towards 'certain kinds of solutions to the poverty problem': 'emphasizing income over services, targeting individuals rather than empowering communities, and favouring interventions that worked outside the market'.[28] John Kay has characterized this philosophy as 'redistributive market liberalism' (RML): the belief that the competitive market is normally the most efficient system of production, but that the state has an important role to play in matters of distribution.[29]

For much of the post-war period, the influence of RML and the focus on tax-benefit integration blurred the distinctions between different income guarantee schemes. During the 1970s and 1980s, however, UBI began to attract support from a more radical constituency of feminists, environmentalists, and Claimants' Unions activists who sought to disrupt prevailing conceptions of work and challenge the gender norms which shaped the existing benefit system. As the UBI movement took institutional form in BIRG (established in 1984) and the Basic Income European Network (1986), British campaigners played an important role in establishing the canonical definition of basic income as an unconditional and non-withdrawable payment to every citizen. Even so, the British movement has continued to be marked by a strong focus on developing costed and affordable schemes which would simplify the tax-benefit interface and reduce the importance of means-testing. Until recently, this has tended to crowd out alternative conceptions of UBI, such as the asset-based approach pursued in Alaska, where the state government has used oil revenues to build up a Permanent Fund and pay out a variable annual dividend to its citizens.[30]

[28] Alice O'Connor, *Poverty Knowledge: Social Science, Social Policy, and the Poor in Twentieth-Century U.S. History* (Princeton, 2001), 214.

[29] John Kay, 'Staking a Moral Claim', *New Statesman*, 11 Oct. 1996, 18–20, at 18; see also Samuel Brittan, 'Redistributive Market Liberalism', in *Essays, Moral, Political and Economic*, edited by Samuel Brittan (Edinburgh, 1998), 22–32.

[30] On this 'Alaska model', see Karl Widerquist and Michael W. Howard, eds, *Exporting the Alaska Model: Adapting the Permanent Fund Dividend for Reform around the World* (New York: Palgrave Macmillan, 2012).

Alongside the emergence of more radical conceptions of UBI, the introduction of new forms of conditionality by Conservative and New Labour governments has also made the policy choices clearer. In mainstream social security policy, the expansion of means-tested income supplements has become increasingly closely linked to the 'welfare-to-work' agenda.[31] Universal Credit and UBI have thus come to be seen as polar opposites in contemporary British policy debate—the one as complex, coercive, and technocratic, the other as potentially emancipatory but prohibitively expensive. A historical analysis of these two visions of integration must account not only for their common intellectual roots but also for the ways in which they have diverged over the last century.

The public policy story: Redistribution in an age of neoliberalism

A purely ideational history of guaranteed income, however, can only take us so far. As Daniel Zamora has pointed out, too many histories of UBI link together apparently similar proposals across time and space to construct an artificially neat genealogy, in exactly the way Quentin Skinner warned against half a century ago.[32] In the realm of social policy, it is impossible to understand the evolution of ideas without reference to the messy realities of policy design and implementation. We need to link the ideational story up with a policy story about the changing place of redistribution in the British welfare state and the ways in which policy-makers have sought to rationalize the tax and benefit systems.[33]

For contemporary economists and political scientists, it is natural to think about redistribution in terms of transfer payments from richer to poorer citizens. In Allan Meltzer and Scott Richard's classic rational choice model, the scale of redistribution depends on the economic interests of the median voter. The electorate supports income transfers so long as mean income is higher than median income, up to the point where the mean and median are

[31] Gray and Timmins, *Reforming Working-Age Social Security*.

[32] Daniel Zamora, 'An Intellectual History of the Universal Basic Income: How a Fringe Idea Went Global (1962–1972)', paper delivered at the History and Economics Seminar, University of Cambridge, 6 Feb. 2018; Quentin Skinner, 'Meaning and Understanding in the History of Ideas', *History and Theory* 8/1 (1969), 3–53.

[33] This discussion draws on Peter Sloman, 'Redistribution in an Age of Neoliberalism: Market Economics, "Poverty Knowledge", and the Growth of Working-Age Benefits in Britain, c.1979–2010', *Political Studies* early view (2018).

equal or where the impact on economic efficiency and work incentives cancels out the benefit to the voter at the median.[34] Other scholars have refined Meltzer and Richard's model by relaxing the assumption of perfect information and exploring cross-national variations in institutions. Torben Iversen and David Soskice, for example, have argued that 'middle-class fears of being soaked by the poor' limit transfers in majoritarian systems, 'whereas their incentive to join the poor in soaking the rich' is more easily satisfied under proportional representation.[35]

The period between the 1940s and the late 1970s is widely remembered as an era of unprecedented social equality in Britain, in which the solidarity forged by the Second World War took concrete expression in the welfare state, progressive taxation, and full employment policies. The Gini coefficient for post-tax income fell from 0.43 in 1938 to 0.36 in 1949 and 0.32 in 1976, and the concentration of wealth fell even faster.[36] For much of this post-war 'golden age', however, the scale of cash transfers was relatively small and dominated by National Insurance, which was mainly financed by flat-rate contributions and so involved a 'horizontal' form of risk-pooling within the working population.[37] As David Edgerton has noted, although the welfare state of the 1940s and 1950s was larger, more universal, and more centralized than it had been between the wars, it was still powerfully 'oriented to production' and paid work: the wage packet formed the primary basis of economic security for most working-class households.[38] Insofar as the British state engaged in explicit redistribution, it did so primarily on the tax side—using progressive marginal rates of income tax to cover much of the cost of the two world wars and finance the expansion of social services such as state education and the National Health Service (NHS). (We might call this 'redistribution *from*' rather than 'redistribution *to*'.) Even this was only part of a much larger egalitarian settlement which reduced income differentials through Keynesian economic management, trade union rights, and regional policies, as Jim

[34] Allan H. Meltzer and Scott F. Richard, 'A Rational Theory of the Size of Government', *Journal of Political Economy* 89/5 (1981), 914–27.

[35] Torben Iversen and David Soskice, 'Electoral Institutions and the Politics of Coalitions: Why Some Democracies Redistribute More than Others', *American Political Science Review* 100/2 (2006), 165–81, at 179.

[36] These Gini figures are based on the post-tax income of tax units, and are taken from Anthony B. Atkinson, Joe Hasell, Salvatore Morelli, and Max Roser, 'Economic Inequality in the United Kingdom', The Chartbook of Economic Inequality, accessed 7 May 2018, <https://www.chartbookofeconomicinequality.com/inequality-by-country/united-kingdom/>.

[37] Peter Baldwin, *The Politics of Social Solidarity: Class Bases of the European Welfare State, 1875–1975* (Cambridge, 1990).

[38] David Edgerton, *The Rise and Fall of the British Nation: A Twentieth-Century History* (2018), 302; for the centralization of welfare provision between the 1900s and the 1950s, see 222–45.

Tomlinson has noted.[39] Although data for the 1960s and 1970s is patchy, the UK appears to have had one of the most equal distributions of pre-tax income in the developed world. In the mid-1970s, for instance, the Gini coefficient for market income was lower in the UK (0.38) than either Sweden or Canada (0.39), let alone the United States (0.41) or the Netherlands (0.43).

Since the late 1970s, the UK's political economy has been transformed by deindustrialization and the 'market turn' in economic thought associated with neoliberalism.[40] During the 1980s and 1990s, technological change and financial globalization raised the profit share at the expense of wages in much of the western world, but the Thatcher government's monetarist policies and assault on trade union power meant that the British experience of widening inequality was particularly dramatic.[41] As Figure 1.2 shows, the Gini coefficient for market income rose from 0.38 in 1975 to 0.47 in 1985 and 0.51 in 1994—turning one of the most equal pre-tax income distributions in the developed world into one of the least equal.

This story of rising market inequality since the 1970s is very familiar. In Britain, as in the United States, the incomes of the top 1 per cent have raced away from the rest, aided by tax policies which favour high earners, by windfall gains from shares and housing wealth, and by the rapid growth of the financial sector.[42] At the same time, however, the 'age of neoliberalism' has also witnessed a significant expansion of the redistributive role of the British state. Since Margaret Thatcher took office in 1979, the social security budget has risen from 8 per cent to 11 per cent of GDP (Figure 1.3) and from 19 per cent to 27 per cent of total government spending. This process has been driven partly by the growth in the pensioner population, but also by the expansion of transfer payments to working-age adults and children, which have more than trebled in real terms. As Figure 1.4 shows, National Insurance benefits for working-age claimants have increasingly been supplanted by means-tested transfers to low- and middle-income households, particularly tax credits and Housing Benefit, which are now the second and third largest elements of social

[39] Jim Tomlinson, 'Distributional Politics: The Search for Equality in Britain since the First World War', in *The Contradictions of Capital in the Twenty-First Century: The Piketty Opportunity*, edited by Pat Hudson and Keith Tribe (Newcastle-upon-Tyne, 2016), 167–91.

[40] Avner Offer, 'The Market Turn: From Social Democracy to Market Liberalism', *Economic History Review* 70/4 (2017), 1051–71.

[41] A. B. Atkinson, *Inequality: What Can Be Done?* (Cambridge, Mass., 2015), 82–109; OECD (Organisation for Economic Co-operation and Development), *Divided We Stand: Why Inequality Keeps Rising* (Paris, 2011), 261–98.

[42] Jonathan Hopkin and Kate Alexander Shaw, 'Organized Combat or Structural Advantage? The Politics of Inequality and the Winner-Take-All Economy in the United Kingdom', *Politics & Society* 44/3 (2016), 345–71.

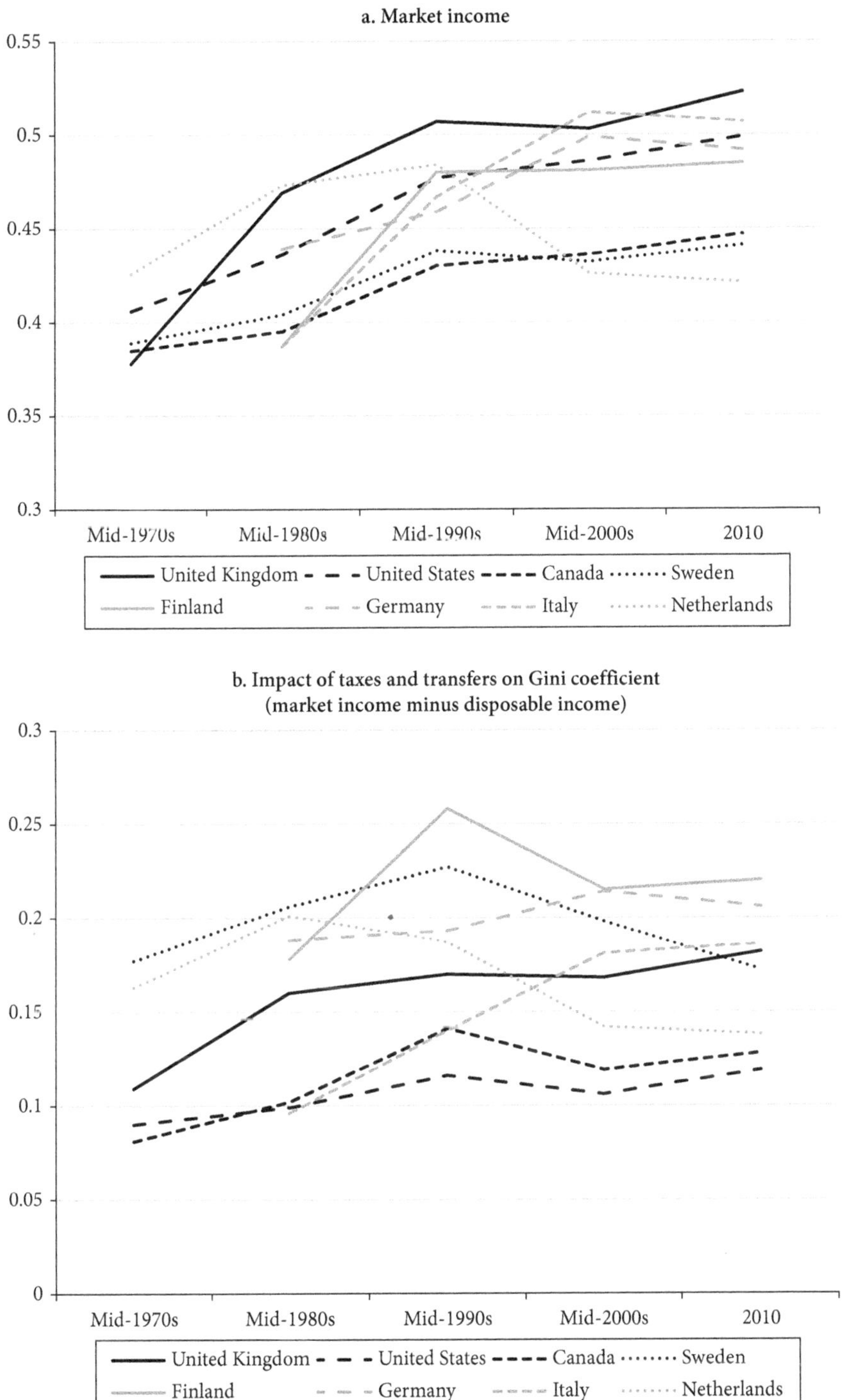

Figure 1.2. Gini coefficient for eight western democracies, mid-1970s to 2010

Source: Author's calculations based on OECD data: <https://stats.oecd.org/>

Selected years: UK 1975, 1985, 1994, 2005, 2010; US 1974, 1984, 1995, 2005, 2010; Sweden 1975, 1983, 1995, 2004, 2010; Finland 1986, 1995, 2005, 2010; Canada 1976, 1985, 1995, 2005, 2010; Germany 1985, 1995, 2004, 2010; Italy 1984, 1995, 2004, 2010; Netherlands 1977, 1985, 1995, 2005, 2010.

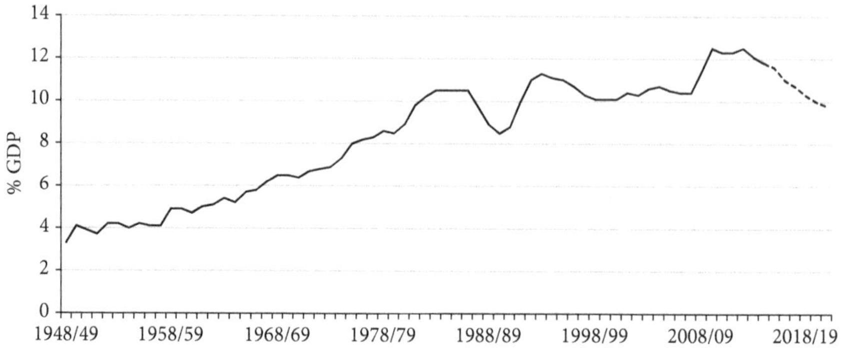

Figure 1.3. Social security expenditure as a share of United Kingdom GDP, 1948/9–2020/1

Source: Institute for Fiscal Studies, 'Fiscal Facts: Social Security Spending', 29 September 2015 <https://www.ifs.org.uk/tools_and_resources/fiscal_facts/public_spending_survey/social_security>

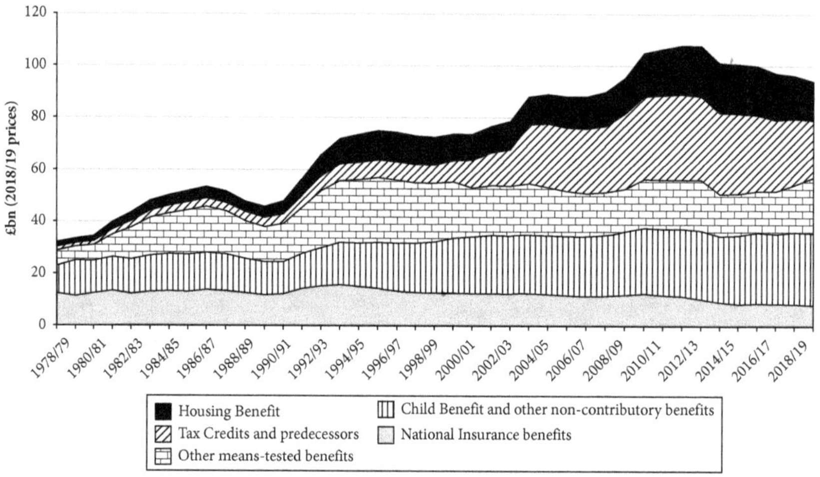

Figure 1.4. Transfer payments to working-age adults and children in Great Britain, 1978/9–2018/19 (real terms, £bn, 2018/19 prices)

Source: Author's calculations based on Department for Work and Pensions, 'Benefit Expenditure and Caseload Tables', Autumn Budget 2018:

<https://www.gov.uk/government/publications/benefit-expenditure-and-caseload-tables-2018>

security spending after the state pension. Despite historically high employment levels and a spate of austerity measures since 2010, cash transfers have come to play a major role in supplementing earned income not only for the very poorest, but for a large minority of working-age households (Figure 1.5). This is particularly true of families with children. Research by the Institute for Fiscal

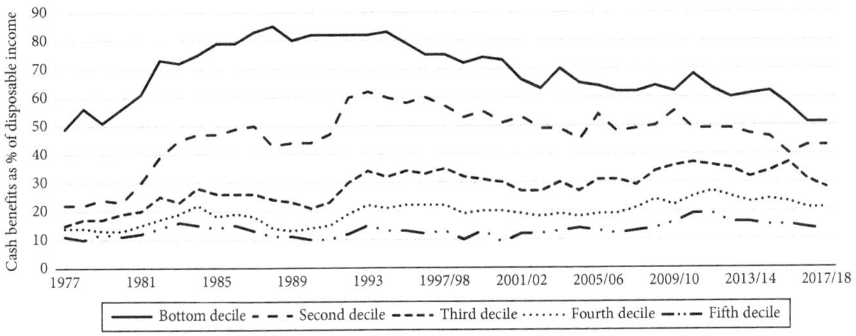

Figure 1.5. Cash benefits as a share of disposable income for working-age households (by decile of equivalized disposable income), 1977–2017/18

Source: Author's calculations based on Office for National Statistics, 'The Effect of Taxes and Benefits on Household Income: Historical Datasets', 20 June 2018, and Office for National Statistics, 'The Effects of Taxes and Benefits on Household Income, Disposable Income Estimate: 2018', 26 February 2019: <https://www.ons.gov.uk/peoplepopulationandcommunity/personalandhouseholdfinances/incomeandwealth/datasets/theeffectsoftaxesandbenefitsonhouseholdincomehistoricaldatasets and https://www.ons.gov.uk/peoplepopulationandcommunity/personalandhouseholdfinances/incomeandwealth/datasets/householddisposableincomeandinequality>

Studies (IFS) suggests that middle-income households with children derived about 30 per cent of their income from tax credits and other benefits in 2014/15, and the widespread under-reporting of benefit income in the Family Resources Survey means that the true figure may be even higher.[43] The sharp rise in the inequality of earnings and investment income has thus been partly offset by the tax and benefit systems.

How should the paradox of rising welfare spending in an age of neoliberalism be explained? It has certainly been driven, in part, by material changes in the UK economy—especially the collapse of the Fordist employment model which was central to British economic and social policy between the First World War and the 1970s. During the early post-war period, almost half of workers were employed in manufacturing or ancillary industries (such as mining and construction), men made up more than two-thirds of the labour force, and gender segregation within the labour market remained strong.[44]

[43] Chris Belfield, Jonathan Cribb, Andrew Hood, and Robert Joyce, *Living Standards, Poverty and Inequality in the UK: 2016* (2016), 49; Adam Corlett, Stephen Clarke, Conor D'Arcy, and John Wood, *The Living Standards Audit 2018* (2018), 48–74. See also Mike Brewer and Liam Wren-Lewis, *Why Did Britain's Households Get Richer? Decomposing UK Household Income Growth between 1968 and 2008–9*. IFS Briefing Note no. 125 (2011).

[44] Charles Feinstein, 'Structural Change in the Developed Countries in the Twentieth Century', *Oxford Review of Economic Policy* 15/4 (1999), 35–55, at 39; Arthur McIvor, *Working Lives: Work in Britain since 1945* (2013), 22.

Since the late 1960s, employment has shifted dramatically from industrial production into services, and Conservative and New Labour governments have accelerated this transition by prioritizing low inflation over industrial competitiveness and reforming employment law to make the labour market more 'flexible'.[45] Although characterizations of the UK as a 'liberal market economy' can be overdone, it seems clear that these policy choices have contributed to the decline of the manufacturing sector and the emergence of a 'precariat' of part-time and casual workers.

This 'meta-narrative' of deindustrialization can be extended to explain rising welfare spending in two ways.[46] First, it is clear that mass unemployment was an important contributory factor in the growth of the benefit bill during the 1980s and 1990s, particularly during the 1980–1 and 1990–1 recessions, when the system 'buckled under the weight of unprecedented inflows' and many older manual workers became long-term benefit claimants.[47] Christina Beatty and Steve Fothergill have shown that the geographical distribution of working-age benefits—especially disability benefits, incapacity benefits, and tax credits—still closely tracks the pattern of job losses during the Thatcher years. Beatty and Fothergill conclude that 'the destruction of industrial Britain in the 1980s' has had 'profound repercussions for present-day public finances' through its legacy of 'persistent worklessness, low wages and an inflated welfare bill'.[48] Comparative studies confirm that deindustrialization has been a major driver of market inequality and 'exerts a consistently significant and substantively large effect on government redistribution' through taxes and transfers.[49]

A second materialist argument focuses on the shift in economic power from trade unions to employers, and the functional role which in-work benefits have come to play in the UK's post-industrial liberal market economy. This shift can be understood in straightforwardly institutionalist terms: for instance, John Myles and Paul Pierson have attributed the growth of NIT

[45] Stewart Wood, 'Labour Market Regimes under Threat? Sources of Continuity in Germany, Britain and Sweden', in *The New Politics of the Welfare State*, edited by Paul Pierson (Oxford, 2001), 368–409.

[46] Jim Tomlinson, 'De-Industrialization not Decline: A New Meta-Narrative for Post-War British History', *Twentieth Century British History* 27/1 (2016), 76–99.

[47] Jonathan Portes, 'Welfare and Work: Continuity and Change', *National Institute Economic Review*, 221 (2012), F4–F9, at F6.

[48] Christina Beatty and Steve Fothergill, 'The Impact on Welfare and Public Finances of Job Loss in Industrial Britain', *Regional Studies, Regional Science* 4/1 (2017), 161–80, at 178.

[49] Cathie Jo Martin and Duane Swank, *The Political Construction of Business Interests: Coordination, Growth, and Equality* (New York, 2012), 239; see also Torben Iversen, 'Economic Shocks and Varieties of Government Responses', in *Varieties of Capitalism: The Institutional Foundations of Comparative Advantage*, edited by Peter Hall and David Soskice (Oxford, 2001), 278–304.

schemes in the United States and Canada to the decline of union power and 'the formation of novel, and unexpected coalitions between those seeking retrenchment, on the one hand, and those concerned about the poor, on the other'.[50] Trade unions have traditionally been highly suspicious of in-work benefits, which they have seen as a threat to the pursuit of a living wage through collective bargaining; the decline of union membership and corporatist policy-making structures has thus made it easier to expand these programmes. From a more critical perspective, political economists such as Bob Jessop and Chris Grover have argued that the profitability of the UK's service sector relies on a ready supply of cheap and flexible labour.[51] In-work benefits support this accumulation regime by encouraging workers to take low-paid jobs and shifting the cost of maintaining these workers from low-wage employers to other taxpayers. If jobseekers' contracts and benefit sanctions form the 'stick' of the activation policies which governments have introduced since the 1980s, tax credits provide a 'carrot' for workers which helps stabilize, reproduce, and legitimize neoliberal capitalism.[52]

Both of these materialist approaches are plausible in their own terms, but they also have significant limitations. Although rising demand as a result of deindustrialization explains some of the growth in working-age benefits, it cannot account for all of it. The scale of cash transfers has also been driven upwards by a series of discretionary policy choices by successive British governments, including the extension of income support to the working poor through Housing Benefit and tax credits. As Jochen Clasen has argued in his recent study of in-work benefits in Germany, 'attributing [these] reforms solely to the prevailing socio-economic environment seems unduly functionalistic'.[53] Likewise, although the decline of trade union power has removed an important obstacle to the expansion of in-work benefits, the evidence that business lobbying has been the main driving force behind policy changes is relatively thin. Indeed, recent work on UK political economy suggests that we should treat this notion with scepticism. Cathie Jo Martin and Duane Swank,

[50] Myles and Pierson, 'Friedman's Revenge', 445.

[51] Bob Jessop, 'From Thatcherism to New Labour: Neo-Liberalism, Workfarism, and Labour Market Regulation', in *The Political Economy of European Employment: European Integration and the Transnationalization of the (Un)employment Question*, edited by Henk Overbeek (2003), 137–53; Chris Grover, *Social Security and Wage Poverty: Historical and Policy Aspects of Supplementing Wages in Britain and Beyond* (Basingstoke, 2016).

[52] Julia Griggs, Andrew Hammond, and Robert Walker, 'Activation for All: Welfare Reform in the United Kingdom, 1995–2009', in *Activation or Workfare? Governance and the Neo-Liberal Convergence*, edited by Ivar Lodemel and Amilcar Moreira (Oxford, 2014), 73–100.

[53] Jochen Clasen, 'Subsidizing Wages or Supplementing Transfers? The Politics and Ambiguity of in-Work Benefits', *Social Policy & Administration* early view (2019).

for instance, have pointed out that British employers have always been 'fragmented and pluralistic'—a tendency reinforced by the Thatcher government's assault on corporatism—and that business groups played only a limited role in the development of Tony Blair's flagship welfare-to-work programme, the 'New Deal'.[54] More generally, Jonathan Hopkin and Kate Alexander Shaw have argued that the UK's highly centralized policy-making process limits the scope for the kind of 'organized combat' between interest groups which Jacob Hacker and Paul Pierson have identified in the United States.[55] Hopkin and Alexander Shaw's study of the growth of the UK financial sector concludes that the liberalization of the City of London associated with the 1986 'Big Bang' is better understood as a state-led process, 'implemented by an ideologically motivated elite that was ahead of the domestic business lobby in its commitment to free markets'.[56]

Whilst recognizing the importance of the material context, then, this book takes its cue from the discursive turn in political science over the past quarter-century and foregrounds the role of ideas in policy change.[57] The restructuring of the UK's welfare state since the 1970s is perhaps best seen (in Paul Pierson's terms) as a 'recalibration' process: an attempt 'to make contemporary welfare states more consistent with contemporary goals and demands for social provision', informed by both the material realities of deindustrialization and the intellectual ascendancy of market liberalism.[58] Successive governments have expanded transfer payments to the working poor whilst pursuing retrenchment and commodification in other parts of the welfare state, from the sale of council houses under 'Right to Buy' to the introduction of university tuition fees. As collective provision has been eroded by market reforms, only the electorally salient (and resource-intensive) core of education and the NHS remains 'free at the point of use'—a shift neatly encapsulated by Labour's 2001 general election slogan 'Schools and Hospitals First'. The UK's reliance on cash transfers as its main instrument of housing policy is particularly striking.

[54] Martin and Swank, *The Political Construction of Business Interests*, 88, 189–207.

[55] Hopkin and Alexander Shaw, 'Organized Combat or Structural Disadvantage?'; Jacob Hacker and Paul Pierson, 'Winner-Take-All Politics: Public Policy, Political Organization, and the Precipitous Rise of Top Incomes in the United States', *Politics & Society* 38/2 (2010), 152–204.

[56] Hopkin and Alexander Shaw, 'Organized Combat or Structural Disadvantage?', 364.

[57] Mark Blyth, 'Structures Do not Come with an Instruction Sheet: Interests, Ideas, and Progress in Political Science', *Perspectives on Politics* 1/4 (2003), 695–706; Vivien A. Schmidt, 'Taking Ideas and Discourse Seriously: Explaining Change through Discursive Institutionalism as the Fourth "New Institutionalism"', *European Political Science Review* 2/1 (2010), 1–25.

[58] Paul Pierson, 'Coping with Permanent Austerity: Welfare State Restructuring in Affluent Democracies', in *The New Politics of the Welfare State*, edited by Paul Pierson (Oxford, 2001), 410–56, at 425.

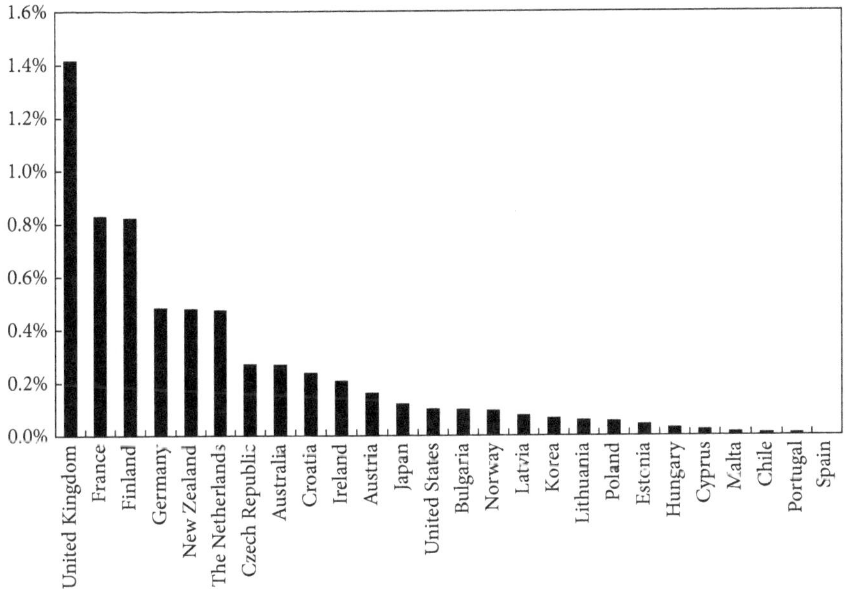

Figure 1.6. Total government spending on housing allowances as a share of GDP, 2015

Source: OECD Affordable Housing Database, December 2016: <http://www.oecd.org/social/affordable-housing-database.htm>

As Figure 1.6 shows, the British government spends far more on housing allowances than any other OECD country.

Bringing the ideational and public policy stories together in this way focuses our attention both on the intellectual context in which policy is made and on the transmission and reception of ideas in political debate. We need to explain why British governments have come to see cash transfers as an effective response to the social challenges thrown up by deindustrialization, and why some forms of transfer payments have been more politically acceptable than others. The relationship between ideas and policy is rarely straightforward, and the translation of guaranteed income proposals into policy has been mediated in at least three ways. Firstly, tax-benefit reform schemes have been drawn up and carried into the political arena by enthusiasts and campaigners: 'policy entrepreneurs' who 'invest their resources—time, energy, reputation, and sometimes money' in hope of securing policy change.[59] Secondly, the reception of these proposals has been shaped by the forms of knowledge and

[59] John Kingdon, *Agendas, Alternatives and Public Policies*, 2nd edn (New York, 1995), 122.

expertise prevailing among policy-makers. For instance, the idea of providing a guaranteed income outside the labour market has been more attractive to neoclassical economists than to other 'epistemic communities' in post-war Britain, such as industrial relations (geared towards wage bargaining) and social administration (which has tended to be more sympathetic to collective provision).[60] Thirdly, policy choices depend not only on elite ideas and interests but also on wider social and cultural values. Brian Steensland has argued that US guaranteed income proposals failed in the 1960s and 1970s partly because they blurred the distinction between the 'deserving' poor and 'undeserving' welfare recipients, especially black single mothers; likewise, British trade unions resisted in-work benefits for much of the twentieth century because they seemed to undermine the dignity of the skilled male breadwinner. Jack Jones of the Transport and General Workers' Union, for instance, warned that 'rely[ing] unduly on changes in social benefits' to eliminate poverty would 'make virtual State pensioners of hundreds of thousands of ordinary, healthy men and women'.[61] The continued resonance of communitarian rhetoric about reciprocity suggests that the obstacles to UBI are still cultural as much as financial. Indeed, from the Heath government's Family Income Supplement to Universal Credit, British governments have consistently presented in-work benefits as an *alternative* to welfare dependency—a way of respecting and reinforcing the Protestant work ethic by 'activating' citizens for the labour market.[62]

From 'tax state' to 'transfer state'

The growth of transfer payments to working-age households which has taken place since the 1970s has important implications for how we think about the British state. In quantitative terms, it has made UK government policy much more 'welfare orientated' (as David Edgerton has recently pointed out); in qualitative terms, the shift from social insurance to means-tested support for

[60] John Kay, 'The Left is Still Searching for a Practical Philosophy', *Financial Times*, 5 May 2010, 13; David Donnison, 'Research for Policy', *Minerva* 10/4 (1972), 519–36. For a recent review of the 'epistemic communities' literature associated with Peter Haas, with a particular focus on the economics profession, see Daniel Hirschman and Elizabeth Popp Berman, 'Do Economists Make Policies? On the Political Effects of Economics', *Socio-Economic Review* 12/4 (2014), 779–811.

[61] Steensland, *The Failed Welfare Revolution*, 234–9; Marjorie Levine-Clark, *Unemployment, Welfare, and Masculine Citizenship: 'So Much Honest Poverty' in Britain, 1870–1930* (Basingstoke, 2015); Jack Jones, 'Wages and Social Security', *New Statesman*, 7 Jan. 1972, 7.

[62] Grover, *Social Security and Wage Poverty*, *passim*.

the working poor has helped to construct and legitimize a particular form of post-industrial liberal capitalism.[63] The British state has thus become not only a 'welfare state' and a 'regulatory state' (and, indeed, many other things as well) but also a 'transfer state'.[64] Like these parallel concepts, the notion of a 'transfer state' can be operationalized on two different levels. Sociologically, it highlights how fiscal transfers have shaped the state's relationship with citizens and society; institutionally, it focuses our attention on the departments responsible for raising tax and administering benefit payments.

The classic starting point for the sociological analysis of fiscal policy is Joseph Schumpeter's discussion of 'The Crisis of the Tax State'. Writing at the end of the First World War, Schumpeter argued that the modern state had been brought into being by the need to raise revenue for military action and public order: 'Tax bill in hand, the state penetrated the private economies and won increasing dominion over them.'[65] For Schumpeter, the tax state was characteristic of a market economy in which public and private spheres were sharply delineated, and the scope for revenue extraction was limited by the needs of social reproduction and private entrepreneurship: the market system would collapse if the 'economic parasite' of the state pushed its demands too far.[66] 'The Crisis of the Tax State' has been a foundational text for the field of fiscal sociology, taken up both by market liberals such as Alan Peacock and Jack Wiseman and by Marxist critics of capitalism such as James O'Connor.[67] Peacock and Wiseman's study of *The Growth of Public Expenditure in the United Kingdom* (1961) highlighted the 'displacement effect' of the two world wars in persuading British voters to accept a higher tax burden, whilst O'Connor warned of a 'fiscal crisis of the state' during the 1970s as the state's twin functions of supporting and legitimating capitalist accumulation came into conflict.

Schumpeter's analysis implies that tax is a discrete activity of the state, geared towards revenue raising. Since the middle decades of the twentieth century, however, economists and sociologists have increasingly come to see

[63] Edgerton, *The Rise and Fall of the British Nation*, 478.

[64] Daniel Wincott, 'Original and Imitated or Elusive and Limited? Towards a Genealogy of the Welfare State Idea in Britain', in *Analysing Social Policy Concepts and Languages: Comparative and Transnational Perspectives*, edited by Daniel Béland and Klaus Petersen (Bristol, 2014), 127–41; Michael Moran, 'The Rise of the Regulatory State in Britain', *Parliamentary Affairs* 54/1 (2001), 19–34.

[65] Joseph Schumpeter, 'The Crisis of the Tax State' [1918], in *Joseph Schumpeter: The Economics and Sociology of Capitalism*, edited by Richard Swedberg (Princeton, 1991), 99–140, at 108.

[66] Schumpeter, 'The Crisis of the Tax State', 112.

[67] John L. Campbell, 'The State and Fiscal Sociology', *Annual Review of Sociology* 19/1 (1993), 163–85; Alan T. Peacock and Jack Wiseman, *The Growth of Public Expenditure in the United Kingdom* (Princeton, 1961); James O'Connor, *The Fiscal Crisis of the State* (New York, 1973).

tax and public expenditure as interdependent. If the capitalist state is required to complement and sustain the market economy, as Schumpeter argued, then one of the principal ways it does so is by redistributing resources—both 'vertically', from rich to poor, and 'horizontally' between citizens at different points in the life cycle. As James Meade and his colleagues put it in their 1978 study of *The Structure and Reform of Direct Taxation*:

> in modern society the distributional effects of a fiscal system are often more pervasive and more purposive than the simple determination of who should bear the burden of an otherwise given level of government expenditures . . .[68]

Public services and benefits in kind play an important part in this redistributive process, but their incidence is difficult to measure, and they tend to be excluded from headline metrics of poverty and inequality, which are based on disposable income. As a result, analysis of the distributional effects of fiscal policy by organizations such as the IFS (and, increasingly, the Treasury itself) has largely focused on cash transfers. This interest in measuring and managing the income distribution reached its apogee under Tony Blair and Gordon Brown's governments, which set a target of eliminating child poverty by 2020 by raising households with children above a relative poverty line (defined as 60 per cent of equivalized median income).

The shift from a tax state to a transfer state can also be traced at an institutional level. Until the late twentieth century, the British government maintained a sharp conceptual and administrative distinction between its tax-raising machinery and its social expenditures. Tax collection was overseen by the Treasury through the annual budget process and carried out by the Board of Customs and Excise and the Inland Revenue, which focused on 'protecting the revenue' by maintaining taxpayers' consent—'plucking the goose with the least amount of hissing'. As Martin Daunton has pointed out, this Revenue ethos chimed closely with the rhetoric of Robert Peel and William Gladstone, who created a 'fiscal constitution' based on 'equity and even-handedness' by emphasizing the probity of the state and presenting the income tax as a source of balance between different classes and interests.[69] Even in the twentieth century, the state defined 'equity' between citizens largely in relation to the distribution of the tax burden. By contrast, social protection was a matter for

[68] J. E. Meade, *The Structure and Reform of Direct Taxation: Report of a Committee Chaired by Professor J. E. Meade* (1978), 12.

[69] Martin Daunton, *Trusting Leviathan: The Politics of Taxation in Britain, 1799–1914* (Cambridge, 2001), 27.

Poor Law officials, who were managed by local Boards of Guardians until 1929 and whose discretionary and personal approach to means-testing survived into the post-war National Assistance system.[70] From 1911, poor relief was complemented by the development of contributory National Insurance, which was financed by a separate Fund and remained institutionally distinct until the 1960s.

The parallel lives of Britain's tax and social security bureaucracies were easy to justify so long as direct taxpayers and benefit claimants formed discrete social groups. Since income tax became a mass tax in the 1940s, however, the case for integration has become increasingly influential.[71] During the 1950s and 1960s, economists such as R. A. Musgrave began to conceptualize redistribution as a single 'tax-transfer process' managed by a 'Distribution Branch', whilst Richard Titmuss argued that tax reliefs and allowances had similar effects to social security benefits and so should be subject to the same political scrutiny.[72] Conservative politicians have generally resisted these arguments on philosophical grounds, insisting (as Margaret Thatcher put it) that there is a fundamental difference between 'the State agreeing that a person should keep more of his own money and . . . bountifully handing some of it back'; nevertheless, the computerization of PAYE and social security records has helped bring about closer links between the two processes.[73] Under New Labour, the Treasury embraced the principle of integration, giving the Inland Revenue (later HM Revenue and Customs) operational responsibility for tax credits and treating them as part of the personal tax system.[74] The Conservatives have reversed this approach since 2010 by placing Universal Credit in the Department for Work and Pensions (DWP), but the technical relationship has in fact become closer, since the monthly assessment of Universal Credit entitlement

[70] Harris, 'From Poor Law to Welfare State?'

[71] Alan Peacock and George Peden, 'Merging National Insurance Contributions and Income Tax: The Lessons of History', *Economic Affairs* 34/1 (2014), 2–13.

[72] Richard A. Musgrave, *The Theory of Public Finance: A Study in Public Economy* (New York, 1959), 3–27, at 22; Richard M. Titmuss, 'The Social Division of Welfare: Some Reflections on the Search for Equity', in Richard M. Titmuss, *Essays on 'the Welfare State'* (1958), 34–55. John Rawls split Musgrave's 'Distribution Branch' into a 'Distributive Branch' which would raise revenue and manage the distribution of wealth and a 'Transfer Branch' which would establish a minimum income: see John Rawls, *A Theory of Justice* (Cambridge, Mass., 1971). For a useful recent survey of economists' approaches to tax and benefit policy, see Alan Hamlin, 'What Political Philosophy Should Learn from Economics about Taxation', in *Taxation: Philosophical Perspectives*, edited by Martin O'Neill and Shepley Orr (Oxford, 2018), 18–36.

[73] Bodleian Library, Oxford, Conservative Party Archive (CPA), CRD3/7/26/14, 'Tax Relief—or Cash Subsidy' by Margaret Thatcher, *Building Societies' Gazette*, Oct. 1967.

[74] Penelope Tuck, Dominic de Cogan, and John Snape, 'A Tale of the Merger between the Inland Revenue and HM Customs & Excise', forthcoming in *Studies in the History of Tax Law*, vol. 9, edited by Peter Harris and Dominic de Cogan (Oxford, 2019).

is based on a Real-Time Information link with PAYE data. Although the vision of a unified transfer branch is not yet a reality, then, the tax and benefit systems have moved a long way in this direction, and the difficulties faced in implementing Universal Credit should not obscure the scale and ambition of the British state's redistributive apparatus.

Plan of the book

The changing place of cash transfers in British social policy since the First World War is a vast story which would be impossible to cover in detail in one book. Many of the most important and familiar elements of the social security system—National Insurance, National Assistance, Child Benefit, and pensions—feature only in passing here: readers interested in the evolution of these benefits will learn much from Nicholas Timmins's excellent 'biography of the welfare state', *The Five Giants*, together with classic works by scholars such as José Harris and Susan Pedersen and newer studies by John Macnicol and Chris Renwick.[75] Housing policy and disability benefits also deserve more attention than it has been possible to give them here, though they have been the subject of important work by social policy specialists and historians such as Peter Malpass, Gareth Millward, and Jameel Hampton.[76] The focus, instead, is on the series of attempts to create a guaranteed income through UBI or NIT, sidestepping the perceived problems of social insurance and means-testing by bringing tax and benefits together.

Chapter 2 clears the intellectual ground for what follows by examining how attitudes to redistribution have changed in Britain since the eighteenth century. It focuses particularly on the history of economic thought, and shows how fiscal redistribution came to the fore among Anglo-American economists during the 1940s and 1950s in reaction to socialist planning and the perceived paternalism of collective provision. It also examines the normative critiques

[75] Nicholas Timmins, *The Five Giants: A Biography of the Welfare State*, 3rd edn (2017); José Harris, *William Beveridge: A Biography*, 2nd edn (Oxford, 1997); Susan Pedersen, *Family, Dependence, and the Origins of the Welfare State: Britain and France, 1914–1945* (Cambridge, 1993); John Macnicol, *Neoliberalising Old Age* (Cambridge, 2015); Chris Renwick, *Bread for All: The Origins of the Welfare State* (2017).

[76] Peter Malpass, *Reshaping Housing Policy: Subsidies, Rents and Residualisation* (1990); Peter Malpass, *Housing and the Welfare State: The Development of Housing Policy in Britain* (Basingstoke, 2005); Gareth Millward, 'Invalid Definitions, Invalid Responses: Disability and the Welfare State, 1965–1995' (Ph.D. thesis, London School of Hygiene and Tropical Medicine, 2014); Jameel Hampton, *Disability and the Welfare State in Britain: Changes in Perception and Policy 1948–79* (Bristol, 2016). For a detailed analysis of the upward trend in disability benefit spending since the 1970s, see CP 2, *Office for Budget Responsibility: Welfare Trends Report, January 2019* (2019).

which conservatives, 'moral economists', Marxists, and social policy experts have levelled at redistributive market liberalism.

Part II draws on archival research to reconstruct the story of three types of guaranteed income schemes which attracted the attention of policy-makers in mid-twentieth-century Britain. Chapter 3 looks at basic income and 'social dividend' schemes, and argues that the idea of UBI took on its characteristic form during the 1940s as a result of Juliet Rhys-Williams's attempt to devise an alternative to the Beveridgean social insurance model. Chapter 4 traces the rise and fall of NIT proposals in Britain during the 1960s in the context of the 'rediscovery of poverty', and shows how attempts to translate Milton Friedman's ideas into policy ran up against the trade unions' suspicion of wage supplements and the structure of the PAYE system. Chapter 5 examines the Heath government's attempt to overcome these problems through a Tax Credit Scheme devised by Arthur Cockfield, then a special adviser to the Chancellor of the Exchequer and later the architect of the European single market. These three episodes might be seen as case studies in failed policy entrepreneurship, but they also shed new light on the contours of British social policy in the post-war 'golden age' and on the obstacles to guaranteed income proposals.

Part III explores how the idea of a guaranteed income has shaped the growth and restructuring of working-age benefits since the 1970s. Chapter 6 argues that despite Margaret Thatcher's ideological suspicion of what she called the 'transfer machine', the Conservative governments of the 1980s and 1990s nevertheless made strategic use of transfer payments to offset the distributional effects of neoliberal reforms, particularly in the housing and labour markets.[77] This expansion was aided by the rationalization of working-age benefits which emerged from Norman Fowler's 1984–5 social security reviews and followed a high-profile debate about the scope for tax-benefit integration. Chapter 7 explores Gordon Brown's efforts to redistribute income to working families with children through tax credits, and examines how this anti-poverty strategy intersected with New Labour's welfare-to-work agenda. Chapter 8 reflects on the backlash against cash transfers which has taken place since the 2008 financial crisis, in the context of new fiscal pressures and demands for a 'living wage', and considers how far this should be understood as a 'crisis of the transfer state'. Although the Conservatives have cut benefits

[77] For the idea of a 'transfer machine', see CPA, CRD4/7/14, 'Taxation and Social Security. Record of a meeting held on Tuesday, 12th December, 1978 at the House of Commons', by P. J. Cropper, 3 Jan. 1979 (copy).

repeatedly over the last decade, the development of Universal Credit suggests that the idea of providing an income floor through cash transfers remains influential. So too does the recent revival of interest in UBI, which is analysed—against the backdrop of earlier debates—in Chapter 9. The concluding Part IV (that is, Chapter 10) returns to the larger themes set out in this introduction and considers the prospects for Britain's transfer state in the twenty-first century.

2

Redistributive Market Liberalism and its Critics

The belief that a civilized society should seek to prevent destitution among its citizens is one of the oldest ideas in politics, yet the idea that this is best achieved by a guaranteed income is relatively new. Indeed, for most of human history rulers have actively sought to avoid any such responsibility. From ancient Israel to the dawn of the industrial age, Jewish and Christian societies expressed their concern for the poor through a mixture of private charity, laws against profiteering and usury, and customary rights of pasture and gleaning. Early modern European states systematized poor relief at a local level, but also stigmatized 'pauperism' through workhouses and intrusive means tests. Even after the industrial revolution, radicals such as Thomas Paine focused on campaigning for universal suffrage and land reform, whilst skilled workers looked to trade union organization to establish their economic security and independence.

This chapter explores the intellectual roots of redistributive market liberalism and traces its emergence as an influence on British social policy. Drawing on work by Samuel Fleischacker, Martin Ravallion, and Alice O'Connor, it argues that the very idea of a guaranteed minimum is a distinctly modern concept, shaped by an Enlightenment conception of distributive justice, an Anglo-American tradition of 'poverty knowledge', and the methodological individualism of neoclassical economics. The ideological breakthrough began in the late eighteenth century with Adam Smith and Immanuel Kant, but it was only after the Second World War that new technologies of income assessment and tax collection made a comprehensive income floor a realistic policy option. Growing evidence of poverty amid plenty, together with a declining faith in planning and collective provision, encouraged governments to pursue their distributional objectives through the tax and benefit systems.

John Kay's concept of redistributive market liberalism provides a useful starting point for this analysis, because it focuses our attention on the ways in which policy-makers have sought to achieve social justice outside the labour market. RML is *liberal* because it takes individual freedom as its starting point

Transfer State: The Idea of a Guaranteed Income and the Politics of Redistribution in Modern Britain. Peter Sloman, Oxford University Press (2019). © Peter Sloman. DOI: 10.1093/oso/9780198813262.001.0001

and treats individual choice as a primary expression of freedom. It is *market-oriented* because it is strongly influenced by the neoclassical model of perfect competition. It is *redistributive* because it believes the state nevertheless has a role to play in alleviating poverty (and perhaps also inequality)—whether on utilitarian grounds, in recognition of social rights, or on the basis of a Rawlsian social contract.

Kay was a leading exponent of RML during his time as director of the Institute for Fiscal Studies (1979–86), but he has since recanted his support and led a growing chorus of criticism. According to Kay's critique, RML ignores the social context in which markets work, places too much faith in rules and transfer payments, and fails to challenge the dominance of individualistic values.[1] Likewise, Elizabeth Anderson has accused egalitarian philosophers of playing into conservatives' hands by focusing on abstract questions of distributive justice instead of building on voters' intuitive desire for equal social status, freedom from oppression, and fair pay for their work.[2] Since the 2008 financial crisis this critique of RML has gained traction on both sides of the Atlantic, spurred on by Jacob Hacker's work on 'predistribution' and high-profile 'living wage' campaigns.[3] Even if the policy climate is turning against cash transfers, however, it is important to understand where the transfer state has come from. The first part of this chapter sets RML in the context of historical approaches to deprivation and poverty, whilst the following sections trace its development in nineteenth- and twentieth-century Britain through debates over Speenhamland, the welfare state, the neoliberal reaction against central planning, and the post-war labour market. A final section examines RML's limitations and the arguments of its critics.

Approaches to poverty

Providing a guaranteed minimum income through transfer payments is a radically modernist response to poverty. It only makes sense if you believe (i) that poverty can be meaningfully conceptualized in terms of income deficiency, (ii) that the state should seek to relieve that deficiency whatever its cause, and (iii) that raising every citizen's income above the 'poverty line' in

[1] John Kay, 'Staking a Moral Claim', *New Statesman*, 11 Oct. 1996, 18–20; John Kay, *The Truth about Markets: Why Some Nations Are Rich but Most Remain Poor* (2003).

[2] Elizabeth S. Anderson, 'What is the Point of Equality?', *Ethics* 109/2 (1999), 287–337.

[3] Jacob Hacker, 'The Institutional Foundations of Middle-Class Democracy', in *Priorities for a New Political Economy: Memos to the Left*, Policy Network (2011), 33–7.

this way is a feasible administrative task. Although these assumptions are commonplace in contemporary poverty research, all of them are open to question. As John Veit-Wilson and Paul Spicker have pointed out, western thinkers have traditionally understood poverty in terms of a deprived lifestyle—vagrancy, malnutrition, idleness, and squalor—rather than inadequate income.[4] Early modern European states were primarily concerned about the threat which 'pauperism' posed to the social order, rather than about poverty per se. Even today, the idea of poverty as income deficiency predominates only among a particular epistemic community of economists and social researchers. Psychologists tend to be more interested in concepts such as individual development and maladjustment, Marxist sociologists in class and power, and continental European policy-makers in social exclusion and integration.[5]

Even where poverty is defined primarily in material terms, as in twentieth-century Britain, raising incomes to the 'poverty line' is only one way of dealing with it. Jean Drèze and Amartya Sen have pointed out that social policy can be geared towards 'entitlement promotion', which builds people's capacity to provide for their own needs in future, as well as 'entitlement protection', which focuses on preventing immediate starvation.[6] It is probably true—as Martin Ravallion suggests—that entitlement protection is the more intuitive response to extreme poverty, but most social thinkers have preferred to focus their longer-term efforts on promotion: dealing with the 'root causes' of poverty rather than the 'symptoms'.[7] This is as true of trade unionists (focused on low pay) as it is of moralists who see poverty as a symptom of behavioural pathologies, or contemporary social policy experts such as Anton Hemerijck who champion a 'social investment' approach.[8]

Although entitlement protection dates back centuries, it has normally been seen as a temporary measure 'to protect poor people against adverse events' until improvements in individual behaviour or the social structure enable them to become self-supporting.[9] This tendency is well illustrated by Juan

[4] John Veit-Wilson, 'Poverty', in *International Encyclopaedia of Social Policy*, vol. 1, edited by Tony Fitzpatrick, Huck-ju Kwon, Nick Manning, James Midgley, and Gillian Pascall (Abingdon, 2006), 1036–42; Paul Spicker, 'Definitions of Poverty: Twelve Clusters of Meaning', in *Poverty: An International Glossary*, 2nd edn, edited by Paul Spicker, Sonia Alvarez Leguizamón, and David Gordon (2006), 229–43.

[5] For an analysis of the 'social exclusion' discourse, see Rob Atkinson and Simin Da Voudi, 'The Concept of Social Exclusion in the European Union: Context, Development and Possibilities', *Journal of Common Market Studies* 38/3 (2000), 427–48.

[6] Jean Drèze and Amartya Sen, *Hunger and Public Action* (Oxford, 1989), 260.

[7] Martin Ravallion, *The Economics of Poverty: History, Measurement, and Policy* (Oxford, 2016), 28.

[8] Anton Hemerijck, *Changing Welfare States* (Oxford, 2013).

[9] Ravallion, *The Economics of Poverty*, 28.

Luis Vives's treatise *De Subventione Pauperum* (1526), one of the earliest detailed proposals for institutionalized poor relief, which stressed the need for a strict work test to prevent malingering and other abuses.[10] Two centuries later, the French philosopher Montesquieu declared that the state 'owes to every citizen a certain subsistence, a proper nourishment, convenient clothing, and a kind of life not incompatible with health', but added that 'transient assistances are much better than permanent foundations' because the latter were likely to discourage work and industrial development.[11]

The idea that the state had a duty to provide for every citizen became more widely accepted in Britain and continental Europe during the second half of the eighteenth century—a period which Ravallion has described as 'the First Poverty Enlightenment'.[12] As Samuel Fleischacker has shown, this period witnessed 'a sea change in attitudes to the poor' in the context of industrialization, revolutionary politics, and the emergence of classical political economy.[13] Though Adam Smith is best known for championing free trade and private property rights, he also insisted that 'no society can…be flourishing and happy of which the far greater part of the members are poor and miserable', and argued that economic growth should be judged primarily by the consumption of commodities.[14] Immanuel Kant, who had read Smith, added a powerful philosophical argument for equal human worth which implied that the state should help citizens realize their potential. Instead of relying on private charity, which reinforced hierarchies of power, Kant urged governments to 'constrain the wealthy to provide the means of subsistence to those who are unable to provide for their most necessary natural needs'.[15]

The French Revolution helped push the idea of social rights to the fore, most famously in Robespierre's declaration that 'the first law of society is that which guarantees the means of existence to all its members'.[16] As Samuel Moyn has pointed out, the 1793 Declaration of the Rights of Man and of the Citizen articulated a powerful vision of basic sufficiency for all, whilst the most ambitious Jacobins—such as 'Gracchus' Babeuf—went even further in

[10] Jean Luis Vives, *De Subventione Pauperum: Sive de humanis necessitatibus libri II* (Antwerp, 1526).

[11] Charles de Secondat, Baron de Montesquieu, *De l'esprit des lois* (Geneva, 1748), quoted in Ravallion, *The Economics of Poverty*, 30.

[12] Ravallion, *The Economics of Poverty*, 35–47.

[13] Samuel Fleischacker, *A Short History of Distributive Justice* (Cambridge, Mass., 2004), 53.

[14] Adam Smith, *An Inquiry into the Nature and Causes of the Wealth of Nations*, 5th edn [1789], ed. Edwin Cannan (1904), Book 1, ch. 8, para. 35.

[15] Immanuel Kant, *The Metaphysics of Morals* (1797), quoted in Fleischacker, *A Short History of Distributive Justice*, 73.

[16] Maximilien de Robespierre, 'Discours sur les troubles frumentaires d'Eure-et-Loir', 2 Dec. 1792, quoted in Albert Soboul, *Précis d'histoire de la Révolution Française* (Paris, 1962), 327.

advocating total material equality.[17] British radicals, in turn, adapted this rhetoric to their own narratives of dispossession, which placed resistance to the Enclosure Acts in the context of an ancient struggle against the 'Norman yoke' and the rise of feudalism. Most famously, Thomas Paine proposed that everyone should receive an endowment of £15 at the age of 21, plus a pension of £10 per annum once they reached the age of 50, as 'compensation . . . for the loss of his or her inheritance, by the introduction of the system of landed property'.[18] Paine's rival Thomas Spence went even further, suggesting that parishes should appropriate all land and buildings in the common interest. The rents could then be used to cover the costs of the state and pay an equal quarterly allowance to each parishioner.[19]

This 'First Poverty Enlightenment' had a powerful impact on British social thought, 'establishing the moral case for the idea of public effort toward eliminating poverty'.[20] As Donald Stabile has shown, practically all the classical economists believed that workers should earn a wage sufficient to maintain themselves and their families. Many of them, including Smith, also adopted a broad definition of subsistence which involved not only the bare essentials of survival and reproduction but also what was necessary for decent and respectable living.[21] At the same time, however, most nineteenth-century economists thought working-class living standards could only be sustainably raised through education, thrift, and population control, not by direct transfer payments. This approach reflected the influence of the 'wage fund' theory popularized by Thomas Malthus, and the way it shaped interpretations of the 'Speenhamland system'.

The shadow of Speenhamland

Until 1834, poor relief in England and Wales was governed by the Elizabethan Poor Law, which required parish authorities to relieve the aged and the sick and to put the able-bodied poor to work. The 1601 Poor Law Act implied that

[17] Samuel Moyn, *Not Enough: Human Rights in an Unequal World* (Cambridge, Mass., 2018), 12–40.

[18] Thomas Paine, *Agrarian Justice* (1797), reprinted in *The Writings of Thomas Paine*, vol. 3, ed. Moncure Daniel Conway (New York, 1894), 322–44, at 331.

[19] Thomas Spence, *The Constitution of Spensonia* (1803), reprinted in *The Political Works of Thomas Spence*, ed. H. T. Dickinson (Newcastle-upon-Tyne, 1982), 104–18.

[20] Ravallion, *The Economics of Poverty*, 47.

[21] Donald Stabile, *The Living Wage: Lessons from the History of Economic Thought* (Cheltenham, 2008), 12–57.

able-bodied paupers should earn their own keep in the workhouse, but during the eighteenth century many parishes began to provide 'outrelief' for low-paid workers. Paying outrelief tended to be cheaper and easier than taking families into the workhouse, and it helped defuse unrest during the Revolutionary and Napoleonic wars with France (1793–1815) and the agricultural depression which followed. As George Boyer has pointed out, the expansion of poor relief may have been particularly attractive to wealthy farmers and landlords because it kept agricultural workers on the land.[22] 'Gilbert's Act' of 1782 removed restrictions on outrelief, and William Pitt the Younger encouraged parishes to extend poor relief to workers with large families on the grounds that this would be more effective and less disruptive than a minimum wage policy.

The most famous system of outrelief for agricultural workers was the scale of support introduced by the Berkshire parish of Speenhamland in May 1795, which guaranteed 'poor and industrious men and their families' a minimum income linked to the price of bread:

> When the Gallon Loaf of Second Flour, Weighing 8lb. 11ozs. shall cost 1s.
>
> Then every poor and industrious man shall have for his own support 3s. weekly, either produced by his own or his family's labour, or an allowance from the poor rates, and for the support of his wife and every other of his family, 1s. 6d.
>
> When the Gallon Loaf shall cost 1s. 4d.
>
> Then every poor and industrious man shall have 4s. weekly for his own, and 1s. and 10d. for the support of every other of his family.
>
> And so in proportion, as the price of bread rise or falls (that is to say) 3d. to the man, and 1d. to every other of the family, on every 1d. which the loaf rise above 1s.

Although 'Speenhamland' became synonymous with generous poor relief, the bread scale was by no means universal. As Mark Blaug showed in an influential 1963 article, the Speenhamland system was only widely adopted in the wheat-growing areas of south-east England, and even here it tended to be used episodically.[23] In 1832, for instance, only about 11 per cent of parishes in 'Speenhamland counties' appear to have supplemented wages directly, and

[22] George Boyer, *An Economic History of the English Poor Law, 1750–1850* (Cambridge, 1990).

[23] Mark Blaug, 'The Myth of the Old Poor Law and the Making of the New', *Journal of Economic History* 23/2 (1963), 151–84.

other forms of relief—such as subsidized job-creation and children's allowances for large families—were much more common.[24] On the other hand, there can be no doubt that total Poor Law expenditures rose sharply in this period—from about 1.59 per cent of England and Wales GDP in 1776 to 2.66 per cent in 1820–1, according to Peter Lindert's calculations.[25] The Speenhamland scale came to symbolize this wider trend in policy.

Karl Polanyi famously held up Speenhamland in *The Great Transformation* (1944) as a 'device contrived by squirearchy' to resist the commodification of labour by industrial capitalism: though 'designed to prevent the proletarianization of the common people', it depressed wages below subsistence level and resulted in 'social catastrophe'.[26] Polanyi's account of 'pauperization' built on Thomas Malthus' famous *Essay on the Principle of Population* (1798), which insisted that poor relief perpetuated poverty in the long run by encouraging population growth which could not be sustained. This critique was underpinned by the theory of the wage fund—that the resources available to support wage-earners in a given year were fixed in relation to the stock of capital—and by the belief that higher real incomes led directly to higher fertility, so that work and wages had to be shared out among more individuals. In fact, modern research suggests that both agricultural productivity and real agricultural wages grew during the late eighteenth and early nineteenth centuries, and that Speenhamland may have played an important role in cushioning rural workers against the disruptive effects of the French wars and the industrial revolution.[27] Nevertheless, the Malthusian interpretation became dominant in political circles during the 1820s and 1830s, perhaps because it served a number of practical purposes: rural landowners were keen to curb the cost of poor relief (and the 'moral economy' which had grown up around it), industrialists resented the subsidy to agricultural labour, and classical economists were keen to divert blame for the post-war agricultural depression away from the 1819 return to the gold standard.[28] The 1832 Royal Commission into

[24] Mark Blaug, 'The Poor Law Report Reexamined', *Journal of Economic History* 24/2 (1964), 229–45, at 236.

[25] Peter H. Lindert, *Growing Public: Social Spending and Economic Growth since the Eighteenth Century*, vol. 1 (Cambridge, 2004), 10.

[26] Karl Polanyi, *The Great Transformation: The Political and Economic Origins of our Time* (New York, 1944), 89, 82, 98.

[27] See, for instance, Fred Block and Margaret Somers, 'In the Shadow of Speenhamland: Social Policy and the Old Poor Law', *Politics & Society* 31/2 (2003), 283–323.

[28] These explanations are suggested, respectively, by Peter Jones, 'Swing, Speenhamland and Rural Social Relations: The "Moral Economy" of the English Crowd in the Nineteenth Century', *Social History* 32/3 (2007), 271–90; Boyer, *An Economic History of the English Poor Law*; and Block and Somers, 'In the Shadow of Speenhamland'.

the Operation of the Poor Laws recommended the abolition of outrelief and a much stricter regime for able-bodied paupers, and the resulting Poor Law Amendment Act had a rapid impact: by 1850 expenditure on poor relief had fallen by more than half.[29]

The Royal Commission's lurid portrayal of Speenhamland inhibited discussion of a guaranteed income for much of the following century, as Fred Block and Margaret Somers have shown.[30] This is perhaps best illustrated by John Stuart Mill's attitude. Like other utilitarians, Mill was keen to improve the lot of the working classes and believed that the distribution of property was a legitimate object of political action, 'since the manner in which wealth is distributed in any given society, depends on the statutes or usages therein obtaining'.[31] Yet Mill's *Principles of Political Economy* (1848) also included a strident attack on the idea of wage supplementation:

> Under the allowance system the people increased so fast, and wages sank so low, that with wages and allowance together, families were worse off than they had been with wages alone ... This deplorable system, worse than any other form of poor-law abuse yet invented, inasmuch as it pauperizes not merely the unemployed part of the population but the whole, received a severe check from the Poor Law of 1834: I wish it could be said that there are no signs of its revival.[32]

Although Mill later recanted his support for the wage fund theory, he never took much interest in direct redistribution to the poor. Instead, Mill put his hopes for the 'futurity of the labouring classes' in education, self-reliance, and the development of producers' cooperatives which would allow workers to share in the profits of the capitalist system.[33]

As Mill's attitude suggests, the New Poor Law came to be seen as one of the landmark achievements of classical political economy and Benthamite social reform. The 1834 Act created what José Harris has called 'the most centralized, professionalized, and regulated system in Europe', financed by compulsory local property taxes and designed to provide a rational and consistent

[29] Lindert, *Growing Public*, vol. 1, 10.

[30] Block and Somers, 'In the Shadow of Speenhamland'.

[31] John Stuart Mill, *Principles of Political Economy* (1848), reprinted in *Collected Works of John Stuart Mill*, vol. 2, ed. J. M. Robson (1965), 21.

[32] Mill, *Principles of Political Economy*, 362.

[33] Mill, *Principles of Political Economy*, Book IV, ch. 7; see also Dale E. Miller, 'Mill's "Socialism"', *Politics, Philosophy & Economics* 2/2 (2003), 231–8.

structure of work incentives.[34] At the same time, Harris notes that the post-1834 regime was less strict than subsequent critics have often supposed: there was much less scope for moral discipline than in continental Europe, and many Boards of Guardians flouted the ban on giving outrelief to the able-bodied poor.[35] More important was the stigma attached to relief, reinforced (up to 1918) by civic disenfranchisement, which encouraged a sharp conceptual distinction between workers and welfare dependants. Skilled workers responded by establishing friendly societies and other forms of collective self-help so that they could avoid the humiliation of the Poor Law.

The liberal collectivists and the welfare state, *c.*1890–1945

The first half of the twentieth century witnessed a dramatic shift in the ethos and structure of British social provision, away from means-tested poor relief and towards the self-consciously inclusive 'welfare state' which T. H. Marshall hailed in the 1940s. The classic narrative of state expansion traces its beginnings to the Liberal governments of 1905–15, which introduced old-age pensions for the over 70s and contributory health and unemployment insurance for workers earning less than £160 a year. Inter-war Conservative and coalition governments developed the system, and Sir William Beveridge's landmark 1942 report on *Social Insurance and Allied Services* set out a far-reaching blueprint for its rationalization. Under the 1946 National Insurance Act, the British state provided a comprehensive system of insurance benefits to tide workers and their families over the contingencies of life: unemployment, sickness, and old age. This social security system was complemented by the government's acceptance of Beveridge's three 'assumptions': Family Allowances, a National Health Service, and the use of demand management to prevent the recurrence of mass unemployment.

Although the growth of welfare provision between 1908 and 1948 was an inherently political process—shaped by total war, mass enfranchisement, and the rise of the Labour Party—it also had important intellectual roots. One

[34] José Harris, 'From Poor Law to Welfare State? A European Perspective', in *The Political Economy of British Historical Experience, 1688–1914*, edited by Donald Winch and Patrick K. O'Brien (Oxford, 2002), 409–37, at 419.

[35] Harris, 'From Poor Law to Welfare State?', 418–27; see also Chris Grover, *Social Security and Wage Poverty: Historical and Policy Aspects of Supplementing Wages in Britain and beyond* (Basingstoke, 2016), 37–41.

influence was early twentieth-century British idealism, which 'subordinate[d] the analysis of specific social problems to a vision of reconstructing the whole of British society' and implied that 'the ultimate sphere of "welfare" in its widest sense was, or ought to be, the institutions of the state'.[36] As José Harris has pointed out, even the work of post-war social scientists such as Richard Titmuss 'was full of muffled resonances of the idealist discourse of the Edwardian age'.[37] At the same time, developments in positivist social research and neoclassical economics laid much of the intellectual groundwork for RML and reinforced the case for tackling poverty through the welfare state.

According to John Veit-Wilson, 'the British discussion of poverty changed its dominant paradigm in the first third of the [twentieth] century, from poverty as deprived *lifestyle* to poverty as subsistence *income*', which made it possible to believe that it could be solved through redistribution.[38] This paradigm shift was largely the result of the pioneering research carried out by Charles Booth in London and Seebohm Rowntree in York during the 1880s and 1890s, which sought to quantify the scale and distribution of poverty in order to analyse its causes.[39] Booth focused on describing living standards street by street and producing 'poverty maps' of the capital, which required him to categorize households into seven (sometimes eight) broad classes. Rowntree, on the other hand, used a team of investigators to identify households 'living in obvious want and squalor', and gathered data on their incomes to reveal how far this was caused by inadequate wages. As Veit-Wilson has pointed out, Rowntree's conception of poverty was 'behavioural and visible', and he constructed his scale of minimal subsistence needs to show that such deprivation was *not* always due to mis-spending.[40] Likewise, the more generous 'Human Needs of Labour' index which Rowntree devised at the end of the First World War was designed to provide a defensible basis for a minimum wage. Other inter-war poverty researchers such as A. L. Bowley followed Rowntree in attempting to quantify basic needs, and Beveridge took a similar approach in *Social Insurance and Allied Services*.[41] Beveridge estimated the

[36] José Harris, 'Political Thought and the Welfare State 1870–1940: An Intellectual Framework for British Social Policy', *Past and Present* 135 (1992), 116–41, at 126, 134.

[37] Harris, 'Political Thought and the Welfare State', 137.

[38] John Veit-Wilson, 'Condemned to Deprivation? Beveridge's Responsibility for the Invisibility of Poverty', in *Beveridge and Social Security: An International Retrospective*, edited by John Hills, John Ditch, and Howard Glennerster (Oxford, 1994), 97–117 at 98.

[39] E. P. Hennock, 'The Measurement of Urban Poverty: From the Metropolis to the Nation, 1880–1920', *Economic History Review* 40/2 (1987), 208–27.

[40] John Veit-Wilson, 'Paradigms of Poverty: A Rehabilitation of B. S. Rowntree', *Journal of Social Policy* 15/1 (1986), 69–99, at 76.

[41] Ian Gazeley, *Poverty in Britain, 1900–1965* (Basingstoke, 2003).

minimum costs of food, rent, clothing, and fuel and light during 'interruption of earnings', added a small 'margin . . . for inefficiency in spending', and claimed that National Insurance benefits set at this level would be 'sufficient . . . to provide the minimum income needed for subsistence in all normal cases'.[42]

The reconceptualization of poverty as income deficiency was aided by the rise of neoclassical economics: that is, the tradition of analysis focused on 'the optimizing behavio[u]r of fully rational and well-informed individuals in a static context and the equilibria that result from that optimization' which emerged from the marginalist revolution of the 1870s.[43] This tradition came to dominate Anglo-American microeconomics in the twentieth century through textbooks such as Alfred Marshall's *Principles of Economics* (1890) and Paul Samuelson's *Foundations of Economic Analysis* (1947). Marginalist analysis focused economists' attention on the preferences and behaviour of individual agents, and the principle of diminishing marginal utility provided a plausible (if contested) justification for redistribution from rich to poor. The sustained rise in working-class living standards and decline in fertility from the mid-nineteenth century onwards strongly undermined the idea of the wage fund and encouraged a more optimistic approach to social improvement: Léon Walras, for instance, dismissed Malthus' theory of population as 'ridiculous'.[44] The pre-eminent British neoclassicist, Marshall, saw poverty as 'a mere passing evil in the progress of man upwards' and questioned 'whether it is really impossible that all should start in the world with a fair chance of leading a cultured life, free from the pains of poverty and the stagnating influences of excessive material toil'.[45] Like other Victorian liberals, Marshall was suspicious of 'administrative' socialism and committed to the improvement of 'character', but accepted that taxation and public expenditure had a role to play in raising the material welfare of the poor.[46]

[42] John Veit-Wilson, 'Muddle or Mendacity? The Beveridge Committee and the Poverty Line', *Journal of Social Policy* 21/3 (1992), 269–301; Cmd. 6404, *Social Insurance and Allied Services: A Report by Sir William Beveridge* (1942), 84–5, 122.

[43] David Colander, Richard P. F. Holt, and J. Barkley Rosser Jr, 'The Changing Face of Mainstream Economics', *Review of Political Economy* 16/4 (2004), 485–99, at 490. The meaning and parameters of neoclassical economics are strongly contested, as the contributions to a recent essay collection show: Jamie Morgan, ed., *What is Neoclassical Economics? Debating the Origins, Meaning and Significance* (Abingdon, 2016).

[44] Quoted in Agnar Sandmo, 'The Principal Problem in Political Economy: Income Distribution in the History of Economic Thought', in *Handbook of Income Distribution*, vol. 2, edited by Anthony B. Atkinson and François Bourguignon (Amsterdam, 2015), 3–65, at 16.

[45] Alfred Marshall, 'Preliminary Statement and Evidence before the Royal Commission on the Aged Poor' [1893], in *Official Papers by Alfred Marshall*, ed. J. M. Keynes (1926), 197–262, at 244; Alfred Marshall, *Principles of Economics* [1890], 8th edn (1920), 4.

[46] For a sensitive analysis of Marshall's social thought, see Donald Winch, *Wealth and Life: Essays in the Intellectual History of Political Economy in Britain, 1848–1914* (Cambridge, 2009), 270–94.

Although many early neoclassical economists were committed to social reform, they also delimited the ways in which poverty and inequality could be tackled by introducing the marginal productivity theory of the labour market. As Deborah Figart, Ellen Mutari, and Marilyn Power have shown, a view of wages as the 'living' which employers owed to their workers was increasingly supplanted by the neoclassical view of wages as a 'price'.[47] Marginalists such as Walras and W. S. Jevons believed that prices were determined by subjective value, and that in this respect the labour market was much like any other. John Hicks expressed the new orthodoxy succinctly in *The Theory of Wages* (1932): 'Wages are the price of labour; and thus, in the absence of control, they are determined, like all prices, by supply and demand.'[48] The marginal productivity theory implied that there was no particular reason why wages should be enough to live on: the value of a worker's labour to an employer might well be below subsistence level. The powerful early twentieth-century drive to 'decasualize' the labour market thus sat uncomfortably with prevailing economic theory. Though neoclassical economists such as Marshall and Hicks recognized that state regulation and trade union activity might sometimes be necessary to prevent exploitation, they believed that any attempt to raise wages *above* the prevailing equilibrium was likely to put less productive workers out of work.

The most systematic analysis of the scope for redistribution in this period came from Marshall's protégé A. C. Pigou, whose study of *Wealth and Welfare* (1912)—later expanded into *The Economics of Welfare* (1920)—'virtually created the study of welfare economics'.[49] Starting with the principle of diminishing marginal utility, Pigou argued that overall welfare could be increased either by expanding the national income or by increasing the share which went to the poor. The challenge for egalitarian policy-makers was to work out how working-class living standards could be raised without reducing the national income—the classic equity/efficiency trade-off. Since a high wage floor was liable to produce unemployment, Pigou believed his goal was best achieved 'by the direct action of the State, in securing for all families of its citizens... an adequate minimum standard in every department of life', including 'some defined quantity and quality of house accommodation, of

[47] Deborah M. Figart, Ellen Mutari, and Marilyn Power, *Living Wages, Equal Wages: Gender and Labor Market Policies in the United States* (2002), 34–51.

[48] J. R. Hicks, *The Theory of Wages* (1932), 1.

[49] David Collard, 'Pigou, Arthur Cecil (1877–1959)', in *Oxford Dictionary of National Biography*, vol. 44, edited by H. C. G. Matthew and Brian Harrison (Oxford, 2004), 296–9, at 297–8.

medical care, of education, of food, of leisure, of the apparatus of sanitary convenience and safety where work is carried on, and so on'.[50]

Pigou was determined to show that not all forms of state welfare would 'tempt the poor into idleness and thriftlessness' by reviving 'the discredited policy of Speenhamland': it depended on the type of social provision and how it was paid for.[51] He argued that a means-tested income guarantee was most damaging because it would 'greatly weaken the motive of many poor people to make provision for themselves', but 'a universal gift to everybody of a sum deemed sufficient to furnish by itself the means of subsistence' was not much better:

> For, if a man of any given presumed capacity knows that he will receive, say, a pound a week as a gift, independently of anything that he may earn for himself, his desire for any *n*th unit of money earned by himself is lowered... It follows that the expectation of a weekly grant will cause the recipient to contract the amount of work that he does, and therewith, his contribution to the national dividend.[52]

Instead, Pigou advocated universal provision of goods and services which citizens might not otherwise have purchased, such as public parks, education, school meals, and children's health care.[53] Not only would these benefits in kind have less impact on incentives, but they could also improve workers' efficiency (or human capital) at a time when 'many poor people [were] unable, through lack of knowledge, to invest resources in themselves or their children in the best way'.[54]

Pigou's collectivist approach to redistribution was widely followed during the inter-war years—a period in which high unemployment and industrial strife meant that the problem of poverty was never far from the fore. His Cambridge colleague John Maynard Keynes, for instance, was keen to reduce inequalities of income and wealth and was confident that mankind's 'struggle for subsistence' could eventually be solved.[55] Although Keynes believed the wage cuts imposed by employers after the First World War were likely to be

[50] A. C. Pigou, *The Economics of Welfare*, 4th edn (1932), 618, 759.
[51] Pigou, *The Economics of Welfare*, 720.
[52] Pigou, *The Economics of Welfare*, 728, 722, 725.
[53] Pigou, *The Economics of Welfare*, 725–8.
[54] Pigou, *The Economics of Welfare*, 753.
[55] Stephen Pressman, 'Keynes and Antipoverty Policy', *Review of Social Economy* 49/3 (1991), 365–82; the quotation is from John Maynard Keynes, 'Economic Possibilities for our Grandchildren' [1930], in John Maynard Keynes, *Essays in Persuasion* (1931), 358–73, at 366.

self-defeating, he shared Pigou's fear that the large wage increases sought by trade unions would damage the competitiveness of British industry and so destroy jobs. 'If we want to better the condition of the working class', he argued in 1930,

> there are plenty of alternative ways of doing it, and plenty of ways of assigning to them a larger proportion of the total national income than they have enjoyed in the past otherwise than by increasing their wages.[56]

So long as Britain had an open capitalist economy, Keynes felt that 'the Liberal solution' to poverty—using taxes to pay for 'useful expenditure' on health and education, housing subsidies, and social benefits—would be more effective than 'the Trade Union solution' of higher wages.[57] Beveridge was similarly 'sceptical of all forms of minimum wage theory' during the 1920s and 1930s, and preferred to focus on improving National Insurance and the social services.[58]

Economists' suspicion of the unions' wage-based strategy was reinforced by the problem of family size. Even advocates of a minimum wage, such as Seebohm Rowntree, recognized that it could not account for variations in family responsibilities, so some sort of allowance would be needed to help workers with large numbers of children. The Family Endowment Society, founded by Eleanor Rathbone in 1917, popularized the idea of a national system of Family Allowances, to which Beveridge and Keynes became enthusiastic converts. Jane Lewis and Susan Pedersen have shown that Rathbone was inspired by a maternalist vision: the desire to reward motherhood and bolster housewives' economic position by providing them with an independent income.[59] Much of the wider appeal of Family Allowances, however, came from the scope for alleviating child poverty outside the labour market and ensuring that men with large families were better off in work. Indeed, John Macnicol has argued that Rathbone's campaign only finally succeeded during the Second World War because ministers recognized that Family Allowances would improve work incentives and help defuse pressure for a minimum wage.[60]

[56] John Maynard Keynes, 'The Question of High Wages', *Political Quarterly* 1/1 (1930), 110–24, at 121.

[57] Keynes, 'The Question of High Wages', 119.

[58] José Harris, *William Beveridge: A Biography*, 2nd edn (Oxford, 1997), 307.

[59] Jane Lewis, 'Models of Equality for Women: The Case of State Support for Children in Twentieth-Century Britain', in *Maternity and Gender Policies: Women and the Rise of the European Welfare States, 1880s–1950s*, edited by Gisela Bock and Pat Thane (1991), 73–92; Susan Pedersen, *Family, Dependence, and the Origins of the Welfare State: Britain and France, 1914–1945* (Cambridge, 1993).

[60] John Macnicol, *The Movement for Family Allowances, 1918–45: A Study in Social Policy Development* (1980), 202.

The idea of a separate allowance for the mother was dropped, and the child allowances were set below subsistence level to keep down the cost and maintain the principle of parental responsibility.

The welfare state which assumed its classic form at the end of the Second World War thus rested on four complementary pillars. The first was state provision of key services, which reflected the 'reluctant collectivism' of utilitarians such as Pigou and the belief that collective provision was more efficient than direct income transfers.[61] R. H. Tawney, for example, argued in his influential study of *Equality* (1931) that 'collective expenditure makes possible results which would be unattainable, were an identical sum distributed . . . in fractional additions to individual incomes'.[62] Trade unions also tended to prefer public services to cash transfers, because it was harder for employers to take account of collective provision in wage negotiations, and the rhetoric of universal provision concealed the extent to which the welfare state subsidized working-class living standards. As well as implementing the 1944 Education Act and creating the NHS, Clement Attlee's Labour government maintained wartime subsidies for staple foodstuffs (which cost £400 million, or more than 3 per cent of GDP, by the late 1940s) and relied predominantly on council house-building to relieve the post-war housing shortage. As a result, the growth in public spending on the welfare state between 1938 and 1951 stemmed almost entirely from higher spending on service provision, rather than increases in cash transfers (Figure 2.1).

The second pillar of the 1940s welfare state was Sir William Beveridge's National Insurance scheme, which provided flat-rate benefits to contributing workers and their families during 'interruptions of earnings'. As José Harris and Peter Baldwin have pointed out, Beveridge's approach attracted support from across the social spectrum: both from middle-class voters who were reassured by the contributory principle, and from trade unionists who welcomed the fact that it gave unemployed workers a right to benefit.[63] Beveridge's vision of social security was enormously powerful, though in fact the National Insurance system was never as generous nor as inclusive as his rhetoric implied. The wartime coalition government rejected the notion that insurance benefits should be adequate for subsistence, and those without a full

[61] Vic George and Paul Wilding, *Ideology and Social Welfare* (1976), 42–61; Tudor Jones, '"Reluctant" or Liberal Collectivists? The Social Liberalism of Keynes and Beveridge, 1922–1945', *Journal of Liberal History* 78 (Spring 2013), 32–41.

[62] R. H. Tawney, *Equality* (1931), 172.

[63] Harris, *William Beveridge*; Peter Baldwin, *The Politics of Social Solidarity: Class Bases of the European Welfare State, 1875–1975* (Cambridge, 1990), 116–34.

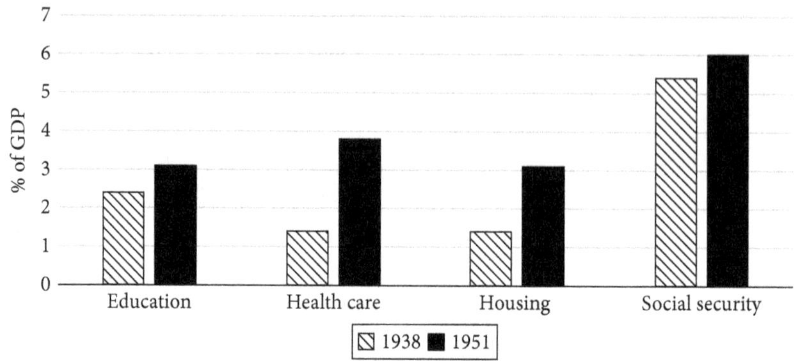

Figure 2.1. Public expenditure on major social services as a share of GDP, 1938 and 1951

Source: Peter Townsend, *Poverty in the United Kingdom: A Survey of Household Resources and Standards of Living* (1979), 155.

contributory record—such as single mothers, irregular workers, and many of the disabled—were still forced to rely on means-testing.[64] Though Family Allowances were introduced on a non-contributory basis, they were confined to second and subsequent children and uprated only twice between 1945 and 1968.

Thirdly, the welfare state was designed to complement rather than subvert trade union wage bargaining. This was perhaps the most significant way in which post-war practice departed from inter-war economists' expectations. Labour's entry into the wartime coalition in 1940—and especially Ernest Bevin's tenure of the Ministry of Labour—marked a transformation in the relationship between the unions and the state, as the TUC established itself as an essential partner in the governing process.[65] Although the British unions were strongly committed to voluntarism, the post-war state came to underwrite their bargaining power in a variety of ways: not only through the legal immunities established by the 1906 Trade Disputes Act, but also by sustaining full employment, supporting central bargaining, and adopting a conciliatory stance towards industrial relations.[66] Partly for this reason, union membership rose from just over 6 million in 1939 to more than 9 million by the late 1940s. This shift in the balance of power between capital and labour was not, of

[64] Veit-Wilson, 'Condemned to Deprivation?'

[65] Keith Middlemas, *Politics in Industrial Society: The Experience of the British System since 1911* (1979).

[66] Chris Howell, *Trade Unions and the State: The Construction of Industrial Relations Institutions in Britain, 1890–2000* (Princeton, 2005).

course, universally welcomed, but the buoyancy of the world economy during the 1950s and 1960s helped defuse distributional tensions. Successive British governments were thus able to combine full employment with low inflation, and rising take-home pay with rising spending on the social services.

Finally, the post-war welfare settlement was underpinned by the government's use of economic and fiscal policy to take control of the 'commanding heights' of the economy and maintain full employment for male industrial workers. As Jim Tomlinson has pointed out, Tawney's 'strategy of equality' centred on the use of public ownership to secure democratic control of economic power; four decades later, the February 1974 Labour manifesto called for 'a fundamental and irreversible shift in the balance of power and wealth in favour of working people and their families'.[67] Nationalization played an important role in eroding the social and political power of private employers and *rentiers*; so too did a highly progressive income tax regime which differentiated between earned and unearned income. High marginal tax rates not only raised revenue but also shaped the underlying economic structure through their impact on managerial behaviour and wealth accumulation. The share of total net wealth held by the top 1 per cent fell from 53.1 per cent in 1937 to 43.4 per cent in 1949 and 21.2 per cent in 1978, whilst the top 1 per cent share of gross income fell from 17 per cent to 11.5 per cent to 5.7 per cent over the same period.[68]

In the context of post-war economic expansion, these policy institutions helped bring about a sharp reduction in the post-tax Gini coefficient—from 0.43 in 1938 to 0.32 in 1976—and broad-based improvements in UK living standards. Critics of the post-war settlement have, perhaps, been too ready to minimize the scale of this achievement. At the same time, however, it is clear that the supposedly universalist welfare state was less comprehensive than it sometimes seemed. The benefit system provided inadequate support for larger families and none at all for low-paid childless workers, whilst the housing subsidy regime created sharp disparities between council and private tenants. These 'gaps in the welfare state' left open the door for alternative visions of a social minimum.

[67] Jim Tomlinson, 'Distributional Politics: The Search for Equality in Britain since the First World War', in *The Contradictions of Capital in the Twenty-First Century: The Piketty Opportunity*, edited by Pat Hudson and Keith Tribe (Newcastle-upon-Tyne, 2016), 167–91, at 168–9; Labour Party, *Let Us Work Together—Labour's Way out of the Crisis* (1974), reprinted in *Labour Party General Election Manifestos, 1900–1997*, edited by Iain Dale (2000), 183–92, at 192.

[68] Anthony B. Atkinson, Joe Hasell, Salvatore Morelli, and Max Roser, 'Economic Inequality in the United Kingdom', The Chartbook of Economic Inequality, accessed 7 May 2018, <https://www.chartbookofeconomicinequality.com/inequality-by-country/united-kingdom/>.

The neoliberal reaction, *c*.1945–1965

Many of the intellectual foundations of RML—the methodological individualism of neoclassical economics, the marginal productivity theory of wages, and the reconceptualization of poverty as income deficiency—were well established by the 1930s. It was after the Second World War, however, that the doctrine really came into its own. The early post-war period marked the beginning of what Ravallion has called the 'Second Poverty Enlightenment'—an era in which growing affluence and an explosion of social science research fostered a new optimism about the state's ability to eliminate poverty.[69] The 1948 Universal Declaration of Human Rights declared that everyone had 'the right to a standard of living adequate for the health and well-being of himself and of his family', and many western liberals sought to use welfare provision to legitimize capitalism in the face of the communist challenge.[70] At the same time, however, the 1940s and 1950s also saw an increasingly vociferous reaction against central planning, fostered by free-market economists and groups such as the Mont Pèlerin Society (MPS), which culminated in the emergence of the New Right. RML stood at the intersection of these two trends, as policy-makers looked for ways of rationalizing social provision and reducing the need for direct interference in the market system.

If the 1940s were the founding moment of the social democratic welfare state, they also represent a starting point for the modern debate over guaranteed income. In the United States, Milton Friedman and George Stigler devised the Negative Income Tax as an alternative to the minimum wage; in Britain, Juliet Rhys-Williams persuaded Conservative ministers to commission the first serious analysis of a basic income. Why did the idea of a guaranteed income begin to gain traction in this period? One important reason was the sharp rise in the tax burden on both sides of the Atlantic during the Second World War, which was designed to reduce private consumption—as Keynes had recommended in *How to Pay for the War* (1940)—as well as to finance military spending.[71] Income tax became a mass tax for the first time, and both the British and US governments were forced to overhaul their tax assessment procedures in order to collect it at source from weekly wage-earners. Rhys-Williams presented her scheme as a solution to this problem before the Inland Revenue introduced Pay-As-You-Earn in 1944, and Friedman spent two years

[69] Ravallion, *The Economics of Poverty*, 80–91.

[70] Moyn, *Not Enough*, 41–67; the quote from the Universal Declaration is at 59.

[71] John Maynard Keynes, *How to Pay for the War: A Radical Plan for the Chancellor* (1940).

in the US Treasury (1941–3) where he helped develop the payroll withholding system.[72] The development of these real-time deduction systems encouraged the belief that a guaranteed income was technically possible, whilst the growing overlap between taxpayers and social security claimants suggested that it might produce administrative savings.

Alongside these practical developments, the 1940s saw the beginning of a free-market counter-offensive against the central planning methods which western governments had adopted during the war and in some cases sought to maintain after it. As Ben Jackson and Angus Burgin have pointed out, the first generation of neoliberal intellectuals who met at Mont Pèlerin in Switzerland in April 1947—such as Friedrich Hayek, Ludwig von Mises, Aaron Director, Wilhelm Röpke, and Lionel Robbins—were primarily concerned with restoring the legitimacy of market economics in the face of 'hot' socialist planning.[73] Within this group, attitudes towards welfare provision differed widely. Some, such as Mises and Röpke, rejected redistribution altogether in the belief that it would destroy independence and work incentives—creating what Röpke called a 'proletarianised society'.[74] Hayek, however, took a more nuanced line, suggesting in *The Road to Serfdom* (1944) that 'security against severe physical privation'—'some minimum of food, shelter, and clothing, sufficient to preserve health and the capacity to work'—could reasonably be 'assured to everybody', and Friedman and Stigler went even further in their enthusiasm for NIT.[75]

Friedman outlined his vision of NIT in a paper on 'Taxation, Poverty and Income Distribution' at the first Mont Pèlerin meeting. Even in a perfectly competitive economy, he argued, there would still be people who could not earn an adequate market income, and '[n]o democratic society' was likely to 'tolerate people starving to death, if there is food with which to feed them'. Friedman was highly sensitive to the ways in which 'the problem of poverty' had been used to justify state intervention, and warned his fellow neoliberals that they had to take this seriously. 'Measures to break up unions', for instance,

[72] Milton and Rose Friedman, *Two Lucky People: Memoirs* (Chicago, 1998), 105–8, 119–23. In later life, Friedman had 'no idea from what source I drew the concept of the negative income tax' but believed that 'negative income taxes were probably discussed at the Treasury in 1941 to 1943 when I was a member of the Tax Research staff': Hoover Institution Archives, Stanford University, Friedman papers, 201.5, Milton Friedman to Dennis J. Ventry Jr., 3 Dec. 1996 (copy).

[73] Ben Jackson, 'At the Origins of Neo-Liberalism: The Free Economy and the Strong State, 1930–1947', *Historical Journal* 53/1 (2010), 129–51; Angus Burgin, *The Great Persuasion: Reinventing Free Markets since the Depression* (Cambridge, Mass., 2012).

[74] Wilhelm Röpke, *Civitas Humana: A Humane Order of Society*, English edn (1948).

[75] Friedrich Hayek, *The Road to Serfdom* (1944), 124–5.

would 'bring success' only if market economists could 'combat the evils which unions were designed to counteract' in another way.[76] Using the income tax apparatus to pay direct supplements to low-income households would be much simpler. Friedman stressed that he saw NIT as a 'substitute' for other forms of social policy, including unemployment benefit and old age pensions, but denied that it was merely an 'expedient', since any 'liberal society' would have to find some way of helping the poor.[77] He also pointed out that it could serve as a Keynesian macroeconomic regulator, providing an 'anti-cyclical' boost to households' purchasing power during a recession.[78]

Friedman's proposal was viewed with suspicion by other Mont Pèlerin delegates, who worried that the income floor would drift too high and have damaging 'psychological effects'—as 'the *good* citizen, who *pays* his taxes, has to pay for the poor'.[79] Outside the MPS, however, the notion that cash transfers were preferable to collective services and subsidies gained wide traction within the economics profession. After all, the argument that market pricing was normally more efficient than collective provision had been widely rehearsed during the socialist calculation debate, and formed the basis of the 'neoclassical synthesis' associated with Paul Samuelson. In Britain, James Meade's book *Planning and the Price Mechanism* (1948) is perhaps the clearest statement of this view. Though Meade was a Labour Party member, he believed that 'money and the pricing system' were 'among the greatest social inventions of mankind', and insisted (in contrast to Pigou and Tawney) that 'the method of control by the quantitative allocation of resources... is bound to be clumsy, inefficient and wasteful as compared with a properly functioning price system'.[80]

The neoclassical case for market pricing was reinforced by a political reaction against the paternalism of the post-war state. In a Cold War world, many liberals and conservatives began to emphasize the moral value of consumer choice as a form of individual agency, which allowed citizens to give expression to their own preferences and values. British Conservatives were particularly effective at exploiting voters' frustration with rationing and austerity by promising to 'set the people free' from socialist planning.[81] In the

[76] Hoover Institution Archives, Stanford University, Mont Pèlerin Society records, 5.12, 'Taxation, Poverty and Income Distribution. Tuesday April 8th, 8.30 p.m.', notes of discussion, 1.

[77] Mont Pèlerin Society records, 5.12, 'Taxation, Poverty and Income Distribution', 2, 3, 4.

[78] Mont Pèlerin Society records, 5.12, 'Taxation, Poverty and Income Distribution', 9.

[79] William Rappard in Mont Pèlerin Society records, 5.12, 'Taxation, Poverty and Income Distribution', 8.

[80] J. E. Meade, *Planning and the Price Mechanism: The Liberal-Socialist Solution* (1948), 9, 7.

[81] Ina Zweiniger-Bargielowska, 'Rationing, Austerity, and the Conservative Party Recovery after 1945', *Historical Journal* 37/1 (1994), 173–97.

welfare sphere, critics of the Attlee government fastened on Douglas Jay's incautious claim that 'in the case of nutrition and health, just as in the case of education, the gentleman in Whitehall really does know better what is good for people than the people know themselves'.[82] When Jay wrote these words in *The Socialist Case* (1937) they elicited almost no reaction, but by the late 1940s they were widely cited as a symbol of Fabian arrogance.[83] 'Is it right that the State should appropriate so large a proportion of the citizens' income and spend it on their behalf', asked the Liberal journalist Elliott Dodds, 'instead of leaving them to spend it according to their own free choices?'[84]

The concept of redistribution attracted growing interest from economists during the 1940s and 1950s for both theoretical and practical reasons. Lionel Robbins's powerful critique of interpersonal utility comparisons meant that redistribution could no longer be justified on narrowly utilitarian grounds, but in the heady aftermath of war the political demand for greater equality seemed irresistible. Other developments in welfare economics kept fiscal transfers to the fore: the Kaldor–Hicks criterion, for instance, focused attention on the possibility of compensating the losers from policy change through cash transfers, whilst the 'second welfare theorem' developed by Harold Hotelling and Kenneth Arrow suggested that any Pareto-optimal outcome could be achieved by the competitive market after an initial reallocation of endowments.[85] In macroeconomics, Keynes's concept of the marginal propensity to consume also gave underconsumptionist arguments for redistribution some credence.

This theoretical interest in transfer payments was matched by a wave of empirical research into income distribution, which was closely linked to the development of national income accounting. In the USA, the Conference on Research in Income and Wealth established in 1936—with Simon Kuznets as its driving force and Friedman as its first secretary—covered both national income and distributional issues.[86] In Britain, Colin Clark, Richard Stone, and James Meade's pioneering work on national accounts was followed by attempts to quantify the effects of the growing welfare system.[87] The Hungarian émigré economist Tibor Barna framed the issue in his study of *Redistribution*

[82] Douglas Jay, *The Socialist Case* (1937), 317.

[83] Richard Toye, '"The Gentleman in Whitehall" Reconsidered: Douglas Jay's Views on Economic Planning and Consumer Choice, 1937–1947', *Labour History Review* 67/2 (2002), 187–204.

[84] Elliott Dodds, 'The Welfare State', *The Fortnightly*, Sept. 1949, 172–8, at 173.

[85] Mark Blaug, 'The Fundamental Theorems of Modern Welfare Economics, Historically Contemplated', *History of Political Economy* 39/2 (2007), 185–207.

[86] Carol S. Carson, 'The Conference on Research in Income and Wealth: The Early Years', in *Fifty Years of Economic Measurement: The Jubilee of the Conference on Research in Income and Wealth*, edited by Ernst R. Bendt and Jack E. Triplett (Chicago, 1990), 3–8.

[87] Tomlinson, 'Distributional Politics', 171–2.

of Incomes through Public Finance in 1937 (1945), which began life as a wartime Ph.D. thesis under Nicholas Kaldor's supervision, and argued that it was essential 'to regard the whole process of redistribution as something integral'.[88] Barna emphasized the progressivity of the British state's activities on the eve of war, estimating that it transferred at least £200 million from those with incomes of above £250 a year to those with incomes below that level through a mixture of National Insurance benefits, poor relief, and social services.[89] Barna believed that 'want... could have been abolished by a further redistribution of incomes of a relatively modest proportion', but argued in classic socialist vein that it was better to attack the 'causes' of inequality—especially unemployment, low wages, and the unequal ownership of capital.[90] By contrast, free-market commentators suggested that the patchwork of services and benefits which had emerged in Britain by the late 1940s was unnecessarily complex. Bertrand de Jouvenel, for instance, argued that much of the redistribution carried out by the post-war British state was 'oblique' rather than 'vertical', and served mainly to concentrate power in the hands of government ministers.[91] A 'pure' form of redistribution, he argued, 'would merely transfer income from the richer to the poorer', and 'could conceivably be achieved by a simple reverse-tax or subsidy handed to the recipients of lower incomes'.[92]

The case for RML was articulated in Britain by a cluster of neoclassical economists—Roy Harrod and John Hicks at Oxford, Dennis Robertson at Cambridge, and Meade and Robbins at the London School of Economics—who urged the Attlee government to pursue its distributional objectives through cash transfers rather than physical planning. Food subsidies, rent controls, and council house subsidies were the lowest-hanging targets for liberal reformers, since the distortions involved were manifest and the benefits only weakly targeted on the poorest households. The Conservative governments of 1951–64 sought to liberate market forces by abolishing food

[88] Tibor Barna, *Redistribution of Incomes through Public Finance in 1937* (Oxford, 1945), 2; Howard Glennerster, *Tibor Barna: The Redistributive Impact of Taxes and Social Policies in the UK: 1937–2005*. CASE Paper 115 (2006).

[89] Barna, *Redistribution of Incomes through Public Finance in 1937*, 233.

[90] Barna, *Redistribution of Incomes through Public Finance in 1937*, 234, 236.

[91] Bertrand de Jouvenel, *The Ethics of Redistribution* (Cambridge, 1951), 90.

[92] De Jouvenel, *The Ethics of Redistribution*, 72. De Jouvenel's empirical analysis was echoed by Findley Weaver, but contested by Alan Peacock and P. R. Browning: Findley Weaver, 'Taxation and Redistribution in the United Kingdom', *The Review of Economics and Statistics* 32 (1950), 201–13; Alan T. Peacock and P. R. Browning, 'The Social Services in Great Britain and the Redistribution of Income', in *Income Redistribution and Social Policy*, edited by Alan T. Peacock (1954), 139–77.

subsidies, encouraging councils to replace rent subsidies with rebates for the poorest tenants, and partly deregulating private rented housing.[93]

More radical neoliberals hoped that these changes were only the beginning of a wider liberalization process. The growth of consumer affluence during the 1950s fostered the belief that many citizens would soon be able to provide for their own welfare needs through saving and private insurance, so the state could increasingly confine itself to providing a safety net for the poor—a view associated with Peter Goldman of the Conservative Research Department, but also shared by some free-market Liberals.[94] Alan Peacock, for instance, argued that Beveridge's contributory National Insurance model was deceptive because only a portion of benefits were really 'earned' by contributions.[95] Peacock was also keen to open up health and education to private providers, and attempted to show how Friedman's proposal for education vouchers might work in Britain.[96] The Liberal leader Jo Grimond was cautious about making immediate changes, but agreed that there was 'no reason why we should not look forward to the time when the only Social Service is a straight payment to bring everyone's income (including that of children) up to a national minimum'.[97] From the late 1950s onwards this agenda was taken up by Arthur Seldon of the Institute of Economic Affairs (IEA) in a long series of pamphlets and articles on 'choice' in welfare.[98] Seldon insisted that 'topping up incomes' through cash transfers was 'not merely a palliative', but part of 'a great experiment in emancipation from standardised, unresponsive, autocratic State services'.[99] In line with Seldon's approach, IEA authors generally saw redistribution as a necessary evil which could help 'to ease the introduction of pricing into government services and then in time to shift them into the market'.[100]

[93] Harriet Jones, 'New Tricks for an Old Dog?' The Conservatives and Social Policy, 1951–5', in *Contemporary British History 1931–61: Politics and the Limits of Policy*, edited by Anthony Gorst, Lewis Johnman, and W. Scott Lucas (1991), 33–43; Peter Weiler, 'The Rise and Fall of the Conservatives' "Grand Design for Housing", 1951–64', *Contemporary British History* 14/1 (2000), 122–50; Peter Malpass, *Reshaping Housing Policy: Subsidies, Rents and Residualisation* (1990), 89–113.

[94] See especially Peter Goldman, 'Preface', in *The Future of the Welfare State: Seven Oxford Lectures*, Conservative Political Centre (1958), 7–10; George Watson, ed., *The Unservile State: Essays in Liberty and Welfare* (1957).

[95] Alan T. Peacock, *The Economics of National Insurance* (Edinburgh, 1952).

[96] Alan T. Peacock, 'Welfare in a Liberal State', in *The Unservile State*, edited by George Watson, 113–30; Alan T. Peacock and Jack Wiseman, *Education for Democrats* (1964).

[97] Joseph Grimond, *The Liberal Future* (1959), 106.

[98] See, for instance, Arthur Seldon, *Pensions in a Free Society* (1957); Institute of Economic Affairs, *Choice in Welfare* (1963); Arthur Seldon and Hamish Gray, *Universal or Selective Social Benefits* (1967).

[99] Arthur Seldon, 'Why not Top up the Poor Man's Pay?', *Daily Telegraph*, 22 Feb. 1971, 12.

[100] Hoover Institution Archives, Stanford University, Institute of Economic Affairs papers, 368.10, 'Liberalism at/through the Mont Pèlerin Society: The British Experience', paper by Arthur Seldon for Liberty Fund conference on the history of the Mont Pèlerin Society, Freiburg, Mar. 1985, 23.

In the hands of neoliberal intellectuals and activists such as Friedman, de Jouvenel, Peacock, and Seldon, RML took on the character of a market fundamentalist creed, designed to justify a free-market assault on trade union power and collective welfare provision. In reality, however, such a radically individualistic vision was never likely to gain much traction in early post-war Britain. The growing influence of RML during the 1950s and 1960s was thus partly a reflection of its ideological and practical flexibility. Social democrats and 'One Nation' Conservatives could be persuaded of the case for introducing cash transfers at the margins without abandoning a solidaristic core of universal public services. Left-liberal economists such as Meade and Peter Wiles also presented a guaranteed income as a complement to a more direct attack on the causes of inequality, especially the distribution of wealth.[101] Meade, for instance, argued in *Efficiency, Equality and the Ownership of Property* (1964) that the 'Welfare State' approach to social equality was superior to 'the Trade Union-Minimum-Wage method', but that it should be combined with measures to reduce inequalities in unearned income, including the promotion of a 'Property-Owning Democracy'—through death duties and education reform—and the expansion of public ownership.[102] Wiles urged his fellow Liberals to embrace 'a revolutionary distributive principle': that 'granted subsistence for all and no gross inequality of property, *laissez-faire is the just way to distribute earned incomes*'.[103]

The rise of redistributive market liberalism, *c*.1965–2008

As Meade's analysis suggests, the intellectual appeal of RML was rooted in the neoclassical commitment to the price mechanism as an instrument of allocative efficiency. Cash transfers offered 'socially concerned economists' a way of eliminating poverty and reducing inequality whilst maintaining the advantages of market pricing.[104] Between the 1940s and the 1970s, however, this neoclassical approach was strongly contested by other epistemic communities which influenced British public policy. The 'Oxford school' of industrial relations founded by Hugh Clegg and Allan Flanders, for instance, championed an institutionalist reading of the labour market which took collective bargaining as an established fact and reinforced the Ministry of Labour's

[101] Peter Wiles, 'Property and Equality', in *The Unservile State*, edited by George Watson, 88–109.
[102] J. E. Meade, *Efficiency, Equality and the Ownership of Property* (1964), 38, 40, 75.
[103] Wiles, 'Property and Equality', 95, 96.
[104] John Kay, 'The Left is Still Searching for a Practical Philosophy', *Financial Times*, 5 May 2010, 13.

conciliatory approach towards the unions.[105] Social administrators such as Richard Titmuss, Brian Abel-Smith, and Peter Townsend applied a similar empirical and sociological approach to the welfare state, identifying citizens' essential social needs and analysing the extent to which existing welfare institutions were successful in meeting them. Although these sociologists sometimes conceptualized poverty in terms of inadequate resources, their work was coloured by a strong commitment to universalism as a symbol of social citizenship, which was shared by many Department of Health and Social Security officials.[106] (As John Veit-Wilson has noted, Abel-Smith and Townsend's 'expedient' use of the National Assistance scale as a relative poverty line in *The Poor and the Poorest* (1965) coexisted with a 'longer, principled, search for the empirically-based level of minimal participatory adequacy which should supersede it'.[107]) The case for tackling poverty through cash transfers was also challenged from within economics by Labour advisers such as Thomas Balogh and Nicholas Kaldor, who favoured a more interventionist approach to economic management.[108] Kaldor, in particular, encouraged Labour politicians to focus on making the tax system more progressive by clamping down on capital gains and fringe benefits.[109]

The impact of RML on British public policy was limited by the contested status of microeconomics within this crowded epistemic marketplace. The institutional focus of social administration and industrial relations scholars fitted neatly with the public-spirited optimism of post-war Whitehall officials and their sense of administrative realities. From the late 1960s onwards, however, neoclassical approaches to income distribution were propelled to the fore by two major developments. Firstly, the field of social policy research was transformed by the application of microeconomic techniques to the study of poverty and inequality—a process stimulated by the American 'War on Poverty' but quickly taken up by British scholars. As Alice O'Connor has argued, the US study of poverty developed 'from an uncertainly connected bundle of university-based sociological and anthropological community studies, into a precise, federally funded analytic science with national-level data

[105] Peter Ackers, 'Symposium: The Oxford School of Industrial Relations: Fifty Years after the 1965–1968 Donovan Commission. Introduction: Who Were the Oxford School and Why Did They Matter?', *Historical Studies in Industrial Relations* 37 (2016), 201–7.

[106] Martin Bulmer, 'The British Tradition of Social Administration: Moral Concerns at the Expense of Scientific Rigor', *Hastings Center Report* 11/2 (1981), 35–42; private information.

[107] Veit-Wilson, 'Condemned to Deprivation?', 113.

[108] Andrew Graham, 'Thomas Balogh (1905–85)', *Contemporary Record* 6/1 (1992), 194–207; Jim Tomlinson, *The Labour Governments 1964–1970*, vol. 3: *Economic Policy* (Manchester, 2004).

[109] Richard Whiting, *The Labour Party and Taxation: Party Identity and Political Purpose in Twentieth-Century Britain* (Cambridge, 2000), 134–43.

sets and neoclassical economic models at its core'.[110] In Britain, Tony Atkinson sought to quantify the distributional effects of different tax and benefit reforms in *Poverty in Britain and the Reform of Social Security* (1969) and went on to become 'the architect of modern public economics' during the 1970s and 1980s.[111] Tony Atkinson and Joseph Stiglitz's landmark *Lectures on Public Economics* (1980), which developed a general equilibrium analysis of public policy and introduced the concept of a Negative Income Tax at an early stage, 'soon established itself as the dominant graduate text in the field'.[112] Atkinson's politics were egalitarian and social democratic, and he developed close links with the Labour Party and the Child Poverty Action Group, just as Titmuss and Townsend had done before him; indeed, for much of his career he supported the 'back-to-Beveridge' approach to social security favoured by the poverty lobby. Nevertheless, his work was grounded in mainstream welfare economics and helped open up social policy questions to economists trained in the neoclassical tradition, as Stephen Jenkins and Howard Glennerster have noted.[113] Applied work on income distribution was aided by the growing availability of official statistics, such as those compiled by the 1974–9 Royal Commission on the Distribution of Income and Wealth, and bore fruit in the Luxembourg Income Study and other international collaborations.[114]

Secondly, the 'market turn' of the 1970s and 1980s called the UK's post-war settlement into question and helped raise the credibility of microeconomics at the expense of other disciplines. During the long post-war boom, Keynesian demand management seemed to be able to short-circuit the implications of neoclassical labour-market theory by reconciling rising wages with full employment. Although mainstream economists continued to articulate the marginal productivity theory of wages, only right-wing Conservatives and

[110] Alice O'Connor, *Poverty Knowledge: Social Science, Social Policy, and the Poor in Twentieth-Century U.S. History* (Princeton, 2001), 166.

[111] Béatrice Cherrier, 'Remembering Tony Atkinson as the Architect of Modern Public Economics', The Undercover Historian blog, 2 Jan. 2017, accessed 24 Jan. 2017, <https://beatricecherrier.wordpress.com/2017/01/02/remembering-tony-atkinson-as-the-architect-of-modern-public-economics/>.

[112] Anthony B. Atkinson and Joseph E. Stiglitz, *Lectures on Public Economics* (Maidenhead, 1980); Agnar Sandmo, 'Tony Atkinson 1944–2017: A Lifetime Commitment to the Study of Inequality', *European Journal of the History of Economic Thought* 24 (2017), 612–23, at 616.

[113] Stephen P. Jenkins, 'Anthony B. Atkinson (1944–)', in *The Palgrave Companion to Cambridge Economics*, vol. 2, edited by Robert A. Cord (Basingstoke, 2017), 1151–74; Howard Glennerster, 'LSE's Contributions to the Economics of Social Policy', in *The Palgrave Companion to LSE Economics*, edited by Robert A. Cord (Basingstoke, 2018), 145–64.

[114] Tom Kelsey, *An Unexpected Cut: Revisiting the Diamond Commission and Assessing Inequality in Post-War Britain* (2018); A. B. Atkinson with Lee Rainwater and Timothy Smeeding, 'Income Distribution in European Countries', in A. B. Atkinson, *Incomes and the Welfare State: Essays on Britain and Europe* (Cambridge, 1995), 41–63.

neoliberals sought to launch a wholesale assault on trade union rights and privileges.[115] From the late 1960s onwards, however, confidence in Keynesian techniques was weakened both politically (as a result of 'stagflation') and theoretically (by Robert Lucas's critique and the new faith in rational expectations). As a result, even liberal and social democratic thinkers began to regard trade union power and labour-market rigidity as a serious problem.[116] Richard Layard, Stephen Nickell, and Richard Jackman's application of the Non-Accelerating Inflation Rate of Unemployment (NAIRU) to Britain was particularly influential.[117] If the prestige of social scientists depends partly on policy influence, as Henry Farrell and John Quiggin have suggested, then the rise of supply-side economics under Thatcher served to marginalize Keynesians and industrial relations scholars—not to mention sociologists—and to focus public attention on microeconomics.[118]

By the late 1980s, the notion that tackling poverty and inequality through cash transfers was preferable to wage regulation and collective provision was widely held within the British economics profession. Martin Ricketts and Edward Shoesmith's 1989 survey of almost a thousand British economists found that 66 per cent believed the distribution of income in developed countries should be more equal—a higher figure than among either their European or their North American counterparts. At the same time, 60 per cent agreed with the statement that 'cash payments are superior to benefits in kind', and there was much greater enthusiasm for NIT than for a minimum wage or rent controls.[119] Ricketts and Shoesmith concluded that

> British economists seem to combine a respect for the power of price signals (perhaps gleaned from their American textbooks or from the continuing tradition in micro-economics nourished in post-war years by the IEA) with a clear acceptance of the redistributive role of government...[120]

[115] George R. Boyer and Robert S. Smith, 'The Development of the Neoclassical Tradition in Labor Economics', *Industrial and Labor Relations Review* 54/2 (2001), 199–223; Ben Jackson, 'An Ideology of Class: Neo-Liberalism and the Trade Unions, *c.*1930–79', in *Classes, Cultures, and Politics: Essays on British History for Ross McKibbin*, edited by Clare V. J. Griffiths, James J. Nott, and William Whyte (Oxford, 2011), 263–81.

[116] See, for instance, Stephen Meredith, *Labours Old and New: The Parliamentary Right of the British Labour Party 1970–9 and the Roots of New Labour* (Manchester, 2008), 103–36.

[117] Richard Layard, *Unemployment in Britain: Causes and Cures* (1981); Richard Layard, Stephen Nickell, and Richard Jackman, *Unemployment: Macroeconomic Performance and the Labour Market* (Oxford, 1991).

[118] Henry Farrell and John Quiggin, 'Consensus, Dissensus, and Economic Ideas: Economic Crisis and the Rise and Fall of Keynesianism', *International Studies Quarterly* 61/2 (2017), 269–83.

[119] Martin Ricketts and Edward Shoesmith, *British Economic Opinion: A Survey of a Thousand Economists* (1990). See especially figure 9, part II, between 44 and 45.

[120] Ricketts and Shoesmith, *British Economic Opinion*, 50.

In truth, the ascendancy of neoclassical theory among academic economists was never complete, and in some ways it became less so towards the end of the twentieth century as the 'applied' or 'empirical turn' took hold.[121] For instance, David Card and Alan Krueger's famous empirical study of fast-food restaurants in New Jersey and Pennsylvania during the early 1990s suggested that the neoclassical assumption that minimum wages reduced employment was not always robust.[122] Labour-market theory also moved away from a textbook supply and demand framework through growing acceptance of the efficiency wage hypothesis and the development of the 'searching and matching' approach.[123]

Nevertheless, social policy and labour-market analysis in Whitehall was increasingly strongly shaped by microeconomic 'policy devices' and 'styles of reasoning' during the 1980s and 1990s, as shown by the influence of Atkinson and Stiglitz's *Lectures on Public Economics* and Nicholas Barr's classic study of *The Economics of the Welfare State* (1987).[124] A leaked 1996 Treasury strategy paper, for instance, stated frankly that 'Treasury officials have a high level of commitment to the efficiency of the market mechanism, to neo-classical welfare economics and to the utilitarian ethics on which they are based'.[125] The same set of principles underpinned the work of think-tanks such as the Institute for Fiscal Studies, which used econometric modelling to simulate the distributional effects of policy measures in its annual 'Green Budgets'.[126] Labour economists, public finance specialists, and poverty researchers formed overlapping epistemic communities which engaged in a common (if often contested) policy discourse. British policy-makers and advisers also became increasingly closely linked with international debates through academic networks and institutions such as the OECD and the World Bank, which threw their weight behind conditional cash transfers during the 1990s as part of 'best

[121] Roger E. Backhouse, 'The Changing Character of British Economics', *History of Political Economy* 28, Supplement (1996), 33–60; Roger E. Backhouse and Béatrice Cherrier, 'The Age of the Applied Economist: The Transformation of Economics since the 1970s', *History of Political Economy* 49, Supplement (2017), 1–33.

[122] David Card and Alan B. Krueger, 'Minimum Wages and Employment: A Case Study of the Fast-Food Industry in New Jersey and Pennsylvania', *American Economic Review* 84/4 (1994), 772–93.

[123] Steve Fleetwood, 'Reflections upon Neoclassical Labour Economics', in *What is Neoclassical Economics?*, edited by Jamie Morgan, 273–310.

[124] Daniel Hirschman and Elizabeth Popp Berman, 'Do Economists Make Policies? On the Political Effects of Economics', *Socio-Economic Review* 12/4 (2014), 779–811; Stuart Astill, 'Nicholas Adrian Barr (1943–)', in *The Palgrave Companion to LSE Economics*, edited by Robert A. Cord (Basingstoke, 2018), 805–30.

[125] 'Strategic Considerations for the Treasury 2000–2005', quoted in Anatole Kaletsky, 'Why the Treasury Must now be Brought to Heel', *The Times*, 18 July 1996, 27.

[126] J. A. Kay, 'Research and Policy: The IFS Experience', *Policy Studies* 9/3 (1989), 20–6.

practice' job-creation and social protection strategies.[127] As Jane Jenson has shown, the UK Treasury stood at the forefront of a global wave of welfare recalibration during the 1990s and 2000s, drawing on 'the policy discourse of economists' to develop new tax and benefit policies.[128]

If RML was particularly attractive to economists, the idea of a guaranteed minimum also received important flanking support from other sources. In particular, the publication of John Rawls's *A Theory of Justice* (1971) sparked a wave of interest in distributive justice among political philosophers during the 1970s and 1980s. Indeed, Ravallion has described Rawls's book as the most important 'philosophical landmark of the Second Poverty Enlightenment', which 'opened the way to new non-utilitarian thinking on poverty and anti-poverty policy' and focused attention on the ways in which structural inequalities constrained people's life chances.[129] As Jon Mandle and Stuart White have shown, Rawls was primarily interested in enabling citizens to interact as social and political equals, and so was more concerned about the structure of social institutions and access to 'primary goods' (including civil liberties, opportunities to exercise responsibility, and 'the social bases of self-respect') than the distribution of material resources.[130] Yet Rawls's famous 'difference principle'—that inequalities were only justified insofar as they benefited the least advantaged—was frequently conceptualized in income terms, and in *A Theory of Justice* he explicitly suggested that the state should use an NIT to establish a 'social minimum' outside the labour market.[131] Rawlsian political philosophy thus reinforced the focus on income distribution as the primary barometer of social justice, at the expense of older egalitarian concerns about desert, solidarity, and risk-pooling. Atkinson and Stiglitz, for instance, drew on Rawls's difference principle to illustrate how normative values might be applied to public economics.[132] Likewise, Julian Le Grand argued that 'the strategy of promoting equality through public expenditure on the social services ha[d] failed' because spending on health, education, transport, and housing disproportionately benefited the middle classes. Le Grand concluded

[127] Jamie Peck and Nik Theodore, *Fast Policy: Experimental Statecraft at the Thresholds of Neoliberalism* (Minneapolis, 2015); Bob Deacon, *Global Social Policy in the Making: The Foundations of the Social Protection Floor* (Bristol, 2013), 14–17.

[128] Jane Jenson, 'A New Politics for the Social Investment Perspective: Objectives, Instruments, and Areas of Intervention in Welfare Regimes', in *The Politics of the New Welfare State*, edited by Giuliano Bonoli and David Natali (Oxford, 2012), 21–44, at 33.

[129] Ravallion, *The Economics of Poverty*, 87, 91.

[130] Jon Mandle, *Rawls'* A Theory of Justice: *An Introduction* (Cambridge, 2009); Stuart White, 'Democratic Equality as a Work-in-Progress', in *A Companion to Rawls*, edited by Jon Mandle and David A. Reddy (Chichester, 2014), 185–99.

[131] John Rawls, *A Theory of Justice* (Cambridge, Mass., 1971), 275.

[132] Atkinson and Stiglitz, *Lectures on Public Economics*, 340.

that 'a more promising way... of achieving equality *of whatever kind* would be through equalizing incomes'.[133]

Four critiques

Tracing the changing intellectual roots of British social policy through the lens of RML inevitably runs the risk of obscuring other influences. As we shall see, economists' arguments for market pricing have always been contested, and it is impossible to talk about 'the rise of RML' without a good deal of simplification. Nevertheless, the concept provides a useful frame of reference for exploring how developments in social research and economic theory have reshaped attitudes to poverty and inequality. The growing purchase of RML among British policy-making elites helps explain both the mounting interest in guaranteed income as an idea and the growth of the transfer state at the level of public policy.

Before we turn to the impact of RML, however, it is worth pausing to reflect on its limitations as a social philosophy. After all, the attempt to achieve social justice through cash transfers has never been short of critics. These arguments can be categorized under four headings, of which the conservative objection to redistribution on grounds of morality or desert is perhaps most familiar. In its strong form, this resembles Robert Nozick's libertarian defence of absolute property rights: inequalities resulting from unequal endowments and skills are not unjust, and the use of taxation to redistribute resources is 'morally on par with forced labour'.[134] In a weaker form, it takes its cue from the Protestant work ethic—encapsulated in St Paul's injunction that 'if any would not work, neither shall he eat'—and warns against the demoralizing impact of welfare dependency.[135] This fear of encouraging idleness and labour-market withdrawal is widely shared among mainstream policy-makers, who have sought to use work requirements and benefit sanctions to reinforce work incentives.[136]

A second line of criticism relates to the ethical basis of RML: its individualist approach to social justice and its acceptance of market liberalism. John Kay's rejection of RML is founded on the complaint that it is ethically thin, and that the attempt to combine the unrestrained pursuit of profit in the economic

[133] Julian Le Grand, *The Strategy of Equality: Redistribution and the Social Services* (1982), 132, 140.
[134] Robert Nozick, *Anarchy, State, and Utopia* (New York, 1974), 169.
[135] 2 Thessalonians 3:10.
[136] Peck and Theodore, *Fast Policy*, 85–129.

sphere with the pursuit of social justice in the political sphere 'takes a hopelessly implausible view of human nature':

> Can one be a selfish beast at work and a concerned citizen at home? Can you have different personalities in the boardroom and the polling booth? . . . The dichotomy between business virtues and civic virtues cannot be maintained, and in practice one rapidly corrodes the other.[137]

Kay's critique echoes a long tradition of moral critiques of capitalism, which can be traced from Victorian romantics such as Thomas Carlyle and John Ruskin through to twentieth-century Christian socialists such as Tawney. As Tim Rogan has recently shown, these 'moral economists' viewed utilitarian social arithmetic with deep suspicion, and sought to remove not only the material injustices of the capitalist system but also the materialistic values that lay beneath them.[138] Though this critique is characteristic of the anti-capitalist left, it has also found its echoes on the right. Bertrand de Jouvenel saw redistributive politics as 'the end result of utilitarian individualism', unmoored from any ethical vision of the good life, and complained that '[n]othing quite so trivial has ever been made into a social ideal'.[139]

Thirdly, left-wing critics have called attention to the limits of RML as a distributional strategy. Using transfer payments to redistribute the fruits of capitalist production may be attractive to market economists in theory, but it risks exacerbating the classic Marxist problem of the 'structural dependence of the state on capital'.[140] As James Meade pointed out in the 1960s, achieving 'a really substantial equalization of individual incomes . . . solely by redistributive income taxes and subsidies' would require an 'exceptionally progressive' budgetary system.[141] If market liberal policies allow wide inequalities in capital ownership and market income, the scope for redistribution is likely to be constrained both economically by the need to maintain incentives to work and invest and politically by the power of capitalist interests.[142] Winning electoral support for cash transfers may also be a challenge. Where public services blur

[137] Kay, 'Staking a Moral Claim', 18–19.

[138] Tim Rogan, *The Moral Economists: R. H. Tawney, Karl Polanyi, E. P. Thompson, and the Critique of Capitalism* (Princeton, 2017).

[139] De Jouvenel, *The Ethics of Redistribution*, 46, 48.

[140] Adam Przeworski and Michael Wallerstein, 'Structural Dependence of the State on Capital', *American Political Science Review* 82/1 (1988), 11–29.

[141] Meade, *Efficiency, Equality and the Ownership of Property*, 38.

[142] Erik Olin Wright, 'Why Something Like Socialism is Necessary for the Transition to Something Like Communism', *Theory and Society* 15/5 (1986), 657–72.

the relationship between taxpayers and beneficiaries and allow politicians to appeal to voters' sense of solidarity, fiscal redistribution makes the pattern of winners and losers more explicit and so risks inflaming social divisions.

Finally, social researchers such as John Hills have warned that a guaranteed income cannot be a substitute for other forms of social policy. By focusing on meeting people's 'normal' needs at a given point in time, RML not only diverts attention away from wider structural inequalities, but also places the onus on individuals to manage their resources effectively and prepare for life's risks, which is not always a realistic expectation. Hills argues that the welfare state is best understood as a form of risk-pooling through which citizens share the costs of health care, education, and retirement, and insure themselves against the instability of a modern capitalist economy.[143] Despite the decline of the social insurance tradition, the UK benefits system can still be seen 'as a "savings bank", smoothing out resources for the same individuals over the life cycle'.[144] In some cases, collective provision of goods and services may also be more efficient than cash transfers. For instance, effective consumer 'choice' in health and education requires the creation of spare capacity, and the government may be drawn into costly bailouts if private service providers become 'too important to fail'.[145]

All these factors help explain why RML has gone into retreat in Britain since the 2008 financial crisis. Slow economic growth has made redistribution more difficult, Conservative ministers have exploited public suspicion of welfare claimants, and left-wing thinkers have revived older moral critiques of the market. Nevertheless, the recent explosion of interest in UBI suggests that the underlying logic of a guaranteed minimum income remains powerful. Part II steps back into the middle decades of the twentieth century—the heyday of collective social provision, Keynesian economics, and the male-breadwinner employment model—to examine how earlier generations of British policy-makers attempted to put this vision into practice.

[143] John Hills, *Good Times, Bad Times: The Welfare Myth of Them and Us*, revised edn (Bristol, 2017).

[144] John Hills, Howard Glennerster, and Julian Le Grand, *Investigating Welfare: Final Report of the ESRC Welfare Research Programme*, Welfare State Programme Discussion Paper WSP/92 (1993), 2.

[145] Debra Hevenstone, *The American Myth of Markets in Social Policy: Ideological Roots of Inequality* (Basingstoke, 2015), 236.

PART II

IN SEARCH OF A GUARANTEED INCOME

3
Social Dividends and Social Contracts, 1918–1955

Historians of the British welfare state have long seen the 1940s as a critical juncture, in which Winston Churchill's wartime coalition and Clement Attlee's post-war Labour government presided over the formation of a far-reaching social settlement. Sir William Beveridge's 1942 report on *Social Insurance and Allied Services*—alongside the 1944 Education Act and the National Health Service—came to symbolize the state's commitment to supporting citizens 'from the cradle to the grave'. One of the consequences of Beveridge's political success has been to cast into the shadows the alternative visions of welfare which were canvassed by his contemporaries. Yet the fiscal architecture which the British state established during the 1940s, based around contributory National Insurance and progressive income tax, was not without its critics. As this chapter shows, it was in the context of mid-twentieth-century welfare debates that Universal Basic Income first gained traction as a serious policy option. The Quaker engineer Dennis Milner published the first scheme for a tax-funded, subsistence-level UBI at the end of the First World War, and Juliet Rhys-Williams revived the idea in the 1940s as an alternative to Beveridge's proposals.

Dennis Milner and Juliet Rhys-Williams's basic income schemes reflected many of the currents in British social and economic thought examined in Chapter 2, such as the 'poverty line' tradition in British social research, the liberal commitment to consumer choice, and the neoclassical fear that wage regulation and trade union power would distort the labour market. At the same time, the emergence of basic income as a policy option was also shaped by inter-war debates over work and welfare, in which a variety of redistributive devices vied for political attention. In Britain, as in the United States, the 1920s and 1930s saw an array of proposals for reshaping the distribution of income in response to socialist demands for equality and hopes (or fears) that the Great Depression signalled the ultimate crisis of capitalism. Eleanor Rathbone's campaign for Family Allowances attracted wide support among liberals; further left, G. D. H. Cole proposed to distribute two-thirds of national income

Transfer State: The Idea of a Guaranteed Income and the Politics of Redistribution in Modern Britain. Peter Sloman, Oxford University Press (2019). © Peter Sloman. DOI: 10.1093/oso/9780198813262.001.0001

as a 'social dividend' to those who were willing to work, whilst Major C. H. Douglas and his Social Credit movement sought to stimulate consumption through a monthly 'National Dividend'. Policy-makers took some of these ideas more seriously than others, but the relatively slow professionalization of British economics meant that the boundary between expertise and crankery remained permeable. John Maynard Keynes's paean to 'the brave army of heretics' in chapter 23 of his *General Theory* suggested that amateurs still had an important part to play in challenging academic orthodoxies; indeed, as late as the Second World War, the Dorset poet and craftsman A. Romney Green was able to publish his ideas on tax reform in the *Economic Journal.*[1]

The reconstruction debates which took place within Whitehall during the Second World War brought order out of this mêlée of proposals.[2] Beveridge, in particular, held out social insurance as the most realistic means of establishing the 'national minimum' which Beatrice and Sidney Webb had demanded more than thirty years earlier. Much of the Beveridge report's appeal lay in its powerful rhetoric of universal provision, which anticipated T. H. Marshall's vision of the welfare state as a basis for inclusive social citizenship.[3] As José Harris, Jane Lewis, and Susan Pedersen have pointed out, however, the National Insurance model which emerged from the report was in fact gendered and work-oriented—coloured by Beveridge's male-breadwinner assumptions about family structure, his lifelong suspicion of casual labour, and his liberal commitment to individual responsibility.[4] Indeed, Harris notes that Beveridge 'was always much less interested in the relief of poverty *per se* than in the kind of restructuring of the labour market that he hoped would ultimately make relief of poverty unnecessary'.[5] Although this enabled him to find common ground with trade unionists and Whitehall officials, it also created a gap between rhetoric and reality. Much of the

[1] John Maynard Keynes, *The General Theory of Employment Interest and Money* (1936), 371; A. Romney Green, 'The Tax Curve', *Economic Journal* 50/200 (1940), 469–74; A. Romney Green, 'Social Reconstruction by Redistribution of Incomes', *Economic Journal* 52/205 (1942), 37–44.

[2] José Harris, 'Some Aspects of Social Policy in Britain during the Second World War', in *The Emergence of the Welfare State in Britain and Germany, 1850–1950*, edited by W. J. Mommsen (1981), 247–62.

[3] Cmd. 6404, *Social Insurance and Allied Services: A Report by Sir William Beveridge* (1942), 12. Marshall's own discussion of social security was relatively cautious: T. H. Marshall, 'Citizenship and Social Class', in T. H. Marshall, *Citizenship and Social Class and Other Essays* (Cambridge, 1950), 1–85, at 54–6.

[4] José Harris, 'Beveridge's Social and Political Thought', in *Beveridge and Social Security: An International Retrospective*, edited by John Hills, John Ditch, and Howard Glennerster (Oxford: 1994), 23–36; Jane Lewis, 'Gender and the Development of Welfare Regimes', *Journal of European Social Policy* 2/3 (1992), 159–73; Susan Pedersen, *Family, Dependence, and the Origins of the Welfare State: Britain and France, 1914–1945* (Cambridge, 1993).

[5] Harris, 'Beveridge's Social and Political Thought', 32.

subsequent British interest in a guaranteed income has been inspired by the desire to make good the deficiencies of the Beveridge system—extending subsistence benefits from unemployed, sick, and retired workers to the rest of the population.

Beveridge's approach to social security was criticized from the outset by feminist activists such as Elizabeth Abbot and Katherine Bompas of the Women's Freedom League, as well as by Conservatives such as Ralph Assheton who regarded it as dangerously extravagant.[6] Perhaps the most ambitious alternative, however, came from the Liberal activist Juliet Rhys-Williams, who proposed a system of cash allowances for all those willing to work in *Something to Look Forward To* (1943). Rhys-Williams's scheme represented a radical response to the problems of poverty and idleness confronted by Beveridge, which drew on a common stock of concepts—such as universality, contribution, less eligibility, and the national minimum—but configured them very differently. In canvassing support for universal cash transfers, financed by general taxation and designed to replace other forms of social security, Rhys-Williams set the tone for subsequent basic income campaigning. Not only did she force Treasury officials to consider the practicability of basic income, but her campaign also had the effect of squeezing out other conceptions of basic income as a 'social dividend' financed by collective assets. By the early 1950s, tax-benefit integration was firmly established as a market liberal cause, rooted in a critique of both Fabian paternalism and the labourist assumptions of the National Insurance system.

Varieties of basic income, 1918–1939

The idea of a basic income or social dividend circulated widely in Britain between the two world wars. As the Belgian scholar Walter van Trier has shown, UBI-type proposals enjoyed active support from at least three groups of activists: Dennis and Mabel Milner's State Bonus League, C. H. Douglas's Social Credit movement, and socialist intellectuals associated with the New Fabian Research Bureau in the 1930s, such as G. D. H. Cole and James Meade.[7]

[6] Elizabeth Abbot and Katherine Bompas, *The Woman Citizen and Social Security: A Criticism of the Proposals Made in the Beveridge Report as They Affect Women* (1943); José Harris, *William Beveridge: A Biography*, 2nd edn (Oxford, 1997), 421.

[7] Walter van Trier, *Every One a King: An Investigation into the Meaning and Significance of the Debate on Basic Incomes with Special Reference to Three Episodes from the British Inter-War Experience* (Leuven, 1995).

The philosopher Bertrand Russell also developed the idea in *Roads to Freedom* (1918). These enthusiasts all saw themselves as part of the political left, and it is possible to trace connections between them. At the same time, however, they also conceived the nature and purpose of transfer payments in distinctly different ways, reflecting their particular contexts and preoccupations. This section examines the origins and impact of their proposals.

Dennis and Mabel Milner and the 'State Bonus'

According to Walter van Trier, Dennis and Mabel Milner's *Scheme for a State Bonus* (1918) was 'in all probability the earliest full-blown modern basic incomes proposal'.[8] The Milners were a Quaker couple based in York, where Dennis worked as an engineer at Rowntree's chocolate factory. During the First World War, they came up with the idea of extending the wartime system of separation allowances for servicemen's families to the whole community, replacing the existing patchwork of income support through old age pensions, insurance benefits, private charity, and the Poor Law. The couple proposed that 'every individual, all the time, should receive from a central fund some small allowance in money which would be just sufficient to maintain life and liberty if all else failed', 'based on the primal needs of individuals (which are nearly the same for all), namely food, shelter, and a minimum of recreation, say, for instance, what could be bought before the War for 5/- a week'.[9] This 'State Bonus' would be paid for by a proportional tax of 20 per cent on all other income.

For van Trier, the Milners' scheme is marked out as 'modern' by the contrast with Thomas Paine and Thomas Spence's proposals for universal cash allowances at the turn of the nineteenth century. Unlike Paine and Spence, the Milners made no attempt to ground UBI in radical ideas about compensation for enclosure, common rights, or collective landownership. Edward Bellamy's utopian novel *Looking Backward* (1888)—in which equal but conditional cash payments formed part of a modernist vision of productive efficiency—may have been a more important source of inspiration, but the Milners shied away from Bellamy's proposals for industrial conscription and work requirements.[10] The State Bonus was simply a form of redistribution or

[8] Van Trier, *Every One a King*, 31.
[9] E. Mabel Milner and Dennis Milner, *Scheme for a State Bonus: A Rational Method of Solving the Social Problem* (Darlington, 1918), 7.
[10] Van Trier, *Every One a King*, 129–38.

risk-pooling designed to 'solve the social problem': 'the widespread unhappiness of the poorer classes, seen most strikingly in the squalor and the wretchedness of the slums, and forced on our attention by the prevalence of industrial unrest, leading constantly to strikes and even violence'.[11] The Milners argued that universal payments would be more efficient than relying on wage bargaining or the Poor Law, 'where something like 75% is absorbed in organisation and only 25% reaches the pauper!'[12] Only the richest tenth of people in England and Wales—those with incomes of more than £550 a year for a family of five—were likely to lose out. The Milners hoped that they would see this as a price worth paying for industrial peace and social stability.[13]

Dennis Milner left his job in March 1918 to promote the idea full-time and launched the State Bonus League, which employed a travelling organizer and claimed twenty-two branches by the end of the year.[14] He also stood as an independent candidate in the 1918 general election, taking 5 per cent of the vote in the Yorkshire constituency of Barkston Ash, and used his Quaker connections to press the idea on the Labour Party. Chesterfield Trades Council called for Labour to 'give careful consideration to the State Bonus Scheme as outlined by Mr. Dennis Milner' at the 1919 Labour Party conference in Southport, and Milner himself introduced a detailed resolution at the 1920 conference in Scarborough with support from more than a dozen trades councils and local parties.[15] The national Labour leadership, however, viewed the idea with deep suspicion, as a memorandum by the party's Advisory Committee on Trade Policy and Finance shows. The committee argued that the State Bonus was unacceptable in principle because it would 'raise money without any regard to ability to pay and... distribute it without any regard to need'; it was also problematic in practice because it would undermine trade union bargaining, divert resources from the social services, and create unrealistic expectations of what a Labour government could achieve within the capitalist system.[16] Indeed, the attempt to impose a 20 per cent income tax on top of the existing tax burden seemed likely to 'produce a financial, industrial and commercial shock that no Chancellor of the Exchequer could

[11] Milner and Milner, *Scheme for a State Bonus*, 3.
[12] Milner and Milner, *Scheme for a State Bonus*, 13.
[13] Milner and Milner, *Scheme for a State Bonus*, 12.
[14] Van Trier, *Every One a King*, 37–8.
[15] Labour Party, *Report of the Nineteenth Annual Conference. Southport, 1919* (1919), 174; Labour Party, *Report of the Twentieth Annual Conference. Scarborough, 1920* (1920), 185–6; see also van Trier, *Every One a King*, 123.
[16] Labour Party, *Report of the Twenty-First Annual Conference. Brighton, 1921* (1921), 60–2, at 60.

cope with'.[17] 'We have already upon our agenda nationalisation, workers' control, the raising of all wages, the raising of unemployment insurance, to say nothing of the scores of minor measures', the committee concluded, and 'it is more in accord with our principles to establish high wages and high unemployment benefit, than to offer merely the means to live'.[18] This labourist critique of the State Bonus scheme was endorsed by the national executive committee in its report to the 1921 party conference.

The Milners' campaign attracted attention from a number of other social reformers, including G. D. H. Cole, Eleanor Rathbone, Hugh Dalton, and Clara Collett, but after the Labour Party rejected the idea the State Bonus League seems to have fizzled out. By the late 1920s Dennis Milner had left his wife, remarried, and moved to the United States; his most active collaborator, Bertram Pickard, also gave up and moved to Switzerland.[19] The link with Cole is potentially significant, as we shall see, but the State Bonus scheme seems to have had little influence on other basic income proposals.

Bertrand Russell and the 'vagabond's wage'

In the same month that Dennis Milner left Rowntree's to launch the State Bonus League, the philosopher Bertrand Russell was developing the idea of a 'vagabond's wage' in his short book *Roads to Freedom*. Like many left-leaning intellectuals, Russell had been thoroughly disillusioned by the Liberal government's decision to join the First World War and was propelled into socialist and pacifist circles by the struggle against it. After war broke out, Russell set analytic philosophy to one side and threw himself into the work of the Union for Democratic Control and the No-Conscription Fellowship; indeed, he completed *Roads to Freedom* just before he was sent to prison for 'insulting an ally' (by speculating that the government might use American troops to break up strikes) in April 1918.[20] From about mid-1915 onwards, he was also an active member of the Independent Labour Party. In many ways, however, Russell's confrontation with the wartime state reinforced his concern about the statist implications of Marxian and Fabian socialism. The idea of a

[17] Labour Party, *Report of the Twenty-First Annual Conference*, 61.

[18] Labour Party, *Report of the Twenty-First Annual Conference*, 61.

[19] Van Trier, *Every One a King*, 138–42.

[20] Royden Harrison, 'Bertrand Russell: From Liberalism to Socialism?', *Russell* 6/1 (1986), 5–38; Alan Ryan, *Bertrand Russell: A Political Life* (1988). For Russell's imprisonment, see Philip Ironside, *The Social and Political Thought of Bertrand Russell: The Development of an Aristocratic Liberalism* (Cambridge, 1996), 104.

'vagabond's wage' thus emerged as a way of maximizing the scope for individual freedom and creativity within a socialist society.

Russell's vision of economic development was heavily influenced by the Russian anarchist writer Pyotr Kropotkin (1842–1921), who had developed Mikhail Bakunin's anarchist utopianism into a model of social organization in *The Conquest of Bread* (1892) and *Fields, Factories and Workshops* (1898). Kropotkin believed that the economic growth unleashed by the scientific organization of production would allow a radical reduction in working hours and the free distribution of basic commodities to the whole population. Kropotkin sought to create a society where work was both voluntary and enjoyable: 'where each individual is a producer of both manual and intellectual work; where each able-bodied human being is a worker, and where each worker works both in the field and in the industrial workshop'.[21] Without going the whole way with Kropotkin, Russell was inclined to share both his economic optimism and his social vision, agreeing that 'with the help of science... the whole community could be kept in comfort by means of four hours' work a day'. He also thought society should be able to guarantee a 'small income, sufficient for necessities' to everyone, 'whether they work or not', together with a larger payment for those willing to engage in useful work.[22] Wages as such would be abolished, though Russell conceded that a higher income might be justified for those in 'specially disagreeable' occupations.[23]

Russell's primary objective was to provide a foundation for individual creativity and artistic expression, which was the preserve of the rich in a capitalist society and risked being eroded further under state socialism. The unconditional 'vagabond's wage' would give 'artists, writers of books, men devoted to abstract intellectual pursuits—in short, all those whom society despises while they are alive and honours when they are dead'—the freedom to 'pursu[e] their own work regardless of any public recognition of its utility'.[24] At the same time, the basic income would also encourage scientific innovation and give women 'complete economic independence'.[25] As Philip Ironside has noted, Russell was 'concerned above all with the role in society of the exceptional individual' and 'the preservation of certain Liberal values in what he took to be an inimical political environment'.[26] A basic income provided a way

[21] Pëtr Alekseevich, kniaz' Kropotkin, *Fields, Factories and Workshops*, English trans. (1899), 6, quoted in Bertrand Russell, *Roads to Freedom* (1918), 104.

[22] Russell, *Roads to Freedom*, 119, 120.

[23] Russell, *Roads to Freedom*, 120.

[24] Russell, *Roads to Freedom*, 114.

[25] Russell, *Roads to Freedom*, 168–86, 196.

[26] Ironside, *The Social and Political Thought of Bertrand Russell*, 4, 5.

of detaching this aristocratic liberalism from the materialism and social injustice of the capitalist system.

Like the Milners, Russell turned to other interests during the 1920s, particularly education and sexual ethics, where his liberal attitude to cohabitation and birth control came to colour his public reputation.[27] Yet his interest in liberation from work resurfaced in later years, particularly in his 1932 essay 'In Praise of Idleness', and chimed with the libertarian optimism of other Cambridge and Bloomsbury intellectuals such as Keynes, who discussed the prospect of transition to an age of leisure in 'Economic Possibilities for our Grandchildren'.[28] Indeed, when the Fabian banker George Wansbrough suggested paying 'a basic income . . . on a scale equivalent to present unemployment insurance benefits' in 1939, Keynes described it as 'an important and excellent' idea which 'should certainly have a place in any Utopian political programme'.[29] A. Romney Green applied the same logic to a Negative Income Tax scheme in a 1942 article for the *Economic Journal*, arguing that a guaranteed minimum would unleash 'the creative instincts of a free people' and allow men and women 'to find their own vocations'.[30] By setting the case for a 'vagabond's wage' in the twin contexts of individual creativity and technological abundance, Russell and his followers raised their sights beyond tax and benefit policy and anticipated the utopianism of a later generation of UBI proponents.

C. H. Douglas and the 'National Dividend'

A third version of basic income (or something like a basic income) circulated in the Social Credit movement, which emerged at the same time as the Milners' State Bonus League but attracted much wider public attention. The theoretical core of Social Credit lay in the underconsumptionist analysis which C. H. Douglas developed at the end of the First World War, summed up in his famous A+B Theorem: since a firm used its revenue to make payments both to individuals in the form of wages, salaries, and dividends (A) and to other

[27] Ryan, *Bertrand Russell*, 103–23.

[28] Bertrand Russell, 'In Praise of Idleness', *Harper's Monthly Magazine*, Oct. 1932, 552–9; John Maynard Keynes, 'Economic Possibilities for our Grandchildren' [1930], in John Maynard Keynes, *Essays in Persuasion* (1931), 358–73.

[29] King's College, Cambridge, John Maynard Keynes papers, HP/1/87–9, George Wansbrough to John Maynard Keynes, 11 Dec. 1939, at fo. 87; HP/1/90–2, John Maynard Keynes to George Wansbrough, 14 Dec. 1939 (copy), at fo. 90.

[30] Green, 'Social Reconstruction by Redistribution of Incomes', 43.

organizations for costs such as raw materials (B), individuals would never have enough purchasing power to buy all the firm's product (A+B). Douglas proposed to remedy this shortfall in demand by using credit creation to subsidize output (fixing what he called a 'Just Price') and to pay out a monthly 'National Dividend'. Walter van Trier has pointed out that the precise nature of the dividend was extremely fuzzy. Although Douglas's ally A. R. Orage presented it as a citizen's right, Douglas's most detailed exposition of the idea—in his 1932 'Draft Social Credit Scheme for Scotland'—suggested that it would not in fact be universal: anyone whose income was more than four times the National Dividend, or who turned down a reasonable offer of employment in their registered trade, would be excluded from the system.[31]

Douglas's analysis of poverty amid plenty was highly influential during the 1920s and 1930s, and the promise of a National Dividend became central to Social Credit's appeal during and after the Great Depression. Though serious economists dismissed Douglas as a crank, several public figures endorsed his ideas: in particular, William Ward made the dividend the main demand of a League to Abolish Poverty which he launched at Friends House in September 1934, with support from the Marquess of Tavistock, the novelists Storm Jameson and J. B. Priestley, and the Dean of Canterbury, Hewlett Johnson.[32] Social Credit also engaged in grassroots mobilization through John Hargrave's eccentric Green Shirts movement, which had begun life as an offshoot of the Scouts (the 'Kindred of the Kibbo Kift') but became a uniformed political party in the early 1930s.[33] By the Second World War the movement was fading away, weakened by internal splits and the UK's economic recovery, and the experience of the Canadian province of Alberta—where a Social Credit government was elected in 1935—showed how hard it was to put Douglas's ideas into operation. Nevertheless, the high profile which Social Credit enjoyed between the wars made it an important precursor for subsequent basic income campaigns.

G. D. H. Cole and the 'social dividend'

A final source of inter-war interest in UBI can be found in the socialist intellectuals who clustered around G. D. H. Cole during the late 1920s and

[31] Van Trier, *Every One a King*, 159–94; on Orage's view of the dividend, see 278.

[32] Van Trier, *Every One a King*, 306–7.

[33] Mark Drakeford, *Social Movements and their Supporters: The Green Shirts in England* (Basingstoke, 1997).

1930s. Ben Jackson has shown that the idea of equality was central to British socialist thought in this period, as 'a dual commitment to an egalitarian view of social justice and a more co-operative community united the otherwise diverse gradations of progressive ideology'.[34] Marx's famous distributive principle—'from each according to his ability, to each according to his needs'—was one important touchstone; R. H. Tawney's ethical critique of class privilege in *Equality* (1931) was another. Few Labour intellectuals shared George Bernard Shaw's commitment to strict equality of incomes, but almost all sought an expanded role for the state in redistributing socially created wealth (what an earlier generation of radicals had called the 'unearned increment') and establishing a 'national minimum'.[35]

Perhaps the most prolific and influential Labour thinker of the inter-war period was the Oxford political theorist G. D. H. Cole, who developed guild socialism as an alternative to Fabianism during the First World War, gathered a circle of socialist students and graduates (the 'Cole group') around him in Oxford during the 1920s, and launched the New Fabian Research Bureau (NFRB) in 1931 to flesh out Labour's economic policy. The principle of equality lay at the heart of Cole's socialist vision, especially after he set guild socialism aside in the mid-1920s and gravitated towards a more conventional Fabianism.[36] He was attracted to the principle of equal distribution as an alternative to the wage system, and was familiar with both the Milners' ideas (to which he was sympathetic) and Social Credit (of which he was much more critical).

In his book *The Next Ten Years in Social and Economic Policy* (1929), Cole described 'State Bonus' and 'Dividends for All' as 'two names which have been adopted by advocates of giving every citizen, quite apart from his work, a certain minimum claim to a share in the annual social product'.[37] Later, in *Principles of Economic Planning* (1935), he set out a more detailed agenda for 'a planned redistribution of incomes' which reflected 'each citizen's claim as a consumer to share the common heritage of productive power'.[38] The 'first overriding claim upon the available resources of production', Cole argued, was a 'satisfactory minimum of food, fuel, clothing, housing, education and other common services', which could be provided either directly by the state or by

[34] Ben Jackson, *Equality and the British Left: A Study in Progressive Political Thought, 1900–1964* (Manchester, 2007), 18.

[35] Jackson, *Equality and the British Left*, 59–90.

[36] Jackson, *Equality and the British Left*, 63–4.

[37] G. D. H. Cole, *The Next Ten Years in Social and Economic Policy* (1929), 199.

[38] G. D. H. Cole, *Principles of Economic Planning* (1935), 226, 235.

assuring 'a basic minimum income... to everybody'.[39] It would also be 'necessary for everybody to have at least a minimum income which he can devote to buying goods and services' beyond these necessities.[40] Taking these two categories of goods together suggested a social dividend of at least 30/- per week for each adult, 20/- for young people aged 15 to 20, and 10/- for younger children, which would cost more than two-thirds of national income and turn wages into a kind of 'pocket money'.[41] As Jackson has pointed out, however, Cole worried that a strictly universal payment would encourage free-riding.[42] His social dividend was therefore conditional on 'a proven readiness to play [one's] part in the common tasks and duties of the whole community', which for able-bodied adults meant a willingness to accept paid work.[43]

Cole's social dividend reflected the radical egalitarianism of early socialist planners, who sought to prioritize necessities over luxuries and to eliminate what they saw as the arbitrary differentials of the labour market. Even in the 1930s, this was a heroic form of socialist idealism which was never likely to win much support from the trade unions. At the same time, however, a younger generation of left-wing economists—more sensitive than Cole to the advantages of market pricing—developed the idea in a different way. James Meade, for instance, argued in a 1935 paper for the NFRB that a Labour government should leave wages and prices largely to competitive forces, and focus on building up a stock of publicly owned assets which would provide it with an independent revenue stream. Depending on economic circumstances, these profits could be reinvested in the nationalized industries, used to reduce the national debt, or paid out 'as a social dividend... on any desired principle of equality'.[44] As an early enthusiast for Keynesian economics, Meade also raised the possibility of using credit creation to finance a social dividend during a recession in *Consumers' Credits and Unemployment* (1938), effectively incorporating Douglas's National Dividend into a more conventional Keynesian framework.

In parallel with Meade's work, Oskar Lange and Abba Lerner at the London School of Economics (LSE) applied the concept of a social dividend to the socialist calculation debate—attempting to show, *pace* Ludwig von Mises and Friedrich Hayek, that the trial and error procedure of the market could be used to allocate resources in a socialist economy. In his famous 1936 article 'On the

[39] Cole, *Principles of Economic Planning*, 224. [40] Cole, *Principles of Economic Planning*, 225.
[41] Cole, *Principles of Economic Planning*, 235–6.
[42] Jackson, *Equality and the British Left*, 64. [43] Cole, *Principles of Economic Planning*, 252.
[44] J. E. Meade, 'Outline of Economic Policy for a Labour Government', in *The Collected Papers of James Meade*, vol. 1, ed. Susan Howson and Donald Moggridge (1988), 33–78, at 53.

Economic Theory of Socialism', Lange suggested that the profits of nationalized industries should be distributed to individuals as a social dividend in proportion to market wages.[45] Lerner, on the other hand, argued that 'the earnings of the factors of production other than labour' should be shared out equally as a right of citizenship, 'with no questions asked and no exceptions': 'There could be no better safeguard of the freedom and independence of the individual.'[46] Like Meade, Lerner saw the social dividend as a balancing factor in Keynesian demand management—adjusted upwards in slumps and downwards in booms 'to keep total demand at the proper level'—and thought a substantial social dividend could help make wages more flexible.[47]

A variety of different rationales for a system of social dividends thus became intertwined in inter-war socialist circles. For the most ambitious egalitarians, such as Cole and Russell, the idea of equal dividends for those willing to work represented a radical challenge to the inequalities of the wage system. For more cautious economists, such as Meade, Lange, and Lerner, social dividends offered a device for managing a market socialist economy by stabilizing demand and sharing out the profits of public ownership. In any case, it is clear that 'most of the advocates of basic incomes in the inter-war period did not simply and solely see the proposal as a means of providing income security', as van Trier has noted.[48] It was Juliet Rhys-Williams who revived the Milners' conception of UBI as a form of social security and placed it firmly within the context of redistributive market liberalism.

Juliet Rhys-Williams and the 'new social contract'

Juliet Rhys-Williams (1898–1964) was born as Juliette Glyn, younger daughter of the romantic novelist Elinor Glyn and her barrister husband Clayton. From the age of 19 she worked as a private secretary in Whitehall, and at 22 she married Sir Rhys Williams, a South Wales lawyer, coalowner, and Coalition Liberal MP, with whom she had four children.[49] During the 1930s, Rhys-Williams became a leading figure in the maternity and child welfare

[45] Oskar Lange, 'On the Economic Theory of Socialism: Part I', *The Review of Economic Studies* 4/1 (1936), 53–71, at 61.

[46] Abba Lerner, *The Economics of Control: Principles of Welfare Economics* (1944), 267, 268.

[47] Lerner, *The Economics of Control*, 269, 259.

[48] Van Trier, *Every One a King*, 452.

[49] William Nicoll, 'Williams, Dame Juliet Evangeline Rhys (1898–1964)', in *Oxford Dictionary of National Biography*, vol. 59, edited by H. C. G. Matthew and Brian Harrison (Oxford, 2004), 254–5. Sir Rhys changed his surname to Rhys-Williams by deed poll in 1938.

movement as honorary secretary of the National Birthday Trust and the Joint Council of Midwifery, where she helped pave the way for the Midwives Act 1936. The National Birthday Trust was a decidedly elite organization with a flavour of Victorian philanthropy, founded by Lady George Cholmondeley to raise funds for voluntary maternity hospitals, but Rhys-Williams persuaded her colleagues to adopt a broader focus on the problems of maternal mortality and malnutrition.[50] In 1934 she launched an experimental scheme for distributing food supplements to poor expectant mothers in the Rhondda, which sharply reduced the maternal death rate and was subsequently extended to other depressed districts in South Wales and County Durham with support from the Special Areas Commission.[51] Rhys-Williams also served alongside her husband on the Bishop of Llandaff's Committee, which investigated the South Wales unemployment problem, and was an active member of Harold Macmillan's Next Five Years Group—the epitome of 1930s 'middle opinion'.[52] Concern about malnutrition and work incentives pushed her towards a universalist view of welfare, and when she fought the safe Labour seat of Pontypridd as a Liberal National candidate in a February 1938 by-election she emphasized her support for Family Allowances, cheap milk, and better old age pensions.[53] Later that year the Munich agreement shattered her faith in the National Government, and she defected from the Liberal Nationals to the opposition Liberal Party.[54]

Rhys-Williams was an unlikely Liberal, since she was a fervent imperialist and a supporter of tariffs at a time when the party was still strongly committed to free trade.[55] As she explained to her friend Leo Amery during the Second World War,

> My Liberalism is purely on social policy. I think their free-trade ideas are just as absurdly old-fashioned as you do, + their little Englandism (now fairly extinct) quite revolting! It was Conservative complacency over distressed areas which drove me out. Also 'appeasement'.[56]

[50] A. Susan Williams, *Women and Childbirth in the Twentieth Century: A History of the National Birthday Trust Fund 1928–93* (Stroud, 1997).

[51] Williams, *Women and Childbirth in the Twentieth Century*, 74–98; Jane Lewis, *The Politics of Motherhood: Child and Maternal Welfare in England, 1900–1939* (1980), 181–2.

[52] Bodleian Library, Oxford, MS. Macmillan dep. c. 375, fos 185–7, minutes of Next Five Years Group general policy committee, 21 Apr. 1936.

[53] *Manchester Guardian*, 25 Jan. 1938, 5; see also Lewis, *The Politics of Motherhood*, 188.

[54] British Library of Political and Economic Science (BLPES), Rhys-Williams papers, J10/2, Juliet Rhys-Williams to Stanley Evans, 14 Nov. 1938 (copy).

[55] Rhys-Williams papers, J11/2, Juliet Rhys-Williams to Percy Cohen, 10 Jan. 1937 (copy).

[56] Churchill Archives Centre, Cambridge, Amery papers, AMEL2/2/29, Juliet Rhys-Williams to Leo Amery, 27 May 1943.

Despite this ideological ambivalence, Rhys-Williams rapidly became a leading figure within the struggling Liberal Party: honorary secretary of the Women's Liberal Federation (1943–5), chairman of the party's Publications and Publicity Committee (1944–6), prospective candidate for Ilford North, and a member of the party's ruling Council.[57] At the same time, she retained links with leading Conservatives such as Sir Kingsley Wood, with whom she had worked closely on midwifery reform. She exploited these networks to the full in canvassing support for her basic income proposals.

The Second World War provided a newly propitious environment for basic income proposals to gain traction in mainstream policy-making circles, as a result of two developments. The first was that the needs of wartime mobilization prompted the British state to accept much wider responsibility for its citizens' welfare, reflected in the mass evacuation of schoolchildren and in the introduction of rationing and food subsidies. Eleanor Rathbone's campaign for Family Allowances had gained momentum during the late 1930s as Conservatives and Liberals embraced it as an anti-poverty measure, and the trade union movement—which had long feared that Family Allowances would depress wage rates—relaxed its hostility following the outbreak of war.[58] From 1941 the issue was taken up by Beveridge as part of his review of social insurance provision. Beveridge favoured the development of a comprehensive insurance scheme for unemployment, sickness, and old age alongside non-contributory Family Allowances, but there was clearly scope for further simplification. For instance, both Political and Economic Planning (PEP) and the Fabian Society urged him to abandon flat-rate insurance contributions and throw the whole cost of social security onto general taxation.[59]

The prospects for radical tax-benefit reform were also enhanced by fiscal policy developments, as we have seen in Chapter 2. Sir Kingsley Wood's period as Chancellor between 1940 and 1943 was a period of significant innovation, including the adoption of Keynesian inflationary gap analysis to manage demands on resources, as Robert Crowcroft has recently shown.[60] Wood raised income tax rates and cut thresholds and allowances in order to curtail

[57] Nicoll, 'Williams, Dame Juliet Evangeline Rhys'. For a fuller analysis of the Liberal Party's internal politics during the war, see Peter Sloman, *The Liberal Party and the Economy, 1929–1964* (Oxford, 2015), 135–65.

[58] John Macnicol, *The Movement for Family Allowances, 1918–45: A Study in Social Policy Development* (1980), 118–28, 154–60, 176–8.

[59] Cmd. 6405, *Social Insurance and Allied Services: Memoranda from Organisations. Appendix G to Report by Sir William Beveridge* (1942), 34–41.

[60] Robert Crowcroft, 'Financial Policy, Coalition and Sir Kingsley Wood, 1940–1', *Twentieth Century British History* 26/1 (2015), 74–96.

private consumption, drawing many manual workers into the income tax net; the number of income-tax payers thus grew from 3.7 million in 1937/8 to 6 million in 1940/1 and 13 million in 1944/5.[61] This helped hold down wartime inflation, but at the cost of creating another problem. The existing system of collecting income tax in arrears was strikingly ill suited to working-class budgeting habits, and though a rudimentary system of deductions from wages was quickly introduced, the government faced strong pressure from MPs and trade unionists for these to be based on current earnings.[62] The Inland Revenue eventually met this demand by devising cumulative PAYE in 1943, but in the interim there was a ready market for schemes which would allow income tax to be deducted on a current basis. One obvious solution, as *The Economist* pointed out, was to deduct tax at a flat rate from all wages and then to pay personal allowances in cash as a separate operation.[63] The paper seems to have been thinking of vouchers which taxpayers could encash on production of a certificate of tax paid, but from here it was only a relatively small step to a basic income.

It is not clear whether Juliet Rhys-Williams had encountered any of the 'State Bonus' or 'social dividend' proposals which circulated during the inter-war years, or whether her scheme was entirely her own creation. According to her later testimony, she began working on tax-benefit reform in the summer of 1941 out of frustration at the way in which means-tested unemployment assistance had operated in South Wales during the 1930s.[64] She pointed out that the Unemployment Assistance Board simultaneously provided an inadequate income for unemployment workers, prevented them from taking part-time and casual jobs, and discouraged those with large families from returning to work because they would lose the extra allowances they received for their dependants. The solution, she argued, was to abandon the 'strange convention' that the state should only provide material aid to the unemployed and elderly, and 'substitute for it the democratic principle that the State owes precisely the same advantages to every citizen, *and should consequently pay the same benefits to the employed and healthy as to the idle and sick*'.[65] Rhys-Williams

[61] Martin Daunton, *Just Taxes: The Politics of Taxation in Britain, 1914–1979* (Cambridge, 2002), 180.

[62] Under the inter-war system, income tax on wages and salaries for (say) the 1938/9 tax year was generally paid in two equal instalments, one due by 1 January 1940 and the other by 1 July 1940, though slightly different arrangements applied to manual workers: John H. N. Pearce, 'The Road to 1944: Antecedents of the PAYE Scheme', in *Studies in the History of Tax Law*, vol. 5, edited by John Tiley (Oxford, 2011), 193–218.

[63] *The Economist*, 7 Feb. 1942, 176–7, and 24 Apr. 1942, 563–4.

[64] Rhys-Williams papers, J2/4/3, 'Why Did You Evolve this Scheme?', press handout, June 1951.

[65] Juliet Rhys-Williams, *Something to Look Forward To* (1943), 144.

proposed that citizens should pay income tax at a flat rate of 45 per cent (9/- in the £) on all earnings up to the surtax threshold, and in return would receive a weekly cash payment to cover basic subsistence needs, which she estimated at 21/- for a man, 19/- for a woman, and 10/- for a child, with regional variation for rent.[66] At one stroke the scheme would solve a host of intractable problems: tax could be deducted on a current basis, the means test would disappear, the financial relationship between the citizen and the state would be greatly simplified, and much of the bureaucracy of social insurance could be abolished. Mothers and housewives would receive an independent income, low-paid occupations such as agriculture would become more viable, the Treasury would obtain a powerful fiscal regulator, and the highest earners would also gain from cuts in the top rates of income tax and surtax.[67]

Rhys-Williams believed that her scheme would improve work incentives because benefits would not be withdrawn as earnings rose, but she recognized the risk that some citizens might choose to live on their allowances, placing a heavy tax burden on those in paid work. Consequently, though she did not object to a universal payment in principle, she proposed to make the allowances conditional on labour market participation for men and single women.[68] Each adult citizen would sign a contract with the state, promising to work to the best of their ability—full-time for men, part-time for single women and young widows without dependent children—in return for their allowance. Those who chose not to sign or fulfil the social contract would not be eligible for benefits.[69] In today's terms, the scheme thus came closer to Tony Atkinson's 'participation income' than a true basic income.

Beveridge's rival, 1942–1945

Juliet Rhys-Williams first outlined her ideas in a privately printed pamphlet in August 1942, which she circulated to friends including Sir Kingsley Wood and Leo Amery, and was commissioned by the publishers MacDonald and Co. to develop them into a book under the title of *Something to Look Forward To*.[70] By the time the book appeared in May 1943, however, the political landscape

[66] Rhys-Williams, *Something to Look Forward To*, 145, 151–2.
[67] Rhys-Williams, *Something to Look Forward To*, 138–59, 182–208.
[68] Amery papers, AMEL2/2/29, Juliet Rhys-Williams to Leo Amery, 19 May 1943.
[69] Rhys-Williams, *Something to Look Forward To*, 145–6.
[70] Amery papers, AMEL2/2/29, Juliet Rhys-Williams to Leo Amery, 11 Sept. 1942; Rhys-Williams papers, J2/4/3, 'Why Did You Evolve this Scheme?'

had been transformed by the rapturous public reception of the Beveridge report and demands from Labour and Liberal backbenchers for the adoption of 'Beveridge in full'. The unions also strongly supported Beveridge's scheme as a way of providing security for the unemployed and retired without challenging the importance of the male-breadwinner wage as the primary source of income for most families. In these circumstances, pressing for the adoption of an alternative form of social security was bound to be an uphill struggle. Nevertheless, Beveridge was not without his critics even in progressive circles: for instance, PEP argued that flat-rate social insurance contributions were regressive and inelastic, whilst Seebohm Rowntree pointed out that the scheme would not eliminate poverty among the low-paid and self-employed.[71] The most impassioned critique came from Elizabeth Abbot and Katherine Bompas of the Women's Freedom League, who accused Beveridge of producing 'a man's plan for man', differentiating between married and unmarried women and denying women workers an equal status.[72] Rhys-Williams argued that her approach would make good some of these deficiencies.[73]

One promising constituency for Rhys-Williams's ideas lay in the women's movement, where Eleanor Rathbone and the Family Endowment Society (FES) had long advocated 'wages for housewives' and feminist activists such as Teresa Billington-Grieg continued to press the issue.[74] Rhys-Williams's conception of womanhood was maternalist rather than egalitarian, as her willingness to excuse married women from work requirements showed, but her scheme nevertheless represented a significant advance over Beveridge's strong male breadwinner assumptions. The South Wales Women's Parliament passed a resolution in January 1943 which embodied her criticisms of Beveridge, and in December the Women's Liberal Federation (WLF) endorsed a modified version of the proposals, which it proceeded to press on the Liberal Party itself.[75] Eleanor Rathbone was also favourably impressed, and urged ministers to give the scheme serious consideration.[76] Yet though Rhys-Williams met with representatives from several women's groups in March

[71] *Planning*, no. 205 (20 Apr. 1943), 1–21; B. Seebohm Rowntree, 'Poverty and the Beveridge Plan', *The Fortnightly*, Feb. 1943.

[72] Abbot and Bompas, *The Woman Citizen and Social Security*, 20.

[73] Rhys-Williams, *Something to Look Forward To*, 182–9.

[74] BLPES, Married Women's Association papers, 5MWA/5/2, Juanita Frances to Teresa Billington-Grieg, 12 July 1943.

[75] The National Archives: Public Record Office, Kew (TNA), T161/1461, Juliet Rhys-Williams to Sir Edward Campbell, 31 Jan. 1943; *The Times*, 20 Dec. 1943, 2.

[76] HC Deb., fifth series, vol. 404, 2 Nov. 1944, col. 957.

1944, none of the main feminist organizations took her ideas up.[77] The egalitarian feminists of the Six Point Group had a well-established agenda of their own, centred on equal pay and the marriage bar, whilst the FES was focused on ensuring that Family Allowances were paid to the mother. As Sheila Blackburn has pointed out, most contemporary feminists welcomed the Beveridge report as an important step forward towards comprehensive social security.[78] In any case the government's acceptance of the social insurance model seemed to be a fait accompli, so it made more sense to press for limited changes to the Beveridge scheme which would make it more gender neutral.

Outside feminist circles, it was the possibility of simplifying the relationship between the individual and the state that attracted most attention. Here, Rhys-Williams's scheme tended to be coupled with a similar proposal by a pair of London actuaries, A. T. Haynes and R. J. Kirton, which was also published in May 1943.[79] *The Economist* gave the two schemes sympathetic coverage and suggested that they provided a logical blueprint towards which tax and social security might develop in the long term; so too did W. Manning Dacey in *The Observer*, J. C. Johnstone in the *Daily Telegraph*, and the City editor of *The Times*.[80] The Chancellor of the Exchequer, Sir Kingsley Wood, commissioned a Treasury analysis of the proposals, and the Liberal Party set up a special committee under the chairmanship of Sir Walter Layton, which reported that the version adopted by the WLF was 'sound in principle'.[81] Layton was particularly attracted by the redistributive character of the scheme and the opportunity to move away from regressive flat-rate contributions.[82] The social security expert Sir Ronald Davison praised Rhys-Williams for 'a brilliant piece of sustained thought', whilst the Liberal matriarch Violet Bonham Carter sent a copy of the scheme to John Maynard Keynes, who said that he found the idea 'very attractive'.[83]

[77] *Manchester Guardian*, 2 Mar. 1944, 4.

[78] Sheila Blackburn, 'How Useful are Feminist Theories of the Welfare State?', *Women's History Review* 4/3 (1995), 369–94.

[79] A. T. Haynes and R. J. Kirton, *Income Tax in Relation to Social Security* (1943).

[80] *The Economist*, 11 Sept. 1943, 357–8, and 25 Dec. 1943, 836–7; *The Observer*, 23 May 1943, 3, and 28 May 1944, 7; *The Daily Telegraph*, 29 June 1943, 4, and 21 July 1943, 4; *The Times*, 15 May 1943, 7, and 24 May 1944, 2.

[81] Liberal Party, *Family Allowances and Social Security: Lady Rhys-Williams' Scheme. With the Report of a Liberal Committee thereon* (1944), 4. Laurence Cadbury suspected that Layton was influenced by his wife Dorothy's enthusiasm for the scheme: Borthwick Institute for Archives, University of York, Seebohm Rowntree papers, POV/3/19, L. J. Cadbury to B. S. Rowntree, 9 June 1944.

[82] Rowntree papers, POV/3/21, Sir Walter Layton to B. S. Rowntree, 9 Aug. 1944.

[83] *Manchester Guardian*, 2 Mar. 1944, 4; Bodleian Library, MS. Bonham Carter, 183/24, Keynes to Violet Bonham Carter, 20 Dec. 1943.

Keynes pointed out, however, that support for the principle of tax-benefit integration was very different from accepting the details of particular proposals, and the expert scrutiny which Rhys-Williams had sought brought her scheme's drawbacks into focus. Critical attention centred on the cost of paying subsistence-level allowances to every citizen. E. F. Schumacher, who examined the scheme for the Liberals, estimated that taxation would have to rise to 53 per cent of national income to finance the payments, even if the government managed to pare back its expenditure in other areas such as roads, defence, and agriculture.[84] The editor of *The Economist*, Geoffrey Crowther, was more sympathetic, but agreed that Rhys-Williams was 'going far too fast in extending the scope of social security and using up a great deal of taxable capacity without enquiring whether the objects on which the money is to be spent are really those which should have priority'.[85] Within government, the veteran Treasury official Herbert Brittain made a similar point. Although the finances of the scheme were plausible enough,

> from a general point of view it is highly fantastic that when the total gross payments required, according to Beveridge, to relieve want, sickness, etc. amount to about £700 millions, we should go to the length of paying out £2,280 millions and of having to collect £2,000 millions more in income tax than at present.[86]

At a time when Conservative ministers and Treasury officials were concerned by the cost of Beveridge's proposals, there seemed to be little point in pressing for a more expensive scheme. As the taxation expert László Rostas observed, the Beveridge report had 'a better chance of general acceptance', and if augmented by adequate Family Allowances and minimum wages it 'would probably serve the same big aims'.[87]

The impact of a basic income on work incentives was also felt to be less clear-cut than Rhys-Williams had claimed. It was probably true that it would make it easier for the unemployed to return to work, but Schumacher pointed out that a flat tax would mean higher marginal rates for millions of workers whose incomes currently fell below the tax threshold or only took them into the reduced-rate bands.[88] Edward Hale of the Treasury also warned that the

[84] Rowntree papers, POV/3/9, 'Notes by Mr. E. F. Schumacher on Proposals for Uniting Income-Tax Allowances with Social Security Benefits for Dependants', 30 Dec. 1943.

[85] Rowntree papers, POV/3/18, Geoffrey Crowther to B. S. Rowntree, 6 June 1944.

[86] TNA, T161/1461, Herbert Brittain to Bernard Gilbert, 28 Jan. 1943.

[87] Rowntree papers, POV/3/11, L. Rostas to B. S. Rowntree, 30 Apr. 1944.

[88] Rowntree papers, POV/3/9, 'Notes by Mr. E. F. Schumacher'.

social contract would be difficult to enforce, especially in the case of the self-employed.[89] It may have been for this reason that Rhys-Williams abandoned the formal contract in later versions of her scheme and suggested that workers might have their allowance netted off against tax liability instead.[90] This modification reduced the contractarian flavour of the scheme, but it also introduced a new form of administrative complexity.

The strongest defence of the status quo came from the Board of Inland Revenue, whose chairman Sir Cornelius Gregg dismissed *Something to Look Forward To* as 'special pleading of a soppy sentimental character with no real principle behind it'.[91] In line with its traditional caution, the Revenue argued that the equation of tax allowances with social benefits gave 'an entirely false picture' because the two systems embodied different principles: income tax was based on the concept of taxable capacity, which varied according to family responsibilities as well as income, whereas social security was designed to prevent citizens from suffering material want as a result of unemployment, sickness, or old age.[92] Gregg also articulated the Revenue's traditional concern for the legitimacy of tax collection, insisting that it would be wrong 'to entangle the Income Tax machine in the payment of Social Service benefits' and difficult to collect a flat rate of tax from all incomes.[93] Sir Bernard Gilbert of the Treasury added the political point that a scheme which demolished the argument for a family wage was unlikely to be popular with the trade unions.[94]

Official attitudes towards Rhys-Williams's scheme may have been coloured by sexism and hostility to lay initiative; Eleanor Rathbone certainly suspected as much.[95] Even so, the Treasury and Inland Revenue's criticisms were cogent enough in their own terms, and were accepted as such by Sir Kingsley Wood and his successor Sir John Anderson.[96] Contributory social insurance, progressive income tax, and cumulative PAYE thus became the fiscal building-blocks of the post-war welfare state, supported for different reasons by both Labour and the Conservatives. Even the Liberals' enthusiasm for radical reform waned after Beveridge joined their ranks as MP for Berwick-upon-Tweed in

[89] TNA, T161/1461, 'Draft Reply to Mr. Amery' by Edward Hale, 30 Jan. 1943.

[90] Liberal Party, *Family Allowances and Social Security*, 12–16.

[91] TNA, T161/1461, Sir Cornelius Gregg to Mr Padmore, n.d. [June/July 1943].

[92] TNA, T161/1461, 'Notes on Income Tax Reforms Proposed in a Book Entitled "Something to Look Forward To" by Lady Rhys Williams, and in a Paper Entitled "Income Tax in Relation to Social Security", by A. T. Haynes and R. J. Kirton, of the Institute of Actuaries', Inland Revenue, 16 July 1943.

[93] TNA, T161/1461, Sir Cornelius Gregg to Mr Padmore, 21 Dec. 1943, and 'Notes on Income Tax Reforms', 16 July 1943.

[94] TNA, T161/1461, Sir Bernard Gilbert to Mr Padmore, 30 Dec. 1943.

[95] Pedersen, *Family, Dependence, and the Origins of the Welfare State*, 352–3; HC Deb., fifth series, vol. 404, 3 Nov. 1944, cols 1173–4.

[96] TNA, T161/1461, Sir Kingsley Wood to Juliet Rhys-Williams, 28 July 1943 (copy).

October 1944, since the party could hardly alienate its star recruit. The January 1945 Liberal Assembly passed a resolution which noted the need for tax-benefit integration, but Beveridge took little interest in the idea, and it made no appearance in the party's 1945 election campaign.[97]

'A progressive policy for the right', 1945–1951

The adoption of the insurance model as the basis for post-war social policy was sealed by the landslide Labour victory in the 1945 general election. Though *Let Us Face the Future* did not mention the Beveridge report by name, ninety-seven Labour MPs had voted for its early implementation in the famous February 1943 Commons debate, and the party seemed to have profited from popular enthusiasm for it.[98] Jim Griffiths, who had led the 1943 rebellion, became Minister of National Insurance and piloted a modified version of Beveridge's plan into law as the 1946 National Insurance Act.[99] Griffiths and his colleagues took justifiable pride in implementing wartime reconstruction plans and overcoming the economic difficulties which threatened to destabilize them. At the same time, Hugh Dalton and Sir Stafford Cripps responded to demands for income tax reductions by increasing personal allowances, earned income relief, and the reduced-rate bands: Dalton's first budget, for instance, took about 2 million people—mostly working men—out of income tax altogether.[100] All this suggested that Rhys-Williams's ideas were politically dead—as an LSE economist, H. S. Booker, lamented in the *Economic Journal*.[101]

During the late 1940s, however, tax-benefit reform returned to the political agenda for two reasons. The first was the growth of concern across the political spectrum—including the Trades Union Congress (TUC) and the Federation of British Industries—about the impact of taxation on work incentives.[102] As Richard Whiting and Martin Daunton have shown, this was a central topic of

[97] *Liberal Magazine* (Apr. 1945), 198–9; Rhys-Williams papers, J2/3/1, Juliet Rhys-Williams to Mrs A. O. Scott, 29 Nov. 1944 (copy).

[98] Steven Fielding, 'What Did "The People" Want? The Meaning of the 1945 General Election', *Historical Journal* 35/3 (1992), 623–39.

[99] Kenneth O. Morgan, *Labour in Power 1945–1951* (Oxford, 1984), 170–3.

[100] Daunton, *Just Taxes*, 219–21.

[101] H. S. Booker, 'Lady Rhys Williams' Proposals for the Amalgamation of Direct Taxation with Social Insurance', *Economic Journal* 56/222 (1946), 230–43, at 230.

[102] Modern Records Centre, University of Warwick, Trades Union Congress papers, MSS.292/411/14/1, 'The Effect of Income Tax on Incentive', 30 Apr. 1946, and Federation of British Industries papers, MSS.200/F/1/1/133/160–1, FBI Taxation Committee minutes, 14 Nov. 1946; HC Deb., fifth series, vol. 421, 10 Apr. 1946, cols 1951–8 (George Benson), 1958–66 (Sir Stanley Holmes), 1993–2001 (Hugh Gaitskell).

debate during the Attlee years in the context of the government's production drive and the pressing need to reduce the UK's 'dollar deficit'.[103] Quite apart from the overall tax burden, the structure of PAYE made workers more aware of the marginal rate which they paid on additional earnings and also provided for refunds if wages fell towards the end of the tax year, allegedly discouraging overtime work and encouraging absenteeism. The Conservative MP David Eccles and the former Inland Revenue official Paul Chambers, who had devised PAYE before becoming a director of ICI, both argued that a flat-rate tax on low and middle incomes would solve these problems. Eccles proposed to pay tax allowances through a voucher system, but Chambers pointed out that the standard rate could be reduced to just 15 per cent (3/- in the £) on incomes up to £500 if all allowances were abolished.[104] In either case, the social security system would have to be retained in some form.

Concerns about incentives were reinforced among mainstream economists by frustration with the Attlee government's policy of maintaining wartime food and housing subsidies. As we have seen in Chapter 2, market-oriented Keynesians such as James Meade, Roy Harrod, and Alan Peacock argued that these subsidies offended against both economic efficiency and consumer choice: it would be better to supplement the incomes of the poorest citizens and allow them to spend the money as they chose. Meade viewed tax-benefit integration as a powerful tool for redistributing purchasing power, and included a detailed discussion of the Rhys-Williams scheme in his 1948 book *Planning and the Price Mechanism*; he also canvassed the idea within the Labour Party, though he worried about the impact on work incentives, and suggested retaining a 'poll tax' on the model of National Insurance contributions in order to reduce the income tax rate required.[105] Harrod, who had drifted from Labour to the Liberals during the war and from the Liberals to the Conservatives after it, was also impressed, arguing that the idea of a basic income was 'radically sound' and 'might constitute a genuine rival to that of socialism itself'.[106]

[103] Richard Whiting, *The Labour Party and Taxation: Party Identity and Political Purpose in Twentieth-Century Britain* (Cambridge, 2000), 90–105; Daunton, *Just Taxes*, 217–21.

[104] HC Deb., fifth series, vol. 421, 10 Apr. 1946, cols 2036–45; S. P. Chambers, 'Taxation and Incentives', *Lloyds Bank Review*, new series no. 8, Apr. 1948, 1–12.

[105] J. E. Meade, *Planning and the Price Mechanism* (1948), 42–6; Labour History Archive and Study Centre, Manchester, Labour Party Archive, Research Department memoranda, RD 201, 'Next Steps in Domestic Economic Policy' by J. E. Meade, Nov. 1948; Trades Union Congress papers, MSS.292/750.1/6, Labour Party Policy and Publicity Committee minutes, 15 Nov. 1948.

[106] Bodleian Library, Conservative Party Archive (CPA), LCC2/1/2/3–25, 'Reform of Income Tax and Social Security Payments. "Preliminary Reaction"' by R. F. Harrod, n.d. [June 1950], at fos 14, 15; see also Roy Harrod, 'The Outlook for 1949', *World Review*, Jan. 1949, 15–19.

Rhys-Williams was well placed to take advantage of this renewed interest in her scheme. After the 1945 election she became a central figure in the Design for Freedom movement, which sought to bring about Liberal-Conservative cooperation, as well as honorary secretary of Winston Churchill's United Europe Movement and a small London-based think-tank, the Economic Research Council.[107] During 1948 she met with Paul Chambers and James Meade with a view to devising a mutually acceptable scheme, but the ideological differences between them proved too great.[108] Chambers was preoccupied by the need to reduce tax rates and horrified by the idea of subsistence-level cash allowances, whereas Meade pointed out that it was only the possibility of replacing National Insurance benefits with a basic income that created scope for large administrative savings.[109]

The political reception of these ideas reflected the complex nexus of gender, class, and ideology which lay at the heart of post-war debates about austerity and consumption.[110] The Attlee government showed little interest, since the concept of basic income cut across both elements in Labour's egalitarian strategy: higher wages for working men and collective provision of health, education, and housing. As Amy Black and Stephen Brooke have pointed out, the Labour Party's trade union roots meant that its economic policies 'stressed producers rather than consumers', whilst 'the assumption that the party of welfare was the party of women' fostered a degree of 'complacency' towards female voters.[111] Meade's enthusiasm for market pricing and consumer choice was a minority taste within the party, and his efforts to canvass support for Rhys-Williams's scheme made little headway—though the sociologist Barbara Wootton, the young economist Brian Abel-Smith, and Douglas Houghton of the Inland Revenue Staff Federation recognized its potential, and the Fabian Society's Social Services Group studied it in the early 1950s.[112] At the Treasury,

[107] For the Economic Research Council, see the correspondence in Rhys-Williams papers, J1/15.

[108] As a compromise, Rhys-Williams suggested that a universal payment of 16/- might be topped up by a 10/- tax credit for workers and an extra 10/- cash allowance for the sick, unemployed, and retired, paid for by income tax at 6/8 in the £ (33.3%) and an employee contribution of 3/4: see Juliet Rhys-Williams, *Income Tax Reform. Outline of Lady Rhys-Williams's Proposals* (1949).

[109] BLPES, Meade papers, 3/7/6–7, James Meade to Juliet Rhys-Williams, 8 Sept. 1948 (copy), and 3/7/11–12, S. P. Chambers to James Meade, 22 Nov. 1948. Ursula Hicks agreed with Chambers: Meade papers, 3/7/15, Ursula Hicks to James Meade, 30 Nov. 1948 (copy).

[110] Ina Zweiniger-Bargielowska, *Austerity in Britain: Rationing, Controls, and Consumption, 1939–1955* (Oxford, 2000).

[111] Amy Black and Stephen Brooke, 'The Labour Party, Women, and the Problem of Gender, 1951–1966', *Journal of British Studies* 36/4 (1997), 419–52, at 428, 434.

[112] Barbara Wootton, 'Record of the Labour Government in the Social Services', *Political Quarterly* 20/2 (1949), 101–12; Barbara Wootton, 'The Labour Party and Social Services', *Political Quarterly* 24/1 (1953), 55–67; BLPES, Abel-Smith papers, 4/14, 'The Rhys-Williams Scheme', n.d.; Trades Union Congress papers, MSS 292/411.14/2, Douglas Houghton to Vincent Tewson, 'Income Tax – P.A.Y.E.', 3

both Stafford Cripps and Hugh Gaitskell investigated the possibility of income tax simplification, but the schemes prepared by Inland Revenue officials provided for a series of low flat rates for weekly wage-earners and left National Insurance untouched.[113] In the end, nothing was done in this direction before Labour lost office in 1951. One reason was that Dalton's policy of removing low earners from tax was politically difficult to reverse; another was the TUC's vocal commitment to a single, steeply progressive income tax system.[114]

Rhys-Williams's ideas achieved greater traction in the Liberal Party, which was less sensitive to trade union opinion and more concerned about choice and incentives. Although the Liberals welcomed the Attlee government's flagship social legislation, the National Insurance Act and the creation of the National Health Service, some activists worried that the continued expansion of collective provision would undermine independence and personal responsibility.[115] Like Meade and other economists, Liberal activists were most suspicious of food and housing subsidies, but they recognized that outright opposition to these measures was likely to be seen as an assault on working-class interests. Rhys-Williams's scheme offered a means of squaring the circle by compensating poorer workers and their families for the loss of benefits in kind.[116] Philip Fothergill, the chairman of the party's executive committee, also seems to have hoped that such radical proposals would help attract voters' attention.[117] The 1949 Liberal Assembly thus reaffirmed the principle of tax-benefit integration, and a Taxation Committee—chaired by the London accountant Guy Naylor and including three LSE economists, Alan Peacock, Frank Paish, and Nancy Seear—was tasked with working out the details.[118] Naylor and his colleagues concluded that a subsistence-level scheme would damage work incentives, and instead

June 1948; BLPES, Fabian Society papers, K24/6/3–5, 'Social Services Group. Report of a Meeting on 14th February, 1952'. The Labour thinker and sociologist Michael Young also corresponded with Rhys-Williams: see Rhys-Williams papers, J2/6, Michael Young to Juliet Rhys-Williams, 25 Apr. 1952, and Juliet Rhys-Williams to Michael Young, 2 May 1952 (copy).

113 TNA, T171/397, fo. 97, 'Budget—1949', note by B.E., 15 Sept. 1949; T171/434, Eric Bamford to Sir Edward Bridges, 29 Nov. 1951; and IR40/13894, 'Board's Memorandum 21. Simplification of the Income Tax on Small Incomes', 17 Nov. 1951.

114 TNA, IR75/30, document 37, 'Trades Union Congress. Evidence to the Royal Commission on Taxation of Profits and Income', 2 May 1951.

115 Sloman, *The Liberal Party and the Economy*, 190–5.

116 Sloman, *The Liberal Party and the Economy*, 193.

117 MS. Macmillan dep. c. 566, fos 412–13, Juliet Rhys-Williams to Harold Macmillan, 6 Dec. 1948.

118 *Liberal Magazine* (Apr. 1949), 186–7; Alan Peacock, *Anxious to Do Good: Learning to be an Economist the Hard Way* (Exeter, 2010), 59–66. For the committee's membership, see: Rhys-Williams papers, J10/3/1, minutes of Taxation Committee meeting, 19 July 1949.

proposed to pay a cash allowance of 12/6—about half the basic National Assistance rate, excluding rent, for a single person—to all adults and children. This would be financed by a flat-rate tax of 25 per cent (5/- in the £) on earned incomes up to £600 and the abolition of the food subsidies.[119] Though the committee's report appeared too late for the party to use in the February 1950 election, it was endorsed by the party Council in June 1950, and Rhys-Williams thought it 'quite excellent as an interim step'.[120]

By the late 1940s, however, Rhys-Williams had drifted away from the Liberal Party in frustration at its ambivalence towards the Labour government. In any case, the Liberals were in precipitate decline, and struggled to find an electoral niche for themselves under Clement Davies's leadership; by 1951 the party had just six seats and was 'on the brink of oblivion'.[121] The real prize Rhys-Williams sought was the Conservative Party's backing, and she energetically used her position as Churchill's intermediary with the Liberals to press the merits of reform. 'There is a progressive policy for the right, as well as for the left,' she wrote to the Tory leader in January 1949, 'and this is the time for it.'[122] Rhys-Williams argued that her latest scheme would burnish the Conservatives' appeal to agricultural workers and women voters—two key electoral groups—whilst providing political cover for cuts in surtax and the food subsidies.[123] Framed in these terms, the concept of tax-benefit reform was an appealing one which chimed with the party's rhetoric of 'setting the people free' and offered a means of outflanking Labour on welfare policy. Leading Conservatives such as Harold Macmillan took an interest in Rhys-Williams's ideas, and R. A. Butler commissioned a detailed analysis from David Dear and Reginald Maudling of the Conservative Research Department.[124]

Over time, though, the Conservatives decided against Rhys-Williams's scheme for a number of reasons. First, the idea of a basic income ran up

[119] The plans also included a 6/- tax on unearned income and a supplementary rate on incomes over £600: Rhys-Williams papers, J10/3/1, minutes of Taxation Committee meeting, 29 Dec. 1949; Liberal Party, *Reform of Income Tax and Social Security Payments* (1950).

[120] *Liberal News*, 16 June 1950, 1; Rhys-Williams papers, J2/2/2, Juliet Rhys-Williams to Guy Naylor, 20 Mar. 1950.

[121] David Dutton, 'On the Brink of Oblivion: The Post-War Crisis of British Liberalism', *Canadian Journal of History* 27/3 (1992), 425–50.

[122] Rhys-Williams papers, J11/5, Juliet Rhys-Williams to Winston Churchill, 17 Jan. 1949 (copy).

[123] MS. Macmillan dep. c. 566, fos 381–2, Juliet Rhys-Williams to Harold Macmillan, 1 Mar. 1949; Rhys-Williams papers, J2/1/6, 'Income-Tax Reform as a Means of Introducing a Reduction in Food Subsidies without Hardship', by Juliet Rhys-Williams, 9 Jan. 1950; CPA, LCC2/1/2/29–48, Juliet Rhys-Williams to R. A. Butler, 'Re. The Income Tax Reform Scheme', 26 June 1950, with 'Talking Points'.

[124] Harriet Jones, 'The Conservative Party and the Welfare State, 1942–1955' (Ph.D. thesis, University of London, 1992), 176. David Eccles devised his own proposals, on similar lines to the Liberal scheme: Rhys-Williams papers, J2/9, 'Income Tax Reform. A New Proposal, Based on Lady Rhys-Williams' Scheme. (Put Forward by Mr David Eccles, M.P.)', n.d., and *The Times*, 20 Sept. 1951, 7.

against the party's deep-seated suspicion of redistributive taxation and welfare spending, which had been visible in the debate over the Beveridge report and was accentuated by the middle-class reaction against the Attlee government. If liberal economists were attracted to a basic income as a means of enlarging consumer choice, many Conservatives were alarmed by the prospect of making every citizen 'dependent on and in some degree a pensioner of the State': Sir John Anderson, for instance, saw this as 'a concession to the pestilent Socialist doctrine of re-distribution and a long step on the way to Communism'.[125] Secondly, Churchill was determined not to tie the hands of a future Conservative government by making expensive tax and spending commitments. As a former Chancellor of the Exchequer himself, he insisted that tax changes should be left to the budget process, not fought out on the hustings.[126] Thirdly, Dear and Maudling were unconvinced by the political benefits of the scheme, since it would not only increase the tax burden overall but would also tend to redistribute income from middle earners towards the rich and the poor.[127] In electoral terms, it made better sense for the Conservatives to cut income tax for skilled workers and other middle-income groups, restoring the 'dip' in the incidence of taxation which had existed in the 1920s and 1930s.[128]

The Conservative leadership's rejection of the Rhys-Williams scheme thus reflected a growing confidence in the party's electoral position. The results of the 1950 general election—which reduced Labour to a majority of five—confirmed Churchill's belief that there was no need to enter into a bidding war over social policy, and thereafter he put his faith in 'housing, red meat, and not getting scuppered'.[129] Outside the field of house-building, where the temptation to exploit Aneurin Bevan's perceived failure was irresistible, Conservatives focused on reassuring voters about their intentions towards the welfare state whilst emphasizing the need to control its cost. As a result, the social policy of Churchill's 1951–5 government had (in Timothy Raison's words) 'a curiously uncomplicated flavour'.[130] Butler used his 1952 budget to cut the food subsidies and grant compensatory increases in Family Allowances

[125] CPA, LCC2/1/1/65–76, 'Liberal Party's Scheme for Reform of Income Tax and Social Security Payments', 26 Apr. 1950, at fo. 71; Rhys-Williams papers, J2/8/2, Sir John Anderson to Juliet Rhys-Williams, 28 Aug. 1951.

[126] Rhys-Williams papers, J11/5, Winston Churchill to Juliet Rhys-Williams, 17 Jan. 1950.

[127] MS. Macmillan dep. c. 566, fos 415–17, 'Lady Rhys-Williams's Scheme', n.d. [Nov./Dec. 1948], though see also fos 391–401, 'Lady Rhys-Williams' Proposals for Income Tax Reform (New Version)' by David Dear, n.d. [Feb. 1949].

[128] For the 'dip', see Daunton, *Just Taxes*, 132–41, 167–9.

[129] Quoted in John Ramsden, *The Age of Churchill and Eden, 1940–1957* (1995), 228.

[130] Timothy Raison, *Tories and the Welfare State: A History of Conservative Social Policy since the Second World War* (Basingstoke, 1990), 32.

and National Insurance benefits; he also increased earned income relief and extended the reduced-rate bands, and followed this up with standard-rate income tax cuts in 1953 and 1955.[131] On the social security side, the contributory principle was reaffirmed, partly because it was believed to encourage personal responsibility and partly because the fact that higher benefits would have to be paid for by higher contributions gave the Treasury a powerful lever for reining in spending.[132] Butler's strategy may have amounted to little more than fiscal 'tinkering', but the increased Conservative majorities in 1955 and 1959 suggest that it was politically astute.[133] As Whiting has pointed out, the income tax cuts effectively drove a wedge between the interests of better-paid skilled workers and other working-class groups.[134]

The Royal Commission on Taxation of Profits and Income, 1951–1955

The appointment of a Royal Commission on the Taxation of Profits and Income in 1951 presented a final opportunity for Rhys-Williams to make the case for reform. Although it was established by the Attlee government in response to criticism of its differential profits tax, the Commission was also asked to consider how far the current system of income tax rates and allowances 'distribut[ed] the tax burden fairly among the individual members of the community', and specifically invited evidence on 'whether it would be advantageous to link income tax with social security payments and contributions'.[135] Rhys-Williams, Haynes and Kirton, and the Liberal Party submitted detailed memoranda and were examined at oral hearings in June and July 1951.

The Royal Commission, however, turned out to be no more receptive to the case for tax-benefit integration than Labour and Conservative ministers had been. Although the Commission examined Rhys-Williams's ideas, the social advantages of basic income lay outside its terms of reference, and its chairman Lord Cohen believed that '[t]he Social Security schemes were only relevant' insofar as '(a) the proposals would involve considerable administrative saving

[131] R. C. Whiting, 'Income Tax, the Working Class and Party Politics, 1948–52', *Twentieth Century British History* 8/2 (1997), 194–221.

[132] Jones, 'New Tricks for an Old Dog?'; CPA, CRD2/30/10, 'National Insurance Policy Sub-Committee. Report on the Finance of National Insurance', by John Vaughan-Morgan, Jack Browne, Richard Fort, J. Enoch Powell, and Charles E. Bellairs, n.d. [1953].

[133] Daunton, *Just Taxes*, 277.

[134] Whiting, 'Income Tax, the Working Class and Party Politics'.

[135] Cmd. 9015, *Royal Commission on the Taxation of Profits and Income. Second Report* (1954), 2, 9.

and/or (b) they would remove the disincentive effects of the present graduated [income tax] system at the margins'.[136] UBI was thus evaluated purely in terms of the contribution it could make to tax simplification and administrative economy—a frame of analysis which meant that the scales were tilted against it from the start. The two leading economists on the Commission were also keen to press their own tax reform schemes: Nicholas Kaldor for a progressive expenditure tax, John Hicks for a simple wages tax on the lines suggested by Chambers.[137] The Inland Revenue, on the other hand, was wary of radical reform proposals in general and of tax-benefit integration in particular, and its trenchant memorandum on the Liberal proposals pointed out that the trade-off between incentive and simplification was inescapable:

> If the scheme is satisfactory as social insurance the rate of tax required is so high as to be disincentive. If the rate of tax is kept down on incentive grounds, the benefits which can be given are too small to be effective as social security. No amount of arithmetical skill in constructing a scheme can provide any escape from this dilemma.[138]

The Revenue also used its statistical expertise and contacts within Whitehall to cast doubt on the reformers' estimates of cost and administrative savings: for instance, it claimed that the Liberals had set their tax rate 11*d*. in the £ (4.6 per cent) too low to cover the cost of the allowances, and that any savings from the abolition of PAYE would be offset by the extra work for the Post Office.[139] Arthur Cockfield, the Board's Director of Statistics and Intelligence, later amplified these points in person.[140]

The Inland Revenue memorandum may have been a 'hatchet job', as Liberal adviser Alan Peacock later complained, but its hostility to change was shared by most of the outside organizations which submitted evidence.[141] Though the TUC had previously expressed concerns about the operation of PAYE, it now played down its disincentive effect and rejected the idea of a simple wages tax.

[136] King's College, Cambridge, Kaldor papers, NK/8/2/268–70, minutes of fifth meeting of Royal Commission, 17–19 July 1951, at fo. 70.

[137] Kaldor papers, NK/8/2/351–2, minutes of first meeting of Royal Commission, 9 Jan. 1951, and NK/8/4/200–3, minutes of twelfth meeting of Personal Taxation Committee, 8 Jan. 1953.

[138] *Minutes of Evidence Taken before the Royal Commission on the Taxation of Profits and Income* (1953), 62.

[139] *Minutes of Evidence Taken before the Royal Commission on the Taxation of Profits and Income*, 63–5.

[140] *Minutes of Evidence Taken before the Royal Commission on the Taxation of Profits and Income*, 67–76.

[141] Peacock, *Anxious to Do Good*, 78.

The TUC memorandum also criticized the notion of a basic income paid 'irrespective of need' and argued that the insurance principle was important because it established a right to benefit.[142] From the other side of industry, the British Employers' Confederation warned that the various integration schemes would be 'detrimental to productive effort and industrial relations and would unnecessarily increase the existing pressing burden of taxation', and the FBI echoed this line, though some of its members liked the idea of a flat tax.[143] The economist Ralph Hawtrey spelled out what these groups left implicit, namely a fear of subsidizing the undeserving poor. 'A disadvantage of the cash allowance', Hawtrey argued,

> is that it would be paid to many adults of varying degrees of moral ineligibility: the professional criminals while out of gaol, the tramps, wastrels and spongers, the feckless members of respectable families, who delay settling down to an occupation, have no just claim on public funds.[144]

Hawtrey was also anxious about the impact on gender norms, warning that the cash allowance would be 'regarded as the housewife's pocket money' and 'acclaimed as a trophy in a war of feminism'.[145] Even potential allies disappointed Rhys-Williams: for instance, Geoffrey Crowther backed the principle of reform but refused to commit himself on details, whilst the National Council of Women focused on pressing for the disaggregation of married couples' incomes.[146]

The Royal Commission's rejection of radical reform was sealed by the results of a specially commissioned investigation into the disincentive effects of PAYE which was carried out by the Government Social Survey in February

[142] Nuffield College, Oxford, Papers of the Royal Commission on the Taxation of Profits and Income (RCTPI), document 37, 'Trade Union Congress. Evidence to the Royal Commission on Taxation of Profits and Income', 2 May 1951. Douglas Houghton of the Inland Revenue Staff Federation, who had previously taken an interest in Rhys-Williams and Chambers's ideas, loyally echoed these criticisms: RCTPI papers, document 60, 'Evidence (Part I) Submitted by the Inland Revenue Staff Association', by Douglas Houghton, June 1951; Trades Union Congress papers, MSS.292/411.14/2, Douglas Houghton to Vincent Tewson, 'Income Tax—P.A.Y.E.', 3 June 1948, and MSS.292/411.151/1, Douglas Houghton to Sir Vincent Tewson, 'I.R.S.F. Evidence to the Royal Commission on Taxation', 31 July 1952.

[143] RCTPI papers, document 108, 'British Employers' Confederation. Memorandum of Evidence', 8 Oct. 1951, and document 83, 'First Memorandum by the Federation of British Industries', 18 July 1951; Federation of British Industries papers, MSS.200/F/1/1/135/61–4, FBI Taxation Committee minutes, 15 June 1951.

[144] RCTPI papers, document 134, 'Memorandum from R. G. Hawtrey, C.B.'

[145] RCTPI papers, document 134, 'Memorandum from R. G. Hawtrey, C.B.'

[146] RCTPI papers, document 166, 'Memorandum of Evidence Submitted to the Royal Commission on the Taxation of Profits and Income by Geoffrey Crowther and Roland Bird', and document 65, 'National Council of Women of Great Britain', May 1951.

and March 1952. The survey found that most workers had a hazy understanding of how income tax worked and concluded that its impact on productive effort had been greatly exaggerated.[147] This suggested that the deterrent effects of PAYE were 'illusory', and nothing more than a 'canard... spread by those reformers who wished to combine the income tax and social security systems'.[148] The Commission's second report in April 1954 thus dismissed proposals for integration and recommended only modest changes to remove subsistence earnings from income tax and improve child allowances for higher earners.[149] It thus reaffirmed the conception of progressive income tax which had developed over the previous half-century, under which tax rates, allowances, and reliefs adjusted the burden of income tax to households' 'taxable capacity', and so established a form of equity within the tax system itself.

This apparently authoritative verdict pushed tax-benefit integration to the margins of social policy debate in Britain for almost a decade. Rhys-Williams remained friendly with Macmillan and pressed her scheme on him again after he became Chancellor in 1955, but officials parried the proposals with ease, and the ambitious 'replanning of the welfare state' which took place under Macmillan's government focused instead on health, education, and pensions.[150] Even Rhys-Williams turned her energies elsewhere in the years before her 1964 death, during which she chaired the National Birthday Trust, the United Europe Movement, and the Cwmbran Development Corporation. When interest in a guaranteed income revived in the 1960s, it took a rather different form, inspired by Milton Friedman's Negative Income Tax and the desire to take the stigma out of means-testing.

Conclusion

If the genealogy of UBI can be traced back to the eighteenth century, it was between the First World War and the mid-1950s that the concept took what is now its most characteristic form. Dennis and Mabel Milner detached the idea

[147] Cmd. 9015, *Royal Commission on the Taxation of Profits and Income. Second Report*, 91–124.

[148] Kaldor papers, NK/8/4/204–6, minutes of eleventh meeting of Personal Taxation Committee, 7 Jan. 1953, at fo. 206.

[149] The principle that subsistence earnings should not be taxed had been elaborated by Adam Smith and endorsed by the Royal Commission on the Income Tax in 1920: John Veit-Wilson, 'The Tax Threshold: Policy, Principles, and Poverty', *Twentieth Century British History* 10/2 (1999), 218–34.

[150] TNA, T227/449, fos 1–4, Juliet Rhys-Williams to Harold Macmillan, 19 June 1956, fo. 22, Harold Macmillan to L. Petch, 30 June 1956, and fos 29–30, H. D. Hancock to L. Petch, 27 July 1956; Rodney Lowe, 'The Replanning of the Welfare State, 1957–1964', in *The Conservatives and British Society, 1880–1990*, edited by Martin Francis and Ina Zweiniger-Bargielowska (Cardiff, 1996), 255–73.

of a basic income from its roots in radical discourses of expropriation and restitution, and presented it as a social security policy financed by income tax; Juliet Rhys-Williams came up with a similar scheme twenty years later, and used her personal and political contacts to press it on the British state. Framing basic income as a tax-benefit reform enhanced its credibility in policy-making circles, but it also served to squeeze out alternative conceptions of UBI and to narrow the context within which the idea was judged, closing off potentially far-reaching debates about social rights and the nature of work in favour of a more technical mode of analysis. As van Trier has pointed out, much of the inter-war interest in radical distributive mechanisms among guild socialists, left-wing economists, and Social Credit enthusiasts was forgotten by later commentators. Even James Meade credited the idea to Rhys-Williams in his post-war writings, in a way that obscured his own 1935 proposals for an asset-based 'social dividend'.[151]

In contrast to other contemporary policy entrepreneurs such as Beveridge and Eleanor Rathbone, however, Rhys-Williams was unable to persuade the politicians that mattered to take up her proposals. Why was her campaign unsuccessful? Perhaps the most important obstacle was the political context, and particularly the popularity of the Beveridge report and the power of the assumptions on which it was based. As is now well known, Beveridge's determination to conquer the 'five giants' of want, idleness, ignorance, disease, and squalor was counterbalanced by a more traditional concern to contain the cost of welfare and preserve the liberal ethos of independence and responsibility. His preference for social insurance and his determination to restrict state support to cases of contributory entitlement or manifest need (except in the special case of Family Allowances) were shared by many Whitehall officials, business leaders, and trade unionists. If there was no consensus between Labour and the Conservatives about the ultimate purpose of the welfare state, the evidence submitted to the Royal Commission revealed a substantial measure of agreement on its fiscal architecture, which was 'locked in' by political caution and institutional inertia in the course of the 1950s.

In these circumstances, rallying support for alternative visions of welfare was a formidable task. Rhys-Williams achieved what she did not only because of her social contacts but also because she was an indefatigable campaigner, who adapted her scheme repeatedly to take account of criticisms and exploit new openings. Yet this flexibility was ultimately a weakness as well as a strength, since she sometimes seemed to be more attached to the mechanics

[151] Van Trier, *Every One a King*, 403–7.

of the scheme than to any particular social purpose. The claims which she made for her proposals also invited suspicion: as Hugh Gaitskell pointed out, the notion that almost everyone would benefit seemed 'naïve' and incredible.[152] In an era of growing professionalization, Rhys-Williams made it too easy for policy-makers to dismiss her as a crank, pushing pet ideas onto the agenda through her social and political connections.

These tactical mistakes were compounded by the strategic problem of Rhys-Williams's political conservatism. The most obvious strategy for achieving a substantial basic income in early post-war Britain would have been to enlist support from Labour intellectuals: not only the socialist economists who had floated social dividend schemes in the 1930s, but also welfare experts such as Richard Titmuss and Barbara Wootton who were well aware of the Beveridge report's limitations. Rhys-Williams might have forged an alliance with this group by presenting her scheme as an expression of universal social rights, but her strongly felt hostility to socialism made this impossible. Her own approach implied a very different distributional coalition, uniting Conservatives, Liberals, women voters, and the low-paid against the labourist outlook of the unionized male breadwinner, which was always an unlikely prospect. In the absence of an ethical or philosophical justification for universal payments, centre-right interest in the scheme tended to be shallow and contingent on its electoral potential or its value as a tax reform. When the Conservative leadership and the Royal Commission turned it down, Rhys-Williams's strategy disintegrated. It would be another decade before the 'rediscovery of poverty' sparked a new wave of interest in integration.

[152] *Forward*, 28 Mar. 1953, 2.

4
Negative Income Tax Comes to Britain, 1955–1970

The 1960s witnessed a marked revival of concern about poverty on both sides of the Atlantic. In the United States, Michael Harrington's bestselling study of *The Other America* (1962) drew attention to the deprivation experienced by the 40 million Americans with incomes of less than $3,000 a year, and helped create the political momentum for Lyndon Johnson's War on Poverty.[1] In Britain, young sociologists such as Dorothy Cole (later Dorothy Wedderburn) and Peter Townsend shattered post-war complacency about the success of the welfare state and prompted the formation of a raft of 'poverty lobby' campaign groups.[2] Though the evidence of deprivation in an 'affluent society' shocked many readers, the prevailing mood was one of determined optimism. As economics and sociology departments proliferated in British universities in the wake of the 1963 Robbins report, expertise from across the social sciences was harnessed to the task of analysing the dimensions of poverty and developing policy responses.[3]

One of the most fashionable responses to the rediscovery of poverty in the United States was the concept of a Negative Income Tax, devised by George Stigler and Milton Friedman in the 1940s and popularized by the latter in *Capitalism and Freedom* (1962).[4] Where Juliet Rhys-Williams had envisaged a basic income (or 'participation income') paid for by income tax revenues, NIT would use the tax machinery to raise the incomes of the poor to a more adequate level. As free-market economists, Stigler and Friedman saw NIT as an efficient remedy for poverty which maximized consumer choice and

[1] Michael B. Katz, *The Undeserving Poor: America's Enduring Confrontation with Poverty*, 2nd edn (New York, 2013), 102–55.

[2] Tanya Evans, 'Stopping the Poor Getting Poorer: The Establishment and Professionalization of Poverty NGOs, 1945–95', in *NGOs in Contemporary Britain: Non-State Actors in Society and Politics since 1945*, edited by Nick Crowson, Matthew Hilton, and James McKay (Basingstoke, 2009), 147–63.

[3] Roger Middleton, *Charlatans or Saviours? Economists and the British Economy from Marshall to Meade* (1998), 201–78; A. H. Halsey, *A History of Sociology in Britain: Science, Literature, and Society* (Oxford, 2004), 89–112; John Welshman, *From Transmitted Deprivation to Social Exclusion: Policy, Poverty and Parenting* (Bristol, 2007).

[4] George J. Stigler, 'The Economics of Minimum Wage Legislation', *American Economic Review* 36/3 (1946), 358–65.

Transfer State: The Idea of a Guaranteed Income and the Politics of Redistribution in Modern Britain. Peter Sloman, Oxford University Press (2019). © Peter Sloman. DOI: 10.1093/oso/9780198813262.001.0001

minimized interference with the labour market; indeed, Friedman hoped that it would eventually supersede all other social welfare programmes.[5] Further to the left, activist groups such as the National Welfare Rights Organization saw a guaranteed income as a way of providing income security for the black urban poor, whilst futurists such as Robert Theobald held it up as a response to the emerging 'cybernation revolution', in which technological change threatened to destroy the traditional employment model.[6] By the late 1960s, NIT advocates of one kind or another could be found in all parts of the US political spectrum, as Gareth Davies and Brian Steensland have shown.[7] Even Richard Nixon took up the idea after winning the 1968 presidential election, though his Family Assistance Plan—which combined income supplements with work requirements—was ultimately blocked by critics in the Senate.

Much of the literature on the US guaranteed income debate presents NIT as a distinctively American phenomenon: a product of market-liberal economic expertise which gained traction in response to racial tensions and the deficiencies of state-level social assistance programmes. Yet the possibility of integrating tax and benefits in this way was also central to British social policy during the 1960s and 1970s, as redistributive market liberalism became increasingly influential. Indeed, as Leslie Lenkowsky has pointed out, discussions of NIT in Britain and the United States often 'sounded remarkably alike' as 'social scientists in the two countries moved along parallel paths'—though the distinct political contexts also produced important differences.[8] The depth of contemporary interest in NIT has perhaps been obscured by historians' focus on the 'poverty lobby', and especially on the Child Poverty Action Group's campaign for a universal Child Benefit, which has fostered perceptions of a binary debate between universalists on the Labour left and Conservative advocates of 'selectivity'. In fact, the policy debate was rather more complex than this caricature implies, as Rodney Lowe and Keith Banting have noted: 'neither political party could accept the full logic of either side', and 'the traditional battle-lines between means-tested and universal benefits' were increasingly 'broken down ... by the growing interest in solutions involving the tax system'.[9]

[5] Milton Friedman, *Capitalism and Freedom* (Chicago, 1962), 190–5.

[6] Daniel Zamora, 'An Intellectual History of the Universal Basic Income: How a Fringe Idea Went Global (1962–1972)', paper delivered at the History and Economics Seminar, University of Cambridge, 6 Feb. 2018.

[7] Gareth Davies, *From Opportunity to Entitlement: The Transformation and Decline of Great Society Liberalism* (Lawrence, Kan., 1996); Brian Steensland, *The Failed Welfare Revolution: America's Struggle over Guaranteed Income Policy* (Princeton, 2008).

[8] Leslie Lenkowsky, *Politics, Economics, and Welfare Reform: The Failure of the Negative Income Tax in Britain and the United States* (Lanham, NY, 1986), 11, 173.

[9] Rodney Lowe, *The Welfare State in Britain since 1945*, 3rd edn (Basingstoke, 2005), 161; Keith G. Banting, *Poverty, Politics and Policy: Britain in the 1960s* (1979), 90.

In this era of technocratic optimism and institutional reform, the British government's engagement with NIT passed through three phases. In the first phase, between the mid-1950s and the mid-1960s, policy-makers focused on the possibility of using PAYE codes to provide a guaranteed income for pensioners. In the second phase, attention turned to poverty among working families with children, which Brian Abel-Smith and Peter Townsend highlighted in *The Poor and the Poorest* (1965). It was at this point that transatlantic influences became most apparent, as Friedman's NIT seemed to offer an attractive way of providing an automatic income supplement for poorer families. In the third phase, between 1970 and 1974, Edward Heath's government responded to the technical difficulties involved in implementing NIT by returning to Juliet Rhys-Williams's ideas. This chapter examines policy development during the first two phases; Chapter 5 traces the rise and fall of the Heath government's Tax Credit Scheme.

The limits of Beveridge and the 'rediscovery of poverty'

The rejection of Juliet Rhys-Williams's proposals by the Royal Commission on the Taxation of Profits and Income in 1954 reflected the wide support which Sir William Beveridge's social insurance model enjoyed during the early post-war period. Not only did the contributory principle tap into a strong tradition of working-class self-help, but the welfare state also seemed to have been effective at eliminating poverty. Seebohm Rowntree estimated that the proportion of the population of York living below his poverty line had fallen from 17.7 per cent in 1936 to 1.7 per cent in 1950, partly through the introduction of new welfare measures and partly because of full employment.[10] The Labour manifesto for the 1950 general election boasted that 'destitution' had been 'banished' by National Insurance, National Assistance, and the National Health Service: 'What is needed now is not so much new legislation as the wise development, through efficient and economical administration, of the services provided by these Acts.'[11]

Rowntree's upbeat (though flawed) analysis contributed to the belief that the affluence which emerged during the 1950s might eventually be shared by

[10] B. Seebohm Rowntree and G. R. Lavers, *Poverty and the Welfare State: A Third Social Survey of York Dealing Only with Economic Questions* (1951), 26–36.

[11] Labour Party, *Let Us Win Through Together: A Declaration of Labour Policy for the Consideration of the Nation* (1950), reprinted in *Labour Party General Election Manifestos, 1900–1997*, edited by Iain Dale (2000), 63–72, at 69.

the whole population.[12] Conservative thinkers such as Peter Goldman were particularly attracted to the possibility that the expansion of private insurance and savings could allow the welfare state to 'wither away' into a means-tested safety net.[13] Members of the Liberal Party's Unservile State Group—including party leader Jo Grimond—took a similar view.[14] Even social democratic intellectuals such as Tony Crosland believed that capitalism had been tamed and acknowledged the progress which Britain had made towards greater equality of incomes. With continued economic growth, Crosland thought, 'material want and poverty and deprivation of essential goods will gradually cease to be a problem'.[15] A Labour government could then focus on tackling the underlying causes of inequality in education and inherited wealth, whilst providing 'individual therapy, casework and preventative treatment' for particularly disadvantaged groups.[16]

Such complacency about the effectiveness of the welfare state was steadily undermined during the 1950s and 1960s from three directions. Firstly, policy-makers became increasingly aware of the limitations of the Beveridge model. As Alan Peacock pointed out in his study of *The Economics of National Insurance* (1952), National Insurance was hardly a true insurance scheme, because participation was compulsory and premiums were not adjusted to risk: 'it is, in fact, a social service financed by a poll-tax, by an indirect tax on employers and by general taxation levied by the Government'.[17] Peacock's critique was echoed by Conservative MPs such as Enoch Powell, who complained that Beveridge had created a 'bogus' insurance system.[18] More practically, Beveridge's decision to finance the scheme through flat-rate contributions from workers and employers—with a modest Treasury supplement—made it difficult to pay benefits at an adequate level. This problem was exacerbated by the Attlee government's decision to pay full pensions immediately, instead of phasing them in over twenty years as Beveridge had recommended, and by the

[12] For a critical reassessment of Rowntree's 1950 study, see A. B. Atkinson, J. Corlyon, A. K. Maynard, H. Sutherland, and C. G. Trinder, 'Poverty in York: A Re-Analysis of Rowntree's 1950 Survey', *Bulletin of Economic Research* 33/2 (1981), 59–71.

[13] This became known as 'the Goldman line'. See especially Peter Goldman, 'Preface', in *The Future of the Welfare State: Seven Oxford Lectures*, Conservative Political Centre (1958), 7–10; Bodleian Library, Oxford, Conservative Party Archive (CPA), CRD2/29/8, PCFSS/61/79, 'Policy Committee on the Future of the Social Services. Social Services and the Distribution of Income', by Brendon Sewill, 28 Mar. 1961.

[14] Elliott Dodds, 'Liberty and Welfare', in *The Unservile State: Essays in Liberty and Welfare*, edited by George Watson (1957), 13–26.

[15] Anthony Crosland, *The Future of Socialism*, 2nd edn (1964), 96.

[16] Crosland, *The Future of Socialism*, 96–7.

[17] Alan T. Peacock, *The Economics of National Insurance* (Edinburgh, 1952), 42.

[18] The National Archives: Public Record Office, Kew (TNA), T227/451, fos 10–12, 'The National Insurance Scheme' by JEP/JVM, 21 Feb. 1957, at fo. 11.

Treasury's desire to minimize its own contribution. By the mid-1950s, Treasury officials were alarmed by forecasts of a growing deficit on the National Insurance Fund, and the Conservative government formally rejected the notion that insurance benefits should provide subsistence. Politicians from both main parties began to consider moving away from flat-rate benefits and contributions, either to a means-tested system, to a graduated social security tax, or to universal pensions paid out of general taxation.[19]

The second challenge to the Beveridge design stemmed from the growth of means-tested National Assistance, which had been created in 1948 as the nationally administered successor to the Poor Law. Beveridge had intended National Assistance to play a diminishing role, since National Insurance was 'designed of itself...to guarantee the income needed for subsistence in all normal cases'.[20] Instead, the number of National Assistance claimants rose from 842,000 in 1948 to 1.8 million in 1954, including about a quarter of all retirement pensioners, largely because insurance benefits did not take account of regional variations in housing costs and had not kept up with inflation. By contrast, the Assistance scale was uprated regularly to maintain a minimum income floor, and most claimants had their actual rent paid.[21]

Perhaps most important of all, however, was the growing realization that the welfare state had not managed to eliminate poverty, even in the limited sense defined by the National Assistance scale. A wave of survey research at Cambridge and the London School of Economics drew attention to three major deficiencies in the system: the incomplete take-up of means-tested benefits, the inadequacy of support for the working poor, and the operation of the 'wage-stop', which restricted Assistance payments for unemployed workers to no more than they would have received in work. Dorothy Cole and John Utting's survey of *The Economic Circumstances of Old People* (1962) estimated that 12 per cent of individuals or couples over the retirement age were eligible for National Assistance but did not claim it, partly because of the stigma and intrusiveness of the means test.[22] Three years later, Brian

[19] The best discussions of this debate can be found in Nicholas Timmins, *The Five Giants: A Biography of the Welfare State*, 3rd edn (2017), 132–7 and 192–6, and Paul Bridgen, 'The One Nation Idea and State Welfare: The Conservatives and Pensions in the 1950s', *Contemporary British History* 14/3 (2000), 83–104. For Labour's interest in a social security tax or payment from general taxation, see the Labour Party discussion pamphlet *The Welfare State* (1952) and *The Times*, 14 Oct. 1955, 8.

[20] Cmd. 6404, *Social Insurance and Allied Services: A Report by Sir William Beveridge* (1942), 12.

[21] Alan Deacon and Jonathan Bradshaw, *Reserved for the Poor: The Means Test in British Social Policy* (Oxford, 1983), 98–102 and 120, note 3.

[22] Dorothy Cole and John Utting, *The Economic Circumstances of Old People* (Welwyn, 1962), 98. Cole and Utting's figure related to 'units of old people', which they defined as a man aged 65+, a woman aged 60+, or a married couple in which the husband was aged 65+.

Abel-Smith and Peter Townsend published their landmark study of *The Poor and the Poorest*, which used data from the Ministry of Labour's 1960 Family Expenditure Survey to estimate that 2 million Britons—including 600,000 children—had incomes below the National Assistance scale (after housing costs). If the poverty line was raised to 140 per cent of Assistance rates to account for special additions, the number of 'poor' people rose to almost 7.5 million.[23] Though government ministers disputed these figures, subsequent official surveys suggested they were of the right order of magnitude.[24] Abel-Smith and Townsend's poverty line may even have understated the problem, since some National Assistance Board officials privately believed the scale rates were too low to support an acceptable standard of living.[25]

The rise of selectivity

The period between the late 1950s and the 1973 oil crisis witnessed an unprecedented expansion of the British welfare state, as Figure 4.1 shows.

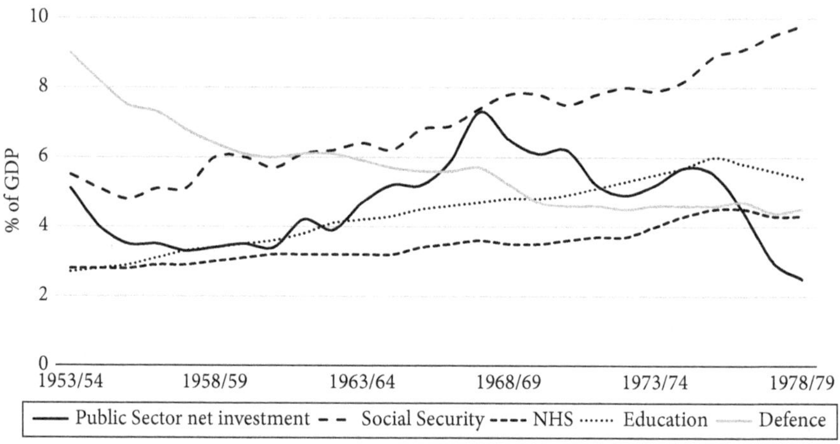

Figure 4.1. Major fields of government spending as a share of GDP, 1953/4–1978/9

Source: *The Guardian* datablog, 'UK public spending since 1963', 19 March 2013: <https://www.theguardian.com/news/datablog/2010/apr/25/uk-public-spending-1963#data>

[23] Brian Abel-Smith and Peter Townsend, *The Poor and the Poorest* (1965).

[24] Ministry of Pensions and National Insurance, *Financial and Other Circumstances of Retirement Pensioners* (1966); Ministry of Social Security, *Circumstances of Families* (1967).

[25] John Veit-Wilson, 'The National Assistance Board and the "Rediscovery" of Poverty', in *Welfare Policy in Britain: The Road from 1945*, edited by Helen Fawcett and Rodney Lowe (1999), 116–57.

Education spending rose from 2.9 per cent of GDP in 1955/6 to 5.5 per cent in 1973/4, NHS spending from 2.8 per cent to 4 per cent, and public sector net investment from 3.5 per cent to 5.2 per cent. Harold Macmillan's Conservative government introduced multi-year budget allocations and launched ambitious plans for building secondary schools, hospitals, and universities; Labour, under Harold Wilson, sought to go further and faster.[26] Demographic changes helped push social security spending upwards at a similar rate: for instance, the number of pensioners rose from about 4.5 million in the mid-1950s to more than 7 million in 1970. Despite elaborate efforts at indicative planning, however, the British economy struggled to achieve the growth rates required to sustain such rapid expansion. A succession of sterling crises sparked repeated attempts to rein in government spending in order to reassure the financial markets, defuse inflationary pressures, and release resources for export. Although the fiscal context of the 1960s and early 1970s looks benign in retrospect, the accumulation of long-term and politically sensitive spending commitments meant that it often felt tight to contemporaries.

One consequence of these fiscal pressures was a burgeoning interest in 'selectivity' across the political spectrum. Many Conservatives and neoliberals regarded means-testing as desirable in principle—as a way of rolling back the frontiers of the state, cutting the tax burden, and encouraging middle-class families to provide for their own welfare—but the case for targeting benefits on the poor could also be made on more practical grounds. Although researchers such as Abel-Smith and Townsend used the National Assistance scale as a convenient way of drawing attention to family poverty, this income-based measure quickly became embedded in public debate, and suggested that poverty could be eliminated relatively cheaply through cash transfers. (As the claimants' activist Bill Jordan pointed out, the 'poverty technicians' who 'analysed poverty in terms of gaps in the Welfare State' sometimes showed 'magnificent disregard for the implications' of their analysis.[27]) When the American sociologist Robert Putnam carried out interviews with ninety-three British MPs in 1967–8, he found that most of them saw poverty 'as a problem of isolated individuals or "problem families"' which could be solved

[26] Rodney Lowe, 'The Replanning of the Welfare State, 1957–1964', in *The Conservatives and British Society, 1880–1990*, edited by Martin Francis and Ina Zweiniger-Bargielowska (Cardiff, 1996), 110–35; Glen O'Hara, *From Dreams to Disillusionment: Economic and Social Planning in 1960s Britain* (Basingstoke, 2007).

[27] Bill Jordan, *Paupers: The Making of the New Claiming Class* (1973), 2, 7.

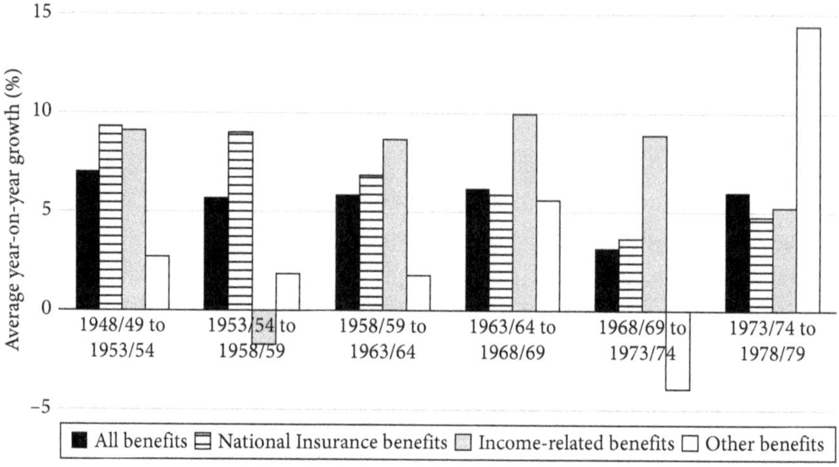

Figure 4.2. Average year-on-year growth in real-terms social security spending by benefit type, 1948/9–1978/9

Source: Author's calculations based on Department for Work and Pensions, 'Benefit expenditure and caseload tables', Autumn Budget 2018: <https://www.gov.uk/government/publications/benefit-expenditure-and-caseload-tables-2018>

by 'patching holes' in the welfare safety net, rather than a structural phenomenon.[28] Once the issue was framed in these terms, it was difficult to deny that means-tested benefits offered 'the most direct approach to the problem of family poverty and in principle the cheapest, if not the only practicable, way of securing that no family need be living below supplementary benefit standards'.[29] As new social problems emerged, then, both Conservative and Labour governments looked to selective benefits to help meet them. Spending on means-tested benefits rose rapidly during the 1960s and early 1970s, as Figure 4.2 shows; indeed, it grew faster than spending on National Insurance benefits in ten of the fifteen years between 1959/60 and 1973/74. Even the left-wing Labour minister Richard Crossman introduced a means-tested rate rebate scheme and encouraged councils to provide rent rebates for lower-income tenants.[30]

Despite its attractions, attempts to expand selectivity faced a number of obstacles. National Assistance was still 'tainted by the old poor law' (as the

[28] Robert D. Putnam, *The Beliefs of Politicians: Ideology, Conflict, and Democracy in Britain and Italy* (New Haven, 1973), 113.

[29] TNA, AST44/1, 'Means Tested Benefit', by S. S. Menneer, May 1970.

[30] Peter G. Richards, 'The Recent History of Local Fiscal Reform', in *The Reform of Local Government Finance*, edited by S. J. Bailey and R. Paddison (1988), 25–41, at 30–3; Peter Malpass, *Reshaping Housing Policy: Subsidies, Rents and Residualisation* (1990), 105–7.

Conservative adviser Charles Bellairs put it in 1962) and the practice of visiting claimants at home to assess their needs reinforced the sense that it was a form of public charity.[31] Sensitivities over targeting were particularly acute within the Labour movement, where memories of the household means test had come to symbolize the indignities which the National Government had inflicted on workers during the 1930s. Although some Labour MPs were ready to slay the 'sacred cow' of universalism, most of the party remained committed to the insurance principle and to the expansion of collective social services.[32] Richard Titmuss's characterization of the universal welfare state as a 'badge of citizenship' provided a powerful justification for this stance; so too did the belief that extending National Assistance to those in work would recreate the evils of 'Speenhamland'.

The appeal of NIT in such a context is not difficult to understand. As the *Manchester Guardian* recognized as early as 1957, anything that removed the stigma and complexity from means-testing would make it easier to target scarce resources on the poor. The challenge was to devise 'a test of needs that is not at the same time felt to be humiliating'. The paper's editorial went on to suggest a possible solution:

> Perhaps a way out might be found by using the machinery of the Inland Revenue... [T]ax collection operates by the most rigorous of all means tests but one which nevertheless is generally accepted. Could not this system be extended down the scale, with cash benefits as a form of 'negative' taxation for those with certain defined categories?[33]

Arthur Seldon of the new Institute of Economic Affairs also thought a 'negative income tax' could help dispel the 'mysticism and folk-lore surrounding the National Assistance means test' by using income tax codes as 'an automatic indicator of entitlement'.[34] James Douglas of the Conservative Research Department (CRD) concurred: '[W]e might consider ways of making the Means Test perhaps [by] another name smell a little sweeter.'[35]

[31] CPA, CRD2/57/7, Charles Bellairs to Sir Michael Fraser, 'Mr. Enoch Powell—Social Policy', 16 Mar. 1962.

[32] Tim Bale, *Sacred Cows and Common Sense: The Symbolic Statecraft and Political Culture of the British Labour Party* (Aldershot, 1999).

[33] *Manchester Guardian*, 27 Mar. 1957, 6. For a speculative antecedent, see letter from Mr O. G. Pickard of Eastbourne in *The Times*, 1 Aug. 1936, 8.

[34] Arthur Seldon, 'Pensions in a Prosperous Society', *Contemporary Review*, Oct. 1959, 134–46, at 142.

[35] CPA, CRD2/29/6, PCFSS/60/11, 'Future of National Insurance Pensions', by James Douglas, 1 Apr. 1960.

'Receive-As-You-Need': Enoch Powell, Douglas Houghton, and the income guarantee for pensioners, 1957–1965

The possibility of paying benefits through the tax system attracted growing attention from British commentators during the late 1950s and early 1960s.[36] Free-market thinkers such as Seldon and Samuel Brittan of *The Observer* were particularly enthusiastic, and shared Friedman's hope that an NIT might eventually replace other benefits and services.[37] Up to the mid-1960s, however, direct references to Friedman's work or other American proposals were relatively rare. At this stage, British interest in a guaranteed income seems to have been largely indigenous, and mostly confined to the narrow question of how to provide income support to pensioners.

Within government, the idea of an income guarantee for those over state pension age was first seriously canvassed by Enoch Powell when Harold Macmillan appointed him Financial Secretary to the Treasury at the beginning of 1957—a few weeks before the *Manchester Guardian* floated the idea. Together with the Chancellor, Peter Thorneycroft, Powell was determined to rein in the growth of government spending in order to reduce inflation and create room for tax cuts.[38] Powell was alarmed by the 'steeply mounting annual deficits' which the National Insurance Fund would face as the population aged, and argued that 'the National Insurance scheme must be radically altered so as to reduce its cost':

> I believe that the only solution is to move over on to the basis of need: to guarantee to all in retirement a minimum income which could and should be substantially above the present National Assistance scales... The means test would be far less of a difficulty than at present, where the insurance pensioner has to go for his supplement to the National Assistance Board. After all, everyone has to prove his circumstances and his income before receiving quite a number of tax reliefs and social benefits. The very universality of the test would negative our old friend the 'stigma of the Poor Law'.[39]

[36] See, for instance, Conservative MP John Eden in HC Deb., fifth series, vol. 604, 20 Apr. 1959, cols 118–28, at cols 124–5; *The Economist*, 16 Feb. 1963, 611.

[37] Samuel Brittan, 'How to Reform the Welfare State', *The Observer*, 10 Nov. 1963, 3; Arthur Seldon, 'Beveridge: 20 Years After', *New Society*, 14 Feb. 1963, 9–12.

[38] Robert Shepherd, *Enoch Powell: A Biography* (1997), 157–8.

[39] TNA, T227/451, fos 10–12, 'The National Insurance Scheme' by JEP/JVM, 21 Feb. 1957, at fos 10–12.

Powell's proposal was rejected by his Conservative colleagues for a mixture of political and practical reasons. Macmillan was impressed by the potential appeal of Labour's new 'National Superannuation' scheme, which promised workers 'half-pay on retirement' through earnings-related contributions, and was determined to offer a constructive alternative. Ministers also worried about the transitional cost of introducing a guaranteed minimum—which would have to be financed out of general taxation—and the difficulties involved in phasing out the National Insurance system. A protracted Whitehall debate in 1957–9 thus produced a modest earnings-related pension scheme, which sat on top of flat-rate National Insurance and helped to plug the Fund's deficit.[40]

Despite this setback, the possibility of replacing Beveridge's system with an income guarantee continued to attract Tory interest. Seldon and the back-bench MP Arthur Tiley campaigned for a 'Retirement grant paid on income codes', and Peter Goldman fleshed this out in more detail in 1963 as part of a pre-election policy development exercise.[41] The Ministry of Pensions and National Insurance—which was institutionally committed to Beveridge—managed to get the idea shelved after Sir Alec Douglas-Home took over as Prime Minister in October 1963, but the 1964 Conservative manifesto nevertheless promised 'a full review of social security arrangements' which left open the possibility of radical reform.[42]

The concept of an income guarantee also attracted growing attention on the Labour side, in this case as a complement to National Insurance rather than a replacement for it. During the late 1950s, Labour had focused its energies on developing and promoting Richard Crossman's National Superannuation scheme, which would include an element of cross-subsidy between higher- and lower-paid workers and so reduce reliance on means-testing.[43] As the chair of the TUC Social Insurance Committee, Sir Alfred Roberts, pointed out, however, it would take time for workers to build up National Superannuation

[40] Bridgen, 'The One Nation Idea and State Welfare'. Even Powell backed away from the idea in a speech to the Conservative Political Centre's 1957 summer school, acknowledging that quasi-universal National Insurance was likely to persist because it could be financed by contributions (rather than general taxation) and was more 'acceptable to public opinion': J. Enoch Powell, 'A Policy of Sewage', in *The Future of the Welfare State*, Conservative Political Centre, 38–47, at 41.

[41] For Seldon, see CPA, CRD2/30/14, Minutes of Conservative Party Health and Social Security Committee, 6 Dec. 1960; for Tiley, see CRD2/29/9, 'Notes on Future Pensions Policy by Mr. Arthur Tiley, M.P.,' 2 Apr. 1962; for Goldman, CRD2/29/10, 'A Guaranteed Minimum Income in Old Age' by Peter Goldman, 2 May 1963. The Bow Group of young Tory graduates also endorsed the idea: see Trevor Weston and Philip Ashworth, *Old People in Britain* (1963).

[42] TNA, PREM11/4685, Richard Wood to Prime Minister, 2 Jan. 1964; Conservative Party, *Prosperity with a Purpose* (1964), reprinted in *Conservative Party General Election Manifestos, 1900–1997*, edited by Iain Dale (2000), 143–60, at 155.

[43] Stephen Thornton, *Richard Crossman and the Welfare State: Pioneer of Welfare Provision and Labour Politics in Post-War Britain* (2009).

rights, and a Labour government could not simply ignore the plight of existing pensioners.[44] Although the party was committed to improving the basic state pension in real terms, floating all pensioners off means-testing in this way would be extremely costly. Even Hugh Gaitskell privately argued that National Assistance was the most realistic way of establishing a national minimum.[45]

Labour took up the idea of an income guarantee in the wake of a 1960 frontbench reshuffle, in which Crossman resigned as social security spokesman in order to champion nuclear disarmament and was replaced by his deputy Douglas Houghton. Though Crossman described him as 'one of the most erratic, explosive men I know', Houghton was widely respected across the Labour movement for his long service as general secretary of the Association of Officers of Taxes (1922–36) and Inland Revenue Staff Federation (1936–60).[46] He had also taken a close interest in Rhys-Williams's ideas during the 1940s, and was intrigued by the possibility of paying benefits through the tax system.[47]

In the face of growing evidence of pensioner poverty, Houghton and the young Labour adviser Tony Lynes devised a plan for a 'pension supplement' which would bring pensioners' incomes up to a more adequate level, reducing National Assistance to the residual role which Beveridge had intended.[48] Lynes initially proposed to pay the supplement to all pensioners and recoup it from better-off households at the end of the year, but Houghton thought this was likely to cause 'hardship and annoyance'.[49] Instead, he suggested that the Inland Revenue could assess eligibility on the basis of an annual income return, and generate codes which would allow the supplement to be added to the basic state pension.[50] Houghton believed that this 'Receive-As-You-Need' approach could make selectivity acceptable to the Labour Party:

> Although this latest proposal is still a means test and not a higher pension 'as of right', the commonsense of it will appeal to most. If we take the tax

[44] *The Times*, 4 Sept. 1957, 14.

[45] Labour History Archive and Study Centre, Manchester, Labour Party Archive (LPA), NEC sub-committee minutes, Box 66, Social Services Sub-Committee minutes and papers 1953–6, 'Joint Meeting with T.U.C. Social Insurance Committee Representatives', 28 Jan. 1955.

[46] Janet Morgan, ed., *The Backbench Diaries of Richard Crossman* (1981), 800; Tam Dalyell, 'Obituary: Lord Houghton of Sowerby', *The Independent*, 2 May 1996.

[47] Modern Records Centre, University of Warwick, Trades Union Congress papers, MSS.292/411.14/2, Douglas Houghton to Vincent Tewson, 'Income Tax—P.A.Y.E.', 3 June 1948.

[48] LPA, NEC sub-committee minutes, Box 66, Study Group on Security and Old Age, RD 216, 'A Draft Social Security Plan', Mar. 1962.

[49] LPA, NEC sub-committee minutes, Box 66, Study Group on Security and Old Age, minutes of fifth meeting, 23 Mar. 1962.

[50] British Library of Political and Economic Science (BLPES), Titmuss papers, 1/15, RD 299, 'National Superannuation and the Guarantee', June 1962.

system—its means test and its methods and principles of calculating total income for tax—only false pride will criticise this as 'humiliating'.[51]

In fact, Houghton privately recognized that the link with the tax system would be largely cosmetic, and Labour advisers such as Richard Titmuss—who liked the idea in principle—became increasingly concerned about the administrative difficulties.[52] Nevertheless, the proposal was included in *New Frontiers for Social Security* (1963), which appeared after Harold Wilson took over as leader, and the 1964 manifesto singled it out as the party's one unequivocal social security commitment, which would not be dependent on the pace of economic growth.[53] The guarantee was thus elevated—in Stephen Thornton's words—from 'a minor proposal to fix a perceived hole in the national superannuation scheme' into 'the centrepiece of Labour's plans for social security'.[54]

Harold Wilson's pension promises may have contributed to Labour's victory in the 1964 general election, but once the new government was in office—with a majority of four—they quickly became a liability. Wilson appointed Houghton as Chancellor of the Duchy of Lancaster and Cabinet 'overlord' for the social services, whilst the Scottish MP Peggy Herbison became Minister of Pensions and National Insurance without a Cabinet seat—an unhappy and anomalous arrangement. Houghton hoped that a detailed scheme could be agreed by mid-1965 so that it could come into operation in April 1966, but within months he was confronted by two sets of problems.[55]

Firstly, it became clear that the technical difficulties involved in linking the guarantee with the tax system were more serious than Houghton had appreciated. Although he had expected civil servants to raise 'snags galore', he was astonished when the Inland Revenue—backed by his one-time union protégé, the new Chancellor Jim Callaghan—refused to have anything to do with the policy.[56] The Chief Inspector of Taxes, Leonard Barford, argued that the tax reforms Callaghan planned to introduce in his 1965 budget would stretch the

[51] LPA, NEC sub-committee minutes, Box 66, Study Group on Security and Old Age, RD 307, 'The Guaranteed Income. Memorandum from Douglas Houghton, M.P.', July 1962.

[52] LPA, NEC sub-committee minutes, Box 66, Study Group on Security and Old Age, RD 743, 'Income Guarantee by Douglas Houghton', Mar. 1964; Titmuss papers, 1/15, '4.3.64. Memorandum. Income Guarantee', note by Richard Crossman. For Titmuss's early enthusiasm see LPA, NEC sub-committee minutes, Box 66, Study Group on Security and Old Age, minutes of sixth meeting, 29 May 1962.

[53] Labour Party, *The New Britain* (1964), reprinted in *Labour Party General Election Manifestos*, 105–25, at 117.

[54] Thornton, *Richard Crossman and the Welfare State*, 103.

[55] TNA, BN72/152, Douglas Houghton to Herbert Bowden, 17 Nov. 1964 (copy).

[56] LPA, NEC sub-committee minutes, Box 66, Study Group on Security and Old Age, RD 743, 'Income Guarantee by Douglas Houghton', Mar. 1964.

Revenue's capacity to its limit, but it was clear that the department's real objections went much deeper: as in the 1940s, tax officials were determined not to become entangled in social security. Barford pointed out that 'The apparent simplicity of the basic idea—P.A.Y.E. in reverse—is illusory' because two-thirds of pensioner households did not pay income tax through PAYE, and tax codes designed to work on a cumulative basis did not provide the 'current information on income, allowance status and need' which the scheme would require.[57] Herbison also insisted that the annual income return could not be made compulsory, and that the guarantee would have to take account of capital assets and housing costs as well as taxable income.[58] Taken together, these changes complicated the scheme and made it difficult to present it as a clean break with National Assistance.

The second problem was that the scope for a major assault on pensioner poverty was significantly reduced by some of the Wilson government's early decisions. The large balance of payments deficit which the government inherited—together with Wilson's reluctance to devalue sterling—meant that it faced sustained pressure from the financial markets, and led Callaghan to impose a 4.25 per cent limit on public spending increases from 1965/6 onwards in an attempt to reassure market opinion.[59] Yet the Cabinet also agreed to a large increase in National Insurance benefits from March 1965, worth 18.5 per cent in nominal terms and more than 12 per cent in real terms, which pre-empted resources that could have been used for the guarantee. Following discussions with the Chancellor, Herbison worked up a modest guarantee scheme which would cost about £100m a year, but this would only raise pensioners 'a few shillings above assistance levels' rather than the 15 per cent difference which Crossman had suggested before the election.[60]

In the end, the income guarantee fell prey to the tight public spending review which Callaghan undertook in the midst of the July 1965 sterling crisis. The Treasury was determined to rein in the social security budget, and believed that earnings-related unemployment benefits were a more important spending priority, since they would boost labour mobility and could be paid

[57] TNA, BN72/152, Leonard Barford to 'Chairman' (Sir Alexander Johnstone), 'Income Guarantee Scheme', 3 Dec. 1964 (copy).

[58] TNA, BN72/152, 'Income Guarantee Scheme. Note of Meeting between Ministers and Officials held on Thursday, 17th December', 23 Dec. 1964.

[59] Jim Tomlinson, *The Labour Governments 1964–1970*, vol. 3: *Economic Policy* (Manchester, 2004), 196.

[60] TNA, BN72/152, Margaret Herbison to Prime Minister, 4 June 1965 (copy); for Crossman's figure see Adrian Webb, 'The Abolition of National Assistance: Policy Changes in the Administration of Assistance Benefits', in *Change, Choice and Conflict in Social Policy*, edited by Phoebe Hall, Hilary Land, Roy Parker, and Adrian Webb (1975), 410–71, at 425.

for by higher contributions; as a result, the income guarantee was squeezed out. The Cabinet's Public Expenditure Committee noted that Herbison's proposal was 'rather different from the scheme originally envisaged' and felt that it 'might well not be very popular', especially if voters saw it as a move away from the insurance principle.[61] (Dorothy Wedderburn, writing in *New Society* magazine, agreed that 'a major extension of income testing...would only be worthwhile if a really generous level of income guarantee were being proposed'.[62]) Though Wilson initially presented the decision as a postponement, the government quickly decided to cut its losses in the run-up to the 1966 general election. In place of the guarantee, Herbison introduced a much cheaper overhaul of National Assistance, renaming it Supplementary Benefit and giving claimants a firm legal entitlement.[63] Though take-up improved slightly, this reform was 'larger in symbolism than substance'.[64]

Adrian Webb has characterized the income guarantee as a textbook case of policy failure—the product of poor preparation by Labour before the election, a failure to establish clear priorities on taking office, Houghton's anomalous institutional position as social policy 'overlord', and the hostility of the Inland Revenue and National Assistance Board.[65] If the first three problems had been avoided, the fourth might not have been insuperable, but the political will was lacking. As Peter Townsend observed in December 1964, ministers' commitment to the scheme had not been strong enough to overcome bureaucratic objections.[66] Labour had taken up the guarantee in opposition as a cheap and temporary solution to pensioner poverty while National Superannuation matured. Once it proved to be neither cheap nor easy, Wilson decided he had more important claims on his political capital.

The Child Poverty Action Group and the debate over family poverty, 1965–1967

We might expect the failure of the income guarantee to have fatally discredited the notion of paying social benefits through the tax system. In practice, it had

[61] TNA, CAB130/232, MISC. 64/3rd Meeting, 8 July 1965; see also Richard Crossman, *The Diaries of a Cabinet Minister*, vol. 1: *Minister of Housing 1964–6* (1975), 276–7, 283.
[62] Dorothy Wedderburn, 'The Old and the Poor', *New Society*, 22 July 1965, 7–8, at 8.
[63] Webb, 'The Abolition of National Assistance'.
[64] Timmins, *The Five Giants*, 227; for the improvement in take-up, see Peter Townsend, *Poverty in the United Kingdom* (1979), 824–6.
[65] Webb, 'The Abolition of National Assistance', 446–9.
[66] Titmuss papers, 1/57, Peter Townsend to Richard Titmuss, 4 Dec. 1964.

no such effect for a number of reasons. Firstly, the announcement of Herbison's Supplementary Benefit scheme was deftly handled, and helped take the sting out of the guarantee fiasco. Secondly, the decision to scrap the guarantee tended to be presented by the government as a financial one, which obscured the technical difficulties involved in linking tax and benefits: as Crossman noted in his diary, the fact that Houghton and Herbison had produced 'a disaster which they wouldn't actually dare to put forward' was 'known only to very few people in Whitehall'.[67] Indeed, Houghton himself believed that he had been thwarted by obscurantist civil servants and that the computerization of PAYE would make it possible to extend the guarantee to the working population. 'Should we not resume our study of income tax in reverse?' he asked his colleagues in a December 1965 memorandum.

> If we have code numbers to pay tax can we not work out a system of code numbers to *receive*? Code numbers tell the employer what to deduct; could not code numbers conversely determine whether rent or rate rebates were due, what supplementary pension should be paid, and what family allowance should be paid?[68]

Thirdly, the growing prominence of NIT in the United States made it increasingly fashionable. As Gareth Davies has shown, the Watts riots of August 1965 revealed the limits of the jobs-based 'service strategy' which had shaped the early War on Poverty and helped propel the Johnson administration towards an 'income strategy' focused on cash transfers.[69] President Johnson himself was wary of this new approach, but the Office of Economic Opportunity (OEO) under Sargent Shriver took a close interest in NIT and sponsored research into income maintenance policies.[70]

Growing awareness of the US War on Poverty coincided with the emergence of family poverty as a political issue in Britain, with the formation of the Child Poverty Action Group (CPAG) in April 1965 and the publication of *The Poor and the Poorest*.[71] Family poverty was a harder nut to crack than pensioner poverty, since it raised complex questions about wage bargaining and work incentives. Post-war policy placed most of the burden of bringing up

[67] Crossman, *Diaries of a Cabinet Minister*, vol. 1, 293.

[68] TNA, PREM12/1209, 'A Re-appraisal of Social Policy', by Douglas Houghton, n.d. [Dec. 1965] (copy).

[69] Davies, *From Opportunity to Entitlement*, 75–104.

[70] Steensland, *The Failed Welfare Revolution*, 52–78.

[71] Rodney Lowe, 'The Rediscovery of Poverty and the Creation of the Child Poverty Action Group, 1962–8', *Contemporary Record* 9/3 (1995), 602–11.

children on the father's wage, in line with the unions' male-breadwinner ethos, though parents were also eligible for child tax allowances (CTAs) and Family Allowances (paid in cash to mothers with two or more children). Tackling family poverty through the wage system was not wholly implausible, since the Wilson government's incomes policy allowed above-average pay increases for low-paid workers, and during the 1960s two interdepartmental working parties examined the possibility of a National Minimum Wage (NMW). On the other hand, most trade unions were opposed to statutory interference with collective bargaining, and officials believed that significant increases in wage rates were likely to exacerbate unemployment and inflation.[72] For instance, the government's 1967–9 working party estimated that a NMW would raise the pay bill by about 11 per cent if the unions attempted to maintain wage differentials.[73] Instead, CPAG focused its attention on the inadequacy of Family Allowances, which had only been increased twice since 1945. Richard Titmuss had already pointed out that state support for families with children was regressive, since CTAs were of much greater value to higher than lower earners: the group thus lobbied the government to equalize these family benefits.[74]

Although CPAG's campaign for higher Family Allowances is justly famous, the group's later commitment to universalism has obscured its early interest in NIT mechanisms. Several of its founder members had been involved in developing the income guarantee and hoped to tackle family poverty in a similar way: Titmuss, after all, had pioneered the analysis of the 'fiscal welfare state', and was determined to break down the distinction between benefits and tax reliefs.[75] In July 1964, for instance, Titmuss sketched out a plan for abolishing Family Allowances and turning CTAs into 'a progressive redistributive system for all parents', with 'direct payment of "tax refunds" for all parents who do not "use"—partly or wholly—the child allowances': in effect, a refundable tax credit.[76] Tony Lynes worked this up into a proposal for a 'tax adjustment' or 'negative income tax' for low-income families during the winter

[72] Dennie Oude Nijhuis, 'Low Pay, Wage Relativities, and Labour's First Attempt to Introduce a Statutory National Minimum Wage in the United Kingdom', *Journal of Policy History* 28/1 (2016), 81–104; see also Colin Duncan, *Low Pay—Its Causes, and the Post-War Trade Union Response* (Chichester, 1981).

[73] Department of Employment and Productivity, *A National Minimum Wage: An Inquiry* (1969); Oude Nijhuis, 'Low Pay', 88.

[74] Richard M. Titmuss, *Income Distribution and Social Change: A Study in Criticism* (1962).

[75] Richard M. Titmuss, 'The Social Division of Welfare: Some Reflections on the Search for Equity', in Richard M. Titmuss, *Essays on 'the Welfare State'* (1958), 34–55.

[76] Titmuss papers, 1/57, 'Family Allowances and Child Allowances', by Richard Titmuss, 20 July 1964.

of 1964–5, and CPAG included it its first memorandum to the government as an alternative to higher Family Allowances.[77] Titmuss wrote about the idea in *The Times* in October 1965, and some civil servants came to view this 'unused allowances' approach as the paradigmatic NIT scheme.[78]

CPAG's attitude towards NIT, however, rapidly hardened, largely because a straightforward increase in Family Allowances seemed so much simpler than a tax-based mechanism.[79] Titmuss's colleague Brian Abel-Smith, for instance, found NIT 'compelling at first sight' but was impressed by the practical difficulties: 'could it ever be possible to bring together the man and the wife's total earnings last week in time to make a payment at the weekend?'[80] More radical members of the group, such as Peter Townsend, also worried that NIT proposals narrowed the focus of social policy onto the 'poor' in a way that legitimized means-testing. As Townsend put it in a Fabian Society essay:

> Our greatest error is in thinking we can meet poverty by considering the poor alone and just developing policies to give them modest additions to cash income . . . The social and economic structure could not be changed except through a more drastic and sophisticated strategy.[81]

Harold Wilson's growth-oriented government was never likely to satisfy Townsend's ambitions for radical social change.[82] The Treasury believed a straight increase in Family Allowances was both wasteful and unaffordable, and favoured a means-tested scheme instead: Jim Callaghan told the Cabinet that 'No practicable increase of family allowances . . . could solve the problem of child poverty as efficiently and economically as the introduction of an income-tested allowance.'[83] Nevertheless, after a year-long debate, Callaghan

[77] Titmuss papers, 1/57, Tony Lynes to Richard Titmuss, 'Family Allowances and Child Allowances', 6 Nov. 1964, and 'Social Security Policy', memorandum by Lynes, n.d. [1965]; Child Poverty Action Group, 'Family Poverty: Memorandum', Nov. 1965, accessed 25 July 2017, available at <http://www.cpag.org.uk/content/family-poverty-memorandum>.

[78] *The Times*, 5 Oct. 1965, 11; TNA, T227/2850, 'Comments on Draft Negative Income Tax Document Dated 7th November, 1969', by P. R. Oglesby, n.d. [1969]. Brian Abel-Smith also encouraged Peggy Herbison to consider the scheme: Sally Sheard, *The Passionate Economist: How Brian Abel-Smith Shaped Global Health and Social Welfare* (Bristol, 2014), 201.

[79] Indeed, an Official Committee on Social Services examined the Titmuss/Lynes scheme in 1966 and ruled that it was too complex: TNA, CAB134/3280, 'Family Endowment. Report by the Official Committee on Social Services', n.d. (*c.* Nov. 1966).

[80] Brian Abel-Smith, 'Paradoxes of the Welfare State', *The Listener*, 30 May 1968, 696–7, at 696.

[81] Peter Townsend, 'The Difficulties of Negative Income Tax', in *Social Services for All? Eleven Fabian Essays*, Fabian Society (1968), 106–11, at 111.

[82] Ilaria Favretto, '"Wilsonism" Reconsidered: Labour Party Revisionism, 1952–64', *Contemporary British History* 14/4 (2000), 54–80; Bale, *Sacred Cows and Common Sense*.

[83] TNA, CAB128/41/67, Cabinet conclusions, 20 Dec. 1966, at 12.

was forced to accept a 7/- increase in Family Allowances. Under the 'clawback' scheme devised by the Cambridge economist and special adviser Nicholas Kaldor, this would be recouped from better-off households by a corresponding reduction in CTAs.[84]

CPAG cautiously welcomed the clawback mechanism, and Roy Jenkins—who succeeded Callaghan as Chancellor in December 1967—hailed it as 'selectivity in a civilised and acceptable form'.[85] Before long, however, a number of problems became apparent. Firstly, the increase in Family Allowances which was granted in this way (7/- in April 1968 and a further 3/- in October) still left an estimated 160,000 families and 250,000 children living below the Supplementary Benefit line.[86] Secondly, clawback involved a substantial shift of resources within families from the husband's pay packet to the wife's purse, which was unpopular with many male workers, including rank-and-file trade unionists.[87] Thirdly, clawback increased both taxation and public expenditure as a share of GDP—an embarrassment for a government which spent much of its time trying to reassure the financial markets of its orthodoxy. Finally, Inland Revenue officials disliked the complexity of the clawback operation and argued that it was bringing the tax system into disrepute.[88] All these factors kept alive the search for an alternative solution.

Transatlantic crossings, 1967–1968

In the midst of this debate over family poverty, NIT briefly became one of the most fashionable ideas in British public policy. As Figure 4.3 shows, references to NIT in Google's Ngram corpus of British publications took off in the late 1960s, lagging the American debate. Interest then fell away after 1972, when the Conservative government unveiled its much-heralded Tax Credit Scheme, before experiencing a revival in the mid-1970s. Analysis of Hansard and leading British newspapers (such as *The Times* digital archive) reveals a similar pattern.[89]

[84] The classic account of the Family Allowances debate is Banting, *Poverty, Politics and Policy*, 66–108.

[85] HC Deb., fifth series, vol. 756, 17 Jan. 1968, cols 1787–805, at col. 1800.

[86] HC Deb., fifth series, vol. 763, 24 Apr. 1968, cols 348, 350.

[87] For instance, Richard Crossman found that many Labour activists in Coventry disliked clawback and would have preferred Family Allowances to be means-tested: Richard Crossman, *The Diaries of a Cabinet Minister*, vol. 2: *Lord President of the Council and Leader of the House of Commons 1966–8* (1976), 638.

[88] TNA, T227/2757, Sir Alexander Johnston to Roy Jenkins, 31 July 1968 (copy).

[89] For instance, the term first appeared in Hansard in November 1967 when Labour MP Gwilym Roberts secured a debate on 'Minimum Income' policy: HC Deb., fifth series, vol. 754, 24 Nov. 1967,

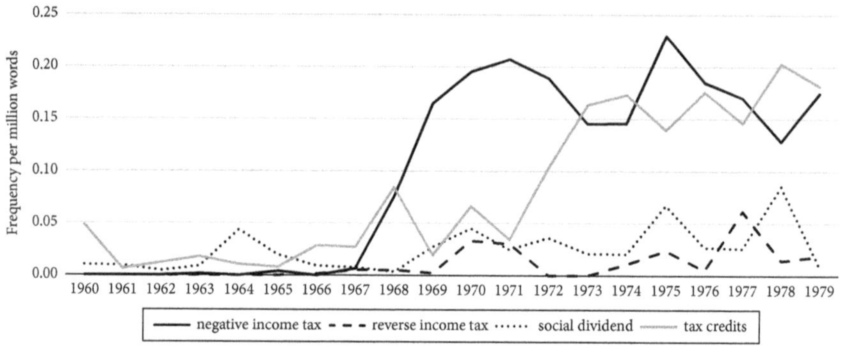

Figure 4.3. Frequency of 'Negative Income Tax' and related terms in the Google Books (British English) corpus by year, 1960–79

Source: Google Books Ngrams, accessed via Brigham Young University online corpora (<http://googlebooks.byu.edu>)

In contrast to the income guarantee for pensioners, which was largely a home-grown initiative, much of this enthusiasm for NIT stemmed from direct engagement with American thinking. Titmuss, for instance, followed the War on Poverty closely through visits to Washington and contact with US scholars such as Martin Rein and Elizabeth Wickenden.[90] The young Treasury official David Hancock spent a year at Harvard University and the Brookings Institution on a Harkness Fellowship in 1965–6, studying the Kennedy and Johnson administrations' tax reforms, and wrote an analysis of Milton Friedman and James Tobin's NIT proposals when he returned to Britain; later he became Roy Jenkins's private secretary.[91] Tony Atkinson was a visiting student at MIT in 1966–7, and then returned to Cambridge to write *Poverty in Britain and the Reform of Social Security* (1969) under the guidance of James Meade.[92] Atkinson defined poverty in relation to the Supplementary Benefit scale and evaluated the likely impact of a range of possible reforms, including NIT, Juliet

cols 1636–42. The term featured in one *Times* article in 1965, one in 1966, and nine articles and two letters in 1967.

[90] See the correspondence with Rein and Wickenden and the notes for 'Washington Seminar' in Titmuss papers, 5/653 and 5/654, and TNA, PIN18/514, 'State Aid to the Family' by Richard Titmuss and Tony Lynes, n.d. [1965]. Philippe Fontaine notes that Titmuss visited the United States in April 1957 and May–July 1966: Philippe Fontaine, 'Blood, Politics, and Social Science: Richard Titmuss and the Institute of Economic Affairs, 1957–73', *Isis* 93/3 (2002), 401–34, at 406, 408.

[91] Sir Douglas Wass, 'Obituary: Sir David Hancock, Civil Servant with Eye for Fiscal Policy', *Financial Times*, 6 Oct. 2013; TNA, T227/2755, 'The Negative Income Tax', extract from report by David Hancock, n.d. (*c*.1966).

[92] Private information; see also King's College Library, Cambridge, Kaldor papers, NK/10/23, 'Low Income Families in Britain: The Case for a Negative Income Tax' by A. B. Atkinson, n.d. (*c*.July 1968).

Rhys-Williams's scheme (which he labelled a 'social dividend'), and CPAG's 'back-to-Beveridge' approach.[93] Brendon Sewill, the director of the CRD, had first encountered NIT in Milton Friedman's work, but a visit to the United States during the summer of 1967 helped crystallize his thinking.[94] Others kept in touch with North American developments through bodies such as the International Committee on Poverty Research and reports in *The Economist* and *New Society*.[95] The launch of several high-profile NIT experiments, beginning in New Jersey and Pennsylvania in 1968, also kept the idea in the news and enhanced its credibility.[96]

The glamour which NIT derived from its American proponents was reinforced by mounting excitement about the potential impact of computerization.[97] Sewill, for instance, believed that automatic data processing would make it possible 'to put on to a single computer system most of the dealings between the State and individual citizens'.[98] Conservative leader Edward Heath was attracted to NIT on similar grounds:

> as a means by which, using a computer, one could make only net payments from the Exchequer and so reduce tax rates by cutting out a lot of unnecessary transfer payments between the State and the individual.[99]

The launch of the Post Office Giro in 1968—with its fully automated payments system and vision of providing banking services for the masses—raised expectations that this might soon be achievable.[100] So too did the Inland Revenue's plans for computerizing PAYE, beginning with Centre 1 at East Kilbride, which opened in 1968 and was intended to be the first of nine

[93] A. B. Atkinson, *Poverty in Britain and the Reform of Social Security* (Cambridge, 1969).

[94] Interview with Brendon Sewill, 14 Sept. 2016; CPA, CRD3/7/26/14, Mr Sewill to Mr Douglas, Mr Bellairs and Mr Hayhoe, 16 Oct. 1967.

[95] See Peter Townsend's comments in Rodney Lowe and Paul Nicholson, 'The Formation of the Child Poverty Action Group', *Contemporary Record* 9/3 (1995), 612–37, at 618–20.

[96] Hoover Institution Archives, Stanford University, Institute of Economic Affairs papers, 253.5, 'A Survey of the Advantages and Disadvantages of a Negative Income Tax or Social Dividend' by Alan K. Maynard, Nov. 1969.

[97] Jon Agar, *The Government Machine: A Revolutionary History of the Computer* (Cambridge, Mass., 2003), 293–342.

[98] CPA, CRD3/7/26/13, 'Reorganisation of Administration of Social Services and Inland Revenue', by Brendon Sewill, 9 Aug. 1965; see also Hilary Sewill, *AUNTIE* (1966).

[99] CPA, CRD3/7/6/3, minutes of Economic Policy Group meeting, 7 Nov. 1968.

[100] Alan Booth and Mark Billings, 'Techno-Nationalism, the Post Office, and the Creation of Britain's National Giro', in *Technological Innovation in Retail Finance: International Historical Perspectives*, edited by Bernardo Bátiz-Lazo, J. Carles Maixé-Altés, and Paul Thomes (Abingdon, 2011), 155–72.

regional computer centres.[101] Tony Benn, then in his technocratic phase as Minister of Technology, predicted that 'The day will come, not long hence, when taxation and social security systems will be capable of complete integration'.[102]

Budding policy entrepreneurs fleshed out their enthusiasm for NIT with a range of specific proposals—'a small flood of panaceas' for the poverty problem.[103] Professor Dennis Lees of University College, Swansea, who had close links with the IEA and spent 1963–4 working alongside Friedman at the University of Chicago, suggested that Family Allowances should be replaced by an NIT for families with children, which would make up half the difference between actual income and the tax threshold.[104] Barney Hayhoe of the CRD proposed to retain Family Allowances and raise incomes one-third of the way towards the tax threshold, whilst Labour MP Gwilym Roberts suggested making up one-fifth of the difference below household income and the minimum full-time industrial wage, which he estimated at £13 per week.[105] The IEA also set up a study group—chaired by the economist George Polanyi, son of Michael and nephew of Karl—which proposed to abolish all cash benefits in favour of a 'Reverse Income Tax' payment equivalent to the Supplementary Benefit scale.[106] As Tony Atkinson pointed out, these schemes reflected rather different conceptions of what NIT meant: for instance, the IEA version was really a guaranteed income with a 100 per cent withdrawal rate, which would not be administered through the tax system.[107] On the other hand, the debate succeeded in focusing attention on the basic welfare trilemma: that 'fully adequate help to the poorest' could only be achieved either at high overall cost or by withdrawing benefits rapidly as income rose, with a consequential impact on work incentives.[108]

Whereas the North American interest in guaranteed income schemes was partly driven by concerns about automation and structural change, the British debate focused more narrowly on poverty relief and benefit simplification. This was true even among the minority of reformers who favoured a UBI-style

[101] Peter W. G. Morris and George H. Hough, *The Anatomy of Major Projects: A Study of the Reality of Project Management* (Chichester, 1987), 159–76.

[102] Speech at Llandudno, 25 May 1968, reported in *The Guardian*, 27 May 1968, 15.

[103] David Barker, 'Negative Income Tax', in *Family Poverty: Programme for the Seventies*, 2nd edn, edited by David Bull (1972), 44–69, at 51.

[104] Brian Chiplin, 'Professor Dennis Lees: Industrial Economist who was a Staunch Believer in the Free Market', *The Independent*, 27 Feb. 2008; D. S. Lees, 'Poor Families and Fiscal Reform', *Lloyds Bank Review*, Oct. 1967, 1–15.

[105] Barney Hayhoe, *Must the Children Suffer?* (1968); HC Deb., fifth series, vol. 754, 24 Nov. 1967, cols 1636–42.

[106] Anthony Christopher, George Polanyi, Arthur Seldon, and Barbara Shenfield, *Policy for Poverty: The Report of an IEA Study Group* (1970).

[107] BLPES, Meade papers, 6/9, 'Negative Income Taxation—A Plain Man's Guide', by A. B. Atkinson, n.d. (*c.*1971).

[108] Christopher et al., *Policy for Poverty*, 41.

approach. Sir Brandon Rhys-Williams, for instance, who was elected Conservative MP for South Kensington in a 1968 by-election, revived his mother Juliet's plan for a basic income paid for by a flat tax, and tried to sell it to colleagues as 'a Business-Efficiency Exercise'.[109] Chuck Brown and Diane Dawson, who developed a similar scheme in a pamphlet for Political and Economic Planning, also focused on the efficiency gains and suggested that the differences between UBI and NIT were largely administrative.[110] One partial exception to this pattern was the Open Group on 'Social Reform in a Centrifugal Society' convened by *New Society* in 1968–9, which included the sociologists Michael Young and Peter Willmott and the urban geographer Peter Hall. The Open Group's plan 'to bring together money transfers in a simpler, unified set of arrangements' drew heavily on Brown and Dawson's work, but Young and his colleagues set this in the context of a wider left-liberal agenda for promoting personal freedom and political participation.[111]

By the winter of 1967–8, a cacophony of voices from across the political spectrum was urging the Wilson government to take NIT seriously. Douglas Houghton reiterated his support for 'an automatic minimum income' in an IEA pamphlet, the Confederation of British Industry urged the Chancellor to explore NIT in its annual pre-budget submission, and backbenchers from both main parties pressed the case in the Commons.[112] During 1968, Labour activists from Deptford and West Stirlingshire submitted party conference resolutions on NIT, and the Conservatives announced that they were studying the idea as a way of targeting benefits more effectively.[113] Ministers thus faced growing pressure to reconsider their sceptical attitude.

Roy Jenkins and the Working Party on NIT, 1968–1970

Up to autumn 1967 the Labour government took the line that, even if NIT was desirable, it was wholly impracticable. An interdepartmental study of family endowment in 1966 found 'serious practical difficulties' in paying Family

[109] Sir Brandon Rhys-Williams, *The New Social Contract* (1968); see also CPA, CRD3/7/26/11, 'Notes on Reform of Redistribution of Income as a Business-Efficiency Exercise', by Sir Brandon Rhys-Williams, 13 May 1969.

[110] C. V. Brown and D. A. Dawson, *Personal Taxation, Incentives and Tax Reform* (1969).

[111] New Society Open Group, *Social Reform in a Centrifugal Society* (1969), 24.

[112] Douglas Houghton, *Paying for the Social Services* (1967), 17; for the CBI, see *Financial Times*, 2 Feb. 1968, 1; for MPs' opinion, see the debate initiated by Gwilym Roberts in HC Deb., fifth series, vol. 754, 24 Nov. 1967, cols 1636–723, and the second reading of the Family Allowances and National Insurance (No. 2) Bill, HC Deb., fifth series, vol. 762, 2 Apr. 1968, cols 182–295.

[113] TNA, T227/2757, R. T. Armstrong to Mr McConnachie, 'Labour Party Conference', 14 Aug. 1968; Conservative Party, *Make Life Better* (1968).

Allowances through the tax system, which the junior social security minister Charles Loughlin set out in the House of Commons: PAYE codes were based on the previous year's earnings, taxable income was not a satisfactory measure of household needs, and many of the poorest workers were outside the tax system altogether.[114] Paying benefits in real time in response to changing circumstances would require a complete overhaul of PAYE, which Loughlin estimated would take nine years.[115] Some left-leaning ministers also objected to wage supplements in principle. The Minister of Social Security Judith Hart, for instance, argued that 'means-tested family allowances would be an explicit subsidy from public funds to low wages' and 'an affront to the human dignity of those to whom they are offered, harshly underlining the failure of a father to meet his children's needs'.[116] Likewise, Richard Crossman told the 1967 Labour Party conference that a successful assault on family poverty would have to include a National Minimum Wage: 'We can't deal with the fundamental evil of low wages through the social security system.'[117]

Such principled opposition to means-testing, however, was less widespread by the late 1960s than it had been twenty or thirty years earlier. Though Titmuss insisted that Socialist and Conservative social policies were 'totally different in their purposes, philosophy and attitudes to people', many on the centre-right of the Labour Party took a more pragmatic approach to selectivity, as Tim Bale has shown.[118] Older trade unionists such as Callaghan and Ray Gunter worried that universal benefits were placing a rising tax burden on skilled workers, whilst younger MPs such as Michael Barnes, Ivor Richard, Peter Archer, and David Marquand shared Houghton's enthusiasm for tax-benefit integration.[119] The decision to reimpose NHS prescription charges in January 1968 showed that Harold Wilson was prepared to break with Labour's traditional universalism in an attempt to demonstrate the party's fitness to govern. The 'neo-revisionist' turn in Labour's social democracy which Stephen Meredith has identified in the 1970s—based on a critical reappraisal of public spending and trade union power—was thus already visible in this period.[120]

[114] TNA, CAB134/3280, 'Family Endowment. Report by the Official Committee on Social Services', n.d. (Autumn 1966), Appendix 3; HC Deb., fifth series, vol. 754, 24 Nov. 1967, cols 1713–21.

[115] HC Deb., fifth series, vol. 753, 8 Nov. 1967, cols 1121–33, at col. 1126.

[116] HC Deb., fifth series, vol. 753, 8 Nov. 1967, cols 1036–48, at col. 1043.

[117] *The Guardian*, 6 Oct. 1967, 5.

[118] Richard M. Titmuss, *Commitment to Welfare* (1968), 116; Bale, *Sacred Cows and Common Sense.*

[119] *The Times*, 21 Aug. 1967, 2; HC Deb., fifth series, vol. 774, 2 Dec. 1968, cols 1023–4; Ivor Richard, 'The Programme Before us', *Socialist Commentary*, June 1966, 11–13; Peter Archer, 'Financing the Social Services', *Socialist Commentary*, Nov. 1967, 20–2; David Marquand, John Mackintosh, and David Owen, 'Change Gear!', supplement to *Socialist Commentary*, Oct. 1967, viii.

[120] Stephen Meredith, *Labours Old and New: The Parliamentary Right of the British Labour Party 1970–9 and the Roots of New Labour* (Manchester, 2008).

After the devaluation of sterling in November 1967, the subordination of Labour's social policy to the needs of economic management became more explicit than ever. The new Chancellor, Roy Jenkins, embarked on a strategy of holding down government spending in order to shift resources into exports and eliminate the balance of payments deficit. Public expenditure thus fell from 44.7 per cent of GDP in 1967/8 to 42.8 per cent in 1969/70 through major cuts in defence and public investment and tighter control of spending on the social services.[121] Jenkins was sympathetic to the extension of selectivity, and saw it as a way of meeting Wilson's pledge to protect the poorest against the inflationary effects of devaluation. Treasury officials were also keen to ensure that the Revenue's plans for computerizing PAYE left open the possibility of tax-benefit integration.[122] Callaghan had used public spending constraints to secure the rejection of Houghton's income guarantee in 1965; under Jenkins, fiscal pressures helped put NIT back on the agenda.

In this context, the Chief Secretary to the Treasury, John Diamond, wrote to the incoming Chancellor to suggest that the time was ripe to study NIT more closely:

> There are mounting pressures, especially as a result of recent decisions arising out of devaluation, to give more help to needy citizens. By adopting negative income tax we could find an acceptable 'means test' without endangering party unity through having yet another bout of argument as to selectivity...
>
> There would, I hope, also be considerable saving in manpower through the integration of services, and I am deeply impressed by the need to achieve this. Finally... I think it is very much in the interests of the Treasury that we should take the initiative on this issue of negative income tax, and not be seen continually as the defenders of a rear-guard action.[123]

Jenkins enthusiastically agreed to a feasibility study, and told the Commons in January 1968 that he hoped to introduce 'full selectivity' for Family Allowances in his 1969 budget.[124]

[121] Tomlinson, *The Labour Governments*, 199–200.

[122] TNA, T227/2755, J. L. Rampton to Mr Phelps, 'Inland Revenue Computer Centres', 20 Sept. 1967, and 'Links between Inland Revenue & M.S.S.' (*c.* Oct. 1967).

[123] TNA, T227/2755, Chief Secretary to the Treasury to Chancellor of the Exchequer, 'Negative Income Tax', 7 Dec. 1967.

[124] TNA, T227/2755, Roy Jenkins to Prime Minister, 8 Jan. 1968 (copy); HC Deb., fifth series, vol. 756, 17 Jan. 1968, cols 1787–805, at col. 1800.

Roy Jenkins's interest in NIT was cautiously welcomed by Treasury economists, who believed that it could offer an efficient solution to family poverty, though they noted that the 'administrative details' would determine whether it was really an improvement on Supplementary Benefit.[125] The Department of Employment and Productivity also felt that any improvement in family support would be 'helpful to incomes policy' by making it easier 'to resist pressure for wage increases' and justify the government's rejection of a NMW.[126] Diamond chaired the Working Group on NIT himself, and hoped to carry out a rapid assessment of its 'desirability and technical feasibility', focusing in the first instance on how it might apply to low-paid workers and pensioners.[127] Progress was hampered, however, by confusion about what NIT actually meant and by the limited coverage of Inland Revenue and Ministry of Social Security statistics, which made it difficult to estimate how many households might benefit.[128] Nicholas Kaldor then diverted the group from its original mission by circulating a plan for a system of refundable child tax credits along the lines of Titmuss and Lynes's 'tax adjustment' scheme.[129]

The Inland Revenue's forthright opposition to any link between tax and benefits made it difficult for Treasury officials to judge how serious the practical objections really were. The Chancellor's Principal Private Secretary, Robert Armstrong, for instance, believed that the Revenue had a vested interest in stifling debate and expressed frustration at its '"dog in the manger" tactics'.[130] As the study went on, however, the Working Group's secretary A. J. Wiggins became convinced that a selective NIT on the lines suggested by Friedman would indeed be 'unworkable' in Britain.[131] Although the cumulative PAYE system adjusted tax liability week by week in response to fluctuating earnings, it would be 'impossible' to pay benefits in the same way because employers lacked information about other sources of income. Making provisional NIT awards on the basis of the previous year's tax data would be

[125] TNA, T227/2755, 'A Negative Income Tax' by Mr Carr and Mr Holmans, n.d. (*c.* Jan. 1968).

[126] TNA, T227/2842, 'Child Tax Credits. Implications for Incomes Policy and a National Minimum Wage', by the Department of Employment and Productivity, 5 Sept. 1968.

[127] TNA, T227/2756, N.I.T. (68) 7, 'Working Group on Negative Income Tax. Note by the Chief Secretary', 26 Mar. 1968; T227/2757, A. J. Wiggins to Mr Jordan Moss and Mr Houghton, 'Working Group on Negative Income Tax', 20 June 1968.

[128] TNA, T227/2756, A. J. Wiggins to Mr Phelps, 'Working Group on Negative Income Tax', 13 Apr. 1968.

[129] TNA, T227/2757, 'Negative Income Tax in Relation to Family Allowances' by Nicholas Kaldor, 28 June 1968. Kaldor claimed that this proposal was modelled on the Danish system: see T227/2842, Nicholas Kaldor to Sir Alexander Johnston, 'Child Tax Credits in Denmark', 16 Sept. 1968.

[130] TNA, T227/2757, R. T. Armstrong to Sir Douglas Allen, 5 Aug. 1968.

[131] TNA, T227/2757, 'Possible Systems of Negative Income Taxation', draft note by A. J. Wiggins, July 1968.

administratively feasible, but a separate means-tested safety net would then be required to deal with unexpected changes of circumstances.[132] Unlike in the USA, where income tax was routinely over-deducted and taxpayers were used to receiving refund cheques at the end of the year, British workers would expect to pay (or be paid) the right amount on time. Nor was computerization likely to solve these problems, since the computerized PAYE system at East Kilbride was based on magnetic tape, and had been organized on the same lines as the old manual records so that tax clerks could link the two together.[133] Even under the Inland Revenue's original timetable (which was subsequently abandoned by the Heath government) this rather primitive system would not be rolled out nationally until the late 1970s, and officials warned that a real-time link with social security was unlikely to be possible for at least twenty years.[134]

These practical obstacles were compounded by the overlap between benefit rates and the tax threshold which had developed during the 1960s. By autumn 1968, the Supplementary Benefit scale rate for a single householder (£4.55 per week or £236.60 per year) was higher than the income tax personal allowance (£220), and the rate for a married couple with two children was only slightly lower than the tax allowances to which they were entitled.[135] An NIT which was based on applying 'negative rates' of tax to workers below the threshold was thus unlikely to lift them to Supplementary Benefit level, and tax allowances would have to be raised substantially in real terms for an NIT to have much effect on poverty. The Working Group's report spelled out these problems in damning terms, and concluded that 'The income tax machinery is at present quite unsuited to the implementation of a negative income tax'.[136]

By the time the Wilson government left office in 1970, then, it had examined NIT from a number of different angles and found it wanting. The selective NIT favoured by Friedman and other American economists proved impossible to operate through PAYE, whilst a universal 'social dividend' or

[132] TNA, T227/2757, 'Possible Systems of Negative Income Taxation'.

[133] Enid Mumford, *Values, Technology and Work* (The Hague, 1981), 162.

[134] TNA, T227/2755, 'Links between Inland Revenue & M.S.S.' (*c.* Oct. 1967).

[135] From April 1968 a married couple with two children aged 5 and 10 would have a tax threshold of £570 (£340 for a married couple and £115 for each child under 11); from October 1968 they could claim £553.80 a year in Supplementary Benefit. This calculation excludes housing costs and the effect of clawback on tax thresholds. See HM Revenue and Customs, 'Tax Structures and Parameters. TA1. Income Tax Personal Allowances and Reliefs, 1948–9 to 1972–2', accessed 28 July 2017, available at <http://webarchive.nationalarchives.gov.uk/20060214102705/http://www.hmrc.gov.uk/stats/tax_structure/00ap_a1a_2.htm>; Institute for Fiscal Studies, 'Fiscal Facts: Income Support and Supplementary Benefit Rates', accessed 28 July 2017, available at <https://www.ifs.org.uk/ff/is.xls>.

[136] TNA, CAB134/3288, 'Negative Income Tax. Report by a Working Group under the Chairmanship of the Chief Secretary to the Treasury', n.d. (1969).

UBI continued to be dismissed as unaffordable. Even more limited attempts to link tax and benefits, such as the income guarantee for pensioners, turned out to be more difficult than they first seemed. As the junior social security minister David Ennals explained in a speech to CPAG in April 1970, the investigation into NIT had highlighted the virtues of the existing benefit system:

> We have spent a great deal of time ... looking at various negative income tax and social dividend schemes. At first sight they have considerable attractions ... But one of the first things one realises when one gets down to detail is that the present system sets very high standards. This is only surprising if one allows oneself to think of it as a complicated system of transfer payments and forgets that it is the result of 60 years of vigorous sophisticated social engineering ... [The Welfare State] is complicated because life in an advanced industrial society is complicated and it provides promptly and efficiently for a great variety of needs. It is very doubtful whether you could adapt the tax system to provide for those needs with anything like the same degree of speed and precision.[137]

Ennals conceded that a rough-and-ready NIT might be useful in a country like the United States, 'where the social security system is much less highly developed'. In Britain, however, 'the elimination of poverty' required a much subtler 'series of adjustments' to taxation, social security, and wage bargaining.[138]

Conclusion

The search for the 'holy grail' of a selective NIT persisted into the 1970s. The 1970 Conservative manifesto accused Labour of 'exaggerat[ing] the administrative problems involved' and promised 'a real effort to find a practical solution'.[139] Neoliberal intellectuals and propagandists such as Seldon and Colin Clark continued to press the idea, and some left-wingers also took it up: Michael Brody of the Amalgamated Union of Engineering Workers, for

[137] TNA, T227/3123, 'Labour and the Poor. Speech by Mr David Ennals MP to the Child Poverty Action Group on 19 April 1970' (copy).

[138] TNA, T227/3123, 'Labour and the Poor'.

[139] Conservative Party, *A Better Tomorrow: The Conservative Programme for the Next 5 Years* (1970), reprinted in *Conservative Party General Election Manifestos*, 177–98, at 191.

instance, hailed NIT as 'a new weapon for socialism' which could bring about a 'massive redistribution of national income'.[140] Within government, however, the verdict of John Diamond's 1968–9 Working Group was regarded as conclusive. NIT could not be introduced without either abandoning cumulative PAYE or waiting for the more sophisticated technology required to forge a real-time link between the tax and benefit systems.

Historians of the US campaign for a guaranteed income have attributed its failure to a mixture of economic and cultural factors. For instance, John Myles and Paul Pierson have pointed out that small business organizations lobbied vigorously against Richard Nixon's Family Assistance Plan, especially in the southern states, fearing that it would weaken work incentives and push up wages.[141] Gareth Davies and Brian Steensland have emphasized the cultural dimension to this opposition, arguing that the idea of a guaranteed income proved politically unacceptable because it 'emphasized entitlement rather than opportunity' and challenged the deep-seated distinction between the deserving and undeserving poor.[142] These fears were reinforced during the 1970s by the results of the field experiments in New Jersey and elsewhere, which appeared to show that NIT reduced working hours and increased rates of marital breakdown.[143]

Cultural and economic considerations also featured in the British debate, though here it was the trade unions that were most suspicious of wage supplementation. As the TUC General Council pointed out in 1971, 'a negative income tax which offered help on an adequately generous scale' would be open to two 'serious practical objections':

> it would comprise a direct and explicit subsidy to low wages, thus tending to inhibit the development of effective collective bargaining among low-paid workers; and it would significantly reduce economic incentives and fair rewards for effort for many low-paid workers.[144]

[140] Institute of Economic Affairs papers, 333.6, Sir Keith Joseph to Arthur Seldon, 3 Jan. 1980; Colin Clark, *Poverty before Politics: A Proposal for a Reverse Income Tax* (1977); Amalgamated Union of Engineering Workers (Engineering Section), *A New Weapon for Socialism—The Negative Income Tax. Revised for 1971–2 Costing and Revenue Figures* (1972), 7.

[141] John Myles and Paul Pierson, 'Friedman's Revenge: The Reform of "Liberal" Welfare States in Canada and the United States', *Politics & Society* 25/4 (1997), 443–72, at 459–61.

[142] Davies, *From Opportunity to Entitlement*, 235; Steensland, *The Failed Welfare Revolution*, 232–46.

[143] Steensland, *The Failed Welfare Revolution*, 213–15.

[144] TNA, T227/3350, 'White Paper: "Reform of Personal Direct Taxation"', memorandum by the TUC General Council (*c.* Aug. 1971).

The more immediate obstacle in Britain, however, was the technical difficulty of assessing and paying benefits through PAYE. As Ennals noted, the main attraction of NIT was the possibility of sidestepping the problems of conventional means-testing. If a guaranteed income had to be administered separately, 'the connection with the tax system would be far too bogus to deceive anyone for very long'.[145] Naive visions of transatlantic policy transfer thus foundered on the distinctiveness and complexity of the UK's tax and benefit institutions.

The failure to devise a satisfactory NIT was politically significant because it made it more difficult to sustain the expansion of selective benefits which had been embarked on by governments of both parties. Even in the late 1960s, Labour ministers were concerned about the complexity of means-tested support and its potential disincentive effects: studies commissioned by Crossman identified forty-three different means tests operated by central and local government, and found that 'at certain critical points on the income scale... an extra £1 or £2 in earnings could produce little or no net gain...when account was taken of tax and the loss of benefits'.[146] The Heath government's decision to introduce Family Income Supplement (FIS)—with a 50 per cent taper—in 1971 made this problem more severe, and the low take-up of FIS also called the cost-effectiveness of means-tested benefits into question. This crisis of confidence in selectivity caused immediate problems for the Conservatives, as we shall see in Chapter 5; but in the longer term it was perhaps even more damaging to Labour, which responded to pressure from CPAG and other campaign groups by redoubling its commitment to universalism. As Martin Rhodes has pointed out, the 1974–9 Labour government's attempts to enlarge the 'social wage' increased the tax cost of the welfare state and exacerbated the difficulty of maintaining public consent for egalitarian policies.[147] By 1979, almost half of working-class men thought welfare benefits had 'gone too far', and the backlash against the politics of 'tax and spend' helped bring Mrs Thatcher to power.[148]

[145] TNA, T227/3123, 'Labour and the Poor'.

[146] TNA, CAB134/3290, 'Report of the Inter-Departmental Working Party on a Multi-purpose Means Test' (*c.* May 1970); CAB134/3285, Ministerial Committee on Social Services, minutes of eighth meeting, 9 July 1969.

[147] Martin Rhodes, 'Desperately Seeking a Solution: Social Democracy, Thatcherism, and the "Third Way" in British Welfare', in *Recasting European Welfare States*, edited by Maurizio Ferrera and Martin Rhodes (2000), 161–86.

[148] Ivor Crewe, Anthony Fox, and Neil Day, eds, *The British Electorate 1963–1992* (Cambridge, 1995), 391.

5

'The Pragmatist's Solution to Poverty'

The Heath Government's Tax Credit Scheme, 1970–1974

On 10 October 1972 the Conservative Chancellor of the Exchequer, Anthony Barber, and the Secretary of State for Social Services, Sir Keith Joseph, unveiled plans for the most radical overhaul of Britain's tax and benefits systems since the Second World War. The government's Tax Credit Scheme, devised by Barber's special adviser Arthur Cockfield, would dramatically simplify the income tax structure and turn the main personal allowances into refundable tax credits, providing an automatic and flexible form of income support for the low-paid. The Tax Credit Scheme was intended to be the capstone of Barber's tax reform programme and a symbol of Joseph's compassionate Conservatism—'the best talisman of the Government's commitment to social justice in its reform of our antiquated tax system'.[1] Samuel Brittan, writing in the *Financial Times*, hailed it as 'The biggest change since Beveridge' and thought that 'if [Edward Heath's] Government is to be remembered in the history books it is more likely to be for this scheme...than for anything else'.[2] *The Times*'s economics editor Peter Jay also welcomed the reform, which showed that the UK Treasury was 'the most talented and imaginative ministry of economics' in the world, while the *Daily Mail* told its readers that 'the Barber plan offers the best chance of helping the low-paid since the Welfare State began'.[3]

The Conservatives' defeat in the February 1974 general election meant that the Tax Credit Scheme never came to fruition, and as a result it has attracted relatively little attention from historians.[4] The scheme is nevertheless of

[1] The quotation is from Patrick Jenkin, the Chief Secretary to the Treasury, in *Financial Times*, 11 Oct. 1972, 24.

[2] *Financial Times*, 11 Oct. 1972, 19.

[3] *The Times*, 11 Oct. 1972, 21; *Daily Mail*, 11 Oct. 1972, 6.

[4] The most detailed study is Leslie Lenkowsky, *Politics, Economics, and Welfare Reform: The Failure of the Negative Income Tax in Britain and the United States* (Lanham, NY, 1986), which draws heavily on contemporaneous interviews with policy-makers. The scheme is also discussed in outline in Rodney Lowe, 'The Social Policy of the Heath Government', in *The Heath Government 1970–4: A Reappraisal*, edited by Stuart Ball and Anthony Seldon (Harlow, 1996), 191–214; Richard Whiting, *The Labour Party and Taxation: Party Identity and Political Purpose in Twentieth-Century Britain* (Cambridge,

Transfer State: The Idea of a Guaranteed Income and the Politics of Redistribution in Modern Britain. Peter Sloman, Oxford University Press (2019). © Peter Sloman. DOI: 10.1093/oso/9780198813262.001.0001

significant interest for a number of reasons. Firstly, it represents the most ambitious blueprint for tax-benefit integration adopted by any British government between the Second World War and the 1990s, and the only serious attempt to depart from the PAYE system since it was introduced in 1944. Secondly, it was the most distinctive British contribution to the search for a Negative Income Tax which preoccupied policy-makers on both sides of the Atlantic during the 1960s and 1970s, and the closest any British government has come to introducing something like a basic income. Troubled by the administrative costs of PAYE and their failure to devise a workable NIT, the Conservatives revived Juliet Rhys-Williams's idea of paying personal allowances in cash as a way of providing income support to low-paid workers and radically simplifying the tax system. Thirdly, the episode provides a valuable insight into the evolution of the Heath government's strategy. Along with the 'Barber boom', the 1972 Industry Act, and Heath's statutory incomes policy, the Tax Credit Scheme came to symbolize the burial of the anti-statist 'Selsdon Man' and the government's reversion to a more inclusive brand of 'One Nation' Conservatism.[5] The failure of this centrist strategy in the 1974 elections sealed Heath's fate, and paved the way for Margaret Thatcher's more radical break with the post-war settlement.

In comparison with the early post-war decades, detailed empirical work on the welfare state in the 1970s has been slow to emerge, though scholars such as Florence Sutcliffe-Braithwaite and Gareth Millward have recently begun to remedy this deficiency.[6] This chapter examines the origins of the Tax Credit Scheme and sets it in the context of the evolving post-war debate about the nature and purpose of a guaranteed income. As sociologist Robert Pinker pointed out at the time, the scheme represented 'the pragmatist's solution to poverty'—'a welfare technician's paper' which provided a new mechanism for income redistribution without grounding it in any particular social philosophy.[7]

2000); Florence Sutcliffe-Braithwaite, 'Neoliberalism and Morality in the Making of Thatcherite Social Policy', *Historical Journal* 55/2 (2012), 497–520.

---

[5] Although David Seawright has recently highlighted the ambivalence of the 'One Nation' tradition, I use it here as shorthand for that centrist strand of Conservative politics which stressed the capacity of elite leadership to defuse social conflict and unite the population around a shared national project. This was also how Heath used it, especially during the second half of his premiership. See David Seawright, *The British Conservative Party and One Nation Politics* (2010), and Conservative Party, *For All the People* (1972).

[6] Sutcliffe-Braithwaite, 'Neoliberalism and Morality'; Gareth Millward, 'Social Security Policy and the Early Disability Movement—Expertise, Disability, and the Government, 1965–77', *Twentieth Century British History* 26/2 (2015), 274–97.

[7] Robert Pinker, 'Social Policy and Social Justice', *Journal of Social Policy* 3/1 (1974), 1–19, at 15–16.

In many ways, this technocratic ambition was characteristic of its era, and reflected the growing influence of redistributive market liberalism in Whitehall and beyond: as Robert Page has observed, '[p]ragmatic, evidence-based, expert-led policy... rather than pure "ideology" was the order of the day' under Heath's 'modern technocratic Conservatism'.[8] Although the scheme was scrapped after Labour returned to office in 1974, it cast a long shadow over both tax and social security policy into the Thatcher years, and left its mark on the tax and benefit systems through more limited forms of simplification.

Competition with compassion: The Heath government's fiscal strategy

The 1970–4 Conservative government came to power with the aim of bringing about what Edward Heath called a 'quiet revolution' in 'the outlook of the British nation'.[9] By encouraging entrepreneurship and making the British economy more flexible, Heath hoped to achieve by free-market methods the faster economic growth that had largely eluded Harold Wilson.[10] Improving incentives to work, save, and invest by reducing direct taxation was central to this economic strategy. As Martin Daunton has pointed out, the Conservatives were also highly attuned to the political value of income tax cuts as a means of satisfying their middle-class base and making inroads into Labour support among increasingly 'affluent' and tax-conscious skilled workers.[11] (Indeed, the party's private polling suggested that 'middle-aged manual workers' played a central role in Heath's surprise election victory.[12]) Heath and his colleagues recognized that lower direct taxation would have to be financed by indirect taxes and public spending cuts, but they hoped to maintain 'balance' and social cohesion by providing more selective support for disadvantaged groups. In Rodney Lowe's phrase, the Conservatives sought to combine 'competition and compassion': means-tested transfer payments would provide a safety net for

[8] Robert M. Page, *Clear Blue Water? The Conservative Party and the Welfare State since 1940* (Bristol, 2015), 62.
[9] John Campbell, *Edward Heath: A Biography* (1993), 311.
[10] Brendon Sewill, 'A View from the Inside: In Place of Strikes', in Ralph Harris and Brendon Sewill, *British Economic Policy 1970–4: Two Views* (1975), 27–64; Sir Alec Cairncross, 'The Heath Government and the British Economy', in *The Heath Government 1970–4: A Reappraisal*, edited by Stuart Ball and Anthony Seldon (Harlow, 1996), 107–38.
[11] Martin Daunton, *Just Taxes: The Politics of Taxation in Britain, 1914–1979* (Cambridge, 2002), 302–28.
[12] Bodleian Library, Oxford, Conservative Party Archive (CPA), SC10, SC/73/17, 'The Strategic/Tactical Situation in 1973', by Sir Michael Fraser and James Douglas, 14 Feb. 1973.

the poor and so underpin the government's pursuit of market liberalism.[13] The Tax Credit Scheme emerged in response to problems which the Conservatives encountered in implementing both parts of this package deal.

Tax reform was arguably the Heath government's biggest success story. Both Heath's first Chancellor, Iain Macleod, and his successor Anthony Barber—who took over after Macleod's untimely death in July 1970—were deeply interested in fiscal policy and hoped to leave a legacy as tax reformers.[14] In opposition, Macleod presided over the development of an elaborate tax package—modelled on a computer by the Conservative Systems Research Centre—which eventually came to revolve around the reduction of income tax and surtax, the abolition of Jim Callaghan's Selective Employment Tax, and the replacement of purchase tax with a French-style Value Added Tax.[15] Barber largely implemented this package in his 1971 and 1972 budgets. He also simplified income tax by replacing the fractional two-ninths earned income relief with a surcharge on investment income, which allowed him to reduce the basic rate to 30 per cent, and then unifying income tax with surtax in a single graduated scale.

Alongside their commitment to reducing income tax, the Conservatives took a keen interest in the possibility of overhauling the system of collection. PAYE achieved relatively accurate deductions from cumulative earnings, but by the late 1960s it was widely held to have two major deficiencies. Firstly, its complexity made it expensive to administer, with 30,000 staff engaged mainly in generating codes and moving files from one local office to another. This problem was exacerbated by the existence of tax reliefs for mortgage interest and life assurance premiums, deductions for work expenses, and additional allowances for children and other dependants, all of which were incorporated in PAYE codes. Partly for this reason, the Inland Revenue faced much higher administrative costs than countries with simpler systems, accounting for 1.45 per cent of the total tax yield in 1968/9 compared with the US Internal Revenue Service's figure of just 0.4 per cent.[16] Secondly, many Conservatives

[13] Lowe, 'The Social Policy of the Heath Government', 198.

[14] Robert Shepherd, *Iain Macleod: A Biography* (1994), 467–77, 526.

[15] CPA, CRD3/7/6/3, EPG/66/85, 'Economic Policy Group. Revised Report on the Reform of Taxation', 30 May 1968, and CRD3/7/26/37, folder A, paper 2, 'Tax Package. The Development of our Thoughts in Opposition', 27 July 1970.

[16] The National Archives: Public Record Office, Kew (TNA), IR40/17750, report on personal taxation in the United States and Canada (RETAX 2) by A. H. Dalton and W. M. Dermit, n.d. [1970]. Christopher Hood and Ruth Dixon have shown that the Revenue's administrative costs rose sharply during the late 1960s and early 1970s, perhaps partly as a result of falling tax thresholds: Christopher Hood and Ruth Dixon, *A Government that Worked Better and Cost Less? Evaluating Three Decades of Reform and Change in UK Central Government* (Oxford, 2015), 92–6.

continued to be troubled by the perceived impact of PAYE on work incentives. In addition to the problem of high marginal rates on overtime encountered during the 1940s, it was difficult to tax short-term benefits such as Unemployment Benefit using PAYE, and the provision for automatic tax refunds where income fell towards the end of the year seemed to provide an undesirable encouragement to strikers.[17] After the 1970 election, Barber commissioned the Revenue to investigate the possibility of moving over to a non-cumulative system based on the US withholding tax. An interdepartmental working group eventually came down against this on the grounds that British taxpayers would find self-coding too complex and would resent having to wait for end-of-year repayments.[18] Non-cumulation nevertheless remained attractive to a government which had made a manifesto pledge to reduce the size of the civil service.

The other element of the Heath government's fiscal strategy was the expansion of 'selectivity'. In the aftermath of the 1964 election defeat, many Tories had encouraged the party leadership to adopt the Friedmanite approach championed by the Institute of Economic Affairs—targeting benefits on poorer households and expanding 'freedom of choice' by opening up services such as health and education to the market.[19] The 1966 Conservative manifesto thus promised 'an entirely new social security strategy designed to concentrate better care and the biggest benefits on those most in need'.[20] Heath was sensitive to the political risks involved in means-testing existing benefits and services, and made it clear that he was mainly interested in applying the principle to the allocation of new resources.[21] At the same time, the Tories recognized that many of their other policies—including the introduction of VAT and changes to agricultural subsidies—were likely to raise the cost of living for poorer families. Selective benefits thus had an important role to play in legitimizing free-market reforms and ensuring that the distributional impact was relatively balanced.

The Conservatives' embrace of RML can be seen most clearly in housing policy, where the 1972 Housing Finance Act required councils to charge 'fair rents' and shift subsidies towards low-income tenants through a system of rent

[17] TNA, IR40/17749, 'Working Group on Personal Taxation. Non-Cumulative PAYE', by A. H. Dalton, July 1970; T328/878, Ralph Howell to Anthony Barber, 20 July 1973 (copy).

[18] TNA, T171/882, 'Report of the Working Group on Non-Cumulative PAYE', draft summary by the Inland Revenue, 28 Oct. 1971.

[19] CPA, CRD2/30/17/63, Tam Galbraith to Ted Heath, 10 Nov. 1964; Conservative Research Department, 'Social Priorities: Report of Working Group on Selectivity and Private Provision in the Social Services', 14 July 1967. I am grateful to Brendon Sewill for lending me a copy of this paper.

[20] Conservative Party, *Action not Words* (1966), reprinted in *Conservative Party General Election Manifestos, 1900–1997*, edited by Iain Dale (2000), 163–73, at 166.

[21] CPA, ACP2/2, Advisory Committee on Policy, minutes of 83rd meeting, 27 July 1967.

rebates and allowances.[22] Alongside housing, Family Allowances also provided an attractive target for reform. Although CPAG presented Family Allowances as the natural solution to family poverty, they enjoyed only limited support among the general population: for instance, 68 per cent of respondents to a May 1968 poll thought they should be confined to poor families.[23] As Barney Hayhoe of the Conservative Research Department pointed out, means-testing Family Allowances—perhaps using an NIT mechanism—would both allow them to be made more generous and free up resources for tax cuts.[24]

The idea of replacing Family Allowances with a means-tested family benefit figured prominently in Conservative thinking in opposition, but some senior Tories became increasingly worried about its political implications. In particular, it was recognized that lower-middle-income families would lose out from the change unless the new benefit extended some way up the income spectrum—in which case the cost savings would be minimal.[25] Shadow Chancellor Iain Macleod was also keen to exploit CPAG's campaign against the Wilson government—with its controversial claim that 'The Poor Get Poorer Under Labour'—in the run-up to the 1970 election. Macleod therefore shelved the plan for a means-tested benefit in March 1970 and proposed to increase family allowances with clawback, pending the development of a workable NIT.[26]

Once the Conservatives were in office, however, they quickly realized that neither of these ideas was practicable. Treasury officials explained that, since the tax threshold was already relatively low, a further instalment of clawback would 'brin[g] into tax many of the people the extra [Family Allowance] is intended to help' whilst having little impact on child poverty.[27] Likewise, Tory ministers' suspicion that Labour had exaggerated the difficulties of NIT was dispelled when they were shown the findings of John Diamond's 1968–9 Working Group. The Chief Secretary to the Treasury, Maurice Macmillan, believed 'that the negative conclusions reached by officials are inescapable, and that whatever the theoretical attractions of NIT in one form or another, the practical objections are likely to be decisive for the foreseeable future'.[28]

[22] Peter Malpass, *Reshaping Housing Policy: Subsidies, Rents and Residualisation* (1990), 114–35.

[23] CPA, LCC4/4, SP/70/8—Addendum, 'Family Allowances', by Barney Hayhoe, 28 Jan. 1970.

[24] CPA, CRD3/7/26/14, 'Family Poverty' by Barney Hayhoe, 14 Sept. 1967.

[25] CPA, CRD3/7/26/41, James Douglas to Edward Heath, 'Selectivity', 20 May 1968, and ACP2/2, minutes of Advisory Committee on Policy meeting, 19 June 1968; Shepherd, *Iain Macleod*, 479–80.

[26] HC Deb., fifth series, vol. 799, 15 Apr. 1970, cols 1391–403, at col. 1400.

[27] TNA, T227/3121, N. Jordan Moss to Mr Henley, 'Family Support', 31 July 1970.

[28] TNA, T227/3132, 'Negative Income Tax', memorandum by the Chief Secretary to the Treasury, n.d. [Oct. 1970] (copy).

Sir Keith Joseph at the Department of Health and Social Security (DHSS) agreed that 'the quest for a negative income tax' was 'not worth pursuing'.[29]

With clawback and NIT closed off, Joseph reverted to a more conventional form of selectivity and took up a proposal for a means-tested Family Income Supplement which officials had developed before the 1970 election.[30] This was introduced in August 1971, initially as a supplement to Family Allowances, though both ministers and officials hoped that it might subsequently be expanded into a 'super-FIS' to replace them.[31] Instead of breaking down public resistance to means-tested benefits, however, FIS became a serious embarrassment for the government. The need to apply to the Supplementary Benefits Commission limited take-up, so that after five months (and despite an expensive publicity campaign) less than half of eligible families were claiming.[32] Critics also drew attention to the 'poverty trap' which FIS created for some workers when its 50 per cent withdrawal rate was superimposed on income tax and other means tests; one Treasury official felt that 'the "marginal tax effect" is becoming politically quite as serious as . . . the number of families in poverty'.[33] CPAG director Frank Field and the Labour MP Michael Meacher waged an impassioned campaign against the benefit, whilst the Tory backbencher Enoch Powell accused the government of reviving 'the evil of relief in supplementation of wages' last seen in the Speenhamland system.[34] Joseph was badly bruised by the experience, and backed away from the idea of 'super-FIS' in the belief that the public would not accept a further expansion of means-testing.[35]

The failure of FIS to provide a solution to family poverty compounded the Heath government's broader political difficulties. Rising unemployment and spending cuts left ministers open to charges of being doctrinaire and divisive—cutting taxes for the rich at the expense of the poor. Harold Wilson accused Heath of leading 'the most reactionary Conservative Government in our lifetime', and Labour opened up a large Gallup Poll lead in the course of

[29] TNA, T227/3132, M. F. H. Stuart to Mr Jordan-Moss, 'Negative Income Tax', 7 Aug. 1970.

[30] TNA, AST36/227, D. C. H. Abbot to 'P.U.S.' [Parliamentary Under-Secretary, MSS], 22 Jan. 1969 (copy); T227/3121, Sir Keith Joseph to Maurice Macmillan, 22 July 1970.

[31] TNA, T227/3121, Maurice Macmillan to P. Mountfield, 31 July 1970; T227/3305, J. H. Gracey to Mr Wright, 'Family Poverty', 25 Feb. 1971; T227/3307, Patrick Jenkin to Chief Secretary to the Treasury, 'Review of Family Poverty', 15 June 1971 (copy).

[32] *The Times*, 22 Dec. 1971, 3.

[33] David Barker, 'The Family Income Supplement', in *Family Poverty: Programme for the Seventies*, 2nd edn, edited by David Bull (1972), 70–82; TNA, T227/3525, M. F. H. Stuart to Mr Widdup, 'Uprating of Pensions: Future Policy: Inter-relationship with Policy for Family Support', 4 Apr. 1972 (copy).

[34] HC Deb., fifth series, vol. 806, 10 Nov. 1970, cols 260–5, at col. 265.

[35] Andrew Denman and Mark Garnett, *Keith Joseph* (Chesham, 2001), 202–5; TNA, T227/3307, 'Note for the Record: Family Poverty Review' by Malcolm Widdup, 24 June 1971.

1971, peaking at 21.5 per cent in July.[36] CRD chairman Sir Michael Fraser warned that the government risked 'becoming type-cast as "hard, efficient, and soulless"', and Heath agreed that it was important to change these perceptions in order 'to avoid being left too far behind on the polls'.[37] This was the context in which Heath launched his famous 'U-turns': reflating the economy, intervening in British industry, and introducing an incomes policy to control inflation. It was also the context that produced the Tax Credit Scheme.

Arthur Cockfield's brainchild, 1971–1972

The Tax Credit Scheme was the brainchild of Arthur Cockfield, a former Inland Revenue official and managing director of Boots whom Iain Macleod had taken into the Treasury as a special adviser. Cockfield was a longstanding enthusiast for income tax reform, and was determined to find a way of replacing PAYE with a non-cumulative system.[38] As the Revenue's Director of Statistics and Intelligence in the early 1950s, Cockfield had been responsible for preparing its critique of Juliet Rhys-Williams's scheme; twenty years on, he recognized that her flat tax and basic income plan could provide the starting point for a drastic simplification. If personal tax allowances were replaced with weekly cash payments or refundable tax credits which could be netted off against tax liability by employers, it would be possible to deduct basic-rate tax on a non-cumulative basis. Cockfield suggested that personal tax allowances should be replaced with weekly tax credits, worth perhaps £2.50 or £3 for each adult and £1.85 for each child, and tax levied at 30 per cent on all incomes up to a higher-rate threshold of about £100 a week. Cockfield's scheme was not quite universal, since he was determined to avoid subsidizing 'the vagrants, the drifters, the drop-outs, the petty criminals', and unprofitable small businessmen. He therefore proposed to restrict the scheme to employees who paid Class I National Insurance contributions, together with those claiming National Insurance benefits such as the state pension—who, with their families, made up about 90 per cent of the population. On a 'no-losers' basis, with £3 adult credits, the net cost would be about £1 billion.[39]

[36] *The Guardian*, 1 Nov. 1971, 5.

[37] CPA, SC9, SC/71/5, 'Public Opinion' by Sir Michael Fraser, 13 Sept. 1971; SC10, SC/71/8, minutes of Steering Committee meeting, 20 Sept. 1971.

[38] CPA, CRD4/7/14, 'A Possible 15% Basic Rate?' by Arthur Cockfield, 19 Dec. 1978 (copy).

[39] TNA, T227/3335, 'The Negative Income Tax', by F. A. Cockfield, 2 Aug. 1971.

Cockfield was critical of the way 'the welfare school ha[d] tended to take over the NIT', and insisted that the purpose of the Tax Credit Scheme was 'not welfare, or poverty, but tax': replacing tax allowances with lump-sum credits would render coding unnecessary for most people and make it easier to tax short-term benefits. Yet he recognized that the scheme also had 'spin off benefits' in the welfare sphere, since it would provide an automatic form of income support for the low-paid, who could receive their unused tax credits in cash on a weekly basis. Employers would deduct tax from earnings at the standard rate, pay unused credits to workers along with the wage packet, and claim reimbursement where necessary from the Inland Revenue. It was unrealistic to think the credits could be high enough to replace National Insurance, as Rhys-Williams had hoped, but it would be possible to abolish Family Allowances and FIS for those within the scheme and greatly reduce reliance on Supplementary Benefit. Cockfield acknowledged that the credits themselves were unselective, but argued that 'the effect of the scheme is exactly and precisely the same as increasing the tax personal allowances combined with help to those below the tax threshold'.[40] The government could thus claim to have fulfilled its manifesto commitment to introduce NIT.

Cockfield submitted his blueprint to the Chancellor in August 1971, and it received a favourable reception from ministers and officials. Though the cost was a cause of some concern, the Financial Secretary to the Treasury, Patrick Jenkin, was 'enormously impressed' by the scheme's ingenuity, whilst Maurice Macmillan thought it could be 'a satisfactory extension of the tax revolution' which Barber had set in hand.[41] Joseph was worried about the exclusion of the self-employed and the uneven distribution of the benefits, but saw 'very great attractions from the social security point of view' in reducing the importance of means-tested benefits and alleviating the poverty trap.[42] Perhaps most importantly, the Inland Revenue chairman Sir Arnold France was attracted by the prospect of saving between 10,000 and 15,000 of the staff currently involved in PAYE work.[43] Whereas previous attempts at tax-benefit integration had been stymied by Revenue opposition, as we have seen in Chapters 3 and 4, France became an enthusiast for the scheme and helped drive it forward.

[40] TNA, T227/3335, 'The Negative Income Tax', by F. A. Cockfield.

[41] TNA, T227/3350, Patrick Jenkin to Chancellor of the Exchequer, 'Negative Income Tax', 4 Oct. 1971 (copy); T227/3335, M. V. Macmillan to Chancellor of the Exchequer, 'Mr Cockfield's NIT Scheme', 5 Oct. 1971 (copy).

[42] TNA, T227/3350, Sir Keith Joseph to Anthony Barber, 1 Oct. 1971 (copy).

[43] TNA, T227/3520, draft letter from Sir Arnold France to Chancellor of the Exchequer, 'TABS and the PAYE Automation Programme', 11 Nov. 1971 (copy).

Barber authorized the formation of a full-time Working Group, chaired by the Inland Revenue official John Green, to examine Cockfield's proposals in detail and report before the 1972 budget. The Working Group endorsed the main principles of Cockfield's scheme with one exception: it felt his proposal to pay a full credit to housewives was much too generous, and instead suggested credit rates of £3 for a single person and £5 for a married couple, with the existing Wife's Earned Income Relief retained in a modified form.[44] The group agreed with Cockfield that the self-employed and workers below the Class I threshold of £8 a week would have to be excluded, the former because their weekly earnings were difficult to measure and the latter because of the risk of abuse; instead, they would continue to be taxed under PAYE and would receive child support through FIS and an expanded system of Child Tax Allowances.[45] Neither of these solutions was particularly elegant, but Green and his colleagues thought it best to set difficult cases aside in order to get the main body of the scheme off the ground. One academic observer, Leslie Lenkowsky, thought the group 'came as close to being partisans of the... scheme as the code of the British civil service would allow'.[46]

Although the Working Group reported in favour of the Tax Credit Scheme, Treasury officials were sharply divided over its merits. On the one hand, John Gracey of the Fiscal Policy Division was alarmed by the budgetary implications: not only would the initial cost have to be accommodated by spending cuts or tax increases, but the scheme would restrict future Chancellors' freedom of action by requiring a wide basic-rate band and making it harder to exploit fiscal drag.[47] The head of the Social Services Division, Malcolm Widdup, was similarly sceptical, pointing out that most of the cost was taken up by raising the tax threshold and that the gains would be least apparent to the very poor, for whom the credits would simply replace FIS and Supplementary Benefit.[48] Cockfield and the second permanent secretary Sir Samuel Goldman, however, turned these arguments upside down, emphasizing the political value of an across-the-board tax cut and suggesting that a more rigid tax system would be 'a useful disciplinary instrument for use against spending

[44] TNA, T227/3521, TAB(SG)(72)5, 'TAB Steering Group. Financial and Budgetary Implications of the TAB Scheme. Note by Working Group', 21 Jan. 1972.

[45] TNA, T227/3520, TAB(SG)(71)1, 'Coverage of the TAB Scheme. Note by the Working Group', 10 Dec. 1971.

[46] Lenkowsky, *Politics, Economics, and Welfare Reform*, 129.

[47] TNA, T227/3520, J. H. Gracey (Treasury) to J. M. Green (IR), 7 Dec. 1971 (copy); T227/3521, J. H. Gracey to Mr Hancock, Mr Beastall, and Mr Rogers, 'TABS', 26 Jan. 1972.

[48] TNA, T227/3522, Malcolm Widdup to M. F. H. Stuart, 'TABS: Advantages and Disadvantages', 31 Jan. 1972.

Ministers'.[49] On balance, the official Treasury advised the Chancellor to take the scheme forward.[50]

Barber had his own reservations about the details of the scheme, but he recognized its potential political value as a means of re-establishing the Conservatives' 'One Nation' credentials.[51] He therefore announced the proposal in his March 1972 budget speech and promised to publish a Green Paper which could be examined by a House of Commons Select Committee. Barber was keen to build a cross-party consensus around the policy, not least because the four-year lead-in time required by the Inland Revenue meant that it could not be introduced until mid-way through the next Parliament.[52] The Cabinet considered a draft Green Paper in June and 'agreed that the scheme would make a constructive and imaginative contribution to the Government's social policy'.[53]

The Green Paper and the Select Committee, 1972–1973

The Green Paper on *Proposals for a Tax-Credit System* finally appeared on 10 October 1972 with a foreword by Barber and Joseph, who hailed it as 'a radical new approach' to the integration of tax and social security 'in which this country is leading the world'.[54] The paper outlined the scheme in detail on the basis of illustrative credits worth £4 for a single person, £6 for a married couple or a single parent, and £2 for each child. At a cost of £1.3 billion—approximately 2 per cent of GDP—the scheme would reduce income tax liability across the board, provide a non-means-tested replacement for Family Allowances and FIS, and float about a million pensioners off Supplementary Benefit.

[49] TNA, T227/3523, 'Note of a Meeting Held in Sir Douglas Allen's Office at 11.15 am on Friday, 11 February 1972', by D. C. Maughan, 15 Feb. 1972, and Sir Samuel Goldman to Sir Douglas Wass, 'TABS', 7 Feb. 1972.

[50] TNA, T227/3523, Sir Douglas Wass to Sir Douglas Allen, 'Tax and Benefits Scheme', 18 Feb. 1972 (copy).

[51] Barber was particularly concerned about the exclusion of the very low-paid and the self-employed: see TNA, T227/3526, J. H. Gracey to Mr Maughan, 'Tax Credit Scheme', 17 May 1972 (copy).

[52] TNA, IR40/17927, A. M. Bailey to Mr Unwin, 'Tax-Credit Scheme', 5 June 1972 (copy).

[53] TNA, CAB128/50/33, Cabinet conclusions, 27 June 1972. Publication was deferred until the autumn because Barber's decision to let sterling float, on 23 June, made it an inauspicious time to announce new spending proposals. Some departmental ministers also seem to have worried that the need to make room for the scheme would squeeze their spending allocations in the forthcoming PESC review: T328/977, Sir Douglas Wass to Mr Corlett, 'Cabinet: Proposals for a Tax-Credit System—CM(72)61', 21 June 1972 (copy).

[54] Cmnd. 5116, *Proposal for a Tax-Credit System* (1972), iii.

Barber and Joseph hoped that the Tax Credit Scheme would allow the government to put the FIS fiasco behind it and regain the initiative in social policy. The general thrust of the Green Paper was well received by most commentators: Conservative newspapers praised ministers for devising a workable NIT, whilst left-wingers such as Frank Field welcomed the government's apparent conversion to universalism.[55] Richard Titmuss commended the tax credit concept in a letter to *The Times*, and the former Labour minister Richard Crossman conceded that it represented a 'notable breakthrough'.[56] Titmuss's protégé Brian Abel-Smith went even further, arguing that the Green Paper proposals would 'represent the largest single step forward in nearly universal provision for the poor and for social dependants since the post-war developments stemming from the Beveridge Report'.[57]

Within days of publication, however, the Green Paper began to attract criticism on a variety of grounds. Perhaps most serious was the Shadow Chancellor Denis Healey's charge that the scheme was 'a gigantic confidence trick' because the government refused to give any indication of how it would cover the cost.[58] The Green Paper suggested that it could be financed by the proceeds of economic growth, but *The Guardian* thought that this came 'dangerously near the Micawber tradition' ('something will turn up').[59] If growth did not materialize, the scheme would have to be paid for by a higher basic rate of tax, higher VAT, or spending cuts elsewhere, in which case its social impact was much less certain. Frank Field and the economist Tony Atkinson highlighted the opportunity cost, arguing that a 'back-to-Beveridge' approach of increasing Family Allowances and National Insurance benefits would have a larger and more immediate impact on poverty.[60] From the opposite perspective, George and Priscilla Polanyi of the IEA called on the government to return to its original selectivity agenda.[61]

Alongside the scheme's £1.3 billion price tag, public criticism focused on the proposals for replacing Family Allowances with child credits. The Green Paper left open the question of whether these would be paid to the father or the

[55] *The Daily Telegraph*, 11 Oct. 1972, 18; *Daily Mail*, 11 Oct. 1972, 6; *Tribune*, 13 Oct. 1972, 3.

[56] *The Times*, 1 Nov. 1972, 14, and 14 Oct. 1972, 17.

[57] *Parliamentary Papers*, 1972–3, vol. 34, 'Select Committee on Tax Credit: Volume II—Evidence', 349–58, at 358.

[58] *The Times*, 11 Oct. 1972, 1.

[59] *The Guardian*, 11 Oct. 1972, 12.

[60] A. B. Atkinson, *The Tax Credit Scheme and the Redistribution of Income* (1973); TNA, T227/3999, 'Implications for Families of Proposed Tax Credit Scheme. Paper Given by Frank Field, Director of Child Poverty Action Group, at Conference Held on 29th November, 1972 [by the] British Union of Family Organisations'.

[61] George and Priscilla Polanyi, 'Tax Credits: A Reverse Income Tax', *National Westminster Bank Quarterly Review*, Feb. 1973, 20–34.

mother, but it strongly hinted that the former option was preferable because it would minimize administrative costs. Civil servants were also keen on payment to fathers because it would increase rather than reduce men's take-home pay, and so help moderate wage demands, but—as Barber had feared—this provoked a storm of protest from CPAG and women's groups.[62] More than 300,000 people signed petitions in favour of payment to the mother, and the veteran Labour peer Edith Summerskill led a cross-party assault on the government in the House of Lords.[63] In the face of these protests Barber began a tactical retreat, using his March 1973 budget speech to indicate that the government would not allow mothers to be made worse off. [64] The Select Committee went further by recommending that the whole child credit should be paid to the mother in cash through the Post Office, on the same basis as Family Allowances, and that child credits should be available to all families, including the self-employed.

A third point of controversy was the Green Paper's proposal to retain PAYE for working wives instead of giving them a full credit of their own. Not only did the National Council of Women and the Conservative Women's Advisory Committee object to this on feminist grounds, but the Confederation of British Industry protested that employers could not be expected to operate two separate tax systems.[65] The Select Committee proposed that working couples should be allowed to opt for two £4 single credits, and the government promised to investigate the idea. However, the Working Group concluded that this would be administratively impossible with manual records, so the Green Paper approach would have to be followed until the system was fully computerized.[66]

A final set of criticisms, voiced especially by the Labour opposition, focused on the scheme's implications for the wider tax system. Though many of the Labour Party's social policy advisers were enthusiastic about tax credits in principle, the party's tax experts were much more sceptical: in particular, Nicholas Kaldor warned that the Green Paper version would '"freeze" the

[62] TNA, T227/3526, M. A. Johns to Mr Corlett, 'GEN 112(72)5. Tax-Credit Scheme: Draft Green Paper. Payment of Child Credits to Father or Mother', 25 July 1972; T227/3523, J. H. Gracey to Mr Maughan, 'Treatment of the Family in the TABS Scheme', 7 Feb. 1972.

[63] *Parliamentary Papers*, 1972–3, vol. 34, 'Select Committee on Tax Credit: Volume I—Report and Proceedings of the Committee', 20; HL Deb., fifth series, vol. 338, 24 Jan. 1973, cols 157–205.

[64] TNA, T328/874, A. M. Bailey to Miss Seammen, 'Tax Credit Scheme: Child Credits', 18 Dec. 1972 (copy); T227/3999, Anthony Barber to William Clark, 8 Mar. 1973 (copy).

[65] TNA, T227/3999, R. R. Martin to Mr Corlett, 'Report by the Women's National Commission on the Tax-Credit Scheme', 6 Apr. 1973; Modern Records Centre, University of Warwick, Confederation of British Industry papers, MSS.200/C/3/EMP/5/8, L.92.73, 'Tax Credits. CBI Evidence to the Select Committee' by D. M. Rea, 14 Mar. 1973 (copy).

[66] TNA, T227/3999, R. R. Martin (IR) to Mr Corlett, 'Tax Credit Scheme: Treatment of Married Women', 31 July 1973 (copy).

income tax system into a mould which reduces it to a simple proportionate tax' for all but the highest earners, erecting 'a firm and lasting barrier to progressive taxation'.[67] The possibility that tax credits would subsidize low wages also aroused hostility from some Labour MPs and trade unionists: Barbara Castle, for instance, declared that wage subsidies were 'repugnant in a modern society'.[68] These criticisms meant that the Select Committee split on party lines, with three of the four Labour members—Castle, Joel Barnett, and Robert Sheldon—opposed to the scheme and only Douglas Houghton and the Liberal MP John Pardoe giving it qualified support.[69] In the end, the government had to rely on the built-in Conservative majority to secure a favourable report.

'Doing Something for Everyone', 1973–1974

By the time the Select Committee completed its work in July 1973, the Tax Credit Scheme had lost much of its original gloss, as concerns about cost and the payment of child credits allowed critics to question whether it was really a progressive measure. It was clear that the government could only go forward with the scheme if it paid child credits to the mother, but the resulting reduction in pay packets (from the abolition of CTAs) would be at odds with the Conservatives' desire 'to promote a greater sense of personal responsibility on the part of the individual wage-earner'.[70] At the same time, Treasury officials had revised their cost estimates upwards and were now convinced that the scheme would require countervailing tax rises—either increasing the basic rate of income tax to 34 per cent or more than doubling VAT—to pay for it.[71] Finally, modifications to the Green Paper design had eroded some of the projected staff savings.[72] The permanent secretary at the Treasury, Sir Douglas Allen, pointed out that it was 'very much a political decision for Ministers, whether to proceed with the scheme in the face of the Opposition's hostility'.[73]

[67] 'Select Committee on Tax Credit: Volume II—Evidence', 211–37, at 212, 217.

[68] 'Select Committee on Tax Credit: Volume I—Report and Proceedings of the Committee', 77–84, at 82.

[69] TNA, T328/877, J. H. Gracey to Mr Jones, 'Select Committee on the TCS', 27 June 1973 (copy).

[70] TNA, CAB128/52/37, Cabinet conclusions, 17 July 1973.

[71] TNA, T328/872, D. W. G. Wass to Sir Douglas Allen, 'Phasing in the Tax Credit Scheme', 10 July 1973 (copy), and T328/873, 'Working Group on Phasing-in the Tax Credit Scheme. Report of the Working Group', 6 July 1973.

[72] In addition to the extra cost of paying child credits to the mother, the CBI had insisted that the Inland Revenue should continue to send tax codes directly to employers: see TNA, T328/1147, 'Tax Credit Scheme', draft brief by A. J. G. Isaac, Somerset House, 26 Sept. 1974.

[73] TNA, T328/877, Sir Douglas Allen to Mr Bailey, 'Report by the Select Committee on Tax Credit', 29 June 1973 (copy).

Barber recognized that it was a finely balanced decision, especially in the context of a mounting budget deficit, but in the end he was more impressed by the political dangers of dropping the scheme.[74] 'To abandon it at this stage', he warned the Cabinet,

> would leave the Government without a comprehensive strategy in these important areas of social and fiscal policy, and would be liable to reopen questions about family support, provision for the elderly and the taxation of short-term benefits, the last of which was a question of particular concern among the Government's supporters.[75]

Other ministers felt that 'the Government stood to gain substantial political credit from proceeding with the scheme' and pointed out that it could be phased in as resources allowed.[76] With Cabinet approval, Barber announced in July 1973 that the government would go ahead with the scheme on the basis of universal child credits paid in cash to the mother.[77] Preparations went forward with a view to including legislation in the 1974 Finance Bill, introducing child credits in April 1976, and completing the changeover two years later. After some wrangling, it was agreed that the Inland Revenue and DHSS would be jointly responsible for implementation. The Treasury also agreed to treat the credits as deductions from revenue rather than additional public expenditure—a major departure from traditional accounting conventions, which social policy experts such as Titmuss had been seeking for more than a decade.[78]

Having invested so much political capital in the Tax Credit Scheme, Heath and Barber hoped to yield the benefit in the run-up to a 1974 or 1975 general election. Ministers saw the scheme as 'a major vote winner, with a particular appeal to women voters', especially now that child credits would be paid to the mother, and Heath's public relations adviser Michael Wolff thought 'it *ought* to be a feather in our election manifesto'.[79] Together with rising spending on existing services such as health and education, and well-publicized *coups de théâtre* such as a £10 Christmas bonus for pensioners, the tax credit proposals

[74] The junior Treasury minister John Nott later confessed to Joseph that Barber had been hesitating about the cost, which by the time of the 1973 PESC exercise was estimated at £2.5 billion: see CPA, KJ10/21, John Nott to Sir Keith Joseph, 'Tax Credits', 25 June 1975.

[75] TNA, CAB128/52/37, Cabinet conclusions, 17 July 1973.

[76] TNA, CAB128/52/37, Cabinet conclusions, 17 July 1973.

[77] *The Times*, 20 July 1973, 1.

[78] TNA, T328/976, TCM (74) 1st Meeting, minutes of Ministerial Group on Tax Credits, 11 Jan. 1974; see also correspondence in T328/1149 on this accounting question.

[79] *The Guardian*, 31 Oct. 1973, 1; Churchill Archives Centre, Cambridge, Wolff papers, WLFF3/3/78, Michael Wolff to Lord President of the Council, 'Tax Credit Scheme', 27 Feb. 1973 (copy).

symbolized the government's determination to ensure that the benefits of growth were widely shared: as the party's 1973 advertising campaign put it, the Conservatives were 'Doing Something For Everyone'.[80] With the onset of recession in the winter of 1973–4, however, the Tax Credit Scheme turned from an asset into a liability. In the crisis atmosphere of the February 1974 election, Heath's tough line against the miners cast social policy into the shadows and reinforced perceptions that the government was 'divisive' and 'bloody-minded'.[81] Not only did the Conservatives struggle to arouse interest in the scheme, but Denis Healey was able to use its cost to deflect criticism of Labour's own spending plans.[82] Whitehall officials became increasingly convinced that the Green Paper proposals were unaffordable, and warned the incoming Chancellor that even a scaled-back version would pose 'a very significant budgetary problem'.[83] When Labour took office, Healey duly scrapped the scheme, retaining only the child credit proposals under the title of Child Benefit.

Afterlife

The Heath government's defeat and the collapse of the long post-war boom dealt a death blow to Cockfield's grand design. The bleak economic climate of the late 1970s made the scheme seem impossibly extravagant, and both the main parties became more sceptical about 'big bang' proposals for eliminating poverty. By rejecting the Tax Credit Scheme and maintaining PAYE, the Wilson and Callaghan governments were able to revive Labour's traditional fiscal strategy of making income tax more progressive whilst raising extra revenue for public services through fiscal drag.[84] On the social security side, Barbara Castle and David Ennals pursued the 'back-to-Beveridge' approach favoured by CPAG and trade union leaders such as Jack Jones: improving National Insurance, replacing Family Allowances with Child Benefit, and creating SERPS as an earnings-related addition to the state pension.[85] Brian

[80] CPA, SC11, SC/73/21 'Manifesto Themes' by Tony Newton, 18 July 1973.

[81] Ivor Crewe, Bo Särlvik, and James Alt, 'The Why and How of the February Voting', *New Society*, 12 Sept. 1974, 669–72, at 670.

[82] *The Guardian*, 14 Feb. 1974, 8.

[83] TNA, T328/1147, 'Tax Credit Scheme'. Note by Somerset House, 28 Feb. 1974 (copy).

[84] Whiting, *The Labour Party and Taxation*, 246–58.

[85] Polly Toynbee and David Walker, 'Social Policy and Inequality', in *New Labour, Old Labour: The Wilson and Callaghan Governments, 1974–79*, edited by Anthony Seldon and Kevin Hickson (Abingdon, 2004), 105–22; Helen Fawcett, 'Jack Jones, the Social Contract and Social Policy 1970–4', in *Welfare Policy in Britain: The Road from 1945,* edited by Helen Fawcett and Rodney Lowe (Basingstoke, 1999), 158–83.

Abel-Smith, who advised Castle at the DHSS, argued that this focus on universal benefits was expensive and would leave many poorer families and pensioners reliant on means-testing for the foreseeable future, but Labour ministers showed little interest in his efforts to devise a more progressive version of Cockfield's proposals.[86]

Despite its rejection, the Tax Credit Scheme 'lived on in a strange half-life' during the late 1970s, as Florence Sutcliffe-Braithwaite has noted.[87] The policy came to function as a concrete example of what tax-benefit integration might achieve, and as with NIT a decade earlier, the practical difficulties identified within Whitehall were only dimly understood outside it. During the Callaghan government's Supplementary Benefits Review in 1976–9, for instance, DHSS officials found that there was 'still a widely-held belief among our staff and the public that a tax credits system could be introduced quickly and would be an alternative solution to most of our problems'.[88] Self-consciously 'progressive' Conservatives such as the Tory Reform Group continued to canvass support for Cockfield's scheme, and the party's 1979 manifesto promised to seek 'the fulfilment of our original tax credit objectives as and when resources become available'.[89] In truth, however, the writing had been on the wall for the scheme within the Conservative Party as soon as Margaret Thatcher replaced Heath as leader in 1975. Thatcher feared that 'once a Tax Credit Scheme had been introduced, a Government would find itself under pressure to widen its application (e.g. to cover the disabled) and other groups', pushing it down a 'slippery slope' towards a UBI.[90] Even Cockfield's very limited approach risked exacerbating trends which Thatcher viewed with suspicion: the growth of the 'transfer machine', the 'removal of the motive to personal thrift' and 'the further socialisation of income'.[91]

[86] TNA, IR40/18565, Barbara Castle to Denis Healey, 15 May 1974 (copy), and NIT(74) 1st Meeting, 'Note of Meeting on Thursday 13 June 1974 in the Board Room, Somerset House. Working Group on Negative Income Tax', by M. Symons, 17 June 1974; British Library of Political and Economic Science (BLPES), London, Abel-Smith papers, 7/11, Brian Abel-Smith to Mr Radford and Mr Overend, 'Cost of Improvements in Social Security and Related Benefits', 29 July 1975 (copy), Bryan Ellis to Brian Abel-Smith, 'Planning for 1980–5', 14 Nov. 1975 (copy), RE 388, 'Costed Options for Social Security—Michael Meacher's Comments', 8 Dec. 1975, and RE 417, 'Future Social Security Strategy', by David Piachaud, Jan. 1976.

[87] Sutcliffe-Braithwaite, 'Neoliberalism and Morality', 507.

[88] TNA, T366/488, A. J. C. Crocker to A. H. Lovell, 'Tax Credits: Second Draft Report', 1 Dec. 1978.

[89] Tory Reform Group, *Tax Credit Report* (1979); Conservative Party, *The Conservative Manifesto 1979* (1979), reprinted in *Conservative Party General Election Manifestos 1900–1997*, edited by Iain Dale (2000), 265–82, at 280.

[90] CPA, CRD4/4/136, 'Tax Credits. Minutes of a Meeting Held on 20th February 1978 in the House of Commons', by Christopher Mockler, 31 Mar. 1978.

[91] CPA, CRD4/7/14, 'Taxation and Social Security. Record of a Meeting Held on Tuesday, 12th December, 1978 at the House of Commons', by P. J. Cropper, 3 Jan. 1979 (copy).

By the late 1970s, the scheme's appeal to the Treasury and the Inland Revenue was also waning. As the world economy slowed and budgetary pressures grew in the wake of the 1973 oil crisis, the Treasury reverted to its traditional fiscal conservatism and came to prize the flexibility of the existing tax system. Fiscal drag also exacerbated the overlap between means-tested benefits and the tax threshold, and meant that replacing FIS with a system of refundable tax credits became prohibitively expensive. By 1976–7 the Cockfield scheme was projected to cost more than £5 billion, and permanent secretary Sir Douglas Wass dismissed it as 'a blunderbuss instrument'—'very costly in terms of the limited results it could buy in terms of floating people off other means-tested benefits'.[92] At the same time, Inland Revenue officials pointed out that most of the staff savings Cockfield promised came from the computerization and simplification of tax collection, rather than the Tax Credit Scheme per se.[93] Plans for computerizing cumulative PAYE, which Barber had scrapped, resumed in 1977 and were confirmed by the Thatcher government after the Conservatives returned to office.[94]

Looking back from the vantage point of 1984, however, the Inland Revenue's deputy chairman John Isaac reflected that 'the tax credit experience between 1971 and 1974 was *not* wholly negative'. Although the scheme was a relic of 'the heady days before the 1974 crash' when 'the Treasury did not see money as a constraint', its 'radical nature and social promise' had given the Revenue 'the muscle to suggest changes which in other contexts might have been unthinkable'.[95] In particular, Cockfield's attempt to devise a non-cumulative system made it easier to simplify the tax treatment of pensioners (in 1975), to abolish CTAs (in 1979) and life assurance premium relief (in 1984), and to remove mortgage interest relief from PAYE codes (in 1983) by applying it at source. Together with other efficiency measures, these changes helped the Revenue stabilize its administrative costs and begin to reverse the increase in its cost-to-yield ratio which had taken place during the early 1970s.[96]

[92] TNA, T364/42, N. C. Price to Sir Douglas Wass, 'Study of the Administration of Tax and Social Security', 3 Dec. 1976 (copy), enclosing 'Paper 1—Tax Credit Scheme'; T364/90, 'Steering Committee on Study of Administration of Tax and Social Security. Minutes of a Meeting Held at 11 am on Tuesday 25 January', by HM Treasury, 31 Jan. 1977 (copy).

[93] TNA, T364/90, 'Steering Committee on Study of Administration of Tax and Social Security. Minutes of a Meeting Held at 11 am on Tuesday 25 January'.

[94] Peter W. G. Morris and George H. Hough, *The Anatomy of Major Projects: A Study of the Reality of Project Management* (Chichester, 1987), 159–76.

[95] TNA, T530/110, A. J. G. Isaac to Financial Secretary to the Treasury, 'Bringing Together the Tax and Benefit Systems', 18 Apr. 1984 (copy).

[96] Hood and Dixon, *A Government That Worked Better and Cost Less?*, 93, 95.

Isaac concluded that 'Many of the big administrative savings which we have made in PAYE over the last decade . . . can be traced back to the tax credit work':

> It is not to the discredit of the scheme that, as things turned out, we have now pocketed most (though not yet quite all) of the staff savings, without having to recruit additional staff for the tax credits themselves.[97]

On the social security side, Cockfield's scheme also marked an important staging-post in the introduction of universal Child Benefit.

This legacy of simplification was significant in its own terms, but Isaac's analysis also demonstrated the narrow way in which the Tax Credit Scheme had been understood within Whitehall. Although it would have provided a modest guaranteed income for most of the population, the scheme was set within a narrowly technocratic frame of reference which prioritized rationality and administrative savings over any wider social objectives. Cockfield and his colleagues had never seen refundable tax credits as desirable for their own sake, let alone as the first step towards a fully-fledged UBI, but simply as 'the administrative key which opened the door' to tax reform.[98] As with Juliet Rhys-Williams's basic income scheme and Milton Friedman's NIT, the emancipatory potential of guaranteed income was rapidly obscured within the policy-making process.

Even in the 1970s, this rationalist approach to redistribution was being overtaken by events. Yet if 'expensive, universal, socialistic' tax credit schemes went out of fashion, cash transfers remained an essential instrument for British policy-makers.[99] Indeed, the rise of mass unemployment and the collapse of trade union power during the early 1980s not only increased the demands on the social security system, but also reduced the constraints which corporatist institutions placed on the British state.[100] The Thatcher government and its successors used this new-found autonomy to break decisively with the Beveridgean welfare settlement, expanding means-tested benefits for the working poor as a way of flanking and legitimizing free-market policies.

[97] TNA, T530/110, A. J. G. Isaac to Financial Secretary to the Treasury, 'Bringing Together the Tax and Benefit Systems'.

[98] CPA, CRD4/7/13, 'Personal Tax Policy—The Alternative Approaches' by F. A. Cockfield, 18 Jan. 1978 (copy).

[99] TNA, PREM19/1638, David Willetts to Prime Minister, 'Child Support', 22 Mar. 1985.

[100] Jim Bulpitt, 'The Discipline of the New Democracy: Mrs Thatcher's Domestic Statecraft', *Political Studies* 34/1 (1986), 19–39.

PART III

CASH TRANSFERS IN POST-INDUSTRIAL BRITAIN

6

Redistribution in a Cold Climate

The Politics of Guaranteed Income in the 1970s and 1980s

The 1970s was the hinge decade of post-war economic history, in Britain as across the western world. The 1973 oil crisis brought the long post-war boom to a halt and sparked a crisis of confidence in both Keynesian policies and the UK's governing institutions. Patterns of deindustrialization which had begun in the previous decade became increasingly pronounced as technological change and global competition intensified and governments focused on bringing inflation down.[1] Unemployment rose from just over 500,000 claimants during the 'Barber boom' to more than 1 million from 1976 onwards and over 3 million by the early 1980s, as Figure 6.1 shows. Trade union power, which peaked under the Labour government's 'social contract', was squeezed after 1979 by recession and Conservative reforms which outlawed secondary picketing and the closed shop: collective bargaining coverage thus fell from more than 70 per cent of employees in the early 1980s to less than 40 per cent by the end of the century.[2] Income inequality grew and regional differences widened as the UK moved towards a service-based economic model, underpinned by consumer credit, housing wealth, and the deregulation of the City of London.[3]

The harsher economic climate which emerged during this period transformed the context in which social policy was made, as the optimism of the Wilson and Heath years gave way to a more moralistic and ideological approach to poverty. David Donnison, who chaired the Supplementary Benefits Commission from 1975 to 1980, thought the early 1970s saw 'the end of a way of seeing things' which had shaped his professional life: the assumption that the

[1] Jim Tomlinson, 'De-Industrialization not Decline: A New Meta-Narrative for Post-War British History', *Twentieth Century British History* 27/1 (2016), 76–99.

[2] Chris Wrigley, 'Industrial Relations', in *Work and Pay in Twentieth-Century Britain*, edited by Nicholas Crafts, Ian Gazeley, and Andrew Newell (Oxford, 2007), 203–24, at 210.

[3] Helen Thompson, 'The Thatcherite Economic Legacy', in *The Legacy of Thatcherism: Assessing and Exploring Thatcherite Social and Economic Policies*, edited by Stephen Farrall and Colin Hay (Oxford, 2014), 33–68.

Transfer State: The Idea of a Guaranteed Income and the Politics of Redistribution in Modern Britain. Peter Sloman, Oxford University Press (2019). © Peter Sloman. DOI: 10.1093/oso/9780198813262.001.0001

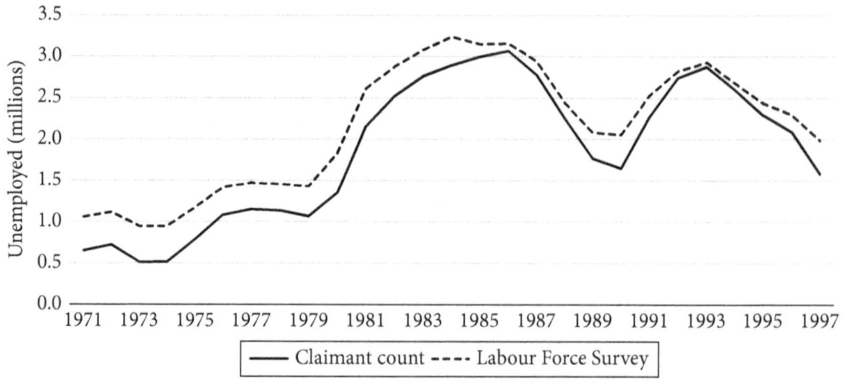

Figure 6.1. UK unemployment, 1971–97
Source: Office for National Statistics time series BCJD and MGSC

welfare state would continue to expand under expert leadership.[4] One of the foundations of Margaret Thatcher's electoral success—as of other New Right politicians across the west—was a public backlash against welfare spending and the taxes required to pay for it. As Bernhard Rieger has shown, the desire to 'activate' the unemployed and reduce 'welfare dependency' led to both out-of-work benefit cuts and the development of new forms of conditionality.[5]

Despite these shifts, the idea of a guaranteed income continued to resonate in three important ways during the 1970s and 1980s. Firstly, the decline of the UK's manufacturing sector and the collapse of the post-war employment model opened up a wide-ranging debate about the future of work, and basic income began to attract significant support as a way of underpinning the transition to a more flexible labour market. Although Conservative enthusiasts such as Sir Brandon Rhys-Williams continued to present UBI as a tax-benefit reform, set firmly within the parameters of redistributive market liberalism, radical groups such as the Claimants Unions and the Ecology Party increasingly highlighted its transformative potential. The formation of the Basic Income Research Group (now the Citizen's Basic Income Trust) in 1984 brought liberal reformers together with New Left activists and gave institutional form to an emerging basic income movement.

Secondly, developments in economics and social research highlighted the growth of poverty under Margaret Thatcher's governments and focused

[4] David Donnison, *The Politics of Poverty* (Oxford, 1982), 19.

[5] Bernhard Rieger, 'Making Britain Work Again: Unemployment and the Remaking of British Social Policy in the Eighties', *English Historical Review* 133/562 (2018), 634–66.

attention on tax-benefit reform as a possible solution. As 'stagflation' pushed policy-makers back to the neoclassical theory of the labour market, economists such as Richard Layard and think-tanks such as the Institute for Fiscal Studies (IFS) pointed out that a guaranteed income could help reconcile wage flexibility with social justice. Tax-benefit integration came to be seen as a 'fashionable' approach to social security—a way of sounding 'progressive and well-informed' at dinner parties—and new microsimulation techniques allowed researchers to quantify the distributional effects of different policies.[6] Of course, this analysis also underlined the political difficulties of reform by drawing attention to the cost of UBI and NIT schemes and the complex pattern of winners and losers.

Thirdly, despite Mrs Thatcher's well-documented hostility to redistribution, cash transfers ultimately became more rather than less central to public policy during these years. Total benefit spending rose from 6.6 per cent of GDP in 1973/4 to 8.3 per cent in 1978/9 and 10.1 per cent in 1996/7, driven largely by the growth of means-tested benefits for working-age adults and children.[7] This was partly a by-product of structural change and macroeconomic choices, which created severe unemployment in former mining districts and other industrial regions, but it also reflected the continuing influence of RML on Conservative policy. Many Tory ministers recognized that an effective social safety net could help smooth the introduction of free-market reforms, including the assault on trade union power, the creation of a more flexible labour market, and the deregulation of private rented housing. Indeed, the streamlined system of means-tested benefits which emerged from Norman Fowler's 1984–5 social security reviews can be seen as a step towards the kind of selective NIT which Friedman had envisaged and the IFS had come to champion—albeit one with significant gaps, and with benefit rates that many poverty researchers saw as wholly inadequate.

Curbing the growth of the 'transfer machine'? Thatcherism and social security

The prevailing approach to social policy within the Conservative Party changed sharply after Margaret Thatcher replaced Edward Heath as leader

[6] Andrew Dilnot, 'A New Sense of Security', *The Guardian*, 4 May 1994, A12.

[7] This and other statistics in the chapter are based on Department for Work and Pensions, Benefit Expenditure and Caseload Tables, Autumn Budget 2018, accessed 20 December 2018, <www.gov.uk/government/publications/benefit-expenditure-and-caseload-tables-2018>.

in January 1975, as Florence Sutcliffe-Braithwaite and Robert Page have shown.[8] As anxieties about inflation, economic decline, and national solvency mounted, the 'modern technocratic Conservatism' of the Heath years gave way to a moralistic emphasis on personal responsibility which matched the monetarist prescription of monetary discipline and spending cuts.

Mrs Thatcher's approach to social security was strongly coloured by her Methodist upbringing in Grantham, which instilled a lifelong commitment to the Victorian virtues of thrift and self-reliance. Like many other New Right politicians, Thatcher saw poverty as a social pathology and strongly resisted attempts to define and measure it in relative income terms. She always believed that self-help was preferable to state provision: as she put it in one of her earliest speeches, in Dartford in 1949, 'the security a family could have by saving its own money, buying its own house and investing, was far greater than . . . one would get from any national scheme'.[9] As party leader, Thatcher claimed that the expansion of out-of-work benefits risked eroding the personal responsibility which formed the basis of Christian morality:

> A man is now enabled to choose between earning his living and depending on the bounty of the state, a choice which comes about because benefits rise and remain tax-free, while earnings rise more slowly if at all, and tax is high at very low income levels . . . This doesn't produce a responsible or a moral society.[10]

Thatcher's biographer Charles Moore has pointed out that her hostility to social security was not absolute: in principle she recognized that National Insurance was a form of collective self-help and, unlike means-tested benefits, did not penalize thrift.[11] Yet this insight tended to be overwhelmed in practice by her twin fears—'that the "shirkers" would tend to benefit at the expense of the workers, and that the cost, if not carefully controlled, would produce

[8] Florence Sutcliffe-Braithwaite, 'Neoliberalism and Morality in the Making of Thatcherite Social Policy', *Historical Journal* 55/2 (2010), 497–520; Robert Page, *Clear Blue Water? The Conservative Party and the Welfare State since 1940* (Bristol, 2015).

[9] Margaret Thatcher, Speech to Dartford Conservative Association AGM, 31 Mar. 1949, reported in *Dartford Chronicle*, 8 Apr. 1949, accessed 16 Jan. 2019, available at <http://www.margaretthatcher.org/document/100822>.

[10] Margaret Thatcher, speech to Greater London Young Conservatives (Iain Macleod Memorial Lecture), 4 July 1977, accessed 16 Jan. 2019, available at <http://www.margaretthatcher.org/document/103411>

[11] Charles Moore, *Margaret Thatcher: The Authorized Biography*, vol. 1 (2013), 164. As a junior pensions spokesman in the 1960s, Thatcher opposed the income guarantee on the grounds that it would discourage saving: Bodleian Library, Oxford, Conservative Party Archive (CPA), CRD2/30/15, Conservative Parliamentary Health and Social Security Committee minutes, 15 Dec. 1964.

national ruin'.[12] Indeed, Thatcher thought a guaranteed income of any kind was likely to be 'a shirker's charter'.[13]

Thatcher's critique of welfare dependency chimed with a broader wave of concern about 'scroungers' during the 1970s, fuelled by high-profile cases such as 'King Con' Derek Deevy, who was convicted of drawing £36,000 in fraudulent benefits.[14] Tory MP Iain Sproat claimed that 20 per cent of social security claims were bogus, and his colleague Ralph Howell called for a benefit cap and strict work requirements to tackle what he called 'the "Why Work?" syndrome'.[15] Thatcher's education spokesman Rhodes Boyson was even more emphatic:

> We are now in 1977 back to a Speenhamland system. There is no workhouse or real work test and although the theory of less eligibility is proclaimed... it is not applied in practice. We thus have a system which encourages idleness and scrounging... Hundreds of thousands of families are forced into dependence on the state. What can their children know of self-reliance and pride?[16]

Daniel Benjamin and Levis Kochin's 1979 article 'Searching for an Explanation of Unemployment in Interwar Britain', which claimed that the benefit regime had exacerbated the Great Depression, lent academic credence to the concept of an 'unemployment trap' in which workers were better off on the dole.[17] Likewise, Patrick Minford of the University of Liverpool used a rational expectations model of the UK economy to estimate that every 10 per cent increase in real benefit rates added half a million to the unemployment rolls.[18] Empirical research into replacement rates by John Flemming and Tony Atkinson suggested that the picture was rather more complex, but many Tory MPs instinctively warmed to the notion that cutting benefits would force the unemployed to price themselves into work.[19]

[12] Moore, *Margaret Thatcher*, vol. 1, 165.

[13] The National Archives: Public Record Office, Kew (TNA), PREM19/1640, Lord Young of Graffham (Minister without Portfolio) to Nigel Lawson, 'Study of Tax and Social Security Systems', 6 June 1985 (copy), with annotations by Thatcher.

[14] Alan Deacon, 'The Scrounging Controversy: Public Attitudes towards the Unemployed in Contemporary Britain', *Social and Economic Administration* 12/2 (1978), 120–35; Auberon Waugh, 'A Red-Toothed Pioneer', *The Spectator*, 23 July 1976, 6.

[15] Deacon, 'The Scrounging Controversy', 122; Ralph Howell, *Why Work? A Challenge to the Chancellor* (1976).

[16] Rhodes Boyson, *Centre Forward: A Radical Conservative Programme* (1978), 106–7.

[17] Daniel K. Benjamin and Levis A. Kochin, 'Searching for an Explanation of Unemployment in Interwar Britain', *Journal of Political Economy* 87/3 (1979), 441–78.

[18] Churchill Archives Centre, Cambridge, Thatcher papers, THCR1/5/10, 'The Problem of Unemployment' by Patrick Minford, n.d. (c.1981), 15.

[19] A. B. Atkinson and J. S. Flemming, 'Unemployment, Social Security and Incentives', *Midland Bank Review*, Autumn 1978, 6–16; TNA, PREM19/1637, Alan Walters to Prime Minister,

The political reaction against welfare spending was reinforced by the growth of tax resistance among sections of the working class. The tax threshold for a married man with two children fell from 100 per cent of average earnings in 1950 to 79 per cent in 1960, 52 per cent in 1970, and 35 per cent in 1980, largely as a result of rising wages and fiscal drag, but also because of the abolition of Child Tax Allowances and the creation of Child Benefit during the late 1970s.[20] At a time of rapid inflation and disputes over wage restraint, Thatcher was able to appeal to many skilled workers' desire for higher take-home pay.

Perhaps the most important decision which the Conservatives took in opposition was to prioritize economic recovery above all else, which meant 'i) getting the P[ublic] S[ector] B[orrowing] R[equirement] right and ii) bringing down marginal tax rates at all levels'.[21] This strategy required a deep squeeze on social security spending, starting with the decoupling of the state pension from earnings growth in 1979 and going on to include real-terms cuts in Child Benefit (frozen until November 1980), the taxation of Unemployment Benefit and Sickness Benefit (from July 1982), and the abolition of the Earnings-Related Supplement for the short-term unemployed which had been introduced in the 1960s. Indeed, one study counted thirty-eight changes to Unemployment Benefit rules during the government's first nine years in office.[22] These savings were designed to release resources for income tax cuts, including the reduction of the standard rate from 33 per cent to 30 per cent in Sir Geoffrey Howe's 1979 budget and the abolition of 'punitive' marginal rates on higher earners.

The early 1980s recession blew the Thatcher government's fiscal and economic strategy off course in important respects, since the monetarist policies adopted to squeeze inflation out of the economy hampered its efforts to unleash entrepreneurial dynamism and reduce public spending. Unemployment Benefit spending doubled in real terms between 1980 and 1982, and ministers searched desperately for ways of raising revenue and cutting administrative costs

'Unemployment, Benefits and the Change from the 1950s to the 1970s', 3 Dec. 1981; CPA, CRD4/7/14, Nigel Lawson to Sir Geoffrey Howe, 15 Feb. 1979 (copy).

[20] CPA, CRD4/4/200, 'The Origins of the Poverty Trap and the Unemployment Trap', by Conservative Research Department, n.d. (Jan. 1983).

[21] CPA, CRD4/7/14, 'Record of a Meeting Held on 7th March 1979', by P. J. Cropper, 14 Mar. 1979 (copy).

[22] Tony Atkinson and John Micklewright, 'Turning the Screw: Benefits for the Unemployed 1979–88', in *The Economics of Social Security*, edited by Andrew Dilnot and Ian Walker (Oxford, 1989), 17–51.

in order to bring the Public Sector Borrowing Requirement down, as Christopher Hood and Rozana Himaz have shown.[23] (Indeed, some of these administrative cuts may have exacerbated the growth of the claimant count by reducing pressure on the unemployed to look for work: for instance, between 1982 and 1986 Unemployment Benefit claimants were not required to sign on at Job-centres.[24]) Yet Thatcher's commitment to re-establishing the authority of the state and resetting wage expectations ruled out a repeat of the Heath government's Keynesian U-turn. Instead, ministers looked to supply-side reforms to reduce the 'natural rate of unemployment' and coax workers into lower-paid jobs. Minford, for instance, told Thatcher that the only sustainable way to get unemployment down was to confront trade union power, deregulate the housing market, and cut taxes and social security benefits.[25] Thatcher's second Chancellor, Nigel Lawson, echoed this analysis in his June 1984 Mais Lecture:

> It is the rediscovery of the enterprise culture, operating within the framework of markets progressively liberated from rigidities and distortions, that will provide the only answer to the curse of unemployment, and the only true generator of new jobs.[26]

Lawson was particularly impressed by the growth of service-sector employment in the United States, which reflected 'more efficient, competitive, innovative and adaptive labour and goods markets' together with the willingness of American workers to help raise productivity and reduce costs.[27] Labour-market policy increasingly sought to promote the creation of part-time, temporary and casual roles, which critics derisively labelled 'McJobs'. Between 1984 and 1997 the number of part-time workers rose from 5 million to 6.7 million and the number of self-employed from 2.7 million to 3.5 million.[28] Many of the new service-sector jobs were filled by women, whose activity rates rose from 44.6 per cent in 1971 to 50.3 per cent in 1984 and 54.2 per cent in 1997.[29] This was bound to have implications for the structure of social security.

[23] Christopher Hood and Rozana Himaz, *A Century of Fiscal Squeeze Politics: 100 Years of Austerity, Politics, and Bureaucracy in Britain* (Oxford, 2017), 141–51.

[24] William Wells, 'From Restart to the New Deal in the United Kingdom', in *Labour Market Policies and the Public Employment Service*, OECD (Paris, 2001), 241–62, at 248.

[25] Thatcher papers, THCR1/5/10, 'The Problem of Unemployment', 1; see also Patrick Minford with David Davies, Michael Peel, and Alison Sprague, *Unemployment: Cause and Cure* (Oxford, 1983).

[26] Nigel Lawson, 'The British Experiment', Mais Lecture at City University Business School, 18 June 1984, accessed 16 Jan. 2019, available at <http://www.margaretthatcher.org/document/109504>.

[27] Lawson, 'The British Experiment'.

[28] Office for National Statistics—Labour Force Survey, series YCBH and MGRQ.

[29] Office for National Statistics—Labour Force Survey, series MGWI.

The Claimants Unions, the 'future of work' debate, and the revival of UBI

The pursuit of labour-market 'flexibility' through deregulation and the dismantling of collective bargaining was characteristic of the Thatcher government's neoliberal political economy, but the New Right was not alone in questioning the continued relevance of the post-war employment model. Social democratic economists such as James Meade and Richard Layard agreed that wage rigidity contributed to unemployment and sought 'a revolutionary change in political attitudes' to work, 'shifting the emphasis from industrial action over wage-fixing to political action over fiscal measures as the recognised means for achieving a more equitable distribution of income'.[30] 'The proper way to redistribute incomes', Layard argued, 'is by the system of taxes and benefits, and not by trying to alter the pattern of pre-tax wages.'[31] From a more radical perspective, the environmental movement questioned the sustainability and value of conventional economic growth, whilst second-wave feminists challenged male-breadwinner norms and demanded the recognition and reallocation of care and household work.[32] In an age of deindustrialization and mass unemployment, established conceptions of work—as a full-time, long-term, predominantly male activity which provided a stable household income—seemed increasingly untenable. This 'future of work' debate not only prompted new interest in UBI, but also opened up the political space in which it could be seen as a radically emancipatory measure—a foundation for new ways of life and new forms of personal freedom.

The new wave of left-wing support for UBI began in the Claimants Unions movement which emerged out of late 1960s student activism and the early 1970s recession. The first Claimants Union, in Birmingham, was set up by law and social work students during the winter of 1968–9 as a way of mobilizing Supplementary Benefit claimants and helping them assert their welfare rights.[33] Six unions formed the National Federation of Claimants Unions (NFCU) in March 1970, and their numbers grew rapidly as unemployment

[30] J. E. Meade, *The Intelligent Radical's Guide to Economic Policy: The Mixed Economy* (1975), 61.

[31] Richard Layard, *More Jobs, Less Inflation: The Case for a Counter-Inflation Tax* (1982), 64.

[32] Sarah Stoller, 'Forging a Politics of Care: Theorizing Household Work in the British Women's Liberation Movement', *History Workshop Journal* 85 (2018), 95–119.

[33] Hilary Rose, 'Up against the Welfare State: The Claimant Unions', *Socialist Register* 10 (1973), 179–203, at 183–4.

rose during the Heath recession, reaching sixty-four by September 1971.[34] Although student activists played a leading role at the outset, the unions quickly developed an aggressively proletarian culture, restricting membership to claimants themselves and launching strident (and potentially libellous) broadsides at DHSS officials.[35] Representation in benefit offices and tribunals was the main focus, encapsulated in the injunction to 'Never meet the S.S. alone', but the NCFU also adopted a four-point national programme which set out more ambitious policy demands:

1. The right to an adequate income without means test for all people.
2. A free welfare state for all with its services controlled by the people who use it.
3. No secrets and the right to full information.
4. No distinction between so-called 'deserving' and 'undeserving'.[36]

The demand for a 'Guaranteed Minimum Income' remained a central theme of Claimants Union activism throughout the 1970s.[37]

The Claimants Unions' enthusiasm for a guaranteed income may have reflected the influence of North American welfare rights campaigners, but it also had distinctly British roots. For instance, the Barnsley activist Joe Kenyon—'a one-man Citizen's Advice Bureau, benefits consultant and agitator' who became one of the claimants' leading spokesmen—had been involved in the National Unemployed Workers' Movement during the 1930s.[38] Kenyon presented basic income as an expression of the old socialist demand for 'work or maintenance':

> I'm not saying that a man should want to work for its own sake; he should have the right to refuse and say 'This isn't the type of job I want.' But we haven't the technical ability to afford that as much as we should like to be

[34] 'National Federation of Claimants Unions', *Journal of the National Federation of Claimants Unions* 1 (Aug. 1970), 31; Rose, 'Up against the Welfare State', 193–4.

[35] For instance, Kentish Town Claimants Union portrayed the local social security officer as 'SS Kommandant P. Rat Boucher', complete with a cartoon of an SS officer wearing a Nazi armband: see Kentish Town Claimants Union, *S.S. Times* (Spring 1972).

[36] 'National Federation of Claimants Unions', 31.

[37] The movement faded away during the 1980s, and by this point the idea of basic income seems to have disappeared; indeed, the activist Bill More claimed in 1989 that 'very little of B[asic] I[ncome] R[esearch] G[roup]'s ideas have reached claimants'. See Modern Records Centre, University of Warwick, Trades Union Congress papers, MSS.292E/116/9, 'BIRG Study Group: BI and the Labour Market. Minutes of First Meeting, 5 Oct 89 at NEDO'.

[38] Austin Mitchell, *Calendar Boy* (Barnsley, 2014), 121.

> able to, and if a man's got to have a job to have his stake in the world, then he must be given a job. If he can't be given a job—and this is what we're arguing for—then he should be given his stake regardless.[39]

For others, such as the unmarried and deserted mothers who figured prominently in many unions, the demand for a guaranteed minimum seemed like a natural response to the 'intimidation', 'mystification', and intrusiveness of the benefit system.[40] Although the replacement of National Assistance with Supplementary Benefit in 1966 had given those outside the labour market a legal right to a means-tested minimum income, in practice officials continued to exercise considerable discretion in applying the DHSS's unpublished guidelines (known as the 'A' code). As Bill Jordan put it in his participant-study of the Newton Abbot union, claimants sought the dignity of 'a real living income... that would not have to be crawled and grovelled for at the feet of a bureaucratic overlord'.[41] The idea of a basic income also provided a conceptual basis for more focused social security campaigns—for instance, against the wage stop and the DHSS's treatment of cohabiting couples.

The Claimants Unions stood on the fringe of the wider New Left, as a loose federation of local groups with an anarchic internal culture which ultimately fizzled out during the 1980s. As Toru Yamamori has shown, however, claimants' activists also played a key role in building wider support for UBI through the Women's Liberation Movement.[42] The Birmingham Claimants Union sent a delegate to the first National Women's Liberation Conference at Ruskin College, Oxford, in 1970, and declared that 'Economic emancipation' required 'Personal Allowances' for adults as well as 'Universal Welfare facilities as of right' (such as crèches) and Family Allowances of at least £2 per child.[43] The Claimants Unions were well represented at subsequent conferences, and sought to tap into the debate stirred up by Selma James's controversial 'Wages for Housework' campaign.[44] The 1974 National Women's Liberation Conference in Edinburgh committed the movement to the 'fifth demand' of 'legal and financial independence for all women', and at the 1977 conference

[39] Tony Gould and Joe Kenyon, *Stories from the Dole Queue* (1972), 176.

[40] West London Claimants Union, 'The Claimants Unions', *Journal of the National Federation of Claimants Unions* 1 (Aug. 1970), 10–14, at 11.

[41] Bill Jordan, *Paupers: The Making of the New Claiming Class* (1973), 73.

[42] Toru Yamamori, 'A Feminist Way to Basic Income: Claimants Unions and Women's Liberation Movements in 1970s Britain', *Basic Income Studies* 9/1–2 (2014), 1–24.

[43] Birmingham Claimants Union, 'Female Liberation Statement', *Journal of the National Federation of Claimants Unions* 1 (Aug. 1970), 24.

[44] Selma James, *Women, the Unions and Work, or, What is not to be Done* (1972).

women claimants succeeded in carrying a resolution calling for a guaranteed annual income.[45] Yet UBI encountered stiff opposition from middle-class feminists such as Patricia Hewitt, who—like previous generations of egalitarian feminists—defined 'legal and financial independence' in terms of equal pay and access to the professions. Claimants' activists blamed class prejudice, but others saw basic income as a utopian idea which risked dividing the movement and hampering its pursuit of more realistic objectives. Suspicions of Trotskyist influence may have seemed alarmist, but were not wholly unjustified. The International Marxist Group appears to have been active in some Claimants Unions, and the NFCU's handbook *Women and Social Security* described UBI as a 'transitional demand' which was 'incompatible with a capitalist society based on private profit and competition'.[46]

Some middle-class radicals outside the feminist movement were more receptive to basic income. This was particularly true of the environmental groups which developed in the wake of the oil crisis, influenced by studies such as *The Limits to Growth* (1972) and E. F. Schumacher's *Small is Beautiful* (1973). The earliest predecessor of the Green Party, Tony Whittaker and Teddy Goldsmith's PEOPLE, included a 'National Income scheme' in *A Manifesto for Survival* (1974), declaring that 'every person resident in Britain is entitled to a basic subsistence income, without any qualification'.[47] The idea survived into the Ecology Party's *Manifesto for a Sustainable Society* (1978) and gained a wider audience through the 'Turning Point' conferences organized by James Robertson and Alison Pritchard. Where the Claimants Unions grounded basic income in a philosophy of welfare rights, environmentalists saw it as a way of helping citizens adapt to a post-industrial society with little or no economic growth. Robertson, for instance, argued that the hyper-modernism of the 1960s and early 1970s had been based on 'a dangerous masculine fantasy—exploitative, elitist and unsympathetic'—and that 'the line of social progress shaped by the technical and economic imperatives of the industrial age' had 'reached its limit'.[48] In a world of slow growth and rapid automation, 'full employment of the conventional kind' was gone for good, and the puritan work ethic should give way to a 'new paradigm of work' based on self-development and human satisfaction.[49] A guaranteed income would encourage job-sharing

45 This discussion is based on Yamamori, 'A Feminist Way to Basic Income'.

46 Rose, 'Up against the Welfare State', 199; Federation of Claimants Unions, *Women and Social Security*, revised edn (1982), 26 and inside back cover.

47 PEOPLE, *A Manifesto for Survival* (Coventry, 1974), 18.

48 James Robertson, *The Sane Alternative: A Choice of Futures*, revised edn (Ironbridge, 1983), 23.

49 Robertson, *The Sane Alternative*, 76, 74.

and allow individuals to combine 'irregular paid work or regular part-time employment' with informal work and greater self-sufficiency.[50]

Although much of the mainstream left sought to defend manufacturing employment and the male-breadwinner model, some Marxist and post-Marxist thinkers joined feminists and environmentalists in rethinking the nature of work. In particular, the Austro-French journalist André Gorz urged Marxists to grapple with the impact of technological change in *Adieux au Proletariat* (1980), suggesting that automation could bring about a 'liberation of time' and the 'abolition' (or at least radical reduction) of paid work.[51] Like the Claimants Unions in Britain, Gorz believed that deindustrialization was eroding Marx's proletariat and creating a 'non-class of non-workers' who jealously guarded their autonomy.[52] Gorz supported a guaranteed social income, but he warned that this was no guarantee of social equality or liberation unless it was set at an adequate level. He also argued that it should be combined with a right *and obligation* to carry out a minimum amount of socially necessary work:

> The guarantee of an income independent of a job will be emancipatory or repressive, from the Left or the Right, according to whether it opens up new spaces for individual and social activity or whether, on the contrary, it is only the social wage for compulsory passivity.[53]

The possibility of breaking the link between work and income quickly became a central theme of a burgeoning literature which Adrian Little has labelled 'post-industrial socialism'.[54] In particular, the Dutch economist Robert van der Veen and the Belgian political philosopher Philippe van Parijs suggested that UBI might be the best way to fulfil Marx's distributive objectives—'from each according to his ability, to each according to his needs'. Their 1986 article 'A Capitalist Road to Communism' provided the starting point for a vigorous debate on the economic and political feasibility of basic income.[55]

[50] Robertson, *The Sane Alternative*, 83–4.

[51] André Gorz, *Farewell to the Working Class: An Essay on Post-Industrial Socialism*, trans. Michael Sonenscher (1982), 1.

[52] Gorz, *Farewell to the Working Class*, 7, 10–11.

[53] André Gorz, *Paths to Paradise: On the Liberation from Work* (1985), 40, quoted in Adrian Little, *The Political Thought of André Gorz* (Abingdon, 1996), 182.

[54] Adrian Little, *Post-Industrial Socialism: Towards a New Politics of Welfare* (1998).

[55] Robert van der Veen and Philippe van Parijs, 'A Capitalist Road to Communism', *Theory and Society* 15/5 (1986), 635–55.

By the early 1980s, pessimistic analyses of the future of work were proliferating across the political spectrum. The management theorist Charles Handy convened a series of consultations on the subject at St George's House, Windsor Castle, and suggested that a basic income could help underpin a shift to 'portfolio lives' in a new kind of society which was 'less job-fixated in its values'.[56] The operations researcher Stephen Cook and the physicist Keith Roberts saw UBI as the best way to solve the unemployment problem, and Peter Ashby of the National Council for Voluntary Organisations thought it would 'provide major incentives for job creation' because employers 'would no longer be required to pay the subsistence component of income'.[57] This was the context in which a small group of activists founded the Basic Income Research Group in 1984, as we shall see in Chapter 9. For many others, however, the principle of full employment remained a touchstone. The Bishop of Liverpool, David Sheppard, for instance, discussed the possibility of 'paying everyone a basic social wage' in his 1984 Dimbleby Lecture, but concluded that 'we must do better than that' because there was still 'a strong connection between earning a wage and self-worth', especially among manual workers.[58] Likewise, Ruth Lister of CPAG thought the work ethic was 'deeply rooted' and that basic income risked shifting power 'to the state as paymaster, and away from Trade Unions as wage bargainers'. At best, UBI 'should be viewed as an ideal against which to measure our plans and progress'.[59]

Poverty research and the pursuit of integration: The Institute for Fiscal Studies, the Fowler reviews, and the 1986 Social Security Act

In the midst of these ideologically charged debates over work and welfare, academic research into poverty and inequality continued to advance. Alice O'Connor has shown that federal funding for poverty research in the United States rose from $3 million in 1965 to almost $200 million in 1980, 'most

[56] Charles Handy, *The Future of Work: A Guide to a Changing Society* (Oxford, 1984), ix; Charles Handy, *Myself and Other More Important Matters* (2006), 96–9.

[57] S. L. Cook, *Can a Social Wage Solve Unemployment?* (Birmingham, 1979); Keith Roberts, *Automation, Unemployment and the Distribution of Income* (Maastricht, 1982); Peter Ashby, *Social Security after Beveridge—What Next?* (1984), 17.

[58] David Sheppard, 'The Poverty that Imprisons the Spirit', *The Listener*, 19 Apr. 1984, 8–12, at 11.

[59] Trades Union Congress papers, MSS.292D/163.2/9, 'What Principles for the Future Benefits System?'—Notes of workshop at Action for Benefits conference, Sheffield, 14 Feb. 1987, by Martin Fitch, 18 Feb. 1987.

designated for the "applied" purposes of measurement, program evaluation, and policy analysis'.[60] Though Britain's 'poverty research industry' was smaller and more eclectic, it followed a similar trajectory of growth and professionalization. As late as 1972, David Donnison thought British social policy needed 'more economists' to evaluate 'the economic repercussions of social programmes' and explore 'the opportunities for attaining policy objectives through intelligent use of fiscal procedures and market mechanisms'; by the 1980s the application of microeconomic analysis to these questions was firmly established.[61] Applied work on public economics expanded rapidly under Tony Atkinson's influence, especially at Cambridge, Essex, and the LSE, where the Suntory-Toyota Centre (STICERD) hosted a major programme of econometric research on 'Taxation, Incentives and the Distribution of Income' funded by the Social Science Research Council (SSRC).[62] During the 1980s and 1990s, a team led by Atkinson and Holly Sutherland developed a series of tax-benefit models—including POLIMOD (a static microsimulation model), LIFEMOD (a dynamic model based on 4,000 simulated life histories), and the European Union-wide EUROMOD—in order to analyse the distributional effects of policy changes.[63] Over time, these researchers formed an increasingly coherent and influential epistemic community.

The social administration tradition established by Richard Titmuss and the close links between researchers and the 'poverty lobby' during the 1960s and 1970s meant that neoclassical approaches to poverty were never as dominant in Britain as in North America. For instance, Peter Townsend's landmark study of *Poverty in the United Kingdom*—begun in the mid-1960s though not published until 1979—used a survey of lifestyles and resources in 2,000 households to identify sixty different indicators of deprivation. In line with his sociological approach and socialist convictions, Townsend emphasized the systemic character of poverty and inequality and the need to adopt a broad definition of income which included assets, benefits in kind, and access to public services. Stewart Lansley and Joanna Mack built on this approach by asking the general public to identify minimum social needs in their 1983

[60] Alice O'Connor, *Poverty Knowledge: Social Science, Social Policy, and the Poor in Twentieth-Century U.S. History* (Princeton, 2001), 213.

[61] David Donnison, 'Research for Policy', *Minerva* 10/4 (1972), 519–36, at 533.

[62] A. B. Atkinson, M. A. King, and H. Sutherland, 'The Analysis of Personal Taxation and Social Security', *National Institute Economic Review* 106 (Nov. 1983), 63–74. The programme was initially based at University College London in 1978–9, but moved to the LSE with Atkinson in 1980.

[63] Gerry Redmond, Holly Sutherland, and Moira Wilson, *The Arithmetic of Tax and Social Security Reform: A User's Guide to Microsimulation Methods and Analysis* (Cambridge, 1998); Holly Sutherland and Francesco Figari, 'EUROMOD: The European Union Tax-Benefit Microsimulation Model', *International Journal of Microsimulation* 6/1 (2013), 4–26.

Breadline Britain survey.[64] Psychological and behavioural explanations of poverty also remained influential. The massive programme of research on 'transmitted deprivation' which Sir Keith Joseph launched in 1972—with £750,000 of funding from the SSRC and DHSS—focused on the intergenerational transmission of poverty within families and communities, and so pushed child development and parenting to the fore.[65] A third current of research focused on the problems of deprived communities, especially in the inner cities, and so adopted a spatial perspective, inspired by the US Community Action Program and its ethos of 'maximum feasible participation'.[66]

Although this eclectic mixture of approaches to poverty persisted into the 1980s, neoclassical techniques and assumptions became increasingly important over time. In particular, the Royal Commission on the Distribution of Income and Wealth established by the Labour government in 1974 compiled a large quantity of statistical data on distributional trends which encouraged policy-makers to focus on raising low incomes.[67] Background research undertaken for the Royal Commission analysed the income distribution in terms of the 'poverty gap' (the cost of lifting all households to Supplementary Benefit level) and 'target efficiency' (the share of transfer payments which went to the poor), and stressed how difficult it was to reduce wage differentials.[68] In similar vein, Richard Layard, David Piachaud, and Mark Stewart of the LSE Centre for Labour Economics argued that there was only a weak relationship between low pay and poverty, so the 'main weight' of egalitarian policy ought 'to be placed on the transfer and tax system'.[69] Indeed, if the government could find a way to 'make the transfer system automatic', then 'the living standards of the working poor, and also of the non-working poor, could within limits be set at whatever level society chose'.[70]

[64] David Gordon, 'The Scientific Measurement of Poverty: Recent Theoretical Advances', in *Researching Poverty*, edited by Jonathan Bradshaw and Roy Sainsbury (Aldershot, 2000), 37–58.

[65] John Welshman, *From Transmitted Deprivation to Social Exclusion: Policy, Poverty and Parenting* (Bristol, 2007).

[66] Pete Alcock, '"Maximum Feasible Understanding"—Lessons from Previous Wars on Poverty', *Social Policy and Society* 4/3 (2005), 321–9.

[67] Cmnd. 7175, *Royal Commission on the Distribution of Income & Wealth. Report No. 6: Lower Incomes* (1978).

[68] Wilfred Beckerman, 'The Impact of Income Maintenance Payments on Poverty in Britain, 1975', *Economic Journal* 89/354 (1979), 261–79; for 'target efficiency', see Royal Commission on the Distribution of Income and Wealth, *Selected Evidence Submitted to the Royal Commission for Report No. 6: Lower Incomes* (1978), 18–22, and TNA, AST44/78, 'An Integrated Benefit to Replace Family Income Supplement and Supplementary Benefit', Mar. 1977.

[69] Richard Layard, David Piachaud, and Mark Stewart, *The Causes of Poverty: Royal Commission on the Distribution of Income and Wealth Background Paper No. 5* (1978), 3. For a recent analysis of the Centre's influence, see Richard Jackman, 'Richard Layard (1934–)', in *The Palgrave Companion to LSE Economics*, edited by Robert A. Cord (Basingstoke, 2018), 743–63.

[70] Layard et al., *The Causes of Poverty*, 3, 134.

The neoclassical approach adopted by Layard et al. was echoed by the IFS, which had been founded by a group of City figures in 1969 to improve public and political understanding of tax policy. Under the direction of Dick Taverne (1970–9) and John Kay (1979–86), the IFS was committed to the conventional assumptions of neoclassical welfare economics, especially the principle that taxes should distort market behaviour as little as possible (known as 'fiscal neutrality').[71] Though politically independent, it tended to use microeconomic analysis to challenge left-wing orthodoxy—for instance, pointing out that high marginal tax rates did not raise much revenue—and to show how progressive goals could be met through the market system. The institute sponsored a committee chaired by James Meade to report on *The Structure and Reform of Direct Taxation* (1978) and followed this up with a research project on the distributional implications of fiscal policy, funded by the Gatsby Foundation, which simulated the effects of different tax-benefit systems on a computer model using data from the 1977 and 1980 Family Expenditure Surveys.[72] Meade (who remained interested in basic income) recommended either a 'New Beveridge' approach to social security or a kind of modified UBI, but the IFS viewed this with scepticism.[73] Taverne thought universalism was 'absurdly wasteful' because it spent 'limited resources' on 'people who do not need benefits at all', and after Kay took over in 1979 the institute threw its weight firmly behind the case for selectivity.[74]

Although redistribution was out of fashion among politicians and much of the British public in the 1980s, then, the tax and benefit systems nevertheless remained central to debates over poverty. For all its limitations, income poverty was much easier to measure than an index of multiple deprivation, and critics of the Thatcher government regularly pointed to the growing numbers of households living below the Supplementary Benefit scales—or, increasingly, below the European Commission's relative poverty line of 50 per cent of median income.[75] The Thatcher government, in turn, sought to make

[71] Dick Taverne, *Against the Tide: Politics and Beyond. A Memoir* (2014), 201–20; J. A. Kay, 'Tax Reform in Context: A Strategy for the 1990s', *Fiscal Studies* 7/4 (Nov. 1986), 1–17.

[72] Dick Taverne, 'Looking Back', *Fiscal Studies* 4/3 (Nov. 1983), 1–6; TNA, T470/49, 'Structure of Income Taxation and Income Support: Recent Work by the Institute for Fiscal Studies', by J. R. King, 2 Apr. 1982 (copy).

[73] J. E. Meade, *The Structure and Reform of Direct Taxation. Report of a Committee Chaired by Professor J. E. Meade* (1978). Meade was sympathetic to basic income in principle, but Atkinson and others seem to have persuaded him that a New Beveridge approach was more realistic in the short and medium term: see correspondence in British Library of Political and Economic Science (BLPES), London, Meade papers, 6/9.

[74] Taverne, 'Looking Back', 5.

[75] A. B. Atkinson, 'Poverty, Statistics and Progress in Europe', in A. B. Atkinson, *Incomes and the Welfare State: Essays on Britain and Europe* (Cambridge, 1995), 64–77.

such calculations more difficult by abolishing the Royal Commission on the Distribution of Income and Wealth, scaling back the production of statistics, and replacing the Low Income Families Tables with a new series on Households Below Average Income.[76] At the same time, the revival of neoclassical labour economics also helped turn the spotlight onto social security. Whereas tackling poverty through the wage system threatened to exacerbate inflation and unemployment, tackling poverty through cash benefits promised to help depoliticize the pay bargaining process.

Alongside the influence of poverty research, the rationalization of the tax and benefit systems remained a live political issue during the 1980s for a number of practical reasons. Although the Thatcher government's reforms sharpened incentives for the unemployed to take paid work, rising National Insurance contributions and growing reliance on means-tested benefits exacerbated the 'poverty trap'. Atkinson and his colleagues estimated that more than 500,000 low-income families faced marginal tax rates of 60 per cent or more, including 40,000 families with marginal rates above 100 per cent, and Treasury officials admitted that the position had worsened since the late 1970s.[77] The Supplementary Benefit and Housing Benefit caseloads grew sharply as a result of the early 1980s recession (as Figure 6.2 shows), and

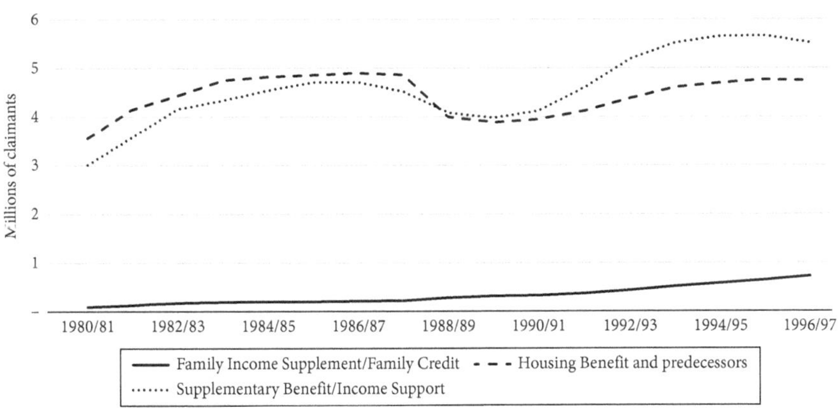

Figure 6.2. Means-tested benefit caseloads (all claimant types), 1979/80–1996/7

[76] Felix Römer, 'Inequality Statistics and Knowledge Production under Thatcher', paper delivered at the Contemporary British History Seminar, Institute of Historical Research, 3 Oct. 2018.

[77] *Parliamentary Papers*, 1982–3, HC 20-II, 'Treasury and Civil Service Select Committee: The Structure of Personal Income Taxation and Income Support. Appendices', Appendix 2, 3–30, at 5, and HC 20-I, 'The Structure of Personal Income Taxation and Income Support. Minutes of Evidence', 242. Atkinson's figures were based on the 1980 Family Expenditure Survey.

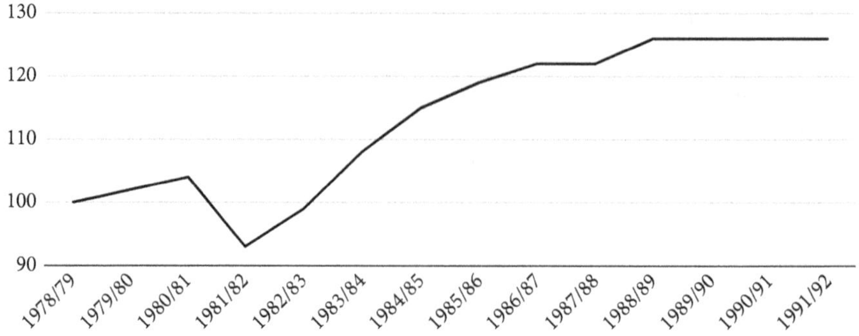

Figure 6.3. Real value of single person's tax allowances, 1978/9–1991/2 (1978/9=100)
Source: Author's chart based on Gavyn Davies et al., *Tax Options for 1992: The Green Budget* (1992), 31: <https://www.ifs.org.uk/comms/comm28.pdf>

though the poverty trap could have been eased by raising the tax threshold, the Treasury was unable to find the money for this until economic growth returned in the middle of the decade (Figure 6.3).

The Conservatives' early attempts to simplify means-tested benefits also proved counter-productive. Thatcher's first Secretary of State for Social Services, Patrick Jenkin, inherited the findings of the Callaghan government's Supplementary Benefits Review, which had sought to adapt Supplementary Benefit to its new 'mass role' by codifying citizens' entitlement in published regulations.[78] Jenkin took up the proposals as a way of reducing civil service numbers, but the attempt to implement them on a cost-neutral basis proved highly embarrassing. Instead of reducing complexity, the 1980 Supplementary Benefit reforms produced 'a horrendous mass of regulations' which neither claimants nor benefit officers could understand, and failed to contain the growth of 'single payments' for furniture and other exceptional needs.[79] Even DHSS officials privately acknowledged that the new system was 'not workable'.[80] Likewise, the decision to create a single system of Housing Benefit for both private and council tenants in 1982 was logical in principle, but ministers' reluctance to increase spending or impose losses meant that the

[78] Department of Health and Social Security, *Social Assistance: A Review of the Supplementary Benefits Scheme in Great Britain* (1978), 5.

[79] John Mesher, 'The 1980 Social Security Legislation: The Great Welfare State Chainsaw Massacre?', *British Journal of Law and Society* 8 (1981), 119–27, at 123; Richard Berthoud, *The Reform of Supplementary Benefit* (1984); Geoffrey Beltram, *Testing the Safety Net: An Enquiry into the Reformed Supplementary Benefit Scheme* (1984).

[80] TNA, BN13/278, 'Yet Another Supplementary Benefit Scheme', by Mrs A. E. Bowtell, Jan. 1983.

unification was only superficial, and local authority housing departments struggled to implement the changes.[81]

One important response to the growing complexity of the interface between tax and benefits came from the Treasury and Civil Service Select Committee, which held an inquiry into 'The Structure of Personal Income Taxation and Income Support' in 1982–3. The former Labour minister Michael Meacher (who chaired the inquiry) was joined by several enthusiasts for tax-benefit reform, such as the Liberal MP Richard Wainwright and the Tory backbencher Ralph Howell, whilst Tony Atkinson and John Kay served as specialist advisers and put their computer models at the committee's disposal.[82] Though Meacher was unable to build a consensus around policy recommendations, the committee's work drew attention to the idiosyncrasies of the status quo and stressed the need for much closer coordination between the Treasury, DHSS, and Inland Revenue.[83] The Select Committee hearings also provided an opportunity for outside groups to canvass proposals for reform. CPAG, for instance, called on the government to phase out the married man's tax allowance to pay for increases in National Insurance and Child Benefit, whilst Sir Brandon Rhys-Williams and his research assistant Hermione Parker worked up a plan for a 'Basic Income Guarantee' which Meacher recommended for further study.[84]

Alongside Rhys-Williams's UBI scheme, the most ambitious plans for tax-benefit integration came from the IFS and the newly formed Social Democratic Party. Leading SDP figures took a close interest in social security from the start, partly because they were determined to show that the Labour left's politics of planning and public ownership was not the only way of achieving social justice. Tax-benefit reform also fitted neatly with the new party's technocratic ethos, since the economists James Meade, Mervyn King, and Richard Layard and the IFS researchers Nick Morris and Evan Davis were

[81] Peter Kemp, 'The Reform of Housing Benefit', *Social Policy & Administration* 21/2 (1987), 171–86.

[82] A. B. Atkinson, 'Taxation and Social Security Reform: Reflections on Advising a House of Commons Select Committee', *Policy and Politics* 12 (1984), 107–18. A sceptical Treasury official saw the inquiry as 'a benefit day for Messrs Howell and Meacher': TNA, T470/49, E. P. Kemp to Mr Norgrove, 'TCSC Enquiry into Income Taxation and Support', 16 Feb. 1982 (copy).

[83] *Parliamentary Papers*, 1982–3, HC 386, 'Third Special Report from the Treasury and Civil Service Select Committee: The Structure of Personal Income Taxation and Income Support, Together with the Proceedings of the Committee relating to the Report from the Sub-Committee', 11 May 1983.

[84] *Parliamentary Papers*, 1982–3, HC 20-I, 'The Structure of Personal Income Taxation and Income Support. Minutes of Evidence', 61–119, 420–59, and HC 386, 'Third Special Report from the Treasury and Civil Service Select Committee: The Structure of Personal Income Taxation and Income Support', xcii.

all involved in developing SDP policy.[85] A working group chaired by Dick Taverne developed plans for a single means-tested Basic Benefit for all claimants, whether in and out of work—an idea which echoed Milton Friedman's NIT and had been floated within Whitehall during the late 1970s.[86] Basic Benefit would effectively merge Supplementary Benefit, Housing Benefit, and FIS into a single payment, withdrawn at a smooth taper of 30 per cent for childless households and 45 per cent for families with children. The scheme would be financed by £4.5 billion of tax increases, including the abolition of the married man's allowance.[87]

The SDP struggled to win support for this selectivist approach during the 1983 general election, partly because it implied a substantial redistribution away from many of the middle-class voters whom the party hoped to win from the Conservatives. Left-wing critics complained that the Basic Benefit would merely 'top up the poor', whilst the SDP's Alliance partners in the Liberal Party favoured a universalist tax credit scheme—netting off a basic income against tax liability—on the lines suggested by Juliet Rhys-Williams and Arthur Cockfield.[88] Despite these obstacles, Andrew Dilnot, John Kay, and Nick Morris of the IFS persisted with the idea and devised an elaborate plan for non-refundable tax and benefit credits, which they published in July 1984 under the title *The Reform of Social Security*. The IFS report was the most sophisticated attempt to date to develop a workable NIT which could replace the whole social security system. Like the SDP scheme, it saw a massive expansion of selectivity as the best way of helping poorer families and relied on computerization to take the stigma out of means-testing. By replacing Child Benefit, the state pension, the married man's allowance, and the additional tax allowance for pensioners with income-related benefit credits, Dilnot, Kay, and Morris proposed to redistribute £4.45bn to low-income households, lifting about 900,000 families above their poverty line (which they set at 120 per cent of Supplementary Benefit).[89] Tony Atkinson complained that the discussion of practical issues (such as the risks of assessing

[85] Albert Sloman Library, University of Essex, Social Democratic Party papers (SDP papers), box 14, 'Working Party on Poverty, Taxation and Social Security', agreed list of members for Policy Committee meeting, 26 Oct. 1981; box 16, 'Policy Committee 12th July 1983. Discussion Paper on Policy Tasks for the SDP', by Wendy Buckley, 7 July 1983 (copy); and box 43F, 'Minutes of the Joint Meeting of the SDP Working Party on Taxation and Social Security and Representatives of the Liberal Party Held on 15th July 1986', by Josephine Hayes.

[86] TNA, AST44/78, RB(77)10, 'An Income Support Scheme for People in and out of Work', March 1977, and M. J. A. Partridge to Mr Crocker, 'Relationship between SB and FIS', 17 Feb. 1978 (copy).

[87] SDP papers, box 16, SDP White Paper 11, 'Attacking Poverty', Mar. 1983.

[88] David Piachaud, 'The SDP's Plan to Top up the Poor', *New Society*, 11 Nov. 1982, 56; Philip Vince, *To Each According: Liberal Tax Credit Proposals* (1979).

[89] A. W. Dilnot, J. A. Kay, and C. N. Morris, *The Reform of Social Security* (Oxford, 1984), 113–43.

benefit entitlement on an annual basis) was superficial, but Samuel Brittan of the *Financial Times* hailed the book as 'an important breakthrough... in moving towards an integrated tax benefit system'.[90]

Some Conservatives and neoliberals also continued to be attracted to integration as a way of dealing with the poverty trap or easing the transition towards a private market in welfare. Ralph Howell, for instance, was keen to replace National Insurance with NIT (though he insisted that there should be sanctions for those who refused to work), whilst the former Foreign Secretary Francis Pym came out in favour of UBI, and other Tory backbenchers continued to hanker after Cockfield's Tax Credit Scheme.[91] When Hugh Bochel and Peter Taylor-Gooby interviewed Conservative MPs towards the end of the 1983 Parliament, 39 per cent of their respondents identified tax-benefit integration as the most important priority in the social security field.[92]

Attitudes towards tax-benefit reform also varied within the Thatcher government. Sir Geoffrey Howe was sympathetic to integration in principle and believed that 'a second Beveridge study' was needed to explore options for 'the long-term interaction of the Social Security and Personal Tax systems'.[93] Not only was Thatcher herself suspicious, however, but the Inland Revenue persuaded ministers that they should postpone structural changes to the tax system until after it had completed the long-delayed computerization of PAYE.[94] In practice, this ruled out a Tax Credit Scheme or any substantial form of integration until the late 1980s. After Nigel Lawson became Chancellor in 1983, the notion that tax and benefits were fundamentally different hardened into Treasury dogma: the 1986 Green Paper on *The Reform of Personal Taxation*, for instance, insisted that it was 'philosophically important not to blur the distinction between reward for effort and support for need, between what individuals gain for themselves and what they receive from the State'.[95] By contrast, the Secretary of State for Social Services, Norman Fowler,

[90] TNA, T530/111, 'IFS Reform of Social Security—Publication Seminar at Regent Palace Hotel, 11 July', note for the record by Stephanie Holmans, 19 July 1984 (copy); Samuel Brittan, 'A One Nation Tax System', *Financial Times*, 12 July 1984, 23.

[91] *Parliamentary Papers*, 1982–3, HC 386, 'Third Special Report from the Treasury and Civil Service Select Committee: The Structure of Personal Income Taxation and Income Support', xciv–ci; *The Times*, 16 Oct. 1985, 16; CPA, CRD4/4/200, minutes of first meeting of Tax and Social Security Policy Group, 24 Nov. 1982, and report, 31 Mar. 1983.

[92] Hugh M. Bochel, *Parliament and Welfare Policy* (Aldershot, 1992), 56. Tax-benefit integration was also mentioned as the top priority by 12% of the Labour MPs and 75% of the Liberal and Social Democrat MPs interviewed.

[93] TNA, T366/754, Sir Geoffrey Howe to Patrick Jenkin, 'Social Security and Personal Tax Systems', 11 Dec. 1980 (copy).

[94] TNA, T366/754, J. H. Gracey to Mr Green and the Chancellor of the Exchequer, '"Why Work" and Associated Social Security and Tax Matters', 17 Nov. 1980 (copy).

[95] Cmnd. 9756, *The Reform of Personal Taxation* (1986), 31.

was keen to keep the door open to integration and believed that tax and benefit reforms should be considered together.[96] Some DHSS officials were also interested in integration. By the 1980s the department's institutional commitment to National Insurance had largely given way to a world-weary pragmatism, reinforced by the promotion of former National Assistance Board officials such as Sir Kenneth Stowe (permanent secretary from 1981 to 1987) and Ann Bowtell (under secretary for Supplementary Benefit in the early 1980s and later permanent secretary herself).[97] If integration could make means-testing easier and more palatable to claimants, then it might well serve the DHSS's interests.

These differences came to a head in the social security reviews which Fowler held in 1984–5, billed as 'the most substantial examination of the social security system since the Beveridge report'.[98] Much of the controversy inside and outside government focused on Fowler's plan to abolish the State Earnings-Related Pension Scheme (SERPS) and liberalize private pensions, but three of the four reviews dealt with means-tested benefits. Thatcher and Lawson were determined to curb the growth of Housing Benefit and Supplementary Benefit spending, which had doubled in real terms between 1980/1 and 1983/4, whilst the DHSS hoped to deal with the administrative problems thrown up by the 1980 and 1982 reforms. Fowler persuaded Thatcher that cuts would be more politically acceptable as part of 'a carefully-considered medium term strategy', though his efforts to include tax policy in the exercise were rebuffed by Lawson.[99] The 1986 Social Security Act which emerged from the reviews replaced Supplementary Benefit with a much simpler system of Income Support, backed up by emergency grants and loans from a discretionary (and highly controversial) Social Fund. Housing Benefit was also simplified and tapered away more quickly as income rose, with a view to saving £500 million a year and cutting the caseload by about a quarter.[100] Fowler then used some of the savings from these changes—together with a freeze in Child Benefit—to improve support for working families with children, replacing FIS with a much larger Family Credit.

[96] TNA, PREM19/1638, Norman Fowler to Nigel Lawson, 'Study of Tax and Social Security Systems', 4 Mar. 1985 (copy).

[97] Private information.

[98] TNA, BN13/278, 'Statement: Social Security Policy Reviews, Monday 2 April 1984'.

[99] TNA, PREM19/1320, Principal Private Secretary to the Prime Minister to Steve Godber, 26 July 1983 (copy); Norman Fowler, *Ministers Decide* (1991), 209–10.

[100] TNA, BN13/301, Note 1A, 'Summary of Proposals as Agreed in MISC 111', Apr. 1985.

The Fowler reviews provoked strenuous criticism from the poverty lobby and other observers on grounds of both process and policy: the review teams were tightly controlled (and in some cases led) by DHSS ministers, their reports were processed in secrecy, and the 1986 Act marked the final abandonment of Beveridge's hope that National Insurance could eventually remove the need for means-tested benefits.[101] Indeed, the Thatcher government adamantly refused to consider whether the rates of benefit were adequate to meet citizens' basic needs. Yet more sympathetic critics, including the IFS, recognized that the reviews also created a more rational and comprehensible structure of income support which would make future integration with the tax system much easier.[102] Evan Davis, for instance, thought the result was 'a first step on an SDP path':

> For the first time, a British government acknowledged the means tested benefits as a central and worthy part of the social security system and as something other than a regrettable and undesirable necessity. For the first time, some rationality was introduced into the structure of means tested benefits and the interactions between the benefits considered in a unified way. Although very mean, the structure of the government's plans... [is] quite defensible.[103]

The scale of redistribution from middle-income households to the poor was much smaller than the SDP and IFS had envisaged, but the influence of their proposals was clear.[104] The 1986 Act aligned the rules and rates of Family Credit, Housing Benefit, and Income Support, and applied the tapers sequentially on net income so that cumulative withdrawal rates could never exceed 100 per cent. Fowler also hoped to administer Family Credit through employers, and told the Social Security Select Committee that paying benefits via PAYE coding was 'the logical next step along the road'.[105]

[101] Ruth Lister, 'The Politics of Social Security: An Assessment of the Fowler Review', in *The Economics of Social Security*, edited by Andrew Dilnot and Ian Walker (Oxford, 1989), 200–23.

[102] E. H. Davis, A. W. Dilnot, and J. A. Kay, 'The Social Security Green Paper', *Fiscal Studies* 6/3 (Aug. 1985), 1–8.

[103] SDP papers, box 43F, 'The Tax and Social Security Proposals of the SDP', by Evan Davis, Mar. 1986.

[104] The IFS proposals were taken particularly seriously in the Central Review Unit led by Ann Bowtell: see TNA, BN133/75, Mrs A. E. Bowtell to Mr Lerner, Mr Stern, and Mr Thompson, 'Handling Tax/Benefit Issues', 16 July 1984, and 'Schemes for Reforming the Tax/Benefit System: Implications for Social Security Reviews', by Central Review Unit, July 1984.

[105] Quoted in Davis et al., 'The Social Security Green Paper', 7.

Reluctant redistributors: The 1979–97 Conservative governments and the growth of the 'transfer state'

The economic legacy of Margaret Thatcher and John Major's governments is often seen through the lens of deindustrialization, globalization, and public-sector retrenchment—the creation of a liberal market economy based on financial services and low-wage service-sector employment. Despite Mrs Thatcher's deep suspicion of welfare benefits, however, the eighteen years of Conservative rule were also a formative period in the development of the UK's transfer state, as growing market inequalities and a succession of policy changes increased the scale of fiscal redistribution. This was particularly true on the benefit side, where social security benefits for working-age households grew from 3.4 per cent of GDP in 1978/9 to 4.9 per cent in 1996/7, and more than doubled in real terms. Spending on Supplementary Benefit (Income Support from 1988), Housing Benefit, and disability benefits rose especially sharply, as Figure 6.4 shows. Alongside this quantitative growth, the 1980s and 1990s also witnessed a number of qualitative shifts in working-age social security: the decline of contributory National Insurance in favour of means-tested benefits, the move 'from highly discretionary decision-marking... to a much more "rules-based" approach', and the pursuit of 'an "active" welfare state' focused on supporting those in work.[106]

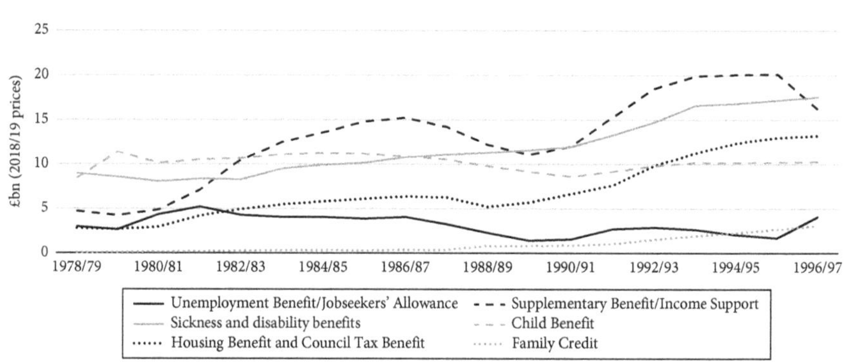

Figure 6.4. Spending on major social security benefits for working-age adults and children, 1978/9–1996/7 (real terms, £bn, 2018/19 prices)

[106] Paul Gray and Nicholas Timmins, *Reforming Working-Age Social Security: Lessons for Policy Makers* (2018), 2–3.

Margaret Thatcher was deeply frustrated by the continued growth of 'welfare dependency'—one area in which her attempt to 'roll back' the state was thwarted by economic difficulties, demographic trends, and political pressures for higher spending.[107] Yet the growth of the social security budget was at least partly a function of the Conservative government's own policies. This is most obviously true of the monetarist shock therapy which Howe applied to the economy after the 1979 election, which accelerated the decline of manufacturing employment, dramatically intensified the social impact of the early 1980s recession, and turned many older industrial workers into long-term benefit claimants.[108] However, the Conservatives' attempt to liberate market forces also increased the burden on the social security system in subtler ways. Many of the Thatcher government's fiscal and economic policies—such as increases in VAT and National Insurance contributions, the abolition of rent controls, and the reduction of transport and fuel subsidies—imposed direct and highly tangible costs on lower-income households. Shrewder ministers recognized that it was easier to implement these regressive reforms if the losers were protected by a means-tested safety net. As Fowler pointed out to Thatcher during the review process, much of the increase in DHSS spending reflected the fact that 'the social security system is having to pick up other people's bills'.[109] Even Thatcher found it politically useful to rebut charges that the poor had grown poorer by pointing to improvements in means-tested benefits.[110] Though she disliked redistribution in principle, it nevertheless formed an important part of her government's statecraft in practice. Promising to '[f]ully protect the sick, the elderly and the poor' helped deflect Labour criticisms of rising inequality and defend the Conservatives' flank against the SDP–Liberal Alliance.[111]

The residual influence of RML on Conservative policy was particularly evident in housing and family support. In housing, the Thatcher and Major governments sought not only to impose free-market principles on a heavily subsidized and highly regulated sector, but also to reshape the electoral landscape by turning council tenants into Conservative-supporting

[107] Margaret Thatcher, *The Path to Power* (1995), 543–8.

[108] Christina Beatty and Steve Fothergill, 'The Impact on Welfare and Public Finances of Job Loss in Industrial Britain', *Regional Studies, Regional Science* 4/1 (2017), 161–80.

[109] TNA, BN13/302, Norman Fowler to Prime Minister, 'Social Security Review', 1 Feb. 1985 (copy).

[110] For instance, TV interview for Panorama, BBC1, 25 Jan. 1988, accessed 12 July 2018, available at <https://www.margaretthatcher.org/document/107028>, and HC Deb., sixth series, vol. 178, 23 Oct. 1990, cols 186–7.

[111] Thatcher papers, THCR1/15/9, Ferdinand Mount to Prime Minister, 'DHSS Seminar', 14 Sept. 1983.

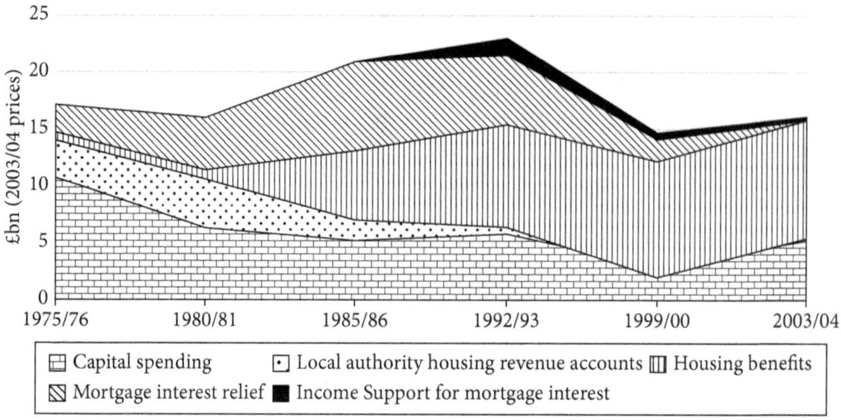

Figure 6.5. UK government spending on housing, 1975/6–2003/4 (real terms, £bn, 2003/4 prices)

Source: Based on table 6.1 in John Hills, *Ends and Means: The Future Roles of Social Housing in England* (2007), 56.

owner-occupiers. Alongside the introduction of the 'Right to Buy' under the 1980 Housing Act, ministers cut the Exchequer subsidy to local authorities' housing revenue accounts and so pushed council rents up sharply, whilst the 1988 Housing Act deregulated new private lettings in an attempt to revive the private rental market.[112] Taking the social and private sectors together, average weekly housing costs for renters trebled in real terms between 1979 and 1997.[113] The cumulative effect of these changes—and the deregulation of mortgage finance—was rapid growth in home ownership, a collapse in construction by local authorities, and the residualization of social housing.

Savings on 'supply-side' housing subsidies, however, were more than offset by the rising cost of Housing Benefit, as Figure 6.5 shows. Since the mid-1950s, Conservative governments had encouraged councils to focus rent subsidies on poorer tenants; Heath had created a national system of rebates and allowances, and the Thatcher government pushed this strategy further after 1979.[114] As Norman Fowler put it, the creation of Housing Benefit in 1982 reflected the belief that it was best for housing subsidies to be treated as a 'form of income

[112] Alan Murie, 'The Housing Legacy of Thatcherism', in *The Legacy of Thatcherism: Assessing and Exploring Thatcherite Social and Economic Policies*, edited by Stephen Farrall and Colin Hay (Oxford, 2014), 143–66; Peter Malpass, *Reshaping Housing Policy: Subsidies, Rents and Residualisation* (1990), 136–60.

[113] See Chris Belfield, Daniel Chandler, and Robert Joyce, *Housing: Trends in Prices, Costs and Tenure*, Institute for Fiscal Studies Briefing Note BN161 (2015), 12, fig. 2.4a.

[114] Belfield et al., *Housing*, 89–113.

support' which could be 'considered in the context of the social security benefit structure and developments as a whole'.[115] The housing minister in John Major's government, Sir George Young, justified the 1988 Act in similar terms:

> Housing benefit will underpin market rents—we have made that absolutely clear. If people cannot afford to pay that market rent, housing benefit will take the strain ...[116]

Though Conservative ministers were surprised by the scale of the increase in Housing Benefit spending during the late 1980s and early 1990s, officials had long warned that deregulation of private rents would add to the benefit bill.[117] In other words, it was always clear that the government's housing policies implied a larger role for social security.

In-work benefits also eased the Thatcher government's labour-market reforms, as Chris Grover has recently argued.[118] A 1982 report on unemployment by the Central Policy Review Staff pointed out that the 'aim of increasing real wage flexibility' was 'likely to run into conflict with trade unions and often with the public's sense of fairness'.[119] In-work benefits could help defuse opposition to wage liberalization by 'breaking the linkage in the public mind between low pay and family poverty':

> An effective mechanism for subsidising the earnings of low income families could encourage the acceptance of low paid jobs, reduce upward wage pressures for family men, increase incentives to seek work and facilitate the growth of part-time employment.[120]

The case for expanding support for working families was strengthened by DHSS research which found that the distribution of low incomes had changed sharply as a result of unemployment and changes in family structure. Between 1971 and 1982 the number of working-age households in the bottom quintile of the equivalized income distribution rose from 2.5 million to 4 million, whilst the number of pensioner households in this group fell from 2.6 million

[115] HC Deb., sixth series, vol. 13, 23 Nov. 1981, col. 651.
[116] HC Deb., sixth series, vol. 184, 30 Jan. 1991, col. 940.
[117] Thatcher papers, THCR1/15/12, Christopher Monckton to Prime Minister, 'A Farewell Report', 25 June 1986.
[118] Chris Grover, *Social Security and Wage Poverty: Historical and Policy Aspects of Supplementing Wages in Britain and Beyond* (Basingstoke, 2016), 108–26.
[119] TNA, CAB184/610, 'Central Policy Review Staff: Report on Unemployment', Sept. 1982, 41.
[120] TNA, CAB184/610, 'Central Policy Review Staff: Report on Unemployment', 46, 80.

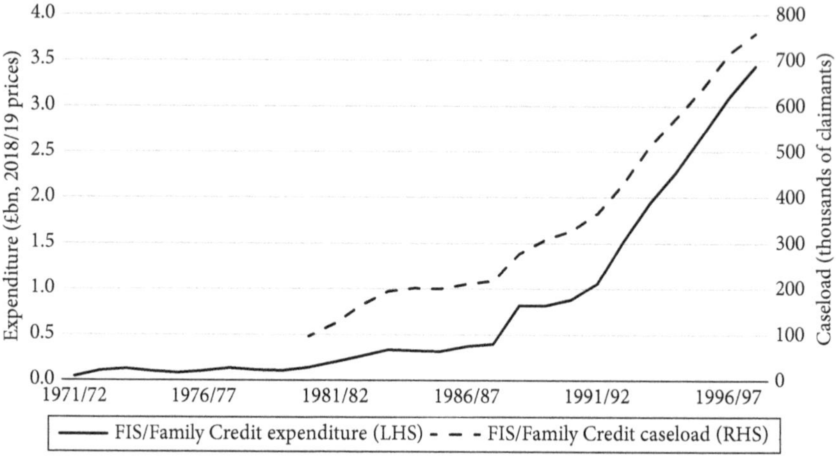

Figure 6.6. The growth of in-work family income support, 1971/2–1997/8

to 1.4 million.[121] Norman Fowler concluded that 'low income families with children, in and out of work, are the group who are now most in need' and persuaded a sceptical Thatcher to redirect resources towards them.[122] FIS was too rudimentary to provide adequate support, since take-up was low, those working fewer than thirty hours a week could not claim it, and it gave disproportionate help to one-child families; Family Credit was designed to solve these problems.[123] Once in place, the benefit grew rapidly, as Figure 6.6 shows. The Major government reduced the qualifying threshold from 24 to 16 hours of work a week in 1992, and Kenneth Clarke expanded the scheme further in his 1993 and 1994 budgets by introducing a bonus for full-time workers and a disregard for childcare costs.[124] Clarke also piloted an Earnings Top-Up scheme for single people and childless couples as a way of smoothing the transition from unemployment into paid work.

The Conservative governments of 1979–97 thus presided over a significant shift away from the Beveridgean vision of contributory National Insurance towards a system of means-tested income support which complemented the neoliberal restructuring of the labour and housing markets. The working-age

[121] TNA, BN13/291, WP1, 'Low Incomes and Social Security', n.d. [1984].

[122] TNA, BN13/302, Norman Fowler to Prime Minister, 'Social Security Review'; for Thatcher's scepticism about Family Credit, see PREM19/1638, David Willetts to Prime Minister, 'Benefits for Children and Young People', 28 Dec. 1984, with annotations by Thatcher.

[123] TNA, BN133/6, 'Review of Benefits for Children and Young People. Note of Sixth Meeting, 2 July 1984', July 1984.

[124] Dorian R. Woods, *Family Policy in Transformation: US and UK Policies* (Basingstoke, 2012), 96–101.

benefit system which emerged from the Fowler reviews bore the imprint of twenty years of NIT campaigning: Patrick Minford thought it was 'close to a negative income tax', and some DHSS officials hoped that it would evolve into 'a single integrated means-tested benefit'.[125] As a form of guaranteed income, however, the system created by the 1986 Act also had some serious limitations. Firstly, Income Support, Housing Benefit, and Family Credit remained structurally distinct both from each other and from PAYE, so the traditional problems of stigma and low take-up persisted. Fowler's hopes of paying Family Credit through employers as an addition to the pay packet were dashed by an alliance of business groups (which objected to the administrative costs) and women's organizations (which insisted on retaining payment to the mother), and claimants continued to face transitional problems in moving from Income Support to Family Credit when they entered paid work.

Secondly, the dramatic expansion in total benefit spending was driven almost entirely by increases in caseload and housing costs, rather than benefit rates. As critics such as Ruth Lister pointed out, the Fowler reviews were constrained by the Treasury's determination to cut costs, and the government made no meaningful attempt to ensure that benefit rates were high enough to lift people out of poverty.[126] Indeed, the extra spending Fowler secured for Family Credit was more than offset by cuts in the generosity of Income Support and Housing Benefit, so that many low-paid workers were worse off overall as a result of the 1986 Act.[127] The replacement of single payments for exceptional needs with discretionary loans and grants from the Social Fund also signalled the end of the principle that out-of-work benefits ought to be adequate for subsistence.

Finally, the extension of transfer payments to working households was increasingly tied up with the 'activation' agenda, which made benefits conditional on paid work or other behavioural choices. From Dennis Milner to the IFS, most twentieth-century enthusiasts for a guaranteed income had been attracted to the idea by its simplicity and unconditionality: indeed, even Milton Friedman was reluctant to impose work requirements on claimants.[128] During

[125] Patrick Minford, 'The Poverty Trap after the Fowler Reviews', in *Improving Incentives for the Low-Paid*, edited by Alex Bowen and Ken Mayhew (Basingstoke, 1990), 121–38, at 122; TNA, BN133/76, Martin Lerner to Mr Walmsley and Mr Thompson, 'Moving towards a Single Integrated Means-Tested Benefit', 31 July 1984.

[126] Lister, 'The Politics of Social Security', 206.

[127] Andrew Dilnot and Steven Webb, 'The 1988 Social Security Reforms', *Fiscal Studies* 9/3 (Aug. 1988), 26–53.

[128] Hoover Institution Archives, Stanford University, Friedman papers, 201.6, Milton Friedman to David Dennis, 17 Feb. 1970 (copy).

the late 1980s and 1990s, however, both 'new paternalist' writers such as Charles Murray and labour economists such as Richard Layard encouraged governments to use sanctions to improve work incentives. The introduction of compulsory 'Restart' interviews in 1988 and the replacement of Unemployment Benefit by Jobseekers' Allowance in 1996 heralded the emergence of increasingly stringent forms of conditionality.[129] This combination of activation and redistribution would become firmly entrenched under New Labour.

[129] Desmond King, *Actively Seeking Work? The Politics of Unemployment and Welfare Reform in the United States and Great Britain* (Chicago, 1995); Julia Griggs, Andrew Hammond, and Robert Walker, 'Activation for All: Welfare Reform in the United Kingdom, 1995–2009', in *Activation or Workfare? Governance and the Neo-Liberal Convergence*, edited by Ivar Lodomel and Amilcar Moreira (Oxford, 2014), 73–100.

7

New Labour's Tax Credits, 1997–2010

The thirteen years of Labour government between 1997 and 2010 may come to be seen by future historians as the zenith of the British transfer state. In other western countries—such as the Netherlands, Sweden, Finland, and Canada—the increase in fiscal redistribution which took place during the 1980s and early 1990s recessions went into reverse during the decade that followed; in the UK, by contrast, the expansion of transfer payments to working-age households was sustained and deepened. Inspired by the Earned Income Tax Credit in the United States, Gordon Brown replaced Family Credit, the married couples' tax allowance, and the child element of Income Support with a complex system of income-related tax credits, which formed a central part of New Labour's strategy for 'making work pay' and eliminating child poverty. Brown also began the process of uniting tax and benefit administration under HM Revenue and Customs to break down what Ed Miliband called the 'Berlin Wall' between the two systems.[1] Brown has claimed in his memoirs that this was 'as near to a revolution in our tax-and-benefit system as we have seen in Britain'.[2] For the first time, the Treasury came to see itself as a social welfare agency, using tax credits and other instruments to achieve explicit distributional objectives. In other words, the idea that the 'tax state' should also be a 'transfer state' finally gained acceptance within government.

The central role which transfer payments came to play in New Labour's policy agenda could not easily have been predicted when the government took office in 1997. The party's 1992–4 Commission on Social Justice argued that a basic income was politically impossible in 'a society with a strong work ethic', and insisted that paid work was 'the best pathway out of poverty'.[3] Tony Blair echoed Labour's traditional suspicion of in-work benefits such as Family Credit in the run-up to the 1997 general election, and accused John Major's

[1] Ed Miliband, Speech to Inland Revenue Senior Managers' Conference, 5 July 2001.

[2] Gordon Brown, *My Life, our Times* (2017), 140.

[3] Commission on Social Justice, *Social Justice: Strategies for National Renewal. The Report of the Commission on Social Justice* (1994), 262, 151.

Transfer State: The Idea of a Guaranteed Income and the Politics of Redistribution in Modern Britain. Peter Sloman, Oxford University Press (2019). © Peter Sloman. DOI: 10.1093/oso/9780198813262.001.0001

government of running up 'the bills of economic failure'.[4] 'Is it not wrong', he asked in his first conference speech as leader,

> that the taxpayer ends up paying more than a billion pounds on benefits to subsidise poverty pay? . . . [T]he people on benefits need and deserve better—not more benefits, but help in getting off benefits, because welfare should be about opportunity and security in a changing world . . . We will put welfare to work—a nation at work not on benefit. That is our pledge.[5]

In similar vein, Gordon Brown declared that New Labour would focus on 'tackling the root causes of poverty and inequality' instead of simply 'us[ing] the tax and benefit system to compensate people for their poverty'.[6]

New Labour's welfare reform programme has been the subject of an extensive literature by political economists and social policy scholars, much of which has taken Blair and Brown's activation rhetoric at face value. Desmond King and Mark Wickham-Jones, for instance, have set tax credits in the context of the government's wider 'welfare-to-work' agenda, which tightened eligibility for out-of-work benefits under the influence of US 'workfare' schemes.[7] Wage supplements for low-paid workers provided a 'carrot' which complemented the 'stick' of work requirements and benefit sanctions. On the other hand, more sympathetic social policy analysts such as Jane Waldfogel and Dorian Woods have pointed out that tax credits can also be seen as a form of 'social investment' in human capital, which complemented progressive initiatives such as Sure Start children's centres and the Education Maintenance Allowances.[8] As Michael Adler and Jane Millar have argued, it was this distinctive combination of activation and large-scale redistribution that set

[4] Quoted in Philip Gould, *The Unfinished Revolution: How the Modernisers Saved the Labour Party* (1998), 222.

[5] Tony Blair, Leader's Speech, Labour Party conference, 4 Oct. 1994, accessed 2 Mar. 2017, available at <http://www.britishpoliticalspeech.org/speech-archive.htm?speech=200>.

[6] Quoted in Martin Powell, 'Introduction', in *New Labour, New Welfare State? The 'Third Way' in British Social Policy*, edited by Martin Powell (Bristol, 1999), 1–27, at 17.

[7] Desmond King and Mark Wickham-Jones, 'Bridging the Atlantic: The Democratic (Party) Origins of Welfare to Work', in *New Labour, New Welfare State? The 'Third Way' in British Social Policy*, edited by Martin Powell (Bristol, 1999), 257–80. On the activation agenda, see also David Dolowitz, *Learning from America: Policy Transfer and the Development of the British Workfare State* (Brighton, 1998); Jochen Clasen and Daniel Clegg, 'Adapting Labour Market Policy to a Transformed Employment Structure: The Politics of "Triple Integration"', in *The Politics of the New Welfare State*, edited by Giuliano Bonoli and David Natali (Oxford, 2012), 135–57; and Julia Griggs, Andrew Hammond, and Robert Walker, 'Activation for All: Welfare Reform in the United Kingdom, 1995–2009', in *Activation or Workfare? Governance and the Neo-Liberal Convergence*, edited by Ivar Lodomel and Amilcar Moreira (Oxford, 2014), 73–100.

[8] Jane Waldfogel, *Britain's War on Poverty* (New York, 2010); Dorian R. Woods, *Family Policy in Transformation: US and UK Policies* (Basingstoke, 2012).

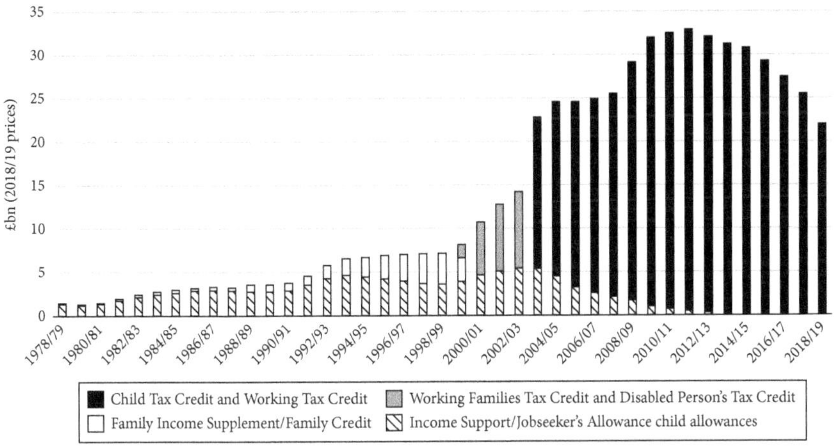

Figure 7.1. Expenditure on tax credits and predecessor benefits, 1978/9–2018/19 (real terms, £bn, 2018/19 prices)

Source: Author's calculations based on Department for Work and Pensions, 'Benefit Expenditure and Caseload Tables', Autumn Budget 2018: <https://www.gov.uk/government/publications/benefit-expenditure-and-caseload-tables-2018>

tax credits apart from traditional social assistance policies.[9] Gordon Brown used the widely supported goals of 'making work pay' and reducing child poverty to justify a major expansion of income support for the working poor, which in turn helped legitimize the growth of low-paid service-sector jobs and spread the benefits of globalization. By the time Labour left office in 2010, tax credits spending was running at about £30 billion a year (Figure 7.1)—as much as the budgets of the Department for Transport, the Home Office, and the Department of Energy and Climate Change put together. Decomposition analysis by Richard Dickens suggests that the reduction in child poverty between 1997/8 and 2008/9 was driven almost entirely by increases in tax credits and other benefits. By contrast, changes in wages and work patterns made a negligible or even a negative contribution.[10]

[9] Michael Adler, 'Combining Welfare-to-Work Measures with Tax Credits: A New Hybrid Approach to Social Security in the United Kingdom', *International Social Security Review* 57/2 (2004), 87–106; Jane Millar, 'Making Work Pay, Making Tax Credits Work: An Assessment with Specific Reference to Lone-Parent Employment', *International Social Security Review* 61/2 (2008), 21–38.

[10] Relative child poverty (before housing costs) fell from 26.2% in 1997/8 to 21.1% in 2008/9. Dickens's analysis suggests that demographics and changes to wages and work patterns pushed child poverty upwards (by 2.1 and 0.8 percentage points), but these effects were more than offset by changes in government benefits (−7.9 percentage points) and taxes (−0.1 percentage points): Richard Dickens, 'Child Poverty in Britain: Past Lessons and Future Prospects', *National Institute Economic Review*, 218 (2011), R7–R19, at R13, table 3.

This chapter examines the origins and development of the tax credits system and sets it in the context of the wider history of guaranteed income proposals. Drawing on archival sources and interviews as well as secondary literature, it highlights the centrality of transfer payments to New Labour's political economy. Under Blair and Brown's leadership, Labour finally broke with the post-war employment model—based on high wages for skilled male industrial workers—and focused on relieving poverty and inequality outside the labour market, as revisionist social democrats such as James Meade, Richard Layard, and Julian Le Grand had recommended since the 1970s. Instead of trying to reverse the decline of manufacturing industry and collective bargaining, the Blair and Brown governments used tax credits and public-sector employment to help cushion the impact of economic change on the traditional Labour heartlands of post-industrial Britain: for instance, Bradford residents received over £350 million of tax credits in 2009/10 alone.[11] John Myles and Paul Pierson have highlighted the value of Negative Income Tax schemes for achieving retrenchment by stealth, since they were 'opaque to the general public' and suited to incremental change, but Brown was more interested in the scope for low-key redistribution.[12] In budget after budget, Brown set aside resources for improving tax credits in an attempt to meet the government's child poverty targets. With the benefit of hindsight, however, the experience also revealed the limits of technocratic redistribution as a social and political strategy. Public confidence in tax credits was undermined by high-profile administrative difficulties, and both opposition MPs and Blairite ministers became increasingly suspicious of the cost and complexity of the system.

Reinventing Labour's social policy, 1987–1997

For most of the eighteen years of Conservative government after 1979, the Labour Party's approach to achieving social justice remained rooted in the assumptions of the late 1960s and 1970s. 'For more than a decade', Nicholas Timmins has argued, 'Labour simply stopped thinking constructively about the welfare state. It was, after all, their welfare state . . . [and] they were damn

[11] Ken Coutts, Andrew Glyn, and Bob Rowthorn, 'Structural Change under New Labour', *Cambridge Journal of Economics* 31/6 (2007), 845–61; author's calculations from HM Revenue and Customs, 'Child and Working Tax Credits Statistics: Finalised Annual Awards. Geographical Analyses, 2009/10', 2011, accessed 3 Oct. 2017, available at <http://webarchive.nationalarchives.gov.uk/20121106034103/http://www.hmrc.gov.uk/stats/personal-tax-credits/cwtc-geog-final-awards-may11.xls>.

[12] John Myles and Paul Pierson, 'Friedman's Revenge: The Reform of "Liberal" Welfare States in Canada and the United States', *Politics & Society* 25/4 (1997), 443–72.

well going to defend it, warts and all . . .'[13] Left-leaning poverty campaigners and social scientists such as Peter Townsend, Ruth Lister, Chris Pond, and Tony Atkinson figured prominently in the party's social policy committees and pressed for a 'back-to-Beveridge' strategy of higher wages and higher universal benefits.[14] CPAG and other 'poverty lobby' groups worked hard to build links with the unions and formed a united front against the Fowler reviews under the banner of 'Action for Benefits'.[15] Likewise, Hugh Bochel and Peter Taylor-Gooby's survey of MPs' attitudes to social security in 1986–7 found that more than nine out of ten Labour MPs wanted to reduce means-testing.[16]

Although Neil Kinnock challenged his party's conventional wisdom in many areas, social policy was not one of them. Indeed, as Labour downplayed and then dropped its commitments to nationalization and unilateral nuclear disarmament, the welfare state became increasingly central to the party's radical identity: pledges to raise Child Benefit and the basic state pension thus featured prominently in the 1987 and 1992 election campaigns. The one new element in the party's social strategy was the adoption of a National Minimum Wage, which the trade unions came to support as the Thatcher government's reforms eroded their bargaining power.[17] The NMW dovetailed neatly with Kinnock's desire to emphasize the linkage between economic efficiency and social justice, and with the vision of 'supply-side socialism' developed by his economic adviser John Eatwell.[18] During the 1992 election campaign, however, both prongs of this anti-poverty strategy caused major problems. On the social security side, the need to pay for improvements in

[13] Nicholas Timmins, *The Five Giants: A Biography of the Welfare State*, 3rd edn (2017), 366.

[14] For instance, Townsend and Lister were members of the party's Social Policy Sub-Committee during the late 1970s and early 1980s; Townsend, Pond, and Atkinson were all members of the Joint Policy Committee on Poverty, Social Security, and Taxation in 1984–6; and Atkinson, Lister, and Pond were advisers to the Economic Equality Policy Review Group in 1987–91. See British Library of Political and Economic Science (BLPES), London, Abel-Smith papers, 7/11–13 (Labour Party Social Policy Sub-Committee, 1975–9); Modern Records Centre, University of Warwick, Trades Union Congress papers, MSS.292D/160.31/4 (Labour Party Social Policy Sub-Committee, 1981–5); Labour History Archive and Study Centre, Manchester, Labour Party Archive (LPA), LP/RD/63/18 (Joint Policy Committee on Poverty, Social Security, and Taxation, 1986) and LP/RD/41/1 (Economic Equality Policy Review Working Group, 1987–90).

[15] Action for Benefits was launched in 1984 and led by the socialist lawyer Tess Gill. It ran alongside a TUC campaign against the Fowler reviews and a separate Union Coalition for Social Security funded by the civil service unions.

[16] Hugh M. Bochel, *Parliament and Welfare Policy* (Aldershot, 1992), 58.

[17] Sheila Blackburn, *A Fair Day's Wage for a Fair Day's Work? Sweated Labour and the Origins of Minimum Wage Legislation in Britain* (Aldershot, 2007), 189–95.

[18] Noel Thompson, *Political Economy and the Labour Party: The Economics of Democratic Socialism, 1884–2005*, 2nd edn (2006), 235–66; Martin Westlake (with Ian St John), *Kinnock: The Biography* (2001), 433–4.

universal benefits forced Shadow Chancellor John Smith to propose tax rises on upper- and middle-income voters—mainly by removing the upper earnings limit on National Insurance contributions—and left the party vulnerable to Conservative warnings of a 'tax bombshell' if Labour took office.[19] On the labour-market side, the proposal for a minimum wage of at least £3.40 a week came under sustained assault from Tory ministers and some economists. Michael Howard's claim that the wage floor would cost up to two million jobs was clearly exaggerated, but more sober assessments from Stephen Bazen of the University of Kent and Walter Eltis of the National Economic Development Office gave credence to the notion that jobs would be lost.[20]

The bruising 1992 election defeat served as a catalyst for more sustained rethinking. One of John Smith's first decisions as Labour leader was to set up an independent Commission on Social Justice to undertake a comprehensive review of the welfare state, based at the centre-left Institute for Public Policy Research (IPPR) and chaired by Sir Gordon Borrie, a former Director-General of Fair Trading. As Catherine Haddon has shown, the Commission's underlying purpose was to 'bury' the spending commitments Smith had made in his ill-fated 'shadow budget'.[21] Although it was unclear how far Smith himself was willing to move away from universalism, younger Shadow Cabinet members such as Tony Blair and Gordon Brown thought it was essential to sacrifice some of the party's sacred cows. Blair and Brown were impressed by the research carried out for Giles Radice's pamphlet *Southern Discomfort*, which found that many floating voters in the south of England feared a Labour government would be soft on 'scroungers', and by the success of Bill Clinton's pledge to 'end welfare as we know it' in the 1992 US presidential election, which suggested that a symbolic repositioning in this sensitive area could transform perceptions of the centre-left.[22] Brown floated the idea of a 'New Deal' for the unemployed at the 1992 party conference, and after Blair took over as leader in 1994 this became the centrepiece of New Labour's social policy, signalling that benefit claimants could no longer expect 'something for

[19] Mark Stuart, *John Smith: A Life* (2005), 195–222.

[20] Conservative Party, 'Michael Howard Warns Labour Minimum Wage Fiasco "Could Double Unemployment"' (press release, 22 Apr. 1991); Stephen Bazen, 'On the Employment Effects of Introducing a National Minimum Wage', *British Journal of Industrial Relations* 28/2 (1990), 215–26; Peter Norman, 'The Poor Cousin of Poverty Fighters', *Financial Times*, 25 June 1991, 16.

[21] Catherine Haddon, 'Making Policy in Opposition: The Commission on Social Justice, 1992–1994', Institute for Government report, Dec. 2012, available at <https://www.instituteforgovernment.org.uk/publications/making-policy-opposition-commission-social-justice-1992–1994>; *The Guardian*, 19 Dec. 1992, 20.

[22] Giles Radice, *Southern Discomfort* (1992); Patricia Hewitt and Philip Gould, 'Learning from Success—Labour and Clinton's New Democrats', *Renewal* 1/1 (Jan. 1993), 45–51.

nothing'. The New Deal built on the 'Restart' interviews and sanctions regime introduced by the Conservatives: men and women under 25 who had been out of work for more than six months would be expected to take a work placement or return to education. The cost of getting 250,000 young people 'off benefit and into work' would be met by a £5 billion windfall tax on the privatized utilities—the only major way in which Blair and Brown pledged to depart from the Conservatives' tax and spending plans.

Welfare-to-work policies appealed to the New Labour leadership for a number of reasons. On a political level, the New Deal represented a symbolic break with the 'tax and spend' politics of the Wilson and Callaghan governments, and lent shape to Blair's communitarian rhetoric of reciprocity and mutual obligation.[23] Attempts by the tabloid press to stoke moral panics around crime, delinquency, and teenage pregnancy during the mid-1990s gave this theme particular resonance. On an economic level, the focus on activation reflected the ascendancy of structural interpretations of unemployment and the wider loss of faith in Keynesian demand management. Richard Layard and Stephen Nickell's emphasis on 'making work pay' chimed with the emerging literature on 'hysteresis', which suggested that the demoralization and skills mismatches created by long-term unemployment could become self-perpetuating.[24] Ed Balls worked on hysteresis at Harvard with Larry Summers and Lawrence Katz before joining the *Financial Times* as a leader-writer in 1990 and then becoming Brown's chief economic adviser.[25]

International agencies played a major role in spreading 'work-first' labour-market policies, most famously through the 1994 OECD Jobs Study, and Blair and Brown took an active interest in policy transfer. The New Deal was partly inspired by Australia's Jobs, Education and Training (JET) programme, which provided job search advice, training, and childcare to help single parents move into paid work.[26] Labour's shadow Treasury team also developed close links with US Democrats and sought to learn from the Clinton administration's efforts at welfare reform. Clinton's approach was particularly significant, since it combined a sharp tightening of out-of-work benefit rules (eventually

[23] Mark Bevir, *New Labour: A Critique* (Abingdon, 2005), 54–82.

[24] William Mitchell and Joan Muysken, *Full Employment Abandoned: Shifting Sands and Policy Failures* (Cheltenham, 2008), 92–102. For a critical analysis of this literature, see David Webster, 'Long-Term Unemployment, the Invention of "Hysteresis" and the Misdiagnosis of Structural Unemployment in the UK', *Cambridge Journal of Economics* 29/6 (2005), 975–95.

[25] Edward Balls, Lawrence F. Katz, and Lawrence H. Summers, 'Britain Divided: Hysteresis and the Regional Dimension of Britain's Unemployment Problem' (unpublished working paper, 1991).

[26] Carol Johnson and Fran Tonkiss, 'The Third Influence: The Blair Government and Australian Labor', *Policy & Politics* 30/1 (2002), 5–18.

enacted in the Personal Responsibility and Work Opportunity Reconciliation Act 1996) with more generous support for working families through the Earned Income Tax Credit. The EITC had been introduced in 1975 as a politically acceptable alternative to President Nixon's Family Assistance Plan, and was expanded in 1986, 1990, and 1993 with bipartisan support.[27] Unlike conventional NIT schemes, EITC can only be claimed by working households, and its value initially increases as earnings rise before levelling off and then phasing out: it thus provides a 'bonus' for low-paid workers. American families claim EITC through their end-of-year tax return, and receive it either as a cheque through the post or as a fully refundable credit against the next year's taxes. Balls was familiar with the policy from his work at Harvard, and British policy-makers were struck by the ease with which Clinton had managed to expand it: 'somehow he was able to persuade the public that it was fine to deliver financial support from the state if you linked it to work and delivered it as a tax credit through the tax system'.[28]

The Commission on Social Justice also looked at more radical options for tax-benefit reform, including the possibility of a basic income. As we shall see in Chapter 9, UBI had attracted significant support during the late 1980s and early 1990s as a way of easing the transition to a service economy and strengthening the bonds of social citizenship. Some members of the Commission, such as David Marquand, Ruth Lister, and Tony Atkinson, were sympathetic to the idea, but it sat uncomfortably with the implicit mandate from the Labour leadership—to reassure voters that a Labour government could control welfare costs.[29] The IPPR's deputy director, Patricia Hewitt, believed universal benefits were intrinsically wasteful and thought basic income could 'deepe[n]... the gendered division of labour' by discouraging married women from seeking paid work.[30] Sir Gordon Borrie was also impressed by 'a widespread feeling in the community that the contributory system has a genuine moral strength'.[31] Hewitt and Borrie's caution was reinforced by an expert study commissioned from Andersen Consulting, which emphasized the technical difficulties of integration and warned that basic income risked encouraging labour-market

27 V. Joseph Hotz and John Karl Scholz, 'The Earned Income Tax Credit', in *Means-Tested Transfer Programs in the United States*, edited by Robert A. Moffitt (Chicago, 2003), 141–97.

28 Interview with Tony Orhnial, 12 Oct. 2016.

29 BLPES, Meade papers, 9/114, David Marquand to James Meade, 7 July 1995; interview with Baroness Lister, 18 July 2018.

30 Alastair Campbell, *The Alastair Campbell Diaries*, vol. 1: *Prelude to Power 1994–1997* (2010), 70; Patricia Hewitt, 'Social Justice in a Global Economy?', in *Citizenship Today: The Contemporary Relevance of T. H. Marshall*, edited by Martin Bulmer and Anthony M. Rees (1996), 249–68, at 259.

31 Susan Raven, 'Which Way Forward? Susan Raven talks to Sir Gordon Borrie', *Citizen's Income Newsletter* 17, Jan. 1994, 13–14, at 13.

withdrawal.[32] The Commission's report acknowledged that it 'would be unwise... to rule out a move to Citizen's Income' if attitudes to work changed in future, and commended Tony Atkinson's idea of a 'participation income' based on a broad test of social contribution, but its main recommendations focused on modernizing social insurance and smoothing the transition from welfare to work.[33]

Up to the 1997 general election, it was never entirely clear whether Labour planned to follow Bill Clinton's lead in expanding income support for low-paid workers. The Borrie Commission criticized the Conservative government for 'offering a permanent subsidy to low wages' through Family Credit, and stressed that its long-term goal was 'to ensure that people earn enough to meet their needs without relying on means-tested benefits'.[34] Ed Balls, on the other hand, pointed out that there was a serious mismatch between unemployed men's ambitions for manual work paying a traditional breadwinner wage and the kind of service-sector jobs that were becoming available. Since reskilling former industrial workers would take 'years rather than months', Balls argued that the government should 'subsidise unskilled employment in the private sector, closing the gap between male wage aspirations (or income from the illegal sector) and what the market will pay'.[35] The 1997 Labour manifesto took refuge in generalities—promising only to 'examine the interaction of the tax and benefit systems so that they can be streamlined and modernised'—but behind the scenes Brown appears to have been set on adopting EITC. He told Paddy Ashdown in December 1996 that he intended to 'adopt the classic Liberal agenda, in favour of competition, in favour of enterprise and centred around equality of opportunity', and that wage supplements had an important part to play:

> I have looked at tax credits. I see there are flaws. But ultimately I think that is the best way forward... If you go to America, you will find that there are millions and millions of people who receive, in one way or another, a top-up for low wages. But in this country topping-up wages is regarded as unacceptable and only for the few. We must change that.[36]

[32] David Clinton, Michael Yates, and Dharminder Kang, *Integrating Taxes and Benefits?* (1994).

[33] Commission on Social Justice, *Social Justice*, 263, 264–5.

[34] Commission on Social Justice, *Social Justice*, 180, 226.

[35] Edward Balls, 'Danger: Men not at Work. Unemployment and Non-Employment in the UK and Beyond', in Edward Balls and Paul Gregg, *Work and Welfare: Tackling the Jobs Deficit* (1993), 1–30, at 27, 29.

[36] Paddy Ashdown, *The Ashdown Diaries*, vol. 1 (2000), 485–6.

Pre-election consultations meant that Treasury and Inland Revenue officials were also well aware of Brown's interest in EITC, and were able to produce detailed notes on policy options within two weeks of Labour's election victory.[37]

Gordon Brown's Treasury and Working Families Tax Credit, 1997–1999

In government, tax-benefit reform quickly became one of Gordon Brown's top priorities. Like the New Deal, tax credits promised to increase the labour supply and reduce the NAIRU, so the government could deliver lower unemployment and faster economic growth 'without the acceleration in average earnings which accompanied similar previous improvements'.[38] This shift in the unemployment–inflation trade-off was essential if New Labour was to fulfil its promise that there would be 'no return to boom and bust'. On an institutional level, the introduction of tax credits also reflected a shift in the Treasury's focus away from macroeconomic 'steering' towards microeconomic policy—a change which had begun under the Conservatives but was pushed further after 1997 as a result of Bank of England independence and Brown's interest in post-neoclassical endogenous growth theory. As Nicholas Deakin and Richard Parry have pointed out, Brown was 'the first Chancellor since Lawson to have a clear sense of a wider role for the Treasury in setting priorities for the government as a whole'.[39] Together with his two special advisers, Ed Balls and Ed Miliband, Brown transformed the Treasury's internal culture, bypassing the civil service hierarchy and expanding the use of '[e]vidence-based microeconomic and distributional analysis'.[40] The Chancellor's former principal private secretary, Nicholas Macpherson, took charge of a new Work Incentives and Poverty Analysis Unit which worked closely with tax policy specialists such as Tony Orhnial at the Inland Revenue. The undignified standoff between Harriet Harman and Frank Field at the Department of Social

[37] Interview with Tony Orhnial; Sir Terence Burns, 'Preparing the Treasury for the Election', *Public Policy and Administration* 13/1 (1998), 1–12.

[38] Ed Balls, Joe Grice, and Gus O'Donnell, *Microeconomic Reform in Britain: Delivering Opportunities for All* (Basingstoke, 2004), 194.

[39] Nicholas Deakin and Richard Parry, *The Treasury and Social Policy: The Contest for Control of Welfare Strategy* (Basingstoke, 2000), 211.

[40] Damian McBride, *Power Trip: A Decade of Policy, Plots and Spin* (2013), 23–6; interview with Tony Orhnial; *Parliamentary Papers*, 1999–2000, HC 492-I, 'Treasury Select Committee: HM Treasury. Minutes of Evidence, 11 May 2000', Memorandum by HM Treasury, paragraph 3.2.

Security (DSS) in 1997–8 also made it easier for Brown to establish the Treasury as the lead actor in social security policy.[41]

The introduction of tax credits can be seen as an audacious attempt at 'fast policy' transfer, using the perceived success of EITC in the USA to push through rapid change in the British welfare system.[42] One of Brown's first acts after the 1997 election was to commission the chief executive of Barclays Bank, Martin Taylor, to review the relationship between tax and benefits with support from an interdepartmental task force—the first of many businessmen he would enlist to provide political cover for new policies. Brown specifically asked Taylor to consider the advantages of a tax credit based on EITC, and the Harvard economist Jeffrey Liebman submitted a paper to the task force which extolled the virtues of the American model. According to Liebman, EITC was cheaper to operate than conventional means-tested benefits, had reduced income inequality, and had helped many lone parents into paid work.[43] These claims were strongly contested, however, by Robert Walker of Loughborough University and Michael Wiseman of the University of Wisconsin, who argued that EITC was beset by problems of fraud and error and only worked because American families were already used to filing end-of-year tax returns.[44] Indeed, the Social Security Select Committee found little support for EITC among British social policy experts. Ruth Lister pointed out that basing EITC eligibility on total household income, as in the United States, would be a 'highly retrograde step'—moving back towards the joint taxation of husband and wife which had been abandoned, after a long feminist campaign, in 1990.[45] In many households, paying EITC to the main earner through the pay packet would also shift the benefit from mother to father. As a result, the Low Pay Unit, CPAG, and TUC all called on the government to retain Family Credit and focus its energies on improving Child Benefit.[46]

Taylor recognized the force of many of these objections, and his March 1998 report acknowledged that the EITC could not be grafted wholesale onto the

[41] Andrew Connell, *Welfare Policy under New Labour: The Politics of Social Security Reform* (2011), 143–57; private information.

[42] The parallels with Michael Bloomberg's attempt to copy Mexico's Oportunidades programme in New York City in 2006–10 are particularly striking: see Jamie Peck and Nick Theodore, *Fast Policy: Experimental Statecraft at the Thresholds of Neoliberalism* (Minneapolis, 2015), 45–84.

[43] Jeffrey Liebman, *Lessons about Tax-Benefit Integration from the US Earned Income Tax Credit Experience* (York, 1997).

[44] Robert Walker and Michael Wiseman, 'The Possibility of a British Earned Income Tax Credit', *Fiscal Studies* 18/4 (1997), 401–25.

[45] *Parliamentary Papers*, 1997–8, HC 283, 'Social Security Committee. First Report. Taxes and Benefits: An Interim Report', 19 Nov. 1997, 105–13, at 108.

[46] HC 283, 'Social Security Committee. First Report. Taxes and Benefits: An Interim Report', 73–82, 82–95, and 178–88.

British tax system. The task force also rejected NIT and UBI in principle, on the grounds that they would 'fail to distinguish sufficiently between participation in work and being out of work'.[47] Taylor did believe, however, that 'the expansion of relatively low-paid jobs' was socially 'beneficial' and that turning Family Credit into a tax credit would help make these jobs more attractive:

> A tax credit will associate the payment in the recipient's mind with the fact of working, a potentially valuable psychological change. I believe that a payment through the tax system, associated with the recipient's work, is likely to prove more acceptable to society at large. And the establishment of a tax credit system is likely to come in useful in future as a broader delivery mechanism, eventually allowing closer integration between the benefit system and conventional income tax.[48]

Taylor thus returned to Norman Fowler's original conception of Family Credit: a benefit awarded for six months on the basis of a separate application, but paid as an addition to the wage packet of the main earner. Treasury officials argued that the purse-to-wallet transfer was a less serious issue than it would have been in the 1970s or 1980s, because the latest figures suggested that six out of ten Family Credit claimants were either single parents or couples where the woman was the main breadwinner.[49] Likewise, the government believed that the introduction of the NMW in April 1999 would reduce the risk of exploitation by employers.[50]

Brown announced plans for a Working Families Tax Credit (WFTC) in his 1998 budget speech and presented it as part of a larger package of measures to make work pay, alongside a 10p starting rate of income tax, an above-inflation increase in Child Benefit for the first child, and changes to the structure of National Insurance Contributions.[51] The extra £1.35 billion a year set aside for WFTC meant that the taper was lower than Family Credit (at 55 per cent of net income rather than 70 per cent) and support for childcare costs was more generous, so the new benefit extended further up the income scale. Moreover, since WFTC would be added to the pay packet and administered by the Inland

[47] HM Treasury, *The Modernisation of Britain's Tax and Benefit System—Number Two. Work Incentives. A Report by Martin Taylor* (1998), 10.

[48] HM Treasury, *The Modernisation of Britain's Tax and Benefit System—Number Two*, 8.

[49] *Parliamentary Papers*, 1997–8, HC 423, 'Social Security Committee. Tax and Benefits. Minutes of Evidence, Wednesday 10 December 1997', 4.

[50] HC 423, 'Social Security Committee. Tax and Benefits. Minutes of Evidence, Wednesday 10 December 1997', 14.

[51] HC Deb., sixth series, vol. 308, 17 Mar. 1998, cols 1097–112.

Revenue, Brown was able to portray it as a 'tax cut for hundreds of thousands of working families on low incomes'.[52] Together with the NMW—initially set at the modest level of £3.60 an hour—WFTC would provide a 'guaranteed income' of £180 a week for parents in full-time work, and would cancel out any income tax liability until the household earned £220.[53]

The political advantages of treating WFTC as a tax credit were clear enough: avoiding the 'stigma and dependence' which many claimants (and voters) associated with means-tested benefits, and instead exploiting what Miliband called 'the badge of citizenship conferred by the tax system'.[54] At the same time, Brown's vision of an integrated tax and transfer agency represented a significant challenge to existing Whitehall cultures, both in the DSS (which lost responsibility for family support) and in the Inland Revenue (which gained it). As we have seen in Chapters 3 and 4, the Revenue was an instinctively cautious department which prized its reputation for fairness and efficiency in tax collection, and when the Blair government took office it was still dealing with the disruption caused by the introduction of income tax self-assessment in 1996.[55] Despite these tensions, Brown and his colleagues—especially Ed Miliband and the Financial Secretary to the Treasury (later Paymaster-General) Dawn Primarolo—leaned heavily on the Revenue to introduce WFTC by October 1999, with payment via employers following in April 2000. The crudeness of the policy design meant that implementation was relatively straightforward, with the Family Credit Unit (based in Preston and Blackpool) transferred from the DSS to the Revenue. The Federation of Small Businesses protested loudly about the administrative burden which WFTC placed on small firms, but otherwise the change provoked few objections.[56] The CBI, for instance, welcomed WFTC 'as an alternative to a minimum wage set too high' and an effective 'means of targeting additional resources towards workers at the bottom of the income scale'.[57]

In policy terms, WFTC was at best a mixed success. Although its increased generosity meant that the number of families eligible for it rose sharply, the take-up rate was initially lower than for Family Credit—despite an expensive

[52] HC Deb., sixth series, vol. 308, 17 Mar. 1998, col. 1104.
[53] HC Deb., sixth series, vol. 308, 17 Mar. 1998, col. 1105.
[54] Miliband, Speech to Inland Revenue Senior Managers' Conference.
[55] Interview with Tony Orhnial.
[56] Modern Records Centre, University of Warwick, Confederation of British Industry papers, MSS.200/C/2008/Box 84, 'Consultative Committee on Employer/Employee Issues. Second Meeting of the Working Group on Working Families Tax Credit. Held on 8 June 1998 at 10 Maltravers Street'.
[57] Confederation of British Industry papers, MSS.200/C/2008/Box 84, 'The Working Family Tax Credit. CBI Evidence to the House of Commons Social Security Committee Tax and Benefits Enquiry', Sept. 1998.

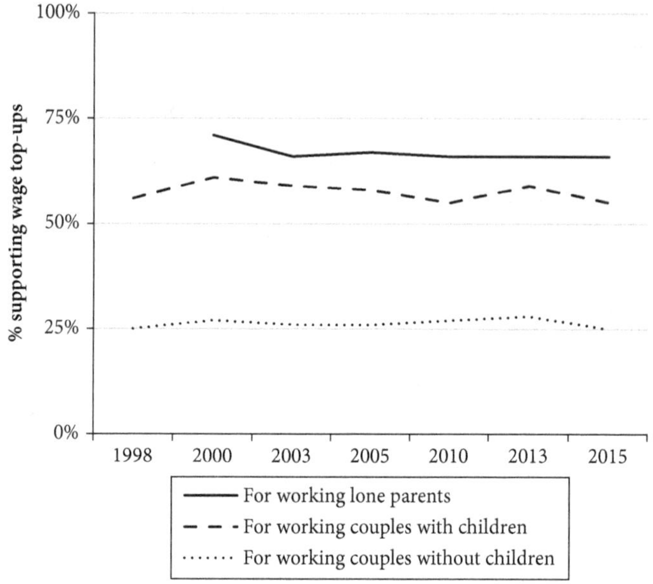

Figure 7.2. Public support for government wage top-ups, 1998–2015
Source: British Social Attitudes Survey, 1998–2015.

advertising campaign—and a study by Citizens Advice Bureaux found little public support for payment via employers.[58] Analysis by the labour economist Richard Blundell also suggested that WFTC had a smaller impact on labour supply than EITC, partly because it had a higher taper (55 per cent compared with a maximum of 21.1 per cent for EITC) and partly because it was fully taken into account when calculating other means-tested benefits.[59] Though WFTC improved incentives for one parent in a household to work, it also raised the marginal tax rates faced by some second earners (who in practice tended to be working wives).[60] On the other hand, the proportion of children living in households with less than 60 per cent of median income (before housing

[58] Stuart Adam and Mike Brewer, *Take-up of Family Credit and Working Families' Tax Credit: Final Report* (2005), accessed 21 Mar. 2017, available at <https://www.gov.uk/government/publications/take-up-of-family-credit-and-working-families-tax-credit>; National Association of Citizens Advice Bureaux, *Work in Progress: CAB Clients' Experiences of Working Families' Tax Credit* (2001). According to Shadow Social Security Secretary David Willetts, the government spent £13.8 million advertising WFTC in 1999/2000 and £7.4m in 2000/1, compared with an average of £4 million a year for all benefits between 1992 and 1997: David Willetts and Nicholas Hillman, *Tax Credits: Do They Add Up?* (2002), 15.

[59] Richard Blundell, 'Earned Income Tax Credit Policies: Impact and Optimality. The Adam Smith Lecture, 2005', *Labour Economics* 13/4 (2006), 423–43.

[60] Richard Blundell, Alan Duncan, Julian McCrae, and Costas Meghir, 'The Labour Market Impact of the Working Families Tax Credit', *Fiscal Studies* 21/1 (2000), 75–104.

costs) fell significantly during the first eighteen months of the programme, from 26 per cent in 1999/2000 to 23 per cent in 2000/1.[61] In political terms, this suited Brown's purposes well, reassuring traditional Labour voters that the government had their interests at heart and boosting family incomes in the run-up to the 2001 general election. The junior minister Chris Mullin, for instance, found that an unemployed shipyard worker in his Sunderland South constituency was surprisingly upbeat because his daughter was '£12 a week better off as a result of Gordon's tax credits'.[62] Despite the longstanding suspicion of in-work benefits within the Labour movement, most voters were willing to support the principle of wage top-ups for working families with children (Figure 7.2).

Redistribution by stealth? The origins of New Tax Credits, 1999–2003

As soon as plans for WFTC were in place, Gordon Brown's ambitions for the policy began to widen. The limitations of WFTC were clear enough: since it was structurally modelled on Family Credit, claimants received fixed awards for six months at a time based on evidence from five weekly payslips or two monthly payslips. Indeed, the Office for National Statistics insisted on treating WFTC as public expenditure rather than revenue foregone—to the Treasury's chagrin—because it was not truly integrated into the tax system.[63] Brown and his advisers always saw it as a stepping-stone to fuller integration, and during 1998 and 1999 Treasury and Inland Revenue officials began to work up longer-term plans, with input from the DSS and the Department for Education and Employment.[64] In December 1998 the Chancellor agreed to abolish the Married Couple's Allowance and replace it with a non-refundable Children's Tax Credit from April 2001, a move which he announced in his 1999 budget.[65] This was followed in 2003 by a wholesale revamp of the system to move it much closer to the NIT model, aligning it with the annual basis of tax assessment and making payments responsive to changes in income and circumstances during the tax year. Working Tax Credit (WTC) provided

[61] Department for Work and Pensions, 'Households below Average Income, 1994/95 to 2015/16: Children Summary', 16 Mar. 2017, accessed 22 Mar. 2017, available at <https://www.gov.uk/government/statistics/households-below-average-income-199495-to-201516>.

[62] Chris Mullin, *A View from the Foothills* (2009), 55.

[63] *Parliamentary Papers*, 1998–9, 'Treasury Committee. Fourth Report. The 1999 Budget', 30 Mar. 1999, x–xi.

[64] Interview with Tony Orhnial.

[65] Robert Peston, *Brown's Britain* (2005), 280–1.

income support through the pay packet to all low-paid workers, including those without children, whilst Child Tax Credit (CTC) subsumed the child elements of Income Support and Jobseekers' Allowance and was paid direct to the main carer.[66]

The development of New Tax Credits reflected not only the technical deficiencies of WFTC but also the government's growing concern about child poverty. As Alan Deacon and John Welshman have pointed out, Tony Blair instinctively shied away from an income approach to poverty and focused instead on tackling the structural causes of deprivation, especially worklessness and 'social exclusion'.[67] The New Deal and the Sure Start programme to support pre-school children in deprived areas were classic expressions of this philosophy. Blair also created a Social Exclusion Unit in the Cabinet Office to coordinate policy development, whilst the Economic and Social Research Council funded a new Centre for Analysis of Social Exclusion (CASE) at the LSE. However, findings presented at joint Treasury/CASE research seminars in November 1997 and November 1998 suggested that income poverty and the intergenerational transmission of disadvantage could not easily be separated.[68] In particular, analysis of longitudinal data from the National Child Development Study by the economists Stephen Machin and Paul Gregg showed that 'family financial distress during the childhood years displays an important association with subsequent economic success or failure': those with low-earning fathers were more likely to leave school without any qualifications, more likely to become lone parents, more likely to get into trouble with the law, and more likely to be unemployed or low earners themselves at the ages of 23 and 33.[69] One of the officials present at the 1998 seminar found this evidence 'startling', and Welshman confirms that 'the data on poverty dynamics had an important influence' on the Treasury's approach to the issue.[70] As a result, the government's rationale (and public

[66] HM Treasury, *The Modernisation of Britain's Tax and Benefit System—Number Six. Tackling Poverty and Making Work Pay—Tax Credits for the 21st Century* (2000).

[67] Alan Deacon, *Perspectives on Welfare: Ideas, Ideologies and Policy Debates* (Buckingham, 2002), 102–18; John Welshman, *From Transmitted Deprivation to Social Exclusion: Policy, Poverty and Parenting* (Bristol, 2007), 205–59.

[68] Anthony Lee and John Hills, eds, *New Cycles of Disadvantage: Report of a Conference Organised by CASE on Behalf of ESRC for HM Treasury* (1998); Centre for Analysis of Social Exclusion, *Persistent Poverty and Lifetime Inequality: The Evidence* (1999).

[69] Stephen Machin, 'Childhood Disadvantage and Intergenerational Transmissions of Economic Status', in Centre for Analysis of Social Exclusion, *Persistent Poverty and Lifetime Inequality: The Evidence*, 17–21, at 20; Paul Gregg, Susan Harkness, and Stephen Machin, *Child Development and Family Income* (York, 1999).

[70] Centre for Analysis of Social Exclusion, *Persistent Poverty and Lifetime Inequality: The Evidence*, 28; Welshman, *From Transmitted Deprivation to Social Exclusion*, 241.

justification) for tax credits began to shift away from active labour-market policy and towards the need for investment in child welfare and human capital.

The beginning of New Labour's assault on child poverty is usually traced to Tony Blair's Beveridge Lecture at Toynbee Hall in March 1999, which set out the ambition to 'end child poverty' in 'a generation', but the prime minister's direct engagement with the issue was relatively limited.[71] Brownites suspected that Alastair Campbell inserted the pledge at the last minute to win a headline, and it certainly sat uneasily with the rest of Blair's speech, which focused on the ways in which the government was already tackling the 'fundamental causes' of poverty and social exclusion.[72] In any case, it was left to the Treasury and the DSS to flesh out a precise income-based target: reducing the proportion of children in households with less than 60 per cent of equivalized median income by a quarter by 2004, halving it by 2010, and pushing it as close to zero as possible—at least among the lowest levels in Europe—by 2020.[73] Though Brown was initially furious that Blair had made the pledge without consultation, he soon realized that it created an opening for him to push forward his own redistributive agenda.[74] One consequence of the child poverty target was an increasingly open and constructive relationship between the government and the poverty lobby. CPAG organized seminars for Treasury officials and was impressed by their engagement with academic research, whilst the group's former deputy director Carey Oppenheim became a senior advisor to Blair at the Number 10 Policy Unit.[75]

New Tax Credits were designed to extend Brown's minimum income guarantee for those in work to households without children and to create a single, highly responsive system of means-tested child support which would cover both working and workless households and would extend well up the income spectrum. *Inter alia*, this would help workless families by levelling up child support to the more generous WFTC level, improve work incentives for

[71] Tony Blair, Speech at Toynbee Hall, London, 18 Mar. 1999.

[72] Steve Richards, *Whatever it Takes: The Real Story of Gordon Brown and New Labour* (2010), 136–7. Campbell's diaries give this theory some credence, though Carey Oppenheim has suggested that the target was 'a last minute addition from Peter Hyman': Alastair Campbell, *The Alastair Campbell Diaries*, vol. 2: *Power and the People 1997–1999* (2011), 686–7; Pat Thane and Ruth Davidson, eds, *The Child Poverty Action Group in the 1990s and 2000s: Witness Seminar* (2016), 25.

[73] As a 2003 consultation on 'Measuring Child Poverty' pointed out, it was 'not feasible to reach a level of zero on any survey-based income measure', since 'the "snapshots" recorded will always classify as poor some with high living standards but transitory low incomes': Department for Work and Pensions, *Measuring Child Poverty* (2003), 20.

[74] Richards, *Whatever it Takes*, 137.

[75] BLPES, Child Poverty Action Group papers, A/29, 'Treasury Review of Support for Children', 12 Dec. 1999; Thane and Davidson, *The Child Poverty Action Group in the 1990s and 2000s*, 23–5.

second earners by switching from a net to a gross income taper (eventually set at 37 per cent), and reduce the 'financial disruption' involved in moving from Income Support into paid work.[76] In designing the new system, Treasury and Inland Revenue officials looked closely at similar programmes in Canada and Australia, both of which reached about 80 per cent of families with children.[77] The Canada Child Tax Benefit (introduced in 1998) was paid monthly on the basis of the previous year's taxable income, giving families a clear sense of what they would receive but forcing those whose incomes fell sharply during the year to rely on provincial social assistance. Australia's Family Tax Benefit (2000), on the other hand, was based on advance estimates of income but subject to end-year reconciliation when workers submitted their tax returns, so those whose incomes were higher than expected were required to make repayments. The UK sought to combine the best of both systems. A provisional award would be made based on the previous year's gross income, and recipients would be required to report major changes in circumstances (such as family composition and childcare costs) to the Inland Revenue. The award would then be reconciled with actual income at the end of the tax year, and any overpayments recovered, subject to a disregard for income increases up to £2,500.

Brown carved out money for improving tax credits in successive budgets, taking advantage of strong economic growth, fiscal drag, and tight control over departmental spending. The number of Jobseekers' Allowance claimants fell from 1.9 million in 1996/7 to less than 900,000 by 2003/4, and as out-of-work benefit spending came down, the Chancellor recycled the savings into in-work benefits.[78] The abolition of Married Couple's Allowance and mortgage interest relief at source (MIRAS) in 2000 provided additional revenue, as did a one-year freeze in the personal tax allowance in 2003/4, allowing Brown to shift resources from single people and childless couples to families with children. Although the poverty lobby remained suspicious of means-testing in principle, it was impressed by the adoption of a relative poverty target and by the scale of Brown's redistributive ambition. The separation of CTC from WTC, so that it could be paid in cash to the main carer and could include workless households with children, satisfied many of CPAG's reservations about WFTC. Likewise, although CTC was means-tested rather than universal, the family element

[76] HM Treasury, *The Modernisation of Britain's Tax and Benefit System—Number Six*, 12.

[77] Interview with Tony Orhnial; Peter Whiteford, Michael Mendelson, and Jane Millar, *Timing it Right: Tax Credits and How to Respond to Income Changes* (York, 2003), 4, 9.

[78] This and other statistics in this chapter are based on Department for Work and Pensions, Benefit Expenditure and Caseload Tables, Autumn Budget 2018, accessed 20 Dec. 2018, <www.gov.uk/government/publications/benefit-expenditure-and-caseload-tables-2018>.

(worth £545) was only withdrawn once household income exceeded £50,000 a year, so that over 90 per cent of families with children were eligible for some kind of payment. Brown and his colleagues characterized this as 'progressive universalism'—providing 'support for all, and most support for those who need it most'—and hoped it would give middle-class families a stake in the system.[79] The Treasury also persuaded CPAG and other children's charities to launch the End Child Poverty coalition to mobilize support for the target of abolishing child poverty by 2020, though this approach to the voluntary sector caused some tensions.[80] For instance, Alison Garnham—then director of policy at One Parent Families and later chief executive of CPAG—felt that 'End Child Poverty was expected somehow to magically summon up public support' to compensate for Brown's reluctance to talk about redistribution.[81]

From 2000 onwards, tax credits became a growing source of controversy within the government itself as Tony Blair sought to establish health and education as his second-term spending priorities. In July 2001, for instance, Blair told Alastair Campbell that he wanted 'more money for schools and hospitals and less for GB's tax credit schemes', and felt that Brown had 'lied' to him about the cost in order to get the policy through.[82] Blairites not only suspected that Brown was using the child poverty target to buttress his left-wing credentials and position himself for the succession, but also questioned whether a strategy based on cash transfers would be politically effective: David Blunkett, for instance, pointed out in Cabinet that middle-aged workers without dependent children gained little benefit from the system.[83] Brown's friend and rival Robin Cook, who hailed him as 'the most redistributionist Chancellor we have ever seen', also feared that 'social justice by stealth' was 'not a sustainable strategy':

> Labour misses the opportunity to consolidate its core vote among the very voters who have benefited most out of this government, because they rarely hear its ministers talking about what Labour has done for them. It is commonplace to come across less well-off families whose weekly budget has been immensely improved by the new system of tax credits, but have no idea that this is not the result of the obscure working of the tax system, but

[79] Brown, *My Life, our Times*, 148; Balls, Grice, and O'Donnell, *Microeconomic Reform in Britain*, 15.
[80] Thane and Davidson, *The Child Poverty Action Group in the 1990s and 2000s*, 49.
[81] Thane and Davidson, *The Child Poverty Action Group in the 1990s and 2000s*, 59.
[82] Campbell, *The Alastair Campbell Diaries*, vol. 3: *Power and Responsibility 1999–2001* (2011), 666.
[83] David Blunkett, *The Blunkett Tapes: My Life in the Bear Pit* (2006), 251–2.

> the direct consequence of a deliberate political decision. It would be a bitter irony if they first discovered how much they owed to Labour when an incoming Conservative government took it away.[84]

Brown has admitted in his memoirs that he 'never succeeded in popularising' tax credits in the way he had hoped, largely because they were 'difficult to explain'. From this perspective, the failure was not one of 'policy' but of 'presentation'.[85]

Tax credits in crisis, 2003–2010

The creation of New Tax Credits was originally seen within the Treasury as part of a larger strategy for the 'step-by-step integration of tax and in-work benefits' under a single agency.[86] The Inland Revenue took over responsibility for National Insurance contributions and Child Benefit as well as tax credits, and then merged with HM Customs and Excise to form HM Revenue and Customs (HMRC) in 2005 in an attempt to improve customer service and generate efficiency savings.[87] Brown also broke with tradition by appointing outsiders to lead the Revenue—first Sir Nicholas Montagu, a civil servant with a background in transport and social security (1997–2004), then Sir David Varney, the former chairman of BT Wireless (2004–6)—and transferring its policy-making functions to the Treasury. Some officials hoped that Housing Benefit and other means-tested benefits could eventually be folded in to the tax credits apparatus, providing a streamlined form of income support for working households which would be closely aligned and publicly associated with the tax system.[88] By the time Brown became prime minister in 2007, however, this grand vision was a distant memory as the policy became a source of political embarrassment.

The most serious setback was the administrative fiasco over the introduction of New Tax Credits in April 2003, which Anthony King and Ivor Crewe have singled out as an object lesson in government ineptitude.[89] The Inland

[84] Robin Cook, *The Point of Departure* (2003), 257, 344.
[85] Brown, *My Life, our Times*, 151.
[86] Miliband, Speech to Inland Revenue Senior Managers' Conference.
[87] Penelope Tuck, Dominic de Cogan, and John Snape, 'A Tale of the Merger Between the Inland Revenue and HM Customs & Excise', forthcoming in *Studies in the History of Tax Law*, vol. 9, edited by Peter Harris and Dominic de Cogan (Oxford, 2019).
[88] Interview with Tony Orhnial.
[89] Anthony King and Ivor Crewe, *The Blunders of our Governments*, revised paperback edn (2014), 141–57.

Revenue had commissioned a bespoke computer system from the American firm Electronic Data Systems (EDS) as part of a ten-year IT services contract worth over £2 billion, but the new system turned out to be highly inflexible and pre-launch testing was rushed.[90] More than 20 per cent of initial awards were miscalculated, and the Revenue had to make 330,000 interim payments to claimants who did not receive their tax credits on time.[91] Treasury ministers faced a storm of public criticism, both from the press and from MPs who had to help their constituents navigate the new system: the Labour MP Gerry Steinberg, for instance, reported that his two secretaries had spent 'all day for about a fortnight or longer dealing with nothing but Tax Credits'.[92] The government's difficulties worsened at the end of the tax year when the Revenue began to demand repayments from some of the 1.9 million claimants who had been paid too much.[93] Even Sir Nicholas Montagu had to admit that the implementation of the new system had gone 'spectacularly wrong'.[94]

Although some of the problems encountered with New Tax Credits reflected deficiencies in government IT procurement, others stemmed from the structure of the system itself. The procedures for claiming tax credits and reporting in-year changes were relatively complex, and families often found it difficult to understand how their tax credits were calculated. Likewise, the system was designed to require end-year reconciliation—as under the US and Australian models—but the scale of under- and over-payments seems to have taken the Treasury by surprise. The Revenue's lack of experience of dealing with poorer households exacerbated these problems, since many low-income families had no savings to fall back on, and overpayments frequently led to cuts in other benefits which claimants were unable to recover.[95] Jane Millar found that the resulting instability made some lone parents 'very anxious and uncertain', and deliberative research carried out for the Fabian Society in February 2005 suggested that tax credits were 'still perceived negatively by many of their recipients'.[96] Although

[90] *Parliamentary Papers*, 1999–2000, HC 431, 'Committee of Public Accounts. Twenty-Eighth Report. Inland Revenue/EDS Strategic Partnership: The Award of New Work', 28 June 2000; *Parliamentary Papers*, 2003–4, HC 89, 'Committee of Public Accounts. Fourteenth Report. Inland Revenue: Tax Credits', 22 Apr. 2004.

[91] *Parliamentary Papers*, 2005–6, HC 124, 'Parliamentary and Health Service Ombudsman. Tax Credits: Putting Things Right', 21 June 2005, 20; HC 89, 'Committee of Public Accounts. Fourteenth Report. Inland Revenue: Tax Credits', Ev. 4.

[92] HC 89, 'Committee of Public Accounts. Fourteenth Report. Inland Revenue: Tax Credits', Ev. 7.

[93] HC 124, 'Parliamentary and Health Service Ombudsman. Tax Credits: Putting Things Right', 37.

[94] HC 89, 'Committee of Public Accounts. Fourteenth Report. Inland Revenue: Tax Credits', Ev. 10.

[95] *Parliamentary Papers*, 2006–7, HC 1010, 'Parliamentary and Health Service Ombudsman. Tax Credits: Getting it Wrong?', 8 Oct. 2007.

[96] Millar, 'Making Work Pay, Making Tax Credits Work', 33; Fabian Society, *Narrowing the Gap: The Final Report of the Fabian Commission on Life Chances and Child Poverty* (2006), 186.

the government revised the system to reduce the need for repayments—not least by raising the disregard for income changes from £2,500 to £25,000—the underlying problems were never fully solved.

The difficulties which the government faced in operating New Tax Credits threw ministers onto the defensive and rapidly dispelled the notion of adding other benefits to the system. Indeed, Brown even retreated from his attempt to pay WTC through the pay packet, and introduced direct payment by HMRC in 2006 in response to pressure from employers. More broadly, the claims which the government made for tax credits began to attract critical scrutiny. Some economists had always been sceptical about the labour-market effects of in-work benefits, and Richard Blundell of University College London repeatedly warned that subsidizing low-paid jobs could discourage workers from investing in their skills. 'With no time limit', Blundell argued, 'tax credit systems can provide a strong negative incentive for wage progression and human capital investment, reducing the chance of longer run self-sufficiency'.[97] Ghazala Azmat at the LSE also presented empirical data which suggested that employers had extracted much of the value of WFTC by holding down claimants' wages, an effect which was most pronounced among male workers.[98] Voices in and around the trade union movement, which had largely acquiesced in the early development of tax credits, could increasingly be found making similar arguments.[99] Catherine Howarth and Peter Kenway of the left-leaning New Policy Institute, for instance, complained that 'tax credits run the danger of undermining efforts to tackle the deeper causes of low pay, including low productivity and weak organisation amongst low paid workers'.[100]

Perhaps the most powerful criticism of tax credits which emerged towards the end of the New Labour years was the sheer cost of eliminating child poverty through direct transfer payments. The government came close to meeting its 2004 interim target of reducing child poverty by a quarter; indeed, recent research by the Resolution Foundation suggests it may even have met it, since the Family Resources Survey data used to measure relative poverty only

[97] Richard Blundell, 'Welfare-to-Work: Which Policies Work and Why?', *Proceedings of The British Academy* 117 (2002), 477–524, at 493; see also Richard Blundell and Costas Meghir, 'Active Labour Market Policy vs Employment Tax Credits: Lessons from Recent UK Reforms', *Swedish Economic Policy Review* 8/2 (2002), 13–37, and Blundell, 'Earned Income Tax Credit Policies'.

[98] Ghazala Azmat, 'The Incidence of an Earned Income Tax Credit: Evaluating the Impact on Wages in the UK', Centre for Economic Performance Discussion Paper no. 724 (May 2006).

[99] For the unions' acquiescence during the Blair government's first term, see Rafael Ziegler and Bill Jordan, 'The Trade Unions, Tax-Benefit Reform and Basic Income: Stumbling towards a Policy?', *Citizen's Income Newsletter* 3 (2001), 2–4.

[100] Catherine Howarth and Peter Kenway, *Why Worry Any More about the Low Paid?* (2004), 38.

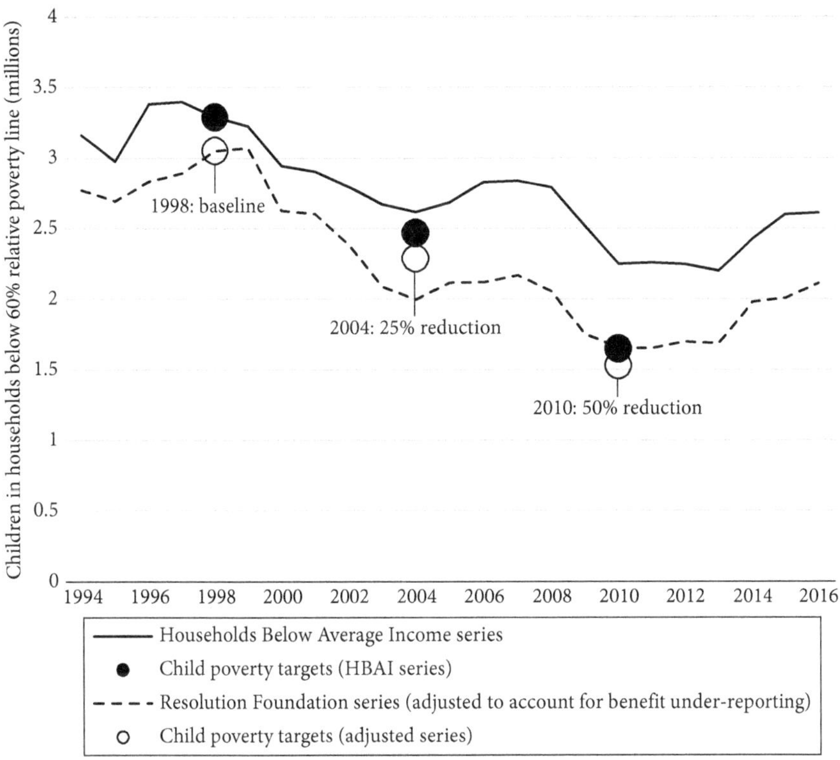

Figure 7.3. Relative child poverty in Britain, 1994–2016

Source: Adam Corlett et al., *The Living Standards Audit 2018* (2018), 68, figure 44. I am grateful to the Resolution Foundation for allowing me to draw on this data series.

captures about 85 per cent of benefit income.[101] As Figure 7.3 shows, however, progress then stalled as wage growth fizzled out and the Treasury focused on fixing the New Tax Credits system. Modelling by the IFS in 2009 suggested that the government would need to spend an extra £4.2 billion a year on tax credits in order to meet its next target of halving child poverty by 2010/11, and at least £19 billion (assuming no behavioural changes) to reduce the child poverty rate to 10 per cent by 2020.[102]

As the UK's public finances deteriorated in the wake of the 2008 financial crisis, further redistribution on this scale came to be seen as increasingly unrealistic. Commentators from across the political spectrum—from the

[101] Adam Corlett, Stephen Clarke, Conor D'Arcy, and John Wood, *The Living Standards Audit 2018* (2018), 48–74.

[102] Institute for Fiscal Studies, 'Cost of Cutting Child Poverty Rises as Families Fall Further below Poverty Line' (press release, 18 Feb. 2009).

Fabian Society on the left to Iain Duncan Smith on the right—called for a more dynamic approach to child poverty, which placed more emphasis on early intervention, social mobility, and 'life chances'.[103] In fact, the Treasury had been moving in this direction since the 2003–4 Child Poverty Review, which added material deprivation indicators to its relative income target and developed a cross-government strategy for tackling the root causes of poverty in education, health, housing, and transport.[104] The *Ending Child Poverty* strategy published in March 2010 broadened this approach out further, emphasizing the need to raise parental employment levels and reduce educational inequalities and setting four new targets for 2020.[105] Even so, Brown's personal commitment to tax credits left him vulnerable to the charge that he was a one-club golfer, over-reliant on the techniques of technocratic utilitarianism.

Conclusion

It is important not to exaggerate the influence of redistributive market liberalism on New Labour. At an ideological level, both Tony Blair and Gordon Brown were strongly committed to paid work as the foundation of household income and to investment in education and skills as the basis of economic growth—a form of supply-side social democracy. Indeed, during its early years in office the government's agenda seemed to be focused on changing the initial distribution of earnings rather than redistributing income through taxes and transfers, as CPAG director Sally Witcher pointed out in a 1998 briefing.[106] This supply-side approach can be seen in the government's enthusiasm for 'activating' the unemployed, as it extended the New Deals from the under-25s and lone parents to other long-term unemployed people, tightened the sanctions regime under Jobseekers' Allowance, and introduced the Work Capability Assessment for disability benefit claimants.[107] In a different way, it also gave rise to social investment policies such as Sure Start and the sharp increase

[103] Fabian Society, *Narrowing the Gap*; Centre for Social Justice, *Dynamic Benefits: Towards Welfare that Works* (2009).

[104] HM Treasury, *Child Poverty Review* (2004); interview with Tony Orhnial.

[105] HM Treasury, Department for Children, Schools and Families, and Department for Work and Pensions, *Ending Child Poverty: Mapping the Route to 2020* (2010).

[106] Child Poverty Action Group papers, A/29, 'Tax Credits—Broad Policy Paper' by Sally Witcher, Jan. 1998.

[107] Griggs, Hammond, and Walker, 'Activation for All'.

in education spending, which were designed to reduce inequality of opportunity and improve the UK's human capital over the long term.[108]

The New Labour government's appetite for reshaping the initial distribution of incomes, however, was always limited by its sensitivity to business opinion and its acceptance of the norms of market liberalism. The introduction of the NMW is a case in point, since Blair and Brown kept its initial rate down in order to limit the impact on business costs and job creation, despite pressure from the unions.[109] The government's larger focus on maintaining macroeconomic stability and low inflation also contributed to the continued decline of manufacturing employment and exacerbated the UK's reliance on the service sector.[110] Even if welfare-to-work and public service reforms would ultimately reduce poverty and inequality, they were unlikely to have much impact in the short term. In this context, the decision to set a child poverty target based on median household income, with demanding interim milestones in 2004 and 2010, effectively compelled the government to make extensive use of cash transfers. By 2009/10, 4.3 million working families with children were receiving tax credits worth an average of £4,378—more than twice as much as the average EITC payment in the USA.[111] As we have seen, this appears to have accounted for the lion's share of the reduction in child poverty achieved during the New Labour years.

In the closing days of the 2010 general election, as Labour desperately sought to shore up its vote, the party finally put tax credits at the heart of its campaigning. A hard-hitting election broadcast entitled 'A Nightmare on your Street' showed grey-suited bureaucrats with clipboards walking up and down a suburban street, explaining the Conservatives' plans to 'stop CTC payments to hundreds of thousands of families on middle and modest incomes'. Together with accompanying direct mailshots, the broadcast played on middle-class

[108] Daniel Wincott, 'Paradoxes of New Labour Social Policy: Towards Universal Child Care in Europe's "Most Liberal" Welfare Regime?', *Social Politics* 13/2 (2006), 286–312.

[109] William Brown, 'The Process of Fixing the British National Minimum Wage, 1997–2007', *British Journal of Industrial Relations* 47/2 (2009), 429–43; Campbell, *The Alastair Campbell Diaries*, vol. 2, 281–2, 415–16, 422.

[110] Coutts, Glyn, and Rowthorn, 'Structural Change under New Labour'.

[111] This figure excludes the 1.5 million out-of-work families with children receiving tax credits or equivalent support for children through the benefit system, and 480,000 childless individuals or couples who received only WTC: see HM Revenue and Customs, 'Child and Working Tax Credits Statistics: Finalised Annual Awards, 2009 to 2010', May 2011, accessed 19 July 2018, available at <http://webarchive.nationalarchives.gov.uk/20121112124508/http://www.hmrc.gov.uk/stats/personal-tax-credits/cwtc-final-awards-may11.pdf>, table 2.2. In US tax year 2009, EITC payments averaged $2,191 (approximately £1,360), though the average payment to families with children is likely to have been somewhat higher: Gene Falk, 'The Earned Income Tax Credit: An Overview', Congressional Research Service report RL31768, 22 Oct. 2014, accessed 19 July 2018, available at <https://fas.org/sgp/crs/misc/RL31768.pdf>, table 2.

voters' fears about David Cameron's deficit-reduction plans and may have helped deny the Conservatives a majority. At the same time, however, 'A Nightmare on your Street' also showed how much the character and presentation of tax credits had changed since the 1990s. What had originally been conceived as a welfare-to-work measure for unemployed men and lone parents, added to the wage packet by the employer, had effectively become a cash benefit for mothers and children. Though Labour could resist Conservative cuts by appealing to voters' loss-aversion, it was difficult to object as a matter of principle to the removal of a means-tested benefit from families earning over £50,000 a year.

If the experience of tax credits illustrates the impact of RML, then, it also reveals its political limitations. During the 1980s and 1990s, social democratic economists such as James Meade had argued that 'a sufficient assured supplement to low pay'—a basic income or a system of wage supplements—would help make flexible labour markets politically acceptable: in other words, redistribution could legitimize market liberalism.[112] In the event, however, the Blair and Brown governments' focus on child poverty did not prevent growing disillusionment among working-class voters, who turned away from Labour in large numbers between 1997 and 2010.[113] As Will Davies has argued, New Labour offered the party's post-industrial heartlands '"redistribution" but no "recognition"': cash transfers could not substitute for the dignity and status which working-class families had once derived from skilled manufacturing work. Though Blair and Brown 'heaped scorn on dependency', their political economy simply transferred it to a macro level, relying on a 'shadow welfare state' to lift workers above the poverty line using tax receipts from the City of London. When boom turned to bust, this 'cultural contradiction' turned out to be unsustainable.[114]

[112] J. E. Meade, *Fifteen Propositions concerning the Building of an Equitable, Full-Employment, Non-Inflationary, Free-Enterprise Economy* (1993), 8.

[113] Geoffrey Evans and James Tilley, *The New Politics of Class: The Political Exclusion of the British Working Class* (Oxford, 2017), 170–7.

[114] Will Davies, 'Thoughts on the Sociology of Brexit', Goldsmiths Political Economy Research Centre blog, 24 June 2016, accessed 19 July 2018, <http://www.perc.org.uk/project_posts/thoughts-on-the-sociology-of-brexit/>.

8

A Crisis of the Transfer State?

Distributional Politics since the 2008 Financial Crisis

The 2008 financial crisis brought an end to fifteen years of continuous economic growth and plunged the British economy into the deepest recession since the Second World War, from which it is still recovering. The 'credit crunch' and the period of austerity that followed have focused public attention on distributional questions and prompted a wide-ranging debate over the sustainability of the UK's economic model, fuelled by a sharp public backlash against the financial sector. In the immediate aftermath of the crisis, Keynesian stimulus policies came back into fashion and social democratic thinkers sought to bring about a 'paradigm shift' away from neoliberalism.[1] Many British politicians and voters, however, came to see the 2008 crash not as a crisis of capitalism but as a crisis of the banking system and, increasingly, a crisis of public debt. This framing was reinforced by developments in the Eurozone and entrenched by the Conservative–Liberal Democrat coalition which took office after the 2010 general election.[2]

One of the consequences of the financial crisis was that the influence of redistributive market liberalism came under challenge from a number of directions. At a practical level, the collapse in UK tax revenues and the rising budget deficit limited the scope for further increases in cash transfers: total public-sector receipts fell by 7.6 per cent in real terms between 2007/8 and 2009/10, driven by a fall of almost one-third in receipts from the finance and

[1] Robert Skidelsky, *Keynes: The Return of the Master* (2009); Andrew Gamble, *The Spectre at the Feast: Capitalist Crisis and the Politics of Recession* (Basingstoke, 2009); Dermot Hodson and Deborah Mabbett, 'UK Economic Policy and the Global Financial Crisis: Paradigm Lost?', *Journal of Common Market Studies* 47/5 (2009), 1041–61; Henry Farrell and John Quiggin, 'Consensus, Dissensus, and Economic Ideas: Economic Crisis and the Rise and Fall of Keynesianism', *International Studies Quarterly* 61/2 (2017), 269–83.

[2] Jim Tomlinson, *Managing the Economy, Managing the People: Narratives of Economic Life in Britain from Beveridge to Brexit* (Oxford, 2017), 110–33; Christopher Hood and Rozana Himaz, *A Century of Fiscal Squeeze Politics: 100 Years of Austerity, Politics, and Bureaucracy in Britain* (Oxford, 2017), 180–99.

Transfer State: The Idea of a Guaranteed Income and the Politics of Redistribution in Modern Britain. Peter Sloman, Oxford University Press (2019). © Peter Sloman. DOI: 10.1093/oso/9780198813262.001.0001

housing sectors.[3] At a discursive level, Conservative politicians such as David Cameron and Iain Duncan Smith successfully challenged New Labour's focus on income poverty—especially the use of 60 per cent of median household income as a relative poverty line—and recast tax credits as a form of 'welfare'.[4] The new Chancellor George Osborne also launched a rhetorical assault on 'shirkers', tapping into longstanding suspicions of the 'undeserving poor' in an attempt to justify benefit cuts and draw a political dividing line with Labour.[5] The coalition government cut working-age benefits and focused on boosting workers' take-home pay through the flagship Liberal Democrat policy of raising the tax threshold to £10,000. At the same time, Labour leader Ed Miliband took up the 'predistribution' agenda championed by the Harvard political scientist Jacob Hacker, based on a renewed interest in the distributional effects of labour and product markets. This reaction against cash transfers culminated in the introduction of the National Living Wage (NLW) in April 2016, which Osborne presented as a way of turning Britain 'from a low wage, high tax, high welfare economy to a higher wage, lower tax, lower welfare society'.[6]

It is tempting to see this era of austerity politics as a 'crisis of the transfer state': a point at which RML went into retreat as public consent for transfer payments reached its limits. Yet such a conclusion would be premature for a number of reasons. Firstly, despite the Conservatives' anti-welfare rhetoric, the period since 2010 has seen the development of Universal Credit—an ambitious attempt to merge tax credits and other working-age benefits into a single system of means-tested income support, subject to new forms of conditionality. Secondly, although the coalition and Conservative governments have cut working-age benefits significantly in real terms since 2010, these efforts to reduce welfare spending have become increasingly fraught. The backlash against the tax credit cuts which George Osborne proposed in his summer

[3] Office for Budget Responsibility, 'Public Finances Databank', 22 Nov. 2017, accessed 12 Dec. 2017, available at <http://budgetresponsibility.org.uk/download/public-finances-databank/>. Total receipts from the financial sector plus housing fell from £59.5 billion in 2007/8 to £41.8 billion in 2009/10: Office for Budget Responsibility, 'July 2011 Fiscal Sustainability Report—Main Report Charts and Tables', 13 July 2011, accessed 12 Dec. 2017, available at <http://budgetresponsibility.org.uk/download/july-2011-fiscal-sustainability-report-main-report-charts-and-tables/>, box 4.1, chart B.

[4] Iain Duncan Smith, 'We've Brought Fairness back to Welfare', *Sunday Telegraph*, 30 Dec. 2012, accessed 23 July 2018, available at <https://www.telegraph.co.uk/news/politics/9772131/Iain-Duncan-Smith-weve-brought-back-fairness-to-welfare.html>.

[5] Richard Hayton and Libby McEnhill, 'Rhetoric and Morality—How the Coalition Justifies Welfare Policy', in *Rhetoric in British Politics and Society*, edited by Judi Atkins, Alan Finlayson, James Martin, and Nick Turnbull (Basingstoke, 2014), 101–15.

[6] George Osborne, Summer Budget Speech, 8 July 2015, accessed 23 July 2018, available at <https://www.gov.uk/government/speeches/chancellor-george-osbornes-summer-budget-2015-speech>.

2015 budget suggests that transfer payments to working families with children retain some political support. Thirdly, the last five years have also witnessed an explosion of public interest in UBI as a way of providing economic security in the face of a new wave of automation.

Redistribution and the 'Anglo-liberal growth model', 1997–2010

Among academic political economists, interpretations of the 2008 financial crisis have been strongly shaped by the 'varieties of capitalism' analysis which Peter Hall and David Soskice developed in the 1990s.[7] The relatively severe impact of the crash on the United States and Britain has been seen as a reflection of the weaknesses of Anglo-American liberal market capitalism, especially short-termist corporate strategies, speculative investment banking, and reliance on high levels of credit to sustain demand. Colin Hay, for instance, has characterized the UK's post-1979 political economy in terms of an 'Anglo-liberal growth model' which combined highly flexible labour and product markets with a massive expansion of mortgage finance and consumer credit.[8] Likewise, Colin Crouch has argued that low interest rates and rising asset prices helped sustain consumer spending in the face of stagnant real wages—a practice he has labelled 'privatised Keynesianism'.[9] During the 1990s and 2000s, the challenge of 'reconciling the uncertainties and instabilities of a capitalist economy with democracy's need for stability in people's lives and capitalism's own need for confident mass consumers' was met by mortgages, credit cards, and personal loans rather than by classic Keynesian policies.[10]

Hay and Crouch's accounts of the UK's pre-crisis growth model say very little about the growth of redistribution: indeed, Hay identifies a trend towards 'welfare residualism' since the mid-1980s, which he illustrates by reference to the decline of social insurance benefits.[11] In the light of the analysis developed in Chapter 7, however, it is clear that tax credits formed an integral part of New Labour's version of the Anglo-liberal regime. The expansion of in-work benefits not only increased labour supply—thereby keeping inflation and

[7] Peter Hall and David Soskice, eds, *Varieties of Capitalism: The Institutional Foundations of Comparative Advantage* (Oxford, 2001).

[8] Colin Hay, *The Failure of Anglo-Liberal Capitalism* (Basingstoke, 2013), 22–32.

[9] Colin Crouch, 'Privatised Keynesianism: An Unacknowledged Policy Regime', *British Journal of Politics and International Relations*, 11/3 (2009), 382–99.

[10] Crouch, 'Privatised Keynesianism', 382.

[11] Hay, *The Failure of Anglo-Liberal Capitalism*, 28–32.

interest rates down—but also provided a direct boost to household incomes which helped offset the effects of widening wage disparities. For many lower-income families, rising tax credit entitlements are likely to have been at least as important as consumer credit in sustaining their spending. As Scott Lavery has recently argued, 'redistributive social policies ... played a key role in reducing relative poverty, constraining income inequality and mitigating the uneven development of "Anglo-liberal" capitalism' during the 1990s and 2000s. New Labour's 'finance-led accumulation strategy' thus went hand-in-hand with a '"One Nation" legitimization strategy'.[12]

The importance of redistribution can be seen by examining changes in household incomes during the pre-2008 boom. Economists such as Jared Bernstein and Joseph Stiglitz have focused attention on the decoupling of median wages from productivity growth in the United States since the 1970s, suggesting that low- and middle-income households have derived little benefit from thirty years of market liberal policies.[13] Although the Thatcher and Blair governments sought to imitate the US labour-market model, however, the trajectory of UK living standards was much more positive.[14] Between 1984 and 2008, real median equivalized disposable income rose by 91.5 per cent in the UK, compared with just 26.1 per cent in the United States.[15] This pattern partly reflected faster growth in GDP per capita, but it was also aided by the expansion of cash transfers. Tax credits played a particularly important role in cushioning household incomes as wage growth slowed during the 2000s, and later mitigated the effects of the 2008–9 recession by acting as an automatic stabilizer.[16] Although the UK's Gini coefficient for market income rose from 0.49 in 1990 to 0.52 in 2010, driven by the continued pulling away of top incomes in the financial sector and elsewhere, the Gini coefficient for disposable income fell slightly (from 0.36 to 0.34) over the same period. As Chris Belfield and his colleagues from the IFS have pointed out, the 'increase in

[12] Scott Lavery, *British Capitalism after the Crisis* (Basingstoke, 2019), 103.

[13] Jared Bernstein, 'Inequality, Mobility, Real Earnings, and Real Anger', *Business Economics* 51/2 (2016), 90–6; Joseph E. Stiglitz, *Rewriting the Rules of the American Economy: An Agenda for Growth and Shared Prosperity* (New York, 2015). For a critical analysis of the 'decoupling' literature, see João Paulo Pessoa and John Van Reenen, 'Decoupling of Wage Growth and Productivity Growth? Myth and Reality', report to the Resolution Foundation Commission on Living Standards, 29 Jan. 2012, accessed 13 Dec. 2017, 31, available at <http://www.livingstandards.org/wp-content/uploads/2012/02/Decoupling-of-wages-and-productivity.pdf>.

[14] Daniel Tomlinson, *You're Hired! Lessons for President Trump from a Comparison of Living Standards and Inequality in the US and the UK* (2017).

[15] Office for National Statistics, 'Middle Income Households, 1977–2010/11', 18 Mar. 2013, accessed 13 Dec. 2017, available at <http://webarchive.nationalarchives.gov.uk/20160107031032/http://www.ons.gov.uk/ons/dcp171776_303386.pdf>, data to figure 2.

[16] Mike Brewer and Liam Wren-Lewis, *Why Did Britain's Households Get Richer? Decomposing UK Household Income Growth between 1968 and 2008–09*, IFS Briefing Note 125 (Dec. 2011), 25, 36.

household earnings inequality' during the late 1990s and 2000s 'was largely unwound by the tax and benefits system'.[17]

On the other hand, labour-market trends during the New Labour years tell a less rosy story. Although Tony Blair and Gordon Brown introduced the National Minimum Wage and sought to 'upskill' the British workforce, there was always a risk that wage subsidies would encourage the expansion of relatively low-paid work and lock the UK economy into a low-cost production regime.[18] Indeed, the MIT economist and Nobel laureate Robert Solow has argued that the Blair government's welfare-to-work policies

> had the effect of increasing the absolute and relative supply of potentially low-wage labor. The net result was little, if any, reduction in the incidence of low-wage work. There must also have been downward pressure on the relative wage of low-end workers.[19]

The presentation of tax credits as 'a hand up, not a hand out' implied that workers would move into better-paid work over time, but in practice the scope for progression in many service-sector occupations appears to have been relatively limited. The labour economist Mark Stewart warned the Treasury in 1998 that low-paid jobs were 'more likely to act as blind alleys than as stepping stones to positions higher up the pay distribution'.[20] Though the NMW was designed to prevent the worst forms of exploitation, studies suggested that many firms in retail, the hotel industry, and food processing responded by flattening their pay structures and treating the minimum wage as the 'going rate'.[21] Analysis of earnings data by Joanne Lindley and Stephen Machin suggests that overall wage inequality continued to rise during the late 1990s and 2000s, despite some evidence of pay compression at the bottom end.[22]

[17] Chris Belfield, Richard Blundell, Jonathan Cribb, Andrew Hood, and Robert Joyce, 'Two Decades of Income Inequality in Britain: The Role of Wages, Household Earnings and Redistribution', *Economica* 84/334 (2017), 157–79, at 170.

[18] On Blair's use of human capital theory, see David Cobham, Christopher Adam, and Ken Mayhew, 'The Economic Record of the 1997–2010 Labour Government: An Assessment', *Oxford Review of Economic Policy* 29/1 (2013), 1–24, at 10–14.

[19] Robert Solow, 'Introduction', in *Low-Wage Work in the United Kingdom*, edited by Caroline Lloyd, Geoff Mason, and Ken Mayhew (New York, 2008), 1–14, at 13–14.

[20] Mark B. Stewart, 'Low Pay, no Pay Dynamics', in Centre for Analysis of Social Exclusion, *Persistent Poverty and Lifetime Inequality: The Evidence* (1999), 71–6, at 76.

[21] Damian Grimshaw, Caroline Lloyd, and Chris Warhurst, 'Low-Wage Work in the United Kingdom: Employment Practices, Institutional Effects, and Policy Responses', in *Low-Wage Work in the United Kingdom*, edited by Caroline Lloyd, Geoff Mason, and Ken Mayhew (New York, 2008), 284–321, at 300.

[22] Joanne Lindley and Stephen Machin, 'Wage Inequality in the Labour Years', *Oxford Review of Economic Policy* 29/1 (2013), 165–77, at 166–9.

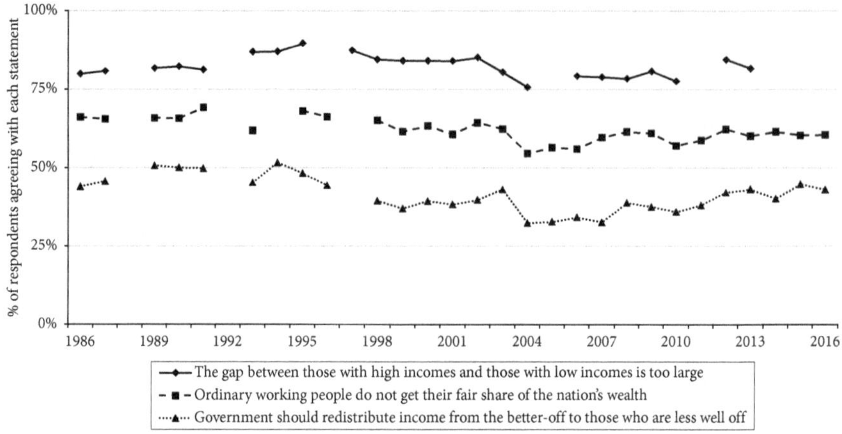

Figure 8.1. Public attitudes to inequality and redistribution, 1986–2016
Source: British Social Attitudes Survey, 1986–2016: proportion of respondents agreeing with each statement.

Lower-income male workers with dependent children seem to have fared particularly badly, relative to both childless male workers and working mothers.[23] Evidence that tax credits have had a dampening effect on wages is inconclusive, but these trends give credence to Bob Jessop and Chris Grover's suspicion that activation policies have encouraged 'low-road' production strategies.[24]

In this context, it is hardly surprising that a deep-seated cultural preference for earned over unearned income appears to have endured among British workers. As Figure 8.1 shows, more than three-quarters of respondents to the British Social Attitudes Survey have consistently said the gap between rich and poor is too large, and about 60 per cent believe that 'ordinary working people do not get their fair share of the nation's wealth', but only about 40 per cent agree that the government should redistribute income from rich to poor. When the 2009 survey asked how policy-makers should reduce income inequality, making the tax system more progressive, raising the NMW, and improving education and job opportunities were much more popular options than improving benefits (Figure 8.2). Although BSAS respondents have generally supported tax credits for lone parents and working couples with

[23] Paul Gregg, Alex Hurrell, and Matthew Whittaker, *Creditworthy: Assessing the Impact of Tax Credits in the Last Decade and Considering What This Means for Universal Credit* (2012), 37–40, 60.

[24] Bob Jessop, 'From Thatcherism to New Labour: Neo-Liberalism, Workfarism and Labour-Market Regulation', in *The Political Economy of European Employment: European Integration and the Transnationalization of the (Un)Employment Question*, edited by Henk Overbeek (2003), 137–53; Chris Grover, *Social Security and Wage Poverty: Historical and Policy Aspects of Supplementing Wages in Britain and beyond* (Basingstoke, 2016).

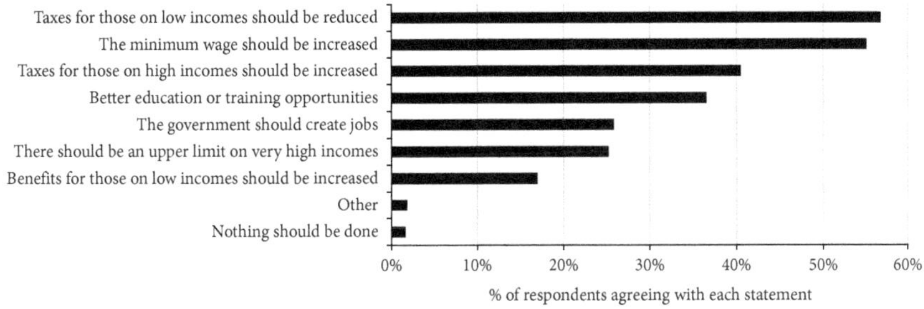

Figure 8.2. What, if anything, should be done to reduce the gap between those on high incomes and those on low incomes? (2009)
Source: British Social Attitudes Survey, 2009: proportion of respondents mentioning each option.

children, a clear majority (64 per cent in 2013) also believe that wage top-ups 'mak[e] it easier for employers to get away with paying low wages'. Public opinion thus appears to be instinctively receptive to a 'predistributive' agenda.

The origins of Universal Credit

Although many Conservatives recoiled against the growth of tax credits under New Labour, it took some time for the party to develop an effective critique of them. After all, Gordon Brown's labour-market strategy was essentially a scaling-up of the Thatcher government's efforts to 'make work pay' and promote service-sector jobs. Some Tories saw Working Families Tax Credit as little more than an expensive rebranding of Family Credit: David Willetts, for instance, argued that the principle of wage supplements for working families was 'very desirable' and complained that Brown's 'restless innovation' had merely added unnecessary complexity to the system.[25] By contrast, William Hague's Shadow Chancellor Francis Maude and Shadow Social Security Secretary Iain Duncan Smith described WFTC as 'economic and social lunacy' and announced that a Conservative government would cut it.[26] The Tory MP Oliver Letwin took a similar line, claiming (in confessional mode) that the Conservatives had been wrong to increase 'dependency and the social security

[25] David Willetts and Nicholas Hillman, *Tax Credits: Do They Add Up?* (2002), 38, 3.

[26] Conservative Party press release, 22 July 1998, quoted in Labour Party, *A Better Deal for Families: Delivered by Labour—Opposed by the Tories* (1999), 6; HC Deb., sixth series, vol. 317, 19 Oct. 1998, col. 951.

budget' between 1979 and 1997: 'we have to change direction and... increase the incentive for people responsibly to look after their own affairs so that they do not need to depend so much on benefit'.[27]

Iain Duncan Smith, who replaced Hague as Conservative leader in 2001, was particularly keen to shift the focus of social policy away from cash transfers, towards a more traditional (and moralistic) analysis of dependency and disadvantage. He praised US president George W. Bush for being 'unafraid of proclaiming the vital importance of family, voluntarism and values in the war on poverty', and hoped that the Centre for Social Justice (CSJ) which he set up after he was ousted from the leadership could draw on the success of Bush's 'compassionate conservatism'.[28] When David Cameron took over as party leader in 2005, he asked Duncan Smith to chair a new Social Justice Policy Group and agreed that the CSJ should provide its secretariat. The group's two reports, *Breakdown Britain* (Dec. 2006) and *Breakthrough Britain* (July 2007), accused the Labour government of neglecting the role of 'the voluntary and community sector' in 'the welfare society' and sharply challenged its use of income-based measures of poverty:

> Labour's definition of poverty based on a single threshold of 60% of median household income has led to a narrow and arbitrary process. Through means testing and tax credits, Labour has prioritised shifting those just below the poverty line to just above it...
>
> The use of income as a sole measure of poverty is inadequate as it fails to properly measure people's quality of life. Whether a person is working or in receipt of benefits matters, for the absence of work and subsequent benefit dependency are themselves a form of social exclusion.[29]

Instead of redistributing resources from rich to poor, *Breakdown Britain* argued that policy should focus on tackling five 'pathways to poverty': educational failure, family breakdown, economic dependency, addiction, and debt.[30] David Cameron enthusiastically took up this analysis, arguing that

[27] HC Deb., sixth series, vol. 331, 20 May 1999, cols 1266–7.

[28] Introduction to Tim Montgomerie, *Whatever Happened to Compassionate Conservatism?* (2004), 6, quoted in Catherine Haddon, 'Making Policy in Opposition: The Development of Universal Credit, 2005–2010', Institute for Government report, Dec. 2012, accessed 11 Feb. 2019, available at <https://www.instituteforgovernment.org.uk/publications/making-policy-opposition-development-universal-credit-2005-2010>.

[29] Social Justice Policy Group, *Breakdown Britain: Interim Report on the State of the Nation* (2006), 14, 18.

[30] Social Justice Policy Group, *Breakdown Britain*, 15.

the problems of 'Broken Britain' could only be solved by building a 'Big Society'.[31] Significantly, the Conservatives' attempts to portray Gordon Brown as a Fabian technocrat were echoed by the Liberal Democrats, who complained that 'the big government, top-down, target-driven approach of the Labour Government... risks ensnaring people in means-tested benefits and welfare dependency'.[32]

Despite its sharp rhetorical critique of New Labour's child poverty strategy, however, *Breakdown Britain* did not propose to abandon redistribution altogether. Instead, one of the CSJ's flagship proposals was the further unification of the benefit system in order to reduce high marginal tax rates and improve work incentives. The case for benefit simplification had gained traction across the political spectrum from 2005 onwards, largely as a result of work by Roy Sainsbury, Professor of Social Policy at the University of York, who canvassed the possibility of a 'Single Working-Age Benefit'.[33] Sainsbury developed the idea in a 2007 pamphlet for the IPPR, co-written with Kate Stanley, which argued that the complexity of the benefit system 'demonstrably hinders the Government's welfare-to-work agenda' and suggested that Income Support, Jobseekers' Allowance, and the new Employment and Support Allowance for disabled people should be replaced by a single means-tested payment.[34] The Department for Work and Pensions set up a Benefit Simplification Unit, and the banker and government adviser David Freud endorsed the idea in an influential report on welfare-to-work policy.[35] Finally, Duncan Smith and the CSJ worked up the proposal in more detail in the 2009 study *Dynamic Benefits*, using dynamic modelling to analyse how benefit reforms might affect citizens' work behaviour over time.[36] *Dynamic Benefits* introduced the title 'Universal Credits', and also widened out Sainsbury's proposal to incorporate tax credits and Housing Benefit. The system would be

[31] Nick Ellison, 'The Conservative Party and the "Big Society"', in *Social Policy Review 23: Analysis and Debate in Social Policy, 2011*, edited by Chris Holden, Majella Kilkey, and Gaby Ramia (Bristol, 2011), 45–62.

[32] Liberal Democrats, *Freedom from Poverty, Opportunity for All* (2007), 5.

[33] University of York, 'Development of the "Single Working Age Benefit" and Impact on Welfare Reform' (impact case study, submission to REF2014), accessed 14 Dec. 2017, available at <https://www.york.ac.uk/spsw/research/research-impact/single-working-age-benefit-impact-case-study/>.

[34] Roy Sainsbury and Kate Stanley, 'One for All: Active Welfare and the Single Working-Age Benefit', in *It's All about You: Citizen-Centred Welfare*, edited by Jim Bennett and Graeme Cooke (2007), 43–56, at 43.

[35] Nicholas Timmins, *Universal Credit: From Disaster to Recovery?* (2016), 18–21; David Freud, *Reducing Dependency, Increasing Opportunity: Options for the Future of Welfare to Work* (2007), 99–105.

[36] Economic Dependency Working Group, *Dynamic Benefits: Towards Welfare that Works* (2009).

administered by 'a single agency based in the Department for Work and Pensions', and benefits withdrawn through the PAYE system.[37]

Both in opposition and in government, Duncan Smith justified Universal Credit in moral terms as a way of tackling worklessness and reducing welfare dependency. *Dynamic Benefits* argued that a single net income taper of 55 per cent—plus more generous earnings disregards or 'work allowances'—would ensure that any amount of work paid, whether or not it took the individual over the tax credit thresholds of 16 and 30 hours per week. Yet Universal Credit was also an ambitious exercise in technocratic rationalization: a fulfilment of half a century of Negative Income Tax proposals and of the simplifying ambitions which lay behind the 1986 Social Security Act. During the Fowler reviews, DHSS officials had seen 'an integrated benefit system' as 'a dot on the horizon'; now the moment had arrived.[38] Roy Sainsbury saw Universal Credit as 'essentially a technocratic change... an apolitical idea that was not rooted in any ideology at all', and the CSJ's preparatory work drew on advice from experts such as the labour economist Mike Brewer (who had helped to develop tax credits in the Treasury before moving to the IFS in 2001) and the accountants PricewaterhouseCoopers.[39]

The troubled history of Universal Credit would merit a book of its own. A full account will have to await the release of official papers under the twenty-year rule, but Nicholas Timmins has written an invaluable interim study for the Institute for Government, based on interviews with ministers and officials, and it is already possible to identify parallels with earlier debates over tax-benefit integration.[40]

Firstly, the origins of Universal Credit illustrate the importance of individual policy entrepreneurs in putting tax-benefit reform on the political agenda. It seems clear that the policy would not have come into being without either Sainsbury's campaigning outside government or Duncan Smith's patronage within it. According to Timmins, the idea did not even feature in the access talks which DWP officials held with the Conservatives before the 2010 election, but Cameron was keen to appoint Duncan Smith as Secretary of State for Work and Pensions, and the former Tory leader insisted that he would only take the post if he could carry out radical simplification.[41] Significantly, Universal Credit also appealed to DWP officials as a way of regaining control

[37] Economic Dependency Working Group, *Dynamic Benefits*, 27.

[38] The National Archives: Public Record Office (TNA), Kew, BN133/52, Martin Lerner to Mr Walmsley, 'Whither the Reviews', 15 Oct. 1984 (copy).

[39] Timmins, *Universal Credit*, 19, 22, 25.

[40] Timmins, *Universal Credit*.

[41] Timmins, *Universal Credit*, 25–6.

of social security policy after being marginalized by the Treasury during the New Labour years.[42] As with Arthur Cockfield's Tax Credit Scheme in 1971–2 and the Fowler reviews in 1984–5, enthusiasts for change were able to exploit both insiders' and outsiders' frustration with the complexity of the means-tested benefit system. Strong support for the principle of reform from Cameron and senior Liberal Democrats, especially Nick Clegg and Danny Alexander, also helped the DWP overcome Treasury resistance.[43]

Secondly, Universal Credit offers a reminder (if one were needed) that the successful delivery of a guaranteed income is heavily reliant on the state's technological capacity. As we have seen, NIT enthusiasts have long hoped that computerization will make it possible to deliver means-tested support in real time in response to fluctuations in income. During the late 2000s Vocalink Ltd—which operates the UK's bank payments systems—developed a prototype Real-Time Information (RTI) system for HM Revenue and Customs which finally promised to meet these expectations. As Timmins puts it, RTI 'was the key to the lock of Universal Credit', making it possible to adjust benefit payments monthly as claimants' earnings and other circumstances changed and so avoiding the over- and under-payments which had beset the tax credits system.[44] Yet 'everything that could go wrong did go wrong' when the DWP tried to develop the IT required to put RTI into practice, partly because of 'optimism bias' within the department, partly because it lacked in-house technical expertise, and partly because the Government Digital Service was determined to adopt a new 'agile' approach to building the system.[45] Duncan Smith's ambitious timetable was repeatedly pushed back, and the National Audit Office, Public Accounts Committee, and Work and Pensions Select Committee published damning reports on the department's lack of progress.[46] Though the RTI system which is now in place appears to be technically viable, the fraught process of IT development has sapped public confidence in Universal Credit and seriously delayed its implementation. The DWP's target for migrating existing claimants from legacy benefits to Universal Credit has slipped from 2017 to 2023, and the department's own research has found that only 54 per cent of claimants are able to complete the online application process without help, so it has had to allocate £170 million to local

[42] Private information. [43] Timmins, *Universal Credit*, 30.

[44] Timmins, *Universal Credit*, 25. [45] Timmins, *Universal Credit*, 34, 71, 68–70.

[46] *Parliamentary Papers*, 2013–14, HC 621, 'National Audit Office. Universal Credit: Early Progress. Report by the Comptroller and Auditor General', 5 Sept. 2013; HC 619, 'Committee on Public Accounts. Thirtieth Report. Universal Credit: Early Progress', 7 Nov. 2013; HC 1209, 'Work and Pensions Committee. Fifth Report, Universal Credit Implementation: Monitoring DWP's Performance in 2012–13', 9 Apr. 2014.

authorities to assist vulnerable claimants.[47] The efficiency gains have thus been lower than expected, and the National Audit Office has warned that 'we cannot be certain that Universal Credit will ever be cheaper to administer than the benefits it replaces'.[48]

Thirdly, Duncan Smith and his colleagues have had to confront the inescapable dilemma faced by generations of would-be welfare reformers: simplifying the benefit system either involves levelling-up, in which case it is expensive, or levelling-down, in which case it imposes losses on claimants. The package set out in *Dynamic Benefits* was costed at £3.6 billion a year gross and £2.7 billion net, once increased tax receipts were taken into account, and the CSJ claimed that this would be offset by 'reduced expenditure on health, crime, policing, and other social costs' as unemployment fell, together with administrative savings.[49] 4.9 million households would be better off by an average of £1,000 a year, and most of the losses would be concentrated on middle-earners receiving the family element of Child Tax Credit, so the overall impact would be progressive.[50] Treasury officials, however, believed that the true cost of the proposals was much greater than the CSJ implied and 'regarded the profile of winners and losers . . . as "horrific"'.[51]

Following fraught negotiations in the run-up to the October 2010 Comprehensive Spending Review, the Treasury agreed to set aside £2.5 billion for the introduction of Universal Credit in return for £12 billion of cuts elsewhere in the DWP budget. To fit Universal Credit within the spending constraints imposed by the government's deficit-reduction plans, however, the original design has been modified in a host of ways: the taper rate raised from 55 per cent to 63 per cent, work allowances cut for many claimants, Council Tax Benefit removed from the system and devolved to local authorities, and (for those with children born after 6 Apr. 2017) the child element restricted to the first two children. Although the deep cuts which George Osborne announced in his July 2015 budget have been eased by Philip Hammond, the cumulative effect has been to make Universal Credit significantly less generous than the system it replaces—to the tune of about £1.5 billion a year by the time it is fully rolled out in 2023/4—unless it succeeds in increasing take-up.[52] Analysis by the Resolution Foundation and the IFS suggests that the new system will

[47] *Parliamentary Papers*, 2017–19, HC 1123, 'National Audit Office. Rolling out Universal Credit. Report by the Comptroller and Auditor General', 15 June 2018, 5, 19, 33, 42.

[48] HC 1123, 'National Audit Office. Rolling out Universal Credit', 56.

[49] Economic Dependency Working Group, *Dynamic Benefits*, 30.

[50] Economic Dependency Working Group, *Dynamic Benefits*, 293–302.

[51] Timmins, *Universal Credit*, 29.

[52] David Finch and Laura Gardiner, *Back in Credit? Universal Credit after Budget 2018* (2018), 9.

provide more support for many working parents with one or two children, especially those in rented housing, and less support for many homeowners, childless workers, and workless families.[53] Ministers have attempted to manage this problem through the time-honoured expedient of transitional protection, so that existing benefit claimants who are transferred to Universal Credit will not lose out in cash terms.

Finally, the case of Universal Credit provides a powerful reminder that the impact of redistribution on people's lives is crucially dependent on policy details. Many, if not most, guaranteed income proposals have been libertarian in ethos, designed to expand citizens' choices as producers and consumers and to remove the stigma and bureaucracy of means-testing. By contrast, Universal Credit embodies the contractarian logic of contemporary activation policy, intensifying the work requirements associated with Jobseekers' Allowance, Working Tax Credit, and successive welfare-to-work schemes. Under the 'claimant commitment', able-bodied Universal Credit recipients are required to spend up to thirty-five hours a week searching for paid work. In-work conditionality has also been introduced, requiring claimants to seek additional work if they earn less than the equivalent of thirty-five hours a week at the NMW, whilst self-employed workers whose incomes fall below a monthly Minimum Income Floor will have their benefit entitlement capped. Published statistics suggest that in any given month about 5 per cent of Universal Credit claimants have had benefit payments reduced as a result of sanctions.[54]

Other design features have further exacerbated the insecurity faced by low-paid workers and fractured the cross-party support which Universal Credit originally enjoyed. In an attempt to promote good budgeting and mimic the world of work, Conservative ministers have insisted that Universal Credit should be paid monthly in arrears and the housing costs element handled by the tenant, instead of being paid directly from the local authority to the landlord, as it is for many Housing Benefit claimants. Predictably enough, the rollout of Universal Credit has led to a sharp increase in rent arrears and many private landlords have become reluctant to accept Universal Credit

[53] Finch and Gardiner, *Back in Credit?*, 8; Tom Waters, 'Personal Tax and Benefit Measures', presentation to IFS budget briefing, 30 Oct. 2018, accessed 16 Jan. 2019, available at <https://www.ifs.org.uk/uploads/budgets/budget2018/tw_budget2018.pdf>.

[54] Department for Work and Pensions, 'Benefit Sanctions Statistics to January 2018', 15 May 2018, accessed 24 July 2018, available at <https://www.gov.uk/government/statistics/benefit-sanctions-statistics-to-january-2018>, table 3.8; David Webster, 'Benefit Sanctions Statistics: Universal Credit, JSA, ESA, and Income Support: February 2018', 20 Mar. 2018, accessed 24 July 2018, available at <https://suwn.files.wordpress.com/2018/03/18-02-sanctions-stats-briefing-d-webster-20-mar-2018.pdf>.

claimants as tenants.[55] Charities and local authorities have also reported cases of serious hardship among new claimants waiting for their first Universal Credit payment, forcing Philip Hammond to introduce a £1.5 billion package of changes in his November 2017 budget, including the reduction of the waiting period from six weeks to five and the introduction of a simpler process for requesting advance payments. A further £1 billion package in the 2018 budget was designed to ease the migration process for self-employed people and those on out-of-work benefits. These concessions have done little to allay critics' fears that the government is less concerned about income maintenance than about social control: 'pimping the precariat', in Hartley Dean's resonant phrase, in order to 'shore up a highly casualised low-wage labour market'.[56]

Predistribution and the National Living Wage

Despite the ambitious rationalization involved in Universal Credit, the fiscal crisis which the British state has experienced since 2008 has highlighted the difficulties of achieving further redistribution through the tax and benefit systems. One of the many consequences of the crisis, then, has been a renewed interest in other ways of tackling poverty and inequality, including direct interventions in labour and product markets. Looking back on thirty years of mounting inequality in the United States in 2011, Jacob Hacker argued that Democratic policy-makers had become over-reliant on tax-benefit reforms to counteract the distributional effects of financial deregulation, declining trade union membership, and the growing market power of large corporations. 'The moral of this story', Hacker concluded,

> is that progressive reformers need to focus on market reforms that encourage a more equal distribution of power and rewards even before government collects taxes or pays out benefits.[57]

Hacker insisted that predistribution was 'not a strategy for doing more with less', since public services such as housing, education, and childcare had a

[55] Michael Savage and Chaminda Jayanetti, 'Revealed: Universal Credit Sends Rent Arrears Soaring', *The Observer*, 17 Sept. 2017, accessed 9 Jan. 2017, available at <https://www.theguardian.com/society/2017/sep/16/universal-credit-rent-arrears-soar>.

[56] Hartley Dean, 'The Ethical Deficit of the United Kingdom's Proposed Universal Credit: Pimping the Precariat?', *Political Quarterly* 83/2 (2012), 353–9, at 358, 354.

[57] Jacob Hacker, 'The Institutional Foundations of Middle-Class Democracy', in Policy Network, *Priorities for a New Political Economy: Memo to the Left* (2011), 33–7, at 35.

major role to play in raising poorer citizens' living standards and earning potential.[58] Nevertheless, the notion that inequality was best tackled at source had obvious attractions for Labour politicians such as Ed Miliband at a time when tax revenues were stagnant and public attitudes to welfare benefits seemed to be hardening.[59] Hacker's analysis chimed with Miliband's long-standing interest in the 'varieties of capitalism' literature and with his perception that the Blair and Brown governments had accepted the case for a flexible labour market too uncritically.[60] It also echoed Elizabeth Anderson's influential 1999 critique of Rawlsian approaches to distributive justice: that most people are less interested in income distribution per se than in the dignity and equality of status provided by shared social institutions.[61] This argument was taken up by Miliband's adviser Marc Stears and 'Blue Labour' thinkers such as Maurice Glasman, along with think-tanks such as the IPPR.[62] The IPPR's 2014 report on *The Condition of Britain*, for instance, complained that New Labour's '[e]xcessive reliance on cash transfers' had left people 'dependent on the spending preferences of the government of the day, rather than experiencing the respect and dignity that comes from earning a living'.[63]

As Labour leader, Miliband drew on the concept of predistribution to justify a wide range of interventionist proposals, including changes to the banking sector, rail franchising, and corporate takeover rules as well as labour-market regulation. Miliband landed an effective hit on the coalition government in his 2013 party conference speech by unveiling plans for a freeze on energy prices to tackle what he called 'the cost of living crisis'.[64] Labour also signalled a desire to shift housing spending 'from benefits to bricks' through increased public investment in housebuilding, as recommended by the charity Shelter.[65] Given Labour's close links with the trade unions, however, wages were always

[58] Jacob Hacker, 'Foreword: The Promise of Predistribution', in *The Predistribution Agenda: Tackling Inequality and Supporting Sustainable Growth*, edited by Claudia Chwalisz and Patrick Diamond (2015), xxi–xxx, at xxii.

[59] Ed Miliband, 'The Inequality Problem', *London Review of Books*, 4 Feb. 2016, 19–20; Nick Pearce and Eleanor Taylor, 'Government Spending and Welfare: Changing Attitudes towards the Role of the State', in *British Social Attitudes: The 30th Report*, edited by Alison Park, Caroline Bryson, Elizabeth Clery, John Curtice, and Miranda Phillips (2013), 33–61.

[60] Tim Bale, *Five Year Mission: The Labour Party under Ed Miliband* (Oxford, 2015), 57–8; Eunice Goes, *The Labour Party under Ed Miliband: Trying but Failing to Renew Social Democracy* (Manchester, 2016), 67–120.

[61] Elizabeth Anderson, 'What is the Point of Equality?', *Ethics* 109/2 (1999), 287–337.

[62] Kayte Lawson, Graeme Cooke, and Nick Pearce, *The Condition of Britain: Strategies for National Renewal* (2014).

[63] Lawson, Cooke, and Pearce, *The Condition of Britain*, 68.

[64] Bale, *Five Year Mission*, 194.

[65] Bale, *Five Year Mission*, 171; Kate Webb, *Bricks or Benefits? Rebalancing Housing Investment* (2012).

likely to be at the heart of any predistributive strategy. Think-tanks such as the Joseph Rowntree Foundation pointed out that paid work was no longer a reliable route out of poverty, since the number of people in working households with incomes below 60 per cent of the median had risen from 5.1 million in 1996/7 to 7.4 million in 2014/15.[66] Miliband made labour-market exploitation a major theme of Labour's 2015 general election campaign by promising to ban zero-hours contracts and raise the NMW to more than £8 per hour by 2019.

Miliband's focus on low pay built on a grassroots 'living wage' movement which had emerged in London during the early 2000s. The East London Community Organisation (TELCO) sought to emulate the success which living wage campaigns had enjoyed in Baltimore and other US cities during the 1990s.[67] By insisting that a wage was not simply the 'price' of labour but should provide a fair reward and an adequate 'living', living wage campaigners tapped into older traditions of labour activism and implicitly challenged New Labour's focus on the distribution of household income.[68] By 2005 the movement enjoyed the patronage of London mayor Ken Livingstone, who established a Living Wage Unit within the Greater London Authority to calculate a London living wage. As take-up among businesses grew, TELCO's successor group London Citizens launched the Living Wage Foundation in 2011 to set the living wage rate outside the capital and accredit living wage employers.[69] At the same time, increases in the statutory NMW became a major priority for the trade unions, and Ed Miliband's commitment to the living wage helped him squeeze past his brother David in the 2010 Labour leadership contest.[70]

The political appeal of the living wage strategy was boosted by the apparent success of the NMW in establishing a wage floor without increasing unemployment, which echoed David Card and Alan Krueger's revisionist findings on minimum wage laws in the United States.[71] One early study by Mark Stewart

[66] Tom MacInnes, Hannah Aldridge, Sabrina Bushe, Peter Kenway, and Adam Tinson, *Monitoring Poverty and Social Exclusion 2013* (York, 2013), 26–7; Adam Tinson, Carla Ayrton, Karen Barker, Theo Barry Born, Hannah Aldridge, and Peter Kenway, *Monitoring Poverty and Social Exclusion 2016* (York, 2016), 20–1.

[67] Jane Wills and Brian Linneker, 'In-Work Poverty and the Living Wage in the United Kingdom: A Geographical Perspective', *Transactions of the Institute of British Geographers* 39/2 (2014), 182–94; Paul John Sellers, 'The UK Living Wage: A Trade Union Perspective', *Employee Relations* 39/6 (2017), 790–9.

[68] Deborah M. Figart, Ellen Mutari, and Marilyn Power, *Living Wages, Equal Wages: Gender and Labor Market Policies in the United States* (2002), 34–51.

[69] Wills and Linneker, 'In-Work Poverty and the Living Wage', 188.

[70] Goes, *The Labour Party under Ed Miliband*, 45–6.

[71] David Card and Alan B. Krueger, *Myth and Measurement: The New Economics of the Minimum Wage* (Princeton, 1995).

found that the introduction of the NMW had 'no significant adverse effect on employment' between 1999 and 2001; another, by Richard Dickens and Alan Manning, showed that it had begun to narrow the gap between the bottom and the middle of the pay distribution.[72] During the mid-2000s, the Low Pay Commission (LPC) persuaded the government to raise the NMW relative to both mean and median earnings, increasing its 'bite' from 45.6 per cent of the median in April 1999 to 50.3 per cent in April 2007.[73] Although this upward trajectory was interrupted by the financial crisis, it resumed under the coalition, reaching 52.5 per cent of median earnings by April 2015. In addition to the living wage campaign, think-tanks such as the Resolution Foundation also helped push the NMW up the political agenda. Founded by the insurance magnate Clive Cowdery in 2005, the Resolution Foundation has become a major centre for research into low- and middle-income households, with a particular focus on financial advice services (during the 2005 Parliament) and living standards (since 2010). In 2013 the Foundation commissioned an expert review of the NMW, *More than a Minimum*, which was chaired by the former LPC chairman Sir George Bain and included the labour economists Paul Gregg, Karen Mumford, and Alan Manning.[74] The Bain review argued that the government should revise the LPC's mandate by setting a medium-term ambition for the NMW, and suggested that raising it to 60 per cent of the median wage over five years would be a realistic objective.[75] The LPC would then become the government's 'watchdog on low pay', advising ministers on how they could remove the obstacles to a higher NMW and on which industries could afford to pay more than the statutory minimum.[76]

Supporters of a higher minimum wage achieved an unexpected breakthrough when George Osborne announced plans for a statutory National Living Wage for workers aged 25 and over in his July 2015 budget. The NLW sits alongside the NMW and is set by the Chancellor, not the LPC, with an initial rate of £7.20 an hour and a target of reaching 60 per cent of

[72] Mark Stewart, 'The Employment Effects of the National Minimum Wage', *Economic Journal* 114/494 (2004), C110–C116, at C116; Richard Dickens and Alan Manning, 'Has the National Minimum Wage Reduced UK Wage Inequality?', *Journal of the Royal Statistical Society*, Series A, 167/4 (2004), 613–26.

[73] Jerold L. Waltman, *Minimum Wage Policy in Great Britain and the United States* (New York, 2008), 100–3; Cm. 9717, *National Minimum Wage: Low Pay Commission Report 2018* (2018), figure 2.5, and supporting data in Low Pay Commission, 'Low Pay Commission 2018 Report Data', 27 Nov. 2018, accessed 9 Jan. 2019, available at <https://assets.publishing.service.gov.uk/government/uploads/system/uploads/attachment_data/file/759273/LPC_2018_Report_data.xlsx>.

[74] Resolution Foundation, *More than a Minimum. The Resolution Foundation Review of the Future of the National Minimum Wage: The Final Report* (2014).

[75] Resolution Foundation, *More Than a Minimum*, 13.

[76] Resolution Foundation, *More Than a Minimum*, 12.

median earnings by 2020. As Donald Hirsch has noted, the introduction of an explicit target for tackling low pay through the NLW represents 'a profound reversal in the policy stance of successive UK governments', qualifying the commitment to labour-market flexibility which dominated Conservative and New Labour policy between 1979 and 2015.[77] Surveys suggest that the idea of a higher wage floor is very popular, and chimes with voters' instinctive support for 'fair' and 'decent' pay.[78] Indeed, during the 2017 general election campaign the two main parties competed to go further and faster on the issue. The Conservatives promised to peg the NLW at 60 per cent of median earnings, whilst Jeremy Corbyn and John McDonnell pledged to extend it to 18–24-year-olds and raise it to 'the level needed for a decent life'—expected to be over £10 an hour by 2020.[79]

Although a £10 minimum wage makes for a powerful campaign slogan, the emerging politicization of low pay is not without risks. The veteran industrial relations scholar William Brown has warned that the introduction of the NLW may have 'fatally compromised' the LPC by abandoning its cautious, evidence-based approach.[80] As the wage floor rises, the risk of displacing low-skilled workers is also likely to become more pressing, particularly in sectors such as hospitality, retail, and social care where the NLW is already over 80 per cent of median earnings.[81] Recent research by Richard Dickens, Rebecca Riley, and David Wilkinson suggests that the employment effects of the NMW may have been understated by previous studies, and that 'large increases in the mid-2000s had damaging effects on employment retention' among part-time female workers.[82] There are also signs that the NLW may have had larger spillover effects than the NMW, though many firms have again sought to manage costs by restructuring supervisory roles and reducing shop-floor differentials.[83]

Even if the NLW does not have a negative impact on employment, the scope for reducing poverty through higher wages is likely to be limited by the

[77] Donald Hirsch, 'The "Living Wage" and Low Income: Can Adequate Pay Contribute to Adequate Family Living Standards?', *Critical Social Policy* 38/2 (2017), 367–86, at 368.

[78] Suzanne Hall, Katrina Leary, and Helen Greevy, *Public Attitudes to Poverty* (York, 2014), 27–9.

[79] Conservative Party, *Forward, Together: Our Plan for a Stronger Britain and a More Prosperous Future* (2017), 16; Peter Walker, 'John McDonnell Announces £10 an Hour Living Wage Plan', *The Guardian* (online edn), 26 Sept. 2016, accessed 10 Jan. 2018, available at <https://www.theguardian.com/politics/2016/sep/26/john-mcdonnell-10-an-hour-living-wage-plan-labour-conference>; Labour Party, *For the Many not the Few: The Labour Party Manifesto 2017* (2017), 47.

[80] William Brown, 'The Toxic Politicising of the National Minimum Wage', *Employee Relations* 39/6 (2017), 785–9, at 785.

[81] Cm. 9717, *National Minimum Wage: Low Pay Commission Report 2018*, 57.

[82] Richard Dickens, Rebecca Riley, and David Wilkinson, 'A Re-examination of the Impact of the UK National Living Wage on Employment', *Economica* 82/328 (2015), 841–64, at 861.

[83] Cm. 9536, *National Minimum Wage: Low Pay Commission Report 2017* (2017), 75–9; Cm. 9717, *National Minimum Wage: Low Pay Commission Report 2018*, 66–72.

mismatch between paid work and household needs which feminists and child poverty campaigners have highlighted for generations. Although George Osborne hoped that the NLW would provide political cover for tax credit and Universal Credit cuts, analysis by the IFS and the Women's Budget Group suggests that the increased wage floor will only partly offset the losses faced by low-income families with children.[84] The government has made no attempt to link the NLW to actual living costs, and even the voluntary living wage set by the Living Wage Foundation—which is based on Loughborough University's Minimum Income Standard—assumes full take-up of the tax credits and other benefits to which workers are entitled.[85] On the public spending side, the Office for Budget Responsibility has estimated that the NLW will reduce total welfare spending by only £500 million (or about 0.2 per cent) by 2020/1.[86] It is difficult to see how any plausible minimum wage would allow a significant reduction in transfer payments without damaging the living standards of workers with high housing costs or large families.

An effective assault on poverty and inequality is thus likely to require either a renewed commitment to income redistribution or a much more wide-ranging set of 'predistributive' policies. As Joe Guinan and Martin O'Neill have pointed out, Jeremy Corbyn's election as Labour leader in 2015 has led to a deepening of the party's 'institutional turn' through new proposals for strengthening trade unions' bargaining power, using local government procurement to build 'community wealth', and extending public ownership.[87] Left-leaning thinkers such as O'Neill, Stewart Lansley, Howard Reed, and Tony Atkinson have suggested a variety of strategies for redistributing wealth, curbing excess profits and corporate pay, and raising wages at the expense of capital.[88] However attractive an 'egalitarian rebalancing of power through a

[84] William Elming, Carl Emmerson, Paul Johnson, and David Phillips, *An Assessment of the Potential Compensation Provided by the New 'National Living Wage' for the Personal Tax and Benefit Measures Announced for Implementation in the Current Parliament*, IFS Briefing Note 175 (2015); Women's Budget Group, 'New Research Shows Universal Credit Failing the "Just About Managing": With Women and BME Households Hardest Hit' (press release, 16 Nov. 2017), accessed 24 July 2018, available at <https://wbg.org.uk/wp-content/uploads/2017/11/pre-budget-press-release-nov-2017-15-11.pdf>.

[85] Donald Hirsch, 'Contemporary UK Wage Floors and the Calculation of a Living Wage', *Employee Relations* 39/6 (2017), 815–24.

[86] Cm. 9341, *Office for Budget Responsibility: Welfare Trends Report, October 2016* (2016), 63.

[87] Joe Guinan and Martin O'Neill, 'The Institutional Turn: Labour's New Political Economy', *Renewal* 26/2 (2018), 5–16.

[88] Martin O'Neill, 'Survey Article: Philosophy and Public Policy after Piketty', *Journal of Political Philosophy* 25/3 (2017), 343–75; Howard Reed and Stewart Lansley, *How to Boost the Wage Share* (2013); Stewart Lansley, Duncan McCann, and Steve Schifferes, *Remodelling Capitalism: How Social Wealth Funds Could Transform Britain* (2018); Anthony B. Atkinson, *Inequality: What Can Be Done?* (Cambridge, Mass., 2015).

reordering of the basic institutions of the economy' might be, though, its political and economic feasibility remains uncertain.[89] In an era of high labour and capital mobility, the most immediate effect of a radically interventionist agenda might well be a weakening of the UK's tax base which further limits the scope for fiscal transfers.

Conclusion

It is not difficult to understand the turn away from RML which has taken place in Britain over the past decade. The decline of tax revenues and living standards in the wake of the financial crisis undermined New Labour's reputation for economic competence and made further instalments of 'redistribution by stealth' politically unsustainable. Calls for higher wages resonated with deeply rooted cultural attitudes and with the emphasis that all recent governments have placed on encouraging paid work. The Conservative–Liberal Democrat coalition was able to gain political traction by characterizing tax credits as a source of welfare dependency and using increases in the personal allowance to boost take-home pay. Indeed, Daniel Clegg has suggested that the NLW and the increased tax threshold might provide the basis for a new 'Make Work Pay consensus', both simpler and more politically durable than New Labour's reliance on transfer payments.[90]

Despite its obvious political appeal, however, the vogue for 'predistribution' also has limitations. Taken by itself, the NLW is unlikely to prompt a decisive shift away from 'low-road' production strategies or to reduce the UK's reliance on low-skilled service-sector jobs. A significant reduction in market inequality would require a much broader engagement with the sources of inequality, including an assault on corporate power, a concerted effort to raise job quality, and an attempt to channel investment into higher-skilled and better-paid sectors. Even if this approach were politically possible, it is difficult to foresee the precise distributional consequences of labour and product market interventions.[91] Nor is it clear how the predistribution agenda would help workers and employers manage the disruptive impact of automation. Indeed, some of the contemporary enthusiasm for a living wage is tinged with nostalgia for a

[89] Guinan and O'Neill, 'The Institutional Turn', 11.

[90] Daniel Clegg, 'The Demise of Tax Credits', *Political Quarterly* 86/4 (2015), 493–9, at 497.

[91] Paul Gregg, 'The Potential and Limits of Predistribution in the UK: Tackling Inequality and Poverty', in *The Predistribution Agenda: Tackling Inequality and Supporting Sustainable Growth*, edited by Claudia Chwalisz and Patrick Diamond (2015), 79–92.

post-war employment model which has been eroded by successive waves of social and technological change.

The redistributive apparatus of the 'transfer state' is thus likely to remain central to British social policy for the foreseeable future. Although the Conservatives have abandoned New Labour's child poverty targets in favour of a focus on worklessness and educational attainment, the Blair government's relative poverty measure remains firmly established in public discourse.[92] Despite a decade of cuts, working-age welfare spending is still high by historical standards, and the introduction of Universal Credit has taken the UK a step closer towards the 'holy grail' of integration. At the same time, disillusionment with the complexity and conditionality of Universal Credit has contributed to growing interest in UBI, as we shall see in Chapter 9.

[92] Feargal McGuinness and Jennifer Brown, 'Child Poverty', House of Commons Library Briefing Note CDP-0256, 15 Dec. 2016.

9

The Return of Universal Basic Income

It is difficult to spend much time in British social policy debates right now without coming across the idea of Universal Basic Income. Over the last five years, basic income has risen from the political margins to attract a wide range of supporters, fuelled by disillusionment with Universal Credit sanctions and cuts and renewed concern about 'the rise of the robots'. Anthony Painter and Chris Thoung of the Royal Society of Arts (RSA), the accelerationist thinkers Nick Srnicek and Alex Williams, and the left-wing broadcaster Paul Mason have all highlighted the potential for UBI to transform the relationship between work, creativity, and leisure in an age of automation.[1] The Green Party put the idea at the heart of its 2015 and 2017 general election campaigns, and four Scottish councils—Glasgow, Fife, North Ayrshire, and Edinburgh—are developing plans for a pilot scheme. Even the TUC has commended the idea for further study, and the Labour Party has set up a working group to explore the implications.[2] 'All of a sudden', Shadow Chancellor John McDonnell has noted, basic income is 'an idea whose time may well have come'.[3]

This chapter explores the history of basic income campaigning in Britain since the 1980s and examines how the idea has moved back up the political agenda. In some respects, the recent surge of interest echoes a similar wave of enthusiasm during the 1970s and 1980s, when (as we have seen in Chapter 6) many claimants' activists, environmentalists, and liberal reformers turned to basic income as a response to the collapse of the Keynesian post-war settlement. The intervening thirty years have seen the development of a global UBI movement, which has taken institutional form in the Basic Income Research

[1] Anthony Painter and Chris Thoung, *Creative Citizen, Creative State: The Principled and Pragmatic Case for a Universal Basic Income* (2015); Nick Srnicek and Alex Williams, *Inventing the Future: Postcapitalism and a World without Work* (2015); Paul Mason, *Postcapitalism: A Guide to our Future* (2015).

[2] Peter Sloman, 'Universal Basic Income in British Politics: From a "Vagabond's Wage" to a Global Debate', *Journal of Social Policy* 47/3 (2018), 625–42; Luke Martinelli and Nick Pearce, 'Basic Income in the UK: Assessing Prospects for Reform in an Age of Austerity', *Social Policy and Society* 18/2 (2019), 265–75.

[3] Ashley Cowburn, 'Labour Sets up "Working Group" to Investigate Universal Basic Income, John McDonnell Reveals', *The Independent*, 5 Feb. 2017, accessed 23 Mar. 2018, available at <https://www.independent.co.uk/news/uk/politics/labour-sets-up-working-group-to-investigate-radical-idea-of-basic-income-john-mcdonnell-reveals-a7563566.html>.

Transfer State: The Idea of a Guaranteed Income and the Politics of Redistribution in Modern Britain. Peter Sloman, Oxford University Press (2019). © Peter Sloman. DOI: 10.1093/oso/9780198813262.001.0001

Group in Britain—now the Citizen's Basic Income Trust—and the Basic Income Earth Network (BIEN). Even so, the current basic income debate is distinctive in at least three respects. Firstly, basic income has moved up the agenda during the recovery from the 2008–9 recession, at a time when the official UK unemployment rate has fallen to its lowest level since the 1970s. Pessimism about the labour market thus stems not so much from joblessness per se—in contrast to the Thatcher years—but from dissatisfaction with the quality of work and fears about the impact of automation. Secondly, UBI has begun to attract much greater support within the Labour Party and the trade union movement than in previous generations. Though some social democrats still see basic income as a Trojan horse for neoliberalism—which would 'discourage work', 'perpetuate inequality', and hasten 'the total, final and irreversible atomisation of labour'—such producerist attitudes are no longer universal.[4] Thirdly, there are signs that some campaigners are beginning to challenge the dominant conception of UBI as a tax-benefit reform designed to provide a guaranteed minimum income. Recent proposals for a variable or time-limited UBI, paid out of a Citizens' Wealth Fund, revive a tradition of asset-based social dividends which dates back to Thomas Paine but has been marginalized in the British debate for much of the last century.

If these shifting attitudes to UBI partly stem from changes in the UK political landscape, they also reflect the fact that basic income debates have taken on a global frame of reference. Where British activists once set the pace in basic income research, the latest wave of interest has been powerfully shaped by developments in the global south, including pilot schemes in Namibia and India and the wider enthusiasm for tackling poverty through cash transfers. The 'new politics of distribution' which James Ferguson has identified in the development community appears to be migrating back to Europe and North America, encouraged by campaigns such as the 2013–14 European Citizens' Initiative for UBI and support from Silicon Valley entrepreneurs such as Sam Altman.[5] The proposed Scottish pilot thus forms part of a growing nexus of research around UBI, drawing on lessons from similar experiments in Finland and the Netherlands and contributing to an ongoing process of policy learning.[6] The lead-in times involved in designing and

[4] Jon Cruddas and Tom Kibasi, 'A Universal Basic Mistake', *Prospect* 224 (July 2016), 50–2, at 50, 51.

[5] James Ferguson, *Give a Man a Fish: Reflections on the New Politics of Distribution* (Durham, NC, 2015).

[6] Jurgen de Wispelaere, 'Basic Income in our Time: Improving Political Prospects through Policy Learning?', *Journal of Social Policy* 45/4 (2016), 617–34; Anna Dent, 'From Utopia to Implementation: How Basic Income Has Progressed from Radical Idea to Legitimate Policy Solution. An Exploratory Study' (MSc dissertation, University of Bristol, 2017).

running pilots make it difficult to describe this as 'fast policy', but it certainly illustrates the intensification of policy transfer which Jamie Peck and Nik Theodore have diagnosed, as 'policy decisions made in one jurisdiction increasingly echo and influence those made elsewhere...and global policy "models"...exert normative power across significant distances'.[7]

Hermione Parker and the Basic Income Research Group

For most of the twentieth century, discussions of basic income in British politics were episodic and conceptually confused, as we have seen in Chapters 3 and 6. Basic income schemes appeared under a wide variety of names, the differences between UBI and NIT were frequently blurred, and some of the most influential proposals either included work requirements (as in Juliet Rhys-Williams's original scheme) or excluded part of the population (as in Arthur Cockfield's). Several of the academics who took an interest in Rhys-Williams's ideas—such as James Meade, the sociologist Michael Young, and the Liberal activist and lecturer Nancy Seear—returned to the fray in the 1970s and 1980s, but this hardly amounted to a basic income movement. The formation of BIRG in 1984 and BIEN (originally the Basic Income *European* Network) in 1986 was an intellectual as well as an institutional turning point. As Figure 9.1 shows, mentions of 'basic income' in British English texts rose almost tenfold between the 1970s and the 1990s, while the older term 'social dividend' fell out of use—a reflection of an increasingly coherent and self-referential literature.

The roots of BIRG lay in Sir Brandon Rhys-Williams's attempt to revive his mother's ideas by encouraging Michael Meacher's Select Committee inquiry to consider a 'Basic Income Guarantee' scheme in 1982–3.[8] Much of the detailed work was carried out by Hermione Parker, a St Andrews PPE graduate who had carved out a career as a research assistant to a string of Conservative MPs.[9] Parker quickly became a basic income enthusiast, and a 1983 conference on income maintenance hosted by the National Council for Voluntary Organisations (NCVO) brought her into contact with other academics and activists

[7] Jamie Peck and Nik Theodore, *Fast Policy: Experimental Statecraft at the Thresholds of Neoliberalism* (Minneapolis, 2015), 3.

[8] British Library of Political and Economic Science (BLPES), London, Rhys-Williams papers, B8/6, 'A New Minimum Income Guarantee: The Tax Credit Solution. Sir Brandon Rhys-Williams MP', n.d. [1981]; *Parliamentary Papers*, 1982–3, HC 20–1, 'The Structure of Personal Income Taxation and Income Support. Minutes of Evidence', 420–59.

[9] Susan Raven, 'Obituary: Hermione Parker', *Citizen's Income Trust Newsletter* 3 (2007).

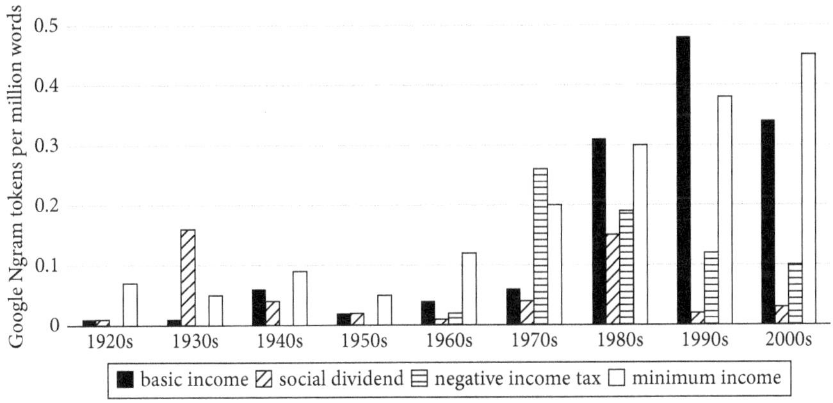

Figure 9.1. Frequency of 'basic income' and related terms in the Google Books (British English) corpus by decade, 1920–2008

Source: Google Books Ngrams, accessed via Brigham Young University online corpora (<http://googlebooks.byu.edu>).

who were interested in the idea.[10] Although the NCVO primarily served as an umbrella group for the voluntary sector, it was drawn into debates over unemployment policy during the 1980s through its involvement in delivering job-creation schemes such as the Community Programme.[11] The NCVO's Policy Analysis Unit also received financial support from the Monument Trust, one of the Sainsbury family's charitable trusts, which was keen to challenge 'the inflexibility of welfare bureaucracies' and 'stimulate fresh thought' about social policy.[12] The head of the Policy Analysis Unit, Peter Ashby, floated the case for UBI in a July 1984 pamphlet and persuaded NCVO to provide seed-funding for a three-year research project: BIRG would 'establish whether a Basic Income scheme would be feasible and whether the costs to be borne by taxation would be capable of commanding a broad consensus'.[13] After the research programme was complete, BIRG remained in existence as an independent charitable trust, changing its name to the Citizen's Income Trust (CIT) in 1992 and Citizen's Basic Income Trust in 2017 to reflect

[10] Interview with Malcolm Torry, 30 Mar. 2017; interview with Annie Miller, 17 Apr. 2018; Rhys-Williams papers, B8/8, 'Mimi' [Parker] to Sir Brandon Rhys-Williams, 14 Oct. 1983.

[11] N. J. Crowson, 'Introduction: The Voluntary Sector in 1980s Britain', *Contemporary British History* 25/4 (2011), 491–8.

[12] London Metropolitan Archives, National Council for Voluntary Organisations papers, LMA/4016/IS/A/01/076, 'Note of Discussion with Hugh de Quetteville (H.) and Tim Riviere (T.R.) on 8th January 1981', by Andrew Purkis, 9 Jan. 1981.

[13] Peter Ashby, *Social Security after Beveridge—What Next?* (1984); *BIRG Bulletin* 2 (1984), 1. Ashby later came to public notice as Peter Mandelson's partner when the couple were outed by the tabloid press during the 1987 general election campaign.

shifting usage. The Joseph Rowntree Charitable Trust provided a major grant during the 1990s, which paid for full-time staff and an office at the LSE, but this lapsed in 2000. Since then, the group has been run on a voluntary basis by its director Malcolm Torry, with an annual budget of about £4,000.[14]

The formation of BIRG brought together UBI enthusiasts from across the political spectrum. Hermione Parker's political instincts were conservative and market-oriented: she shared Margaret Thatcher's sturdy individualism, dismissed proposals for a living wage as 'inflationary nonsense', and wrote pamphlets for the Institute of Economic Affairs.[15] By contrast, Bill Jordan was influenced by the libertarian socialism of the Claimants' Unions, whilst the Scottish economist Annie Miller had reacted against the National Insurance system on feminist grounds, and the South London vicar Malcolm Torry had previously spent two years administering Supplementary Benefit and wanted to do all he could to take people off it.[16] Alongside a core of committed supporters, Parker and Ashby also built up a network of sympathizers from politics and the voluntary sector. About 150 individuals and almost 100 institutions subscribed to BIRG's biannual *Bulletin*, and the SDP MP Charles Kennedy and three future Labour ministers—Malcolm Wicks (Family Policy Studies Centre), Cathy Ashton (Business in the Community), and David Triesman (National Association of Teachers in Further and Higher Education)—could be found among the members of the group's Research Panel.[17]

The institutionalization of the British movement paralleled similar developments elsewhere in western Europe, particularly in the Netherlands, where the radical Christian intellectual Jan Pieter Kuiper and the food-workers' union Voedingsbond FNV canvassed support for UBI.[18] The Belgian philosopher Philippe van Parijs began to work on the idea during the early 1980s, and organized an international conference at Louvain-la-Neuve in September 1986 at which BIEN was formed. BIRG was closely involved in BIEN from the outset—providing four of its twelve founding officers—and its *Bulletin* featured regular reports from international correspondents such as Alexander de

[14] Interview with Malcolm Torry.

[15] Rhys-Williams papers, B8/6, Hermione Parker, 'The BIG Way to Full Employment', 18 June 1983 (copy); Hermione Parker, *The Moral Hazard of Social Benefits: A Study of the Impact of Social Benefits and Income Tax on Incentives to Work* (1982); Hermione Parker, *Taxes, Benefits and Family Life: The Seven Deadly Traps* (1995).

[16] Interview with Bill Jordan, 2 Aug. 2017; interview with Annie Miller; interview with Malcolm Torry.

[17] For *Bulletin* circulation, see Hermione Parker, 'Editorial', *BIRG Bulletin* 5 (1986), 1; for the Research Panel, see *BIRG Bulletin* 2 (1984), 3.

[18] Philippe van Parijs and Yannick Vanderborght, *Basic Income: A Radical Proposal for a Free Society and a Sane Economy* (Cambridge, Mass., 2017), 96–7.

Roo, an adviser to the Green group in the European Parliament who later became an MEP himself.[19] Guy Standing, then working as coordinator of labour market research at the International Labour Organization (ILO) in Geneva, was also a member of the BIEN committee. Where other British welfare reformers looked to the United States and the Commonwealth for inspiration, BIRG built links with fellow European campaigners and sought to exploit the opportunities opened up by European integration. Sir Brandon Rhys-Williams had proposed a European Community-wide basic income as early as 1975, and Meade and van Parijs revived the idea in the early 1990s as a way of levelling up social provision within the single market.[20] Indeed, BIEN remained overtly European in outlook until it became the Basic Income *Earth* Network in 2004.

Arguments for UBI during the 1980s and 1990s took a variety of forms. Perhaps the most important was the belief that the model of stable industrial employment which had shaped British economic policy for much of the twentieth century had gone for good, and that a basic income offered the best way of supporting new working patterns. Hermione Parker, for instance, claimed that her 'Basic Income Guarantee' scheme was

> the only proposal submitted to the Meacher Inquiry which made a real attempt to come to terms with social, demographic and technological change since World War 2... Today's world needs a more flexible labour market, with job sharing, flexible working hours, part-time work by both men and women, and above all a highly skilled workforce with a readiness to change jobs, to train and re-train more frequently.[21]

Parker's enthusiasm for labour-market deregulation had a distinctly Thatcherite ring to it, but others shared her belief that attitudes to work and welfare needed to change. James Meade thought that '[i]n a competitive non-inflationary economy full employment will require severe wage restraints', and hoped that a basic income would ease this process by reducing the

[19] Anne G. Miller, ed., *Basic Income: Proceedings of the First International Conference on Basic Income, Louvain-La-Neuve, Belgium, 4–6 September 1986* (Antwerp, 1986), iv; Alexander de Roo, 'Basic Income Initiatives in the European Parliament', *BIRG Bulletin* 7 (1988), 27; Alexander de Roo, 'Citizen's Income Too Radical for the European Parliament', *BIRG Bulletin* 15 (1992), 19–20.

[20] Sir Brandon Rhys-Williams, 'Economic and Monetary Union: New Approaches', working document for European Parliament Committee on Economic and Monetary Affairs, PE 41.975 (1975); J. E. Meade, *The Building of the New Europe: National Diversity versus Continental Uniformity* (Edinburgh, 1991); Michel Genet and Philippe van Parijs, 'Eurogrant', *BIRG Bulletin* 15 (1992), 4–7.

[21] Rhys-Williams papers, B8/6, Hermione Parker, 'The BIG Way to Full Employment'.

political salience of wage bargaining.[22] Left-wing UBI supporters also talked the language of flexibility, though they were more sympathetic to the possibility that it would encourage labour-market withdrawal and greater self-provisioning. Guy Standing, for instance, argued that a basic income 'need not result in lower wages to the extent that people could more easily reject a job paying a very low wage', whilst Bill Jordan hoped that it would 'provide a platform for a new advance in the battle against exploitation of all kinds' and 'give families ... more choice about how to share home responsibilities'.[23]

A second set of arguments for UBI focused on the dysfunctionality of the existing tax and benefit systems, particularly the low take-up of means-tested benefits and the problem caused by the poverty and unemployment traps. Centre-right enthusiasts for basic income, such as Parker and Rhys-Williams, presented it as a way of rationalizing 'obsolete systems of raising revenue and redistributing income', simplifying the 'vastly expensive welfare jungle', and rewarding 'self-reliance through thrift'.[24] For those with links to claimants' groups, its appeal was rather different: a genuinely unconditional basic income would free the poor from complex benefit rules and fill gaps in the system. Peter Mitchell of the Royal Association for Disability and Rehabilitation (RADAR), for instance, saw a generous UBI as a way of ending the separation of claimants into 'sick sheep and fit goats' and fulfilling disability campaigners' demand for a national disablement income.[25] Likewise, as work conditionality requirements grew during the late 1980s, the cultural theorist Ann Gray suggested that it could serve as a 'mobilizing deman[d]' for the left, giving structure to the unions' struggle against 'economic conscription'.[26]

A third strand of the basic income literature was more utopian in character, echoing Bertrand Russell's vision of a 'vagabond's wage' as a foundation for creativity and personal freedom. André Gorz's discussion of the 'liberation of time' pointed in this direction, but Philippe van Parijs's 'real libertarianism' was perhaps more influential, particularly when he tried to justify UBI by explaining why even 'welfare hippies and Malibu surfers' deserved to be fed.[27]

[22] J. E. Meade, *Fifteen Propositions concerning the Building of an Equitable, Full-Employment, Non-Inflationary, Free-Enterprise Economy* (1993), 5.

[23] Guy Standing, 'An Alternative to Wage-Capping', letter, *BIRG Bulletin* 4 (1985), 19; Bill Jordan, 'Exploitation and Basic Incomes', *BIRG Bulletin* 4 (1985), 12–13, at 13.

[24] Rhys-Williams papers, B8/13, Sir Brandon Rhys-Williams to Nigel Lawson, 6 Jan. 1988 (copy); Hermione Parker, *Goodbye Beveridge?* (1980), i, ii.

[25] Peter Mitchell, 'Sick Sheep, Fit Goats', letter, *BIRG Bulletin* 3 (1985), 17.

[26] Ann Gray, 'Resisting Economic Conscription', *Capital & Class* 12/1 (1988), 119–46, at 119, 131.

[27] Philippe van Parijs, 'Why Surfers Should Be Fed: The Liberal Case for an Unconditional Basic Income', *Philosophy and Public Affairs* 20/2 (1991), 101–31, at 102; Philippe van Parijs, *Real Freedom for All: What (if Anything) can Justify Capitalism?* (Oxford, 1995).

Van Parijs sought to adapt Rawls's difference principle to argue that a society ought to guarantee all citizens 'the means they require for the pursuit of their conception of the good life', since work requirements and means tests risked fatally undermining 'the social bases of self-respect'.[28] This emphasis on autonomy was taken up by pluralist socialists such as Paul Hirst, who argued that UBI could underpin radical decentralization and cooperative experiments in *Associative Democracy* (1994).[29] It also chimed with the instincts of claimants' activists who saw means-testing as a form of 'social control over... working class people'.[30]

All three of these arguments implied that UBI should be a stable and predictable source of income, replacing all or part of the social security system. Alongside this conception of UBI, however, James Meade attempted to revive the inter-war idea of a variable social dividend, based on a public asset or hypothecated revenue stream. Ever since the 1960s, Meade had been concerned by the prospect that automation would increase corporate profits at the expense of the wage share.[31] As the rise of 'Chips and Robots' accelerated in the 1980s, Meade argued that the government should embark on a programme of 'topsy-turvy nationalisation', building up a portfolio of shares and using the profits to pay out an annual dividend to every citizen—an idea taken up by the Social Democratic Party.[32] One obvious model for an asset-based dividend of this type was the Alaska Permanent Fund, which was established in 1976 to invest the state's oil revenues and pay out part of its returns to citizens. Surprisingly, however, Alaska's scheme attracted relatively little interest from British UBI campaigners before the early 1990s.[33] Although the *Financial Times* journalist Samuel Brittan called for 'a people's stake in North Sea oil' in 1978, his plan involved giving citizens free shares rather than an annual dividend, in line with the emerging Thatcherite conception of a 'property-owning democracy'.[34]

[28] Van Parijs, 'Why Surfers Should Be Fed', 103, 105.

[29] Paul Hirst, *Associative Democracy: New Forms of Economic and Social Governance* (Cambridge, Mass., 1994).

[30] East London Claimants' Union, *A Guaranteed Minimum Income: A Socialist Strategy for Social Security* (1980), 1.

[31] J. E. Meade, *Efficiency, Equality and the Ownership of Property* (1964).

[32] J. E. Meade, 'A New Keynesian Approach to Full Employment', *Nationaløkonomisk Tidsskrift* 131/3 (1983), 299–316, at 310; J. E. Meade, *Agathotopia: The Economics of Partnership* (Aberdeen, 1989); Stuart White, '"Revolutionary Liberalism"? The Philosophy and Politics of Ownership in the Post-War Liberal Party', *British Politics* 4/2 (2009), 164–87.

[33] J. Patrick O'Brien and Dennis O. Olson, 'The Alaska Permanent Fund and Dividend Distribution Program', *BIRG Bulletin* 12 (1991), 3–6.

[34] Samuel Brittan and Barry Riley, 'A People's Stake in North Sea Oil', *Lloyds Bank Review*, Apr. 1978, 1–18.

A false dawn: The politics of basic income in the 1980s and 1990s

In common with previous generations of guaranteed income campaigners, the biggest challenge which BIRG faced was to 'get the Basic Income concept discussed as a serious policy option'.[35] Despite the interest which Labour and Conservative governments had taken in NIT and tax credit schemes during the 1960s and 1970s, many social policy experts still dismissed UBI as a panacea hawked by cranks: the trade union researcher Rory O'Kelly, for instance, thought 'tax credit enthusiasts' had a well-deserved reputation as 'the Jehovah's Witnesses of social policy'.[36] Like Juliet Rhys-Williams forty years earlier, Hermione Parker sought to use her political connections and policy analysis techniques to secure mainstream credibility. In particular, she forged close links with Tony Atkinson and Holly Sutherland at the LSE, and used their TAXMOD model to simulate the cost and distributional effects of different policy options.[37] Parker also persuaded Ken Mayhew of the National Economic Development Office to host a study group on basic income and the labour market in 1989–90.[38] Later, after the 1992 election, BIRG organized a two-day seminar for front-bench politicians and other senior policy-makers at St George's House, Windsor Castle.[39]

Parker's determination to establish the credibility of UBI had major implications for the form which BIRG's proposals took. Since many of its members were reacting against the deficiencies of Supplementary Benefit, the group was strongly committed to universality and highly critical of the IFS's plans for a selective guaranteed income.[40] On the other hand, attempts to cost a UBI 'sufficient to permit the abolition of all existing cash benefits, without people on low incomes losing out' suggested that it would require a tax rate of at least 70 per cent, which Parker thought was 'not feasible and probably never will be'.[41] Partly for this reason, the group amended its constitution in 1987–8 to remove a claim that UBI would cover subsistence needs, and focused its efforts

[35] Christopher Hall, 'The Future of Basic Income in Great Britain', in *Basic Income*, edited by Anne G. Miller, 309–13, at 309.

[36] Rory O'Kelly, 'Why Social Dividends are not the Answer', *Policy Studies* 5/2 (1984), 24–30, at 29; interview with Ruth Lister, 18 July 2018.

[37] Rhys-Williams papers, B8/8, 'Mimi' [Parker] to Sir Brandon Rhys-Williams, 14 Oct. 1983.

[38] Hermione Parker, ed., *Basic Income and the Labour Market* (1991).

[39] 'At Home and Abroad', *Citizen's Income Bulletin* 16 (1993), 26–30.

[40] Annie Miller papers, private collection, 'Note of Meeting of the Basic Income Group, Friday 13 July [1984] at 11.30am at NCVO', by Peter Ashby.

[41] Hermione Parker, 'Are Basic Incomes Feasible?', *BIRG Bulletin* 7 (1988), 5–7, at 5, 7.

on showing how a 'partial' payment could reduce reliance on means-testing.[42] Parker, for instance, proposed a basic income of £24 a week at 1985/6 prices—just below the Unemployment Benefit rate for a single person—which would be paid for by a combined income tax and National Insurance rate of 38 per cent, cuts in the personal tax allowance, and the abolition of mortgage interest relief at source.[43] This made it easier to present UBI as a form of supply-side policy, which could help smooth the UK's transition to a service economy, but it also meant that separate means-tested or categorical benefits would have to be maintained for disabled people and other claimants.[44]

Although Parker and Rhys-Williams secured some support from fellow Tories—including a member of the Number 10 Policy Unit, Christopher Monckton—their attempts to press basic income on the Thatcher government were predictably unsuccessful.[45] The Labour Party's social policy advisers were also suspicious, dismissing NIT and UBI as 'essentially fiscal, and largely administrative attempts to tackle poverty' which ignored the 'underlying causes' of low pay and unemployment.[46] As the 1980s went on, however, the political environment became more favourable as politicians began to look to a world beyond Thatcherism. In particular, basic income resonated with two of the main ideological themes which emerged on the centre-left in the wake of the 1987 general election. On the one hand, it fitted well with the left's growing willingness to embrace technological change and the rise of the service economy—a trend typified by *Marxism Today*'s famous 1988 analysis of 'New Times', which suggested that 'the old mass-production Fordist economy' was giving way to 'a new, more flexible, post-Fordist order'.[47] On the other hand, it could also be seen as a concrete embodiment of the new politics of 'citizenship' which underpinned Charter 88's campaign for constitutional reform and which David Marquand championed in *The Unprincipled Society* (1988). The leader of the newly formed Liberal Democrats, Paddy Ashdown, brought these themes together in *Citizen's Britain* (1989)—a book which bore

[42] Tony Walter, 'What are Basic Incomes?', *BIRG Bulletin* 8 (1988), 3–5, at 5.

[43] Parker, 'Are Basic Incomes Feasible?'

[44] Hermione Parker, 'The Tax and Benefit Systems, and their Effects on People with Low Earnings Potential', in *Improving Incentives for the Low-Paid*, edited by Alex Bowen and Ken Mayhew (Basingstoke, 1990), 73–119; Mitchell, 'Sick Sheep, Fit Goats'.

[45] Churchill Archives Centre, Cambridge, Thatcher papers, THCR1/15/12, Christopher Monckton to Prime Minister, 'A Farewell Report', 25 June 1986.

[46] Modern Records Centre, University of Warwick, Trades Union Congress papers, MSS.292D/160.31/4, 'Closing the Stable Door: The Need to Tackle Inequalities at Source', by Chris Pond, Nov. 1984; Labour History Archive and Study Centre, Manchester, Labour Party Archive (LPA), LP/RD/41/1, minutes of Economic Equality Policy Review Group meeting, 28 Jan. 1988.

[47] 'New Times', *Marxism Today*, Oct. 1988, 3.

the strong imprint of discussions with Bill Jordan.[48] Although it might 'take several decades of growing prosperity' to achieve a full basic income, Ashdown argued that 'every step we take towards it' would 'diminish dependency, liberate economic power in the hands of the citizen and cut back on the oppressive power of the state bureaucracies over people's lives'.[49]

For a fleeting moment, what John Kingdon has called the 'policy', 'problem', and 'political' streams seemed to be converging around UBI as a way of supporting labour-market change and mitigating the excesses of Thatcherism.[50] BIRG attempted to exploit this opening by changing its name to the Citizen's Income Trust—a move which helped secure Rowntree funding—and recruiting the former *Tribune* editor Dick Clements as its full-time director.[51] By the mid-1990s, however, the moment of opportunity had passed. The Borrie Commission on Social Justice rejected UBI in its 1994 report, and the Liberal Democrats—who had included the idea in their 1992 manifesto—also backed away from it.[52] 'At no time during the twelve years since the Basic Income Research Group has formed', Parker complained in 1996, 'has the immediate outlook for the introduction of a Citizen's Income in Britain looked weaker.' [53]

Why did basic income fall off the agenda so quickly during the 1990s? One problem was certainly the cost, since the success of the Conservatives' 'tax bombshell' campaign in the 1992 general election made Labour and the Liberal Democrats intensely cautious about new spending commitments. (Parker lamented that 'Anyone can rubbish C[itizen's] I[ncome]. All they need is a computer print-out which says it would cost too much.'[54]) Just as important, however, was the growing influence of communitarian ideas about work obligations and the dangers of dependency, which spread from the United States to Britain during the Thatcher and Major years and shaped New Labour's thinking on welfare.[55] Business and trade union critics had long warned that basic income risked undermining the work ethic, and Charles

[48] Paddy Ashdown, *Citizen's Britain: A Radical Agenda for the 1990s* (1989), iv. Some parts of the book were co-written: interview with Bill Jordan.

[49] Ashdown, *Citizen's Britain*, 83.

[50] John Kingdon, *Agendas, Alternatives and Public Policies*, 2nd edn (New York, 1995).

[51] Interview with Malcolm Torry.

[52] For the Liberal Democrats' rejection of UBI, see Philip Vince, 'After Sixteen Years in Favour of CI, Britain's Liberal Democrats Do a U-Turn', *Citizen's Income Bulletin* 20 (1995), 21, and *The Guardian*, 22 Sept. 1994, 6.

[53] Editorial, *Citizen's Income Bulletin* 22 (1996), 1–2, at 1.

[54] Editorial, *Citizens' Income Bulletin* 21 (1996), 1–2, at 1.

[55] Alice O'Connor, *Poverty Knowledge: Social Science, Social Policy, and the Poor in Twentieth-Century U.S. History* (Princeton, 2001), 242–83; Mark Bevir, *New Labour: A Critique* (Abingdon, 2005), 54–82.

Murray's lurid portrait of a workless 'underclass' revived concerns that it would subsidize the undeserving poor.[56] As the philosopher and Labour peer Raymond Plant pointed out, the 'shift in thinking about social inclusion, from one based on citizenship, status and rights, to one based on obligation and achievement' put UBI advocates on the defensive.[57] Tony Atkinson agreed that 'a major reason for opposition to basic income lies in its lack of conditionality', and tried to accommodate the reciprocity principle for the Borrie Commission by devising a 'participation income' based on a broad test of 'social contribution', but the idea of monitoring citizens' contributions to society raised both practical and theoretical objections.[58] How, for instance, would the state assess the social value of volunteering?[59]

The fate of the Citizen's Income Trust's campaign was sealed by the Major and Blair governments' success in reducing unemployment through economic growth and welfare-to-work measures. The UK unemployment rate fell from 10.4 per cent in 1993 to 6.9 per cent in 1997 and 4.8 per cent in 2004, and the adoption of active labour-market policies in other European countries appeared to have a similar effect, suggesting that—despite the gloomy predictions of post-industrial theorists—full employment was still attainable.[60] As Anton Hemerijck pointed out at the 1998 BIEN Congress, there seemed to be 'no need to introduce a basic income' so long as 'the pathology of "welfare without work"' could be 'resolved through a mix of less expensive policy measures'.[61] The veteran social administrator David Donnison also concluded that the moment for UBI had been and gone. It was 'the great North-West Passage of social policy', which 'had to be explored', but there was 'no way through': 'our whole culture is driving C[itizen's] I[ncome], with its calls for universal benefits financed by a more progressive income tax, off the map of politically feasible options'.[62]

[56] Charles Murray, *The Emerging British Underclass* (1990).

[57] Raymond Plant, 'Citizenship, Employability and the Labour Market', *Citizen's Income Newsletter* 24 (1997), 2–3, at 3.

[58] A. B. Atkinson, 'Beveridge, the National Minimum and its Future in a European Context', in A. B. Atkinson, *Incomes and the Welfare State: Essays on Britain and Europe* (Cambridge, 1995), 290–304, at 300, 301; interview with Malcolm Torry.

[59] Jurgen de Wispelaere and Lindsay Stirton, 'The Case against Participation Income—Political, not Merely Administrative', *Political Quarterly* 89/2 (2018), 262–7.

[60] Olivier Blanchard, 'European Unemployment: The Evolution of Facts and Ideas', *Economic Policy* 21/45 (2006), 6–59.

[61] Anton Hemerijck, 'Prospects for Basic Income in an Age of Inactivity?', in *Basic Income on the Agenda: Policy Objectives and Political Chances*, edited by Robert van der Veen and Loek Groot (Amsterdam, 2000), 137–54, at 153.

[62] David Donnison, 'Is Citizen's Income Still a Serious Option?', *Citizen's Income Bulletin* 25 (1998), 27.

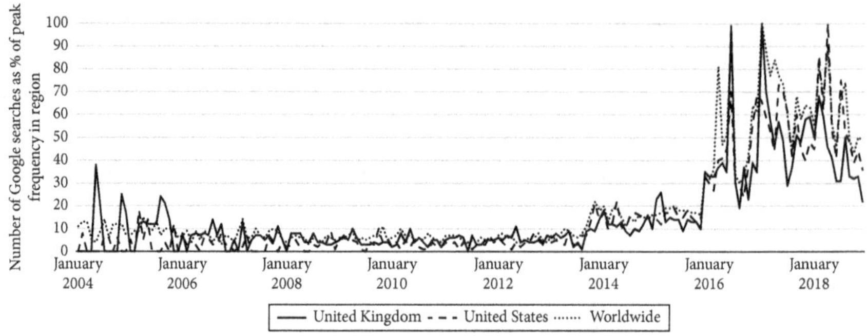

Figure 9.2. Google Trends: Relative frequency of Google searches for 'basic income' in the United Kingdom, the United States, and worldwide, 2004–18
Source: Google Trends data.

Global networks and local experiments: UBI since the 2008 financial crisis

Although interest in UBI has always been cyclical and episodic, the scale of the recent surge is still staggering. Data from Google Trends—set out in Figure 9.2—suggest that the frequency of UK Google searches for 'basic income' doubled in the second half of 2013, doubled again in the winter of 2015–16, and has fluctuated since then at consistently high levels. It is not difficult to identify domestic explanations for the revival of the UBI debate in Britain, such as the troubled implementation of Universal Credit, the election of Jeremy Corbyn as Labour leader, and a renewed appetite for radical ideas on the British left. The close relationship between UK, US, and global searches, however, suggests that it is better understood as part of a much wider trend.

The political geography of the contemporary basic income debate is particularly striking. Though UBI was largely dormant in British (and indeed European) policy debates during the late 1990s and 2000s, the same period witnessed both a deepening of academic work on basic income—much of it fostered by BIEN—and an explosion of interest in cash transfers in the global south. This 'cash transfer revolution' had a number of sources, including political demands for social protection in Latin America and southern Africa and a growing awareness of the limits of traditional social insurance policies within international agencies such as the ILO and the World Bank.[63] As Bob

[63] Joseph Hanlon, Armando Barrientos, and David Hulme, *Just Give Money to the Poor: The Development Revolution from the Global South* (Sterling, Va, 2010); Moritz von Gliszczynski and

Deacon has pointed out, Guy Standing played a particularly important role in forging links with civil society groups in developing countries—such as the Self-Employed Women's Association (SEWA) in India—through the ILO's InFocus Programme on Socio-Economic Security. Standing's commitment to UBI went well beyond ILO policy, but it contributed to a reconceptualization of social policy within the organization, which culminated in a formal recommendation that member states should establish 'social protection floors' in 2012.[64]

The growth of cash transfers in the developing world since the early 2000s has mostly involved categorical benefits such as state pensions and family allowances, often with conditions attached.[65] Brazil's famous Bolsa Familia programme, for instance, provides a means-tested payment to low-income families whose children receive vaccinations and attend at least 85 per cent of school classes.[66] The World Bank's enthusiasm for conditional cash transfers of this kind reflects its focus on poverty alleviation and human capital, an approach which has more in common with New Labour's child poverty strategy than with the basic income movement's commitment to unconditional rights. Nevertheless, the vogue for cash transfers within the development community has paved the way for small-scale experiments with UBI, first in the Namibian village of Otjivero in 2008–9 (with support from the German United Evangelical Mission) and then in the Indian state of Madhya Pradesh in 2011–12 (funded by UNICEF).[67] The Indian pilot, in particular, has shown promising results—including higher levels of small-scale entrepreneurship, higher earned incomes, lower debt bondage, and improvements in school attendance and child nutrition.[68] Of course, these findings are sensitive to the injection of aid money and the particular dynamics of local labour markets, so they cannot be straightforwardly extrapolated to the developed world. Even so, the Namibian and Indian experiments have given UBI credibility and helped raise its profile.

Lutz Leisering, 'Constructing New Global Models of Social Security: How International Organizations Defined the Field of Social Cash Transfers in the 2000s', *Journal of Social Policy* 45/2 (2016), 325–43.

---

[64] Bob Deacon, *Global Social Policy in the Making: The Foundations of the Social Protection Floor* (Bristol, 2013), 31–3, 161.

[65] Von Gliszczynski and Leisering, 'Constructing New Global Models of Social Security'.

[66] Anthony W. Pereira, '*Bolsa Família* and Democracy in Brazil', *Third World Quarterly* 36/9 (2015), 1682–99.

[67] Guy Standing, 'How Cash Transfers Promote the Case for Basic Income', *Basic Income Studies* 3/1 (2008); van Parijs and Vanderborght, *Basic Income*, 138–9.

[68] Sarath Davala, Renana Jhabvala, Soumya Kapoor Mehta, and Guy Standing, *Basic Income: A Transformative Policy for India* (2015).

As we have seen in Chapter 8, the logic of labour-market activation has continued to structure UK social security policy since the 2008 financial crisis. David Cameron and Theresa May's governments have tightened conditionality requirements through Universal Credit and the Work Programme, whilst relying on low-paid service-sector jobs to bring unemployment down. Yet the proliferation of zero-hours contracts and involuntary self-employment has also produced a powerful reaction among left-wing commentators and activists, typified by Guy Standing's influential analysis of *The Precariat* (2011). Despite record levels of employment and a rising minimum wage, data from the Family Resources Survey suggest that about 10 per cent of full-time workers and 20 per cent of part-time workers live below the relative poverty line, and many others drift in and out of poverty over time.[69] One result of this growing concern about economic insecurity is that the traditional social democratic suspicion of UBI has begun to break down, as Daniel Sage has noted.[70] The Unite trade union, for instance, passed a resolution in support of basic income at its 2016 policy conference, tabled by activists from the West Midlands. In the face of 'the growing crisis of low pay, in work poverty and precarity in a labour market increasingly characterised by casualised forms of employment', Unite members welcomed the prospect of an unconditional income floor as a way of liberating workers from 'frequently arbitrary' benefit sanctions and strengthening their bargaining power.[71] Many trade union leaders are still sceptical or hostile, but there are signs of mounting support at grassroots level.[72]

The growth of left-wing interest in basic income has been reinforced by the increasingly pluralistic nature of British UBI campaigning. Although the Citizen's Basic Income Trust remains an important hub for research, other groups have also begun to engage in policy entrepreneurship. Basic Income UK, for instance, was formed in 2013 to canvass support for a petition to the European Parliament (the European Citizen's Initiative for UBI) organized by the Austrian activist Klaus Sambor. Unlike CBIT, it is not a charity, so it has

[69] Joseph Rowntree Foundation, *UK Poverty 2017* (York, 2017), 11; Rod Hick and Alba Lanau, 'Moving in and out of In-Work Poverty in the UK: An Analysis of Transitions, Trajectories and Trigger Events', *Journal of Social Policy* 47/4 (2018), 661–82.

[70] Daniel Sage, 'The Quiet Revolution? The Labour Party and Welfare Conditionality', *Political Quarterly* 90/1 (2019), 99–106.

[71] Kate McFarland, 'UK's Largest Trade Union Endorses Basic Income', BIEN, 11 July 2016, accessed 2 Aug. 2018, available at <https://basicincome.org/news/2016/07/uks-largest-trade-union-endorses-basic-income/>.

[72] Interview with Barb Jacobson, 3 Apr. 2017; Veronica Velez Osorio and Romy Siegert, 'European Trade Union Positions towards Universal Basic Income' (paper delivered at BIEN Congress, University of Tampere, 24–26 Aug. 2018).

been able to engage directly in politics and has built close links with anti-austerity campaigners.[73] The centre-left think-tank Compass has also taken a recurring interest in UBI, and the Green Party focused political attention on the idea by including it in its 2015 manifesto.[74] Perhaps most importantly, the RSA has thrown its weight behind UBI since the 2015 election, highlighting the links between economic security, creativity, and 'decent work' through its 'Power to Create' research programme.[75]

The Labour Party's engagement with basic income has been shaped both by the reaction against precarity and by the 'techno-utopian' vision of 'fully automated luxury communism' championed by left-wing futurists such as Srnicek and Williams.[76] John McDonnell's interest in UBI dates back long before he became Shadow Chancellor; indeed, he briefed the TUC on 'social dividend' proposals as a young researcher in the early 1980s.[77] McDonnell has commissioned Guy Standing to write a report on the idea, and Standing in turn has drawn advice from researchers such as Anthony Painter of the RSA, Stewart Lansley, and Malcolm Torry.[78] Though interest in basic income spans Labour's factional divides, it is perhaps particularly valuable to the left as a way of demonstrating the party's willingness to embrace economic change—giving substance to McDonnell's talk of 'socialism with an iPad' and deflecting charges that Corbyn would 'take Britain back to the 1970s'.

Centre-left enthusiasm for UBI has been even more visible in Scotland, where the social legacy of deindustrialization has become a major driver of support for Scottish independence. The feminist economist Ailsa McKay used her involvement in the Scottish Parliament's 'Scotland's Futures Forum' to put basic income on the agenda during the early 2010s, framing it as an emancipatory measure which could transform gender relations in a 'new Scotland'.[79] The policy was taken up by Radical Independence campaigners as a symbol of their egalitarian ambition in the run-up to the 2014 independence referendum,

[73] Interview with Barb Jacobson.

[74] Howard Reed, *Plan B+1: Rebuilding Britain and a Good Society* (2012), 16; Indra Adnan and Neal Lawson, *New Times: How a Politics of Networks and Relationship Can Deliver a Good Society* (2014), 20; Howard Reed and Stewart Lansley, *Universal Basic Income: An Idea Whose Time Has Come?* (2016); Green Party, *For the Common Good: General Election Manifesto 2015* (2015), 53–6.

[75] Interview with Anthony Painter, 28 Sept. 2017.

[76] Srnicek and Williams, *Inventing the Future*. For a critical analysis of this 'techno-utopian' politics, see Frederick Harry Pitts and Ana Cecilia Dinerstein, 'Corbynism's Conveyor Belt of Ideas: Postcapitalism and the Politics of Social Reproduction', *Capital & Class* 41/3 (2017), 423–34.

[77] Interview with Malcolm Torry; Trades Union Congress papers, MSS.292D/160.11/1, 'Range of Possible Methods for Fulfilling the Functions of Social Security', by Trevor Mawer and John McDonnell, 3 Sept. 1980.

[78] Private information.

[79] Ailsa McKay, *'Welfare to Work' or a Welfare System that Works? Arguing for a Citizens Basic Income in a New Scotland* (Edinburgh, 2013).

and has subsequently received growing attention from the Scottish National Party (SNP) itself. Although most of the social security system—including Universal Credit—is still controlled by Westminster, talking about UBI reinforces the SNP's demands for greater powers and fits neatly with its efforts to identify itself with Scandinavian social democracy.[80] The party's 2016 spring conference noted that UBI could 'potentially provide a foundation to eradicate poverty, make work pay and ensure all our citizens can live in dignity', and Inverclyde MP Ronnie Cowan secured a Westminster Hall debate on the issue.[81] The policy has also attracted support from think-tanks and civil society groups such as Reform Scotland, the Scottish Campaign for Welfare Reform, and the Carnegie Trust, together with a diverse array of MSPs and councillors.[82] The Scottish government has now granted £250,000 to Glasgow, Fife, North Ayrshire, and Edinburgh councils to develop plans for a pilot.[83]

These developments have given UBI a higher profile in British politics than Juliet Rhys-Williams or Hermione Parker ever managed, but they also bear out Jurgen de Wispelaere's warnings about the difficulty of uniting its proponents around a coherent strategy.[84] Much of the contemporary interest in UBI might well be seen as 'cheap', designed to win media coverage and signal a willingness to 'think the unthinkable'. Both the Labour Party and the SNP have carefully avoided explicit commitments to the policy, and the Scottish government does not yet have the power to introduce a national scheme. More seriously, the growing appeal of UBI on the left seems to lie partly in its very transgressiveness, as a symbolic way of challenging the direction of mainstream welfare policy. This might well have the effect of 'contaminating' the policy and making it more difficult to win support among liberals and conservatives. As Samuel Brittan has pointed out, linking basic income with 'fashionable anticapitalist causes such as anti-globalisation and extreme environmentalism' risks 'putting off the enlightened minority among anti-socialist politicians who might otherwise give it some house room'.[85] The implosion of the Green Party's proposals during the 2015 election may already have had

[80] Gill Scott and Gerry Mooney, 'Poverty and Social Justice in the Devolved Scotland: Neoliberalism Meets Social Democracy?', *Social Policy and Society* 8/3 (2009), 379–89.

[81] Jon Stone, 'SNP Conference Backs Universal Basic Income for Independent Scotland', *The Independent*, 15 Mar. 2016, accessed 2 Aug. 2018, available at <https://www.independent.co.uk/news/uk/politics/universal-basic-income-snp-scotland-independent-conference-vote-a6931846.html>; HC Deb., sixth series, 14 Sept. 2016, vol. 614, cols 419WH–434WH.

[82] Interview with Annie Miller.

[83] Carnegie UK, *Exploring the Practicalities of a Basic Income Pilot* (Dunfermline, 2019).

[84] Jurgen de Wispelaere, 'The Struggle for Strategy: On the Politics of the Basic Income Proposal', *Politics* 36/2 (2016), 131–41.

[85] Samuel Brittan, review in *Citizen's Income Trust Newsletter* 2 (2005), 8–9, at 9.

this effect, reinforcing perceptions of the policy as a form of left-wing escapism. The UK government's dismissive response to the Westminster Hall debate on UBI, and the attempt by Scottish Tories to portray pilot schemes as 'an SNP vanity project', suggests that many Conservatives think such a critique is intrinsically damning.[86]

Reframing basic income

Jurgen de Wispelaere is certainly right to warn against naive optimism about the prospects for basic income. A growing sense that radical ideas may be needed to deal with precarity and automation has brought it back on to the policy agenda, but the ethos of unconditionality remains highly controversial, and building a robust coalition of support is still a major challenge. In the light of this context, UBI advocates have become increasingly aware of the importance of framing. As Peter Ashby pointed out thirty years ago,

> The idea of a full BI conjures up powerful symbolic images, such as 'the right not to work', an 'alternative to the work ethic' and 'an acceptance of mass unemployment'. Unless we can repudiate these images, and associate BIs with more positive notions of employment-creation, greater security for flexible workers and part-time working for the unemployed, the idea will be killed before it gets anywhere near the starting post.[87]

As one might expect, surveys suggest that public support varies markedly depending on how basic income is presented and how it would be paid for.[88]

One of the legacies of Juliet Rhys-Williams's work has been to establish a particular conception of basic income—as a universal social security benefit paid for by a relatively proportional income tax—as the paradigmatic form of the scheme in British policy-making circles. Arthur Cockfield's Tax Credit Scheme and Parker's 'Basic Income Guarantee' followed this approach, and Tony Atkinson made it a staple of the public economics literature through his

[86] Damien Hinds in HC Deb., sixth series, 14 Sept. 2016, vol. 614, cols 429WH–434WH; Angus Howarth, 'Scottish Tories want "Unaffordable" Basic Income Pilots Scrapped', *The Scotsman*, 27 June 2018, accessed 2 Aug. 2018, available at <https://www.scotsman.com/news/scottish-tories-want-unaffordable-basic-income-pilots-scrapped-1-4760913>.

[87] Peter Ashby, 'Towards an Income and Work Guarantee', *BIEN Bulletin* 7 (1988), 28–30, at 29.

[88] RSA/Populus Universal Basic Income Survey, 27–29 July 2018, accessed 3 Aug. 2018, available at <https://www.thersa.org/globalassets/pdfs/reports/rsa-populus-basic-income-polling.pdf>.

analysis of 'the basic income/flat tax proposal'.[89] Yet a basic income of this kind is always likely to be difficult to sell politically, since it can so easily be caricatured as an inducement to free-riding—taxing workers in order to pay benefits to those out of work. The conventions of mainstream policy analysis are also unhelpful here, since replacing tax allowances with cash benefits increases both tax and public expenditure, whilst any shift from formal to informal work is liable to reduce GDP (as if it were a straightforward reduction in economic welfare). It is not even clear that replacing existing benefits with a basic income would necessarily reduce headline measures of poverty and inequality. Static microsimulation analysis suggests that the distributional effects are highly sensitive to the parameters chosen, allowing critics to portray UBI as 'a powerful tax engine pulling a tiny cart'—with a complex pattern of gains and losses but only a limited net impact on poverty outcomes.[90]

Ironically, the difficulties of introducing a basic income are exacerbated by the size and structure of the UK's existing transfer state, as a recent OECD study has pointed out.[91] Since tax credits and Housing Benefit provide such large means-tested payments to low-income families, setting UBI at the level of existing benefits would be extremely costly, whilst replacing the benefit system with a cost-neutral basic income would leave many poorer households worse off. Critics can thus point to the 'basic income trilemma' identified by Luke Martinelli (and, indeed, by the Inland Revenue back in 1951): that UBI is either 'inadequate, unaffordable—or not worth the bother'.[92]

Partly for this reason, British campaigners have increasingly attempted to reframe the case for basic income on different lines. The RSA, in particular, has emphasized the need to adopt a dynamic perspective which takes into account the opportunities which a secure regular income can provide. Even if a regular UBI payment is not large enough to lift individuals above the poverty line by itself, it strengthens their ability to make meaningful choices about work and training and so become less reliant on means-tested benefits. Instead of presenting UBI as a path to a post-work utopia, Anthony Painter and his colleagues have suggested that it could become 'one of the institutions supporting good work: that which is fairly remunerated, respected, providing of

[89] A. B. Atkinson, *Public Economics in Action: The Basic Income/Flat Tax Proposal* (Oxford, 1995).

[90] Ian Gough, 'Basic Income: A Powerful Tax Engine Pulling a Tiny Cart', in *It's Basic Income: The Global Debate*, edited by Amy Downes and Stewart Lansley (Bristol, 2018), 101–2.

[91] James Browne and Herwig Immervoll, 'Mechanics of Replacing Benefit Systems with a Basic Income: Comparative Results from a Microsimulation Approach', *Journal of Economic Inequality* 15/4 (2017), 325–44.

[92] Luke Martinelli, 'A Basic Income Trilemma: Inadequate, Unaffordable—or not Worth the Bother?' (paper delivered at BIEN Congress, University of Tampere, 24–26 Aug. 2018).

purpose and with scope for progression'.[93] Painter points to a recent OECD study which suggests that 35 per cent of British workers are over-qualified for their jobs, and that reducing this skills mismatch could improve productivity by 5 per cent.[94] In light of the UK's weak productivity performance since the financial crisis, there are reasons for thinking that the 'work first' philosophy of existing activation policy may be counter-productive, and that allowing workers to be more 'choosy' about the jobs they take might benefit the wider economy.

Shifting the frame of analysis from poverty to economic security offers a way of breaking out of the 'basic income trilemma', because it provides a coherent rationale for a UBI which does not attempt to meet citizens' subsistence needs. Contemporary British basic income campaigners have attempted to build on this insight by developing two types of scheme which would run alongside the existing benefit system. One approach returns to the logic of the 1972 Tax Credit Scheme by turning tax allowances into a UBI or a refundable tax credit. Above-inflation increases in the tax threshold since 2010 mean that the personal allowances for income tax and National Insurance contributions are now worth about £65 a week to the basic-rate taxpayer. Malcolm Torry has calculated that these allowances could be replaced with a basic income of the same cash value by adding just 3p to income tax rates and charging the 12 per cent rate of National Insurance contributions on all earnings. Microsimulation analysis using EUROMOD suggests that this would cut poverty by about one-third and lower the Gini coefficient for disposable income from 0.30 to 0.27.[95] Howard Reed and Stewart Lansley have developed a similar scheme for Compass, whilst Andrew Harrop of the Fabian Society has suggested that the increase in tax rates could be avoided by phasing in the change, for instance over twenty years.[96] In any case, leaving the benefit system in place whilst offsetting UBI against means-tested benefit entitlements ensures that the overall impact is progressive and minimizes the losses to lower-income households.

[93] Anthony Painter, Jake Thorold, and Jamie Cooke, *Pathways to Universal Basic Income: The Case for a Universal Basic Opportunity Fund* (2018), 13.

[94] Painter, Thorold, and Cooke, *Pathways to Universal Basic Income*, 12; Müge Adalet McGowan and Dan Andrews, *Labour Market Mismatch and Labour Productivity: Evidence from PIAAC Data*, OECD Economic Department Working Paper ECO/WKP(2015)27 (Paris, 2015), figures A1 (Panel B) and 3.

[95] Malcolm Torry, *An Update, a Correction, and an Extension, of an Evaluation of an Illustrative Citizen's Basic Income Scheme*, addendum to EUROMOD Working Paper EM 12/17 (Colchester, 2018).

[96] Reed and Lansley, *Universal Basic Income*; Andrew Harrop, *For Us All: Redesigning Social Security for the 2020s* (2016), 142–4.

A second strategy canvassed by Stewart Lansley and the RSA takes its cue from the apparent success of Alaska's Permanent Fund, and echoes James Meade's asset-based social dividend proposals. Lansley has published plans for creating a Citizens' Wealth Fund, financed by a mixture of existing public assets (such as the UK government's stake in Royal Bank of Scotland), corporate fines, personal wealth taxes, and a 'scrip tax'—requiring the top 350 firms to transfer 0.5 per cent of their share capital each year into the fund.[97] The return on the investment could be shared between citizens as a variable annual dividend, or used to make a capital grant to every citizen at the age of 25. In similar vein, the RSA has proposed a Universal Basic Opportunity Fund, from which citizens could draw a time-limited UBI—perhaps for two years out of every ten—to support periods of care-giving, entrepreneurship, and retraining.[98] The main difficulty here is one of scale. Even a Citizens' Wealth Fund of £1.2 trillion, financed by tax receipts of £50 billion a year over twenty years and earning a 4 per cent return, would only generate an annual dividend of £765 per person.[99] 'Topsy-turvy nationalisation' is thus difficult to justify purely on the basis of the dividend it would pay, as opposed to the wider economic case for expanding public ownership.

The problem with pilots

Malcolm Torry's scheme, then, offers perhaps the most realistic path for introducing a basic income in the UK. However, any movement in this direction in the coming years is likely to depend on the success of the proposed Scottish pilot. In an age of evidence-based policy, small-scale experimentation is intuitively attractive, and the local authorities developing the Scottish scheme are working closely with BIEN to draw on international 'best practice'.[100] As Charlie Young and Karl Widerquist have noted, however, this 'policy laboratory' approach also presents its own challenges.[101] One set of constraints reflects the legal and political context of Scottish devolution, since Universal Credit and income tax collection are still controlled by Westminster,

[97] Stewart Lansley, Duncan McCann, and Steve Schifferes, *Remodelling Capitalism: How Social Wealth Funds Could Transform Britain* (2018).

[98] Painter, Thorold, and Cooke, *Pathways to Universal Basic Income.*

[99] Lansley, McCann, and Schifferes, *Remodelling Capitalism*, 32.

[100] Interview with Annie Miller; Carnegie UK, *Exploring the Practicalities of a Basic Income Pilot.*

[101] Charlie Young, *Realising Basic Income Experiments in the UK: A Typology and Toolkit of Basic Income Design and Delivery* (2018); Karl Widerquist, *A Critical Analysis of Basic Income Experiments for Researchers, Policymakers, and Citizens* (Basingstoke, 2018).

and the current Conservative government has so far refused to cooperate. It is difficult to see how the behavioural impact of UBI can be properly tested unless the UK government is prepared to apply a different set of tax and benefit withdrawal rates to people who take part in the pilot.

A second set of limitations relates to the design of the pilot itself. The results from the trials in India and Namibia suggest that the social benefits of basic income are greatest when the scheme is open to everyone in a given area—an approach known as a 'saturation site'. Although this approach is attractive, it raises the question of how to deal with migration in and out of the area, and comparisons with a 'control group' are likely to be less robust than under a randomized controlled trial.[102] More broadly, the long-term impact of a guaranteed income on labour supply, education, and entrepreneurship will only become partly apparent over the course of a two- or three-year experiment. Even a large-scale pilot will thus give an incomplete picture of the effects of a permanent UBI.

If the Scottish pilot goes ahead, then, its results are likely to be ambiguous and politically contested. The experience of the 1970s NIT experiments in the United States and Canada suggests that supporters and critics will cherry-pick figures which support their case—particularly in relation to labour-market withdrawal—and that the public debate over the results will generate more heat than light. In the final analysis, the argument over basic income is a matter of political priorities and social values. Unless UBI proponents can secure public support for the principle of an unconditional income floor, their campaign is unlikely to be bolstered by any number of trials.

[102] Young, *Realising Basic Income Experiments in the UK*, 45–54.

PART IV
CONCLUSION

10
What Kind of Transfer State?

The UK's 2016 vote to leave the European Union has thrown British politics into turmoil, and its implications are likely to preoccupy policy-makers for many years to come. Nevertheless, the debate about economic inequality sparked by the financial crisis continues to rumble on. Whatever the limits of redistributive market liberalism, the tax and benefit systems are now firmly established as the British state's primary tools for shaping distributional outcomes, among working as well as workless households. The political salience of Universal Credit testifies to the central role which cash transfers have come to play in supporting living standards and legitimizing the UK's distinctive form of liberal capitalism.

This book has shown how the idea of a guaranteed income floor has become increasingly central to British social policy over the past century. This process can be understood in ideational terms—as a product of ideas about distributive justice and social rights, the influence of economists on poverty research, and changing attitudes to work and wage determination since the 1970s—but it has also been shaped by a more prosaic history of policy development. Universal Credit can be seen as the latest flowering of a social market tradition in British welfare policy which has intersected with the Beveridgean social insurance tradition but also diverged from it, particularly in its focus on the working poor and its interest in tax-benefit integration.[1] From Dennis Milner to Iain Duncan Smith, successive waves of policy entrepreneurs have sought to overcome the deficiencies of contributory insurance and means-tested benefits through a variety of UBI and NIT schemes and other rationalization proposals.

John Kay's concept of RML has provided a useful starting point for tracing how neoclassical economics, quantitative 'poverty knowledge', and a technocratic interest in tax-benefit reform have shaped the development of British social policy since the First World War. The social market tradition which has emerged at the intersection of these influences has significant strengths—including

[1] Alan Peacock, 'Welfare Philosophies and Welfare Finance', in *The State and Social Welfare*, edited by Thomas and Dorothy Wilson (1991), 37–54, at 42.

Transfer State: The Idea of a Guaranteed Income and the Politics of Redistribution in Modern Britain. Peter Sloman, Oxford University Press (2019). © Peter Sloman. DOI: 10.1093/oso/9780198813262.001.0001

a commitment to giving poor citizens dignity and choice and to tackling poverty whatever its source—but also a number of weaknesses. Enthusiasts for a guaranteed income have tended to prioritize 'sufficiency' over broader conceptions of equity or equality, and have often defined 'sufficiency' narrowly by reference to subsistence needs or the rates set by the existing benefit system.[2] Partly as a result, the UK's 'transfer state' has become unbalanced, focused on raising the incomes of the poor (especially low-paid workers with children) rather than reining in the growth of inequality at the top of the income spectrum. Some tax-benefit entrepreneurs have also come perilously close to treating rationalization as an end in itself, divorced from wider social and political objectives. The troubled rollout of Universal Credit shows what can go wrong when ambitious paper schemes fail to account for the lived experiences of welfare claimants. As Ruth Patrick has shown, top-down exercises in welfare reform are liable to add 'an extra layer of insecurity and uncertainty to the already challenging context of getting by on benefits'.[3]

The guaranteed income proposals which have circulated over the last century have varied widely—in generosity, administrative structure, target populations, income tapers, and work or contribution requirements. UBI schemes have featured prominently in tax-benefit reform debates and have attracted support from across the political spectrum. Yet the dominant trajectory of British welfare policy has been towards a very particular kind of 'transfer state', based on means-tested and conditional support for the working poor, which has reached its apotheosis in Universal Credit. This pattern mirrors global trends in cash transfer policy. As Jamie Peck and Nik Theodore have noted, the 'expert consensus' in institutions such as the OECD and the World Bank 'remains rooted in technocratic approaches to policy design predicated on means testing, targeting, and... conditionalities'.[4]

British policy-makers' preference for targeted benefits is partly a matter of cost: indeed, Treasury officials, Conservative politicians, and business leaders have long been suspicious of universalism for this reason. At a deeper level, however, the growth of selectivity also reflects the narrow conception of poverty fostered by mainstream poverty research, as Bill Jordan warned more than forty years ago.[5] In a static distributional analysis, means-tested benefits will always be the cheapest way of raising individuals above the

[2] Samuel Moyn, *Not Enough: Human Rights in an Unequal World* (Cambridge, Mass., 2018).

[3] Ruth Patrick, *For Whose Benefit? The Everyday Realities of Welfare Reform* (Bristol, 2017), 141.

[4] Jamie Peck and Nik Theodore, *Fast Policy: Experimental Statecraft at the Thresholds of Neoliberalism* (Minneapolis, 2015), 122.

[5] Bill Jordan, *Paupers: The Making of the New Claiming Class* (1973), 2.

'poverty line'. This tendency has been reinforced by the persistent hope that many of the problems traditionally associated with means-testing, such as stigma and low take-up, can be solved by computerizing benefit administration and integrating it with the tax system.

The prevailing commitment to work conditionality can also be understood at two different levels, in terms of both a narrowly economic desire to maximize labour supply and the broader cultural resonance of the Protestant work ethic. Although traditional employment patterns have been transformed by the transition to a service economy, hostility to perceived 'scroungers' remains strong both inside and outside government.[6] Where Beveridge's social insurance model recognized the dignity of full-time workers by *restricting* their access to cash benefits, the Heath, Thatcher, and Blair governments have instead sought to reinforce the work ethic by *creating* new benefits for those in paid employment. Tax credits, in particular, were designed to sidestep the stigma of the benefit system by presenting transfer payments as part of the reward for work and delivering them through the pay packet. In practice, the categorical divide between in- and out-of-work benefits is less sharp than ministers have sometimes suggested, since Housing Benefit and Child Tax Credit are available to both groups of claimants, and Universal Credit will erase many of the remaining distinctions. In the context of in-work conditionality and anti-welfare rhetoric, however, the erosion of these categorical boundaries may simply lead to 'symbolic pollution' by recasting all benefit recipients as 'welfare dependants'.[7]

The consolidation of tax credits, Housing Benefit, and means-tested out-of-work benefits into a single monthly payment through Universal Credit thus marks the culmination of a particular line of development. In the hands of Conservative and New Labour politicians, the expansion of the transfer state has been an elite project, driven forward within Whitehall and exploiting the relative autonomy from trade unions and other interest groups which the British state has enjoyed since the 1980s. For the Thatcher and Major governments, social security provided an unloved but expedient safety net for those hit hardest by deindustrialization, which helped 'take the strain' of mass unemployment and spending cuts in other parts of the public sector. For the

[6] John Hudson and Neil Lunt, with Charlotte Hamilton, 'Nostalgia Narratives? Pejorative Attitudes to Welfare in Historical Perspective: Survey Evidence from Beveridge to the British Social Attitudes Survey', *Journal of Poverty and Social Justice* 24/3 (2016), 227–43.

[7] The classic work on 'symbolic pollution' is, of course, Mary Douglas, *Purity and Danger: An Analysis of the Concepts of Pollution and Taboo* (New York, 1966). Brian Steensland has applied the concept to social security: Brian Steensland, *The Failed Welfare Revolution: America's Struggle over Guaranteed Income Policy* (Princeton, 2008), 15.

Blair and Brown governments, tax credits offered a means of reducing child poverty and redistributing the proceeds of growth without inhibiting job creation. In both cases, the growth of cash transfers went with the grain of the UK's post-industrial economic model—reinforcing incentives to take paid work and avoiding upward pressure on service-sector labour costs. Though some sections of the public and the business community may have welcomed this process, it has largely rested on consent (or indifference) rather than active political mobilization. Indeed, proposals for restructuring means-tested benefits have mostly passed beneath the radar in election campaigns—at least until the 2017 election, when controversy over the Universal Credit rollout placed Theresa May's government on the defensive.

Universal Credit

The centrality of means-testing and work requirements to the UK welfare system presents the historian with a paradox. From any historical or comparative perspective, the British government is now spending a large amount on cash transfers to working-age households—forecast to be £96.8 billion, or 4.4 per cent of GDP, in 2019/20—and Universal Credit represents an ambitious attempt at technocratic rationalization.[8] Despite its formidable scale, however, the UK's transfer state does not in any meaningful sense provide working-age citizens with a guaranteed income. Successive British governments have made only sporadic efforts to ensure that benefits are adequate for subsistence, and their real value has been sharply eroded by a decade of austerity: the cumulative effect of a 1 per cent cap on annual upratings (from 2013 to 2016) followed by a four-year freeze (from 2016 to 2020) has been particularly damaging. Housing Benefit now falls short of rents in many parts of the country, with the shortfall for a two-bedroom property (measured against the 30th percentile of local rents) averaging £43 per week in London and £8 per week outside the capital.[9] The introduction of the household benefit cap (set at £23,000 a year in London and £20,000 outside it) and the two-child limit on CTC and Universal Credit payments (for children born

[8] These figures apply to Great Britain and are taken from Department for Work and Pensions, 'Benefit Expenditure and Caseload Tables 2018', 21 Nov. 2018, available at <http://www.gov.uk/government/publications/benefit-expenditure-and-caseload-tables-2018>.

[9] Patrick Butler, 'Low-Income Tenants Face "Heat, Eat or Pay Rent" Choices', *The Guardian* (online edn), 29 Aug. 2018, accessed 30 Aug. 2018, available at <https://www.theguardian.com/society/2018/aug/29/low-income-tenants-face-heat-eat-or-pay-rent-choices-study>; Chartered Institute of Housing, *Missing the Target: Is Targeted Affordability Funding Doing its Job?* (Coventry, 2018).

after 6 April 2017) has further reduced the adequacy of provision for larger families. Research by Donald Hirsch and his colleagues at Loughborough University suggests that a lone parent with two dependent children, who works full-time on the National Living Wage and claims all the benefits to which he or she is entitled, will still find themselves about £70 a week below the Minimum Income Standard (which is based on public perceptions of the income needed to meet essential needs and participate in society). For those out of work, the deficiency is much greater.[10] One predictable consequence of these cuts is that, after falling under New Labour and levelling off under the coalition, the child poverty rate appears to be rising again.[11]

The patchwork nature of the UK's income support system is exacerbated by restrictions on out-of-work benefits for young people (for instance, most under-18s cannot claim Universal Credit) and by the impact of benefit sanctions. Although the political rationale for attaching conditions to benefit receipt is clear enough, the current sanctions regime does not seem to be functioning effectively even in its own terms. The recent Economic and Social Research Council-funded Welfare Conditionality Project (2013–18) concluded that conditionality was 'largely ineffective in facilitating people's entry into or progression within the paid labour market'. A 'substantial minority' of the claimants interviewed for the study had experienced 'negative behaviour changes and outcomes', such as ill health or 'counterproductive compliance'—applying for or taking unsuitable jobs in order to avoid sanctions. Unsurprisingly, some responded to job search requirements by disengaging from the benefit system entirely.[12]

The immediate policy question concerns the future of Universal Credit. Though it promises to be a significant technical achievement when it is fully rolled out, it has become a source of political embarrassment for Conservative ministers, and it remains unclear whether it will raise employment rates or produce efficiency savings. Indeed, the programme has become so toxic among left-wing activists that Shadow Chancellor John McDonnell has suggested Labour would scrap it.[13] On the other hand, a 2018 report by the

[10] Abigail Davis, Donald Hirsch, Matt Padley, and Claire Shepherd, *A Minimum Income Standard for the UK, 2008–2018: Continuity and Change* (York, 2018), 59, 57.

[11] Adam Corlett, Stephen Clarke, Conor D'Arcy, and John Wood, *The Living Standards Audit 2018* (2018), 46.

[12] Welfare Conditionality Project, *Welfare Conditionality Project, 2013–2018: Final Findings Report* (York, 2018), 4.

[13] Dan Sabbagh, 'John McDonnell Urges Scrapping "Iniquitous" Universal Credit', *The Guardian* (online edn), 7 Oct. 2018, accessed 18 Jan. 2019, available at <https://www.theguardian.com/society/2018/oct/07/john-mcdonnell-says-universal-credit-needs-to-get-scrapped-benefits>.

National Audit Office concluded that there was 'no practical alternative to continuing with Universal Credit', not least because the government had already spent £1.9 billion on infrastructure and running costs and more than 800,000 claimants had already been transferred to the new system.[14] Many of the problems highlighted by critics could be solved within the Universal Credit framework—for instance, by abolishing the Minimum Income Floor for self-employed workers and relaxing in-work conditionality. The system also has 'a great deal of poverty reduction potential which is currently under-utilised', as the CPAG and the TUC have pointed out.[15] An incoming government could exploit the selective structure and wide coverage of Universal Credit to reduce income poverty relatively cheaply and quickly.

Rolling back conditionality requirements and turning Universal Credit into an anti-poverty device would represent a major shift away from the philosophy of activation which has animated the programme to date.[16] On the other hand, the system would still have significant limitations. Even with an effective Real-Time Information feed which adjusts benefits in response to each month's wages, the principles of monthly assessment and payment in arrears mean that family budgets are liable to be destabilized by fluctuations in Universal Credit payments.[17] Likewise, the household basis of Universal Credit risks creating dependency within the family, whilst the exclusion of those with savings above a capital limit (currently set at £16,000) discourages thrift and independence. As Jane Millar and Fran Bennett have pointed out, these design features sit particularly uncomfortably with the needs of today's low-paid workers.[18] One of the ironies of Universal Credit is that it is geared towards a model of regular, monthly paid work which is beginning to pass away. If governments want to help citizens navigate a rapidly shifting labour market, they should prioritize forms of social security which provide a stable and predictable income floor that individuals can build on through work and saving.

[14] *Parliamentary Papers*, 2017–19, HC 1123, 'National Audit Office. Rolling out Universal Credit. Report by the Comptroller and Auditor General', 15 June 2018, 10, 68–9.

[15] Child Poverty Action Group and Trades Union Congress, *Reforms to Universal Credit* (2015), accessed 17 Sept. 2018, available at <https://www.tuc.org.uk/sites/default/files/ReformstoUniversalCredit_0.pdf>.

[16] Jane Millar and Fran Bennett, 'Universal Credit: Assumptions, Contradictions and Virtual Reality', *Social Policy and Society* 16/2 (2017), 169–82.

[17] Millar and Bennett, 'Universal Credit', 172–5.

[18] Millar and Bennett, 'Universal Credit'.

The case for basic income

It is this argument for economic security—the value of a stable, individual foundation for work, care, training, and other life choices—that provides the most powerful case for UBI. Given the structure of the existing UK welfare system, it is difficult to see how a basic income could ever be set high enough to replace the most extensive forms of support for disabled people or low-income families with children. Nevertheless, even a modest basic income would give 'everyone a modicum of basic security in an increasingly insecure world', as Ruth Lister has argued—providing a new source of resilience for the 12 per cent of UK workers who live below the relative poverty line, the 19 per cent who say they struggle to make ends meet because of income volatility, and the 32 per cent who have less than £500 in savings.[19] Indeed, a basic income might complement Universal Credit by placing an individual income floor beneath the more variable, conditional, and household-based system of means-tested benefits. There are good reasons for believing that this would reduce the 'cognitive load' of economic insecurity and so contribute to better nutrition, education, and health outcomes for the most vulnerable citizens.[20]

The most realistic schemes for introducing UBI in the UK—such as Malcolm Torry's plan for replacing tax allowances with a basic income of about £65 per week—bear a close resemblance to Juliet Rhys-Williams and Hermione Parker's partial basic income proposals. It is tempting to think that a basic income of this type might be sold to policy elites as a 'prosaic' form of tax-benefit simplification, in a similar way to Arthur Cockfield's Tax Credit Scheme.[21] In the contemporary context, however, the principles of selectivity and conditionality appear to be too firmly rooted for such a strategy to gain much traction. Even if a basic income were to emerge as a result of an elite-level 'political accident', it would be highly vulnerable to a populist critique of unconditionality.[22] The construction of a 'moralised antagonism' between 'hard working taxpayers' and 'welfare claimants' has become a staple of British

[19] Ruth Lister, 'Coming off the Fence on Universal Basic Income', in *It's Basic Income: The Global Debate*, edited by Amy Downes and Stewart Lansley (Bristol, 2018), 54–7, at 57; Brhmie Balaram and Fabian Wallace-Stephens, *Thriving, Striving, or just about Surviving? Seven Portraits of Economic Security and Modern Work in the UK* (2018), 20, 25.

[20] Evelyn Forget, 'The Basic Income Path to a Healthier Society' (paper delivered at BIEN Congress, University of Tampere, 24–26 Aug. 2018).

[21] Luke Martinelli and Nick Pearce, 'Basic Income in the UK: Assessing Prospects for Reform in an Age of Austerity', *Social Policy and Society* 18/2 (2019), 265–75, at 273.

[22] Malcolm Torry, 'History and the Contemporary Debate in the UK', in *It's Basic Income: The Global Debate*, edited by Amy Downes and Stewart Lansley (Bristol, 2018), 123–7, at 127.

Conservative discourse, as Scott Lavery has recently noted, and centre-right politicians around the world have routinely deployed this rhetoric against UBI.[23]

Although mass mobilization has not featured prominently in British tax-benefit reform to date, then, it may be an unavoidable necessity for basic income advocates today. It is difficult to see how a genuinely unconditional UBI could be introduced and sustained without a significant shift in public attitudes to welfare and social citizenship. Some possible levers for shifting these attitudes are already visible—in public support for universal services such as the NHS, in concern about the 'gig economy' and zero-hours contracts, and in widespread disillusionment with Universal Credit and benefit sanctions. Meeting part of the cost of basic income from outside the personal tax system, for instance through a Citizens' Wealth Fund or carbon tax, might also help defuse resistance from current workers. Nevertheless, much of the political work required to establish UBI as a legitimate option for social security reform among the electorate at large is still to be done. Building popular support for the idea will not be easy, as Luke Martinelli and Nick Pearce have noted: the low-wage 'precariat' is hardly a unified political constituency, and 'many of those who might stand to benefit from BI in material terms might oppose it on normative grounds'.[24] In the face of the contractarian and utilitarian ethos of mainstream welfare policy, however, there is perhaps no alternative.

Twenty-first-century challenges

In a context of automation and rapid labour-market change, the case for a guaranteed minimum income may well be stronger in the twenty-first century than it was in the twentieth. The Fordist model of stable, full-time employment which provided economic security for many people in the post-war 'golden age' seems to be gone for good, and even if predictions of widespread technological unemployment turn out to be exaggerated, cash transfers are likely to have an important role to play in sustaining living standards. Yet tackling poverty and inequality through fiscal policy should not be seen as an easy option. Indeed, there are several reasons for thinking that the

[23] Scott Lavery, 'The Legitimation of Post-Crisis Capitalism in the United Kingdom: Real Wage Decline, Finance-Led Growth and the State', *New Political Economy* 23/1 (2018), 27–45, at 36.
[24] Martinelli and Pearce, 'Basic Income in the UK', 269, 270.

redistributive strategies we have studied in this book are likely to become more difficult in future.

One major challenge stems from the impact of automation on the tax system. As Ryan Abbott and Bret Bogenschneider have recently pointed out, most western states rely heavily on revenue from income and payroll taxes, making their tax bases vulnerable to capital–labour substitution.[25] Shifting the tax burden from labour to capital—either by raising existing corporate taxes or by introducing new levies such as a 'robot tax' or 'data tax'—is intuitively attractive but politically challenging, given the growing concentration of market power and the ability of multinational firms to minimize their tax bills by exploiting transfer pricing.[26] Indeed, the last decade has witnessed a renewed 'race to the bottom' in corporate tax rates—including the reduction of UK corporation tax from 30 per cent in 2007/8 to 17 per cent from April 2020—along with mounting evidence of tax avoidance.[27] The shift in consumption from physical goods towards the 'invisible digital products' produced by technology giants such as Google and Facebook is likely to exacerbate these problems.[28] The need for coordinated global action is clear enough, but the experience of recent anti-avoidance and tax harmonization efforts is not encouraging.

The scope for expanding the UK's 'transfer state' is likely to be further constrained by competing demands on public spending. The Office for Budget Responsibility has projected that the cost of delivering existing government policy (excluding debt interest) will rise from 36.7 per cent of GDP in 2017/18 to 44.6 per cent in 2067/8, driven by increases in health and social care spending (from 8.3 per cent to 15.7 per cent) and benefits for those above the state pension age (from 5.9 per cent to 8.2 per cent) as a result of an ageing population and rising treatment costs.[29] Pressure for improvements in the quality of public services may push these figures even higher. The complaint that a basic income will not solve everything is a lazy critique, but like any other policy it carries an opportunity cost. Winning political support for UBI

[25] Ryan Abbott and Bret Bogenschneider, 'Should Robots Pay Taxes? Tax Policy in the Age of Automation', *Harvard Law & Policy Review* 12/145 (2018), 145–75.

[26] Sara Dillon, 'Tax Avoidance, Revenue Starvation, and the Age of the Multinational Corporation', *The International Lawyer* 50/2 (2017), 275–327.

[27] For the longer-term 'race to the bottom', see Duane Swank, 'Taxing Choices: International Competition, Domestic Institutions and the Transformation of Corporate Tax Policy', *Journal of European Public Policy* 23/4 (2016), 571–603.

[28] Jim Corkery, Jay Forder, Enrico Mercuri, and Dan Svantesson, 'Taxes, the Internet and the Digital Economy', *Revenue Law Journal* 23/1 (2013), 128–43.

[29] Office for Budget Responsibility, *Fiscal Sustainability Report, July 2018* (2018), 75.

may become increasingly difficult as the cost of existing welfare institutions rises and the state struggles to cover this spending through higher taxes.

A third challenge for proponents of a guaranteed income involves the troubled politics of migration. Early UBI and NIT proponents tended to take the boundaries of the nation state for granted, but the growth of migration flows within and beyond the European Union since the 1990s has turned the limits of social citizenship into a live political question. Some basic income campaigners have responded by endorsing border controls, on the grounds that 'there is no fundamental right of free movement': 'As long as the national level is the highest one at which genuine redistribution can be institutionalized, it needs protection against selective immigration.'[30] Others have highlighted the multi-layered character of existing citizenship rights and suggested that a basic income should be paid to all permanent residents or all those on the electoral register.[31] Although the risk that UBI would create a 'welfare magnet' for potential migrants is liable to be overstated, the choice between narrow and inclusive eligibility rules is not an enviable one.[32] In either case, there is a danger of inflaming welfare chauvinism.

In the last analysis, then, the nature and extent of redistribution will always be a political matter. If cash transfers have sometimes appealed to economists and philosophers as a way of eliminating poverty without confronting the distribution of economic power, this technocratic vision is an illusion. As Joseph Schumpeter pointed out a century ago, the budget reflects 'the spirit of a people, its cultural level, its social structure', and ultimately its power relations.[33] Objections to the cost and unconditional nature of UBI have been as persistent and resonant as the idea itself. Only when supporters of basic income manage to surmount these cultural and political obstacles will the idea become a reality.

[30] Philippe van Parijs and Yannick Vanderborght, *Basic Income: A Radical Proposal for a Free Society and a Sane Economy* (Cambridge, Mass., 2017), 220–1.

[31] Malcolm Torry, *Money for Everyone: Why We Need a Citizen's Income* (Bristol, 2013), 195–202; Annie Miller, *A Basic Income Handbook* (Edinburgh, 2017), 75–8; Guy Standing, *Basic Income: And How We Can Make it Happen* (2017), 123–5.

[32] Michael W. Howard, 'Basic Income and Migration Policy: A Moral Dilemma?', *Basic Income Studies* 1/1 (2006).

[33] Joseph Schumpeter, 'The Crisis of the Tax State' [1918], in *Joseph Schumpeter: The Economics and Sociology of Capitalism*, edited by Richard Swedberg (Princeton, 1991), 99–140, at 103.

Bibliography

All books and pamphlets are published in London unless otherwise stated.

Manuscript and archival sources

Albert Sloman Library, University of Essex

Social Democratic Party papers

Bodleian Library, Oxford

Conservative Party Archive (CPA)
MSS. Bonham Carter
MSS. Macmillan

Borthwick Institute for Archives, University of York

Seebohm Rowntree papers

British Library of Political and Economic Science (BLPES)

Abel-Smith papers
Child Poverty Action Group papers
Fabian Society papers
Married Women's Association papers
Meade papers
Rhys-Williams papers
Titmuss papers

Churchill Archives Centre, Cambridge

Amery papers
Thatcher papers
Wolff papers

Hoover Institution Archives, Stanford University

Friedman papers
Mont Pèlerin Society records
Institute of Economic Affairs papers

King's College, Cambridge

John Maynard Keynes papers
Kaldor papers

Labour History Archive and Study Centre, Manchester

Labour Party Archive (LPA)

London Metropolitan Archives

National Council for Voluntary Organisations papers

Modern Records Centre, University of Warwick

Confederation of British Industry papers
Federation of British Industries papers
Trades Union Congress papers

The National Archives: Public Record Office (TNA)

Boards of Stamps, Taxes, Excise, Stamps and Taxes, and Inland Revenue papers (IR)
Cabinet and War Cabinet papers (CAB)
Department of Health and Social Security papers (BN)
Ministry of Pensions and National Insurance papers (PIN)
Prime Minister's Office papers (PREM)
Treasury papers (T)
Unemployment Assistance Boards, the Supplementary Benefits Commission, and related bodies papers (AST)

Nuffield College, Oxford

Papers of the Royal Commission on the Taxation of Profits and Income (RCTPI)

Private Collection

Annie Miller papers

Newspapers and periodicals

BIRG Bulletin
Citizen's Income Bulletin
Daily Mail
The Daily Telegraph
The Economist
Forward

The Guardian (*Manchester Guardian* until 1959)
Liberal Magazine
Liberal News
New Society
The Observer
Planning
Socialist Commentary
The Times
Tribune

Official papers

Cm. 9341, *Office for Budget Responsibility: Welfare Trends Report, October 2016* (2016)
Cm. 9536, *National Minimum Wage: Low Pay Commission Report 2017* (2017)
Cm. 9562, *Office for Budget Responsibility: Welfare Trends Report, January 2018* (2018)
Cm. 9717, *National Minimum Wage: Low Pay Commission Report 2018* (2018)
Cmd. 6404, *Social Insurance and Allied Services: A Report by Sir William Beveridge* (1942)
Cmd. 6405, *Social Insurance and Allied Services: Memoranda from Organisations. Appendix G to Report by Sir William Beveridge* (1942)
Cmd. 9015, *Royal Commission on the Taxation of Profits and Income. Second Report* (1954)
Cmnd. 5116, *Proposal for a Tax-Credit System* (1972)
Cmnd. 7175, *Royal Commission on the Distribution of Income & Wealth. Report No. 6: Lower Incomes* (1978)
Cmnd. 9756, *The Reform of Personal Taxation* (1986)
CP 2, *Office for Budget Responsibility: Welfare Trends Report, January 2019* (2019)
Parliamentary Debates (House of Commons)
Parliamentary Debates (House of Lords)
Parliamentary Papers

Books and articles

Abbot, Elizabeth, and Katherine Bompas. *The Woman Citizen and Social Security: A Criticism of the Proposals Made in the Beveridge Report as They Affect Women* (1943).

Abbott, Ryan, and Bret Bogenschneider. 'Should Robots Pay Taxes? Tax Policy in the Age of Automation'. *Harvard Law & Policy Review* 12/145 (2018), 145–75.

Abel-Smith, Brian. 'Paradoxes of the Welfare State'. *The Listener*, 30 May 1968, 696–7.

Abel-Smith, Brian, and Peter Townsend. *The Poor and the Poorest* (1965).

Ackers, Peter. 'Symposium: The Oxford School of Industrial Relations: Fifty Years after the 1965–1968 Donovan Commission. Introduction: Who Were the Oxford School and Why Did They Matter?' *Historical Studies in Industrial Relations* 37 (2016), 201–7. doi:10.3828/hsir.2016.37.7.

Adalet McGowan, Müge, and Dan Andrews. *Labour Market Mismatch and Labour Productivity: Evidence from PIAAC Data*. OECD Economic Department Working Paper ECO/WKP(2015)27 (Paris, 2015).

Adam, Stuart, and Mike Brewer. *Take-up of Family Credit and Working Families' Tax Credit: Final Report* (2005). Accessed 21 Mar. 2017. <https://www.gov.uk/government/publications/take-up-of-family-credit-and-working-families-tax-credit>.

Adler, Michael. 'Combining Welfare-to-Work Measures with Tax Credits: A New Hybrid Approach to Social Security in the United Kingdom'. *International Social Security Review* 57/2 (2004), 87–106. doi:10.1111/j.1468-246X.2004.00189.x.

Adnan, Indra, and Neal Lawson. *New Times: How a Politics of Networks and Relationship Can Deliver a Good Society* (2014).

Agar, Jon. *The Government Machine: A Revolutionary History of the Computer* (Cambridge, Mass., 2003).

Alcock, Pete. '"Maximum Feasible Understanding"—Lessons from Previous Wars on Poverty'. *Social Policy and Society* 4/3 (2005), 321–9. doi:10.1017/S1474746405002472.

Amalgamated Union of Engineering Workers (Engineering Section). *A New Weapon for Socialism—The Negative Income Tax. Revised for 1971–72 Costing and Revenue Figures* (1972).

Anderson, Elizabeth S. 'What Is the Point of Equality?' *Ethics* 109/2 (1999), 287–337. doi:10.1086/233897.

Archer, Peter. 'Financing the Social Services'. *Socialist Commentary*, Nov. 1967, 20–2.

Ashby, Peter. *Social Security after Beveridge—What Next?* (1984).

Ashby, Peter. 'Towards an Income and Work Guarantee'. *BIEN Bulletin* 7 (1988), 28–30.

Ashdown, Paddy. *Citizen's Britain: A Radical Agenda for the 1990s* (1989).

Ashdown, Paddy. *The Ashdown Diaries*, vol. 1 (2000).

Astill, Stuart. 'Nicholas Adrian Barr (1943–)'. In *The Palgrave Companion to LSE Economics*, edited by Robert A. Cord (Basingstoke, 2018), 805–30.

Atkinson, A. B. *Poverty in Britain and the Reform of Social Security* (Cambridge, 1969).

Atkinson, A. B. *The Tax Credit Scheme and the Redistribution of Income* (1973).

Atkinson, A. B. 'Taxation and Social Security Reform: Reflections on Advising a House of Commons Select Committee'. *Policy and Politics* 12/2 (1984), 107–18. doi:10.1332/030557384782628390.

Atkinson, A. B. 'Beveridge, the National Minimum and its Future in a European Context'. In A. B. Atkinson, *Incomes and the Welfare State: Essays on Britain and Europe* (Cambridge, 1995), 290–304.

Atkinson, A. B. 'Poverty, Statistics and Progress in Europe'. In A. B. Atkinson, *Incomes and the Welfare State: Essays on Britain and Europe* (Cambridge, 1995), 64–77.

Atkinson, A. B. *Public Economics in Action: The Basic Income/Flat Tax Proposal* (Oxford, 1995).

Atkinson, A. B., J. Corlyon, A. K. Maynard, H. Sutherland, and C. G. Trinder. 'Poverty in York: A Re-Analysis of Rowntree's 1950 Survey'. *Bulletin of Economic Research* 33/2 (1981), 59–71. doi:10.1111/j.1467-8586.1981.tb00171.x.

Atkinson A. B., and J. S. Flemming. 'Unemployment, Social Security and Incentives'. *Midland Bank Review* (Autumn 1978), 6–16.

Atkinson, A. B., M. A. King, and H. Sutherland. 'The Analysis of Personal Taxation and Social Security'. *National Institute Economic Review* 106 (Nov. 1983), 63–74. doi:10.1177/002795018310600107.

Atkinson, A. B., with Lee Rainwater and Timothy Smeeding, 'Income Distribution in European Countries'. In A. B. Atkinson, *Incomes and the Welfare State: Essays on Britain and Europe* (Cambridge, 1995), 41–63.

Atkinson, Anthony B. *Inequality: What Can Be Done?* (Cambridge, Mass., 2015).

Atkinson, Anthony B., Joe Hasell, Salvatore Morelli, and Max Roser. 'Economic Inequality in the United Kingdom'. The Chartbook of Economic Inequality. Accessed 7 May 2018. <https://www.chartbookofeconomicinequality.com/inequality-by-country/united-kingdom/>.

Atkinson, Anthony B., and Joseph E. Stiglitz. *Lectures on Public Economics* (Maidenhead, 1980).

Atkinson, Tony (=A. B. Atkinson), and John Micklewright. 'Turning the Screw: Benefits for the Unemployed 1979–88'. In *The Economics of Social Security,* edited by Andrew Dilnot and Ian Walker (Oxford, 1989), 17–51.

Atkinson, Rob, and Simin Da Voudi. 'The Concept of Social Exclusion in the European Union: Context, Development and Possibilities'. *Journal of Common Market Studies* 38/3 (2000), 427–48. doi:10.1111/1468-5965.00229.

Azmat, Ghazala. 'The Incidence of an Earned Income Tax Credit: Evaluating the Impact on Wages in the UK'. Centre for Economic Performance Discussion Paper no. 724 (May 2006).

Backhouse, Roger E. 'The Changing Character of British Economics'. *History of Political Economy* 28, Supplement (1997), 33–60.

Backhouse, Roger E. and Béatrice Cherrier. 'The Age of the Applied Economist: The Transformation of Economics since the 1970s'. *History of Political Economy* 49, Supplement (2017), 1–33. doi:10.1215/00182702-4166239.

Balaram, Brhmie, and Fabian Wallacc-Stcphens. *Thriving, Striving, or just about Surviving? Seven Portraits of Economic Security and Modern Work in the UK* (2018).

Baldwin, Peter. *The Politics of Social Solidarity: Class Bases of the European Welfare State, 1875–1975* (Cambridge, 1990).

Bale, Tim. *Sacred Cows and Common Sense: The Symbolic Statecraft and Political Culture of the British Labour Party* (Aldershot, 1999).

Bale, Tim. *Five Year Mission: The Labour Party under Ed Miliband* (Oxford, 2015).

Balls, Edward. 'Danger: Men not at Work. Unemployment and Non-Employment in the UK and beyond'. In Edward Balls and Paul Gregg, *Work and Welfare: Tackling the Jobs Deficit* (1993), 1–30.

Balls, Ed, Joe Grice, and Gus O'Donnell. *Microeconomic Reform in Britain: Delivering Opportunities for All* (Basingstoke, 2004).

Banting, Keith G. Poverty, *Politics and Policy: Britain in the 1960s* (1979).

Barker, David. 'Negative Income Tax'. In *Family Poverty: Programme for the Seventies*, 2nd edn, edited by David Bull (1971), 44–69.

Barker, David. 'The Family Income Supplement'. In *Family Poverty: Programme for the Seventies,* 2nd edn, edited by David Bull (1971), 70–82.

Barna, Tibor. *Redistribution of Incomes through Public Finance in 1937* (Oxford, 1945).

Bazen, Stephen. 'On the Employment Effects of Introducing a National Minimum Wage'. *British Journal of Industrial Relations* 28/2 (1990), 215–26, doi:10.1111/j.1467-8543.1990.tb00364.x.

Beatty, Christina, and Steve Fothergill. 'The Impact on Welfare and Public Finances of Job Loss in Industrial Britain'. *Regional Studies, Regional Science* 4/1 (2017), 161–80. doi:10.1080/21681376.2017.1346481.

Beckerman, Wilfred. 'The Impact of Income Maintenance Payments on Poverty in Britain, 1975'. *Economic Journal* 89/354 (1979), 261–79. doi:10.2307/2231601.

Belfield, Chris, Richard Blundell, Jonathan Cribb, Andrew Hood, and Robert Joyce. 'Two Decades of Income Inequality in Britain: The Role of Wages, Household Earnings and Redistribution'. *Economica* 84/334 (2017), 157–79. doi:10.1111/ecca.12220.

Belfield, Chris, Daniel Chandler, and Robert Joyce. *Housing: Trends in Prices, Costs and Tenure*. Institute for Fiscal Studies Briefing Note BN161 (2015).

Belfield, Chris, Jonathan Cribb, Andrew Hood, and Robert Joyce. *Living Standards, Poverty and Inequality in the UK: 2016* (2016).

Beltram, Geoffrey. *Testing the Safety Net: An Enquiry into the Reformed Supplementary Benefit Scheme* (1984).

Benjamin, Daniel K., and Levis A. Kochin. 'Searching for an Explanation of Unemployment in Interwar Britain', *Journal of Political Economy* 87/3 (1979), 441–78. doi:10.1086/260773.

Bernstein, Jared. 'Inequality, Mobility, Real Earnings, and Real Anger'. *Business Economics* 51/2 (2016), 90–6. doi:10.1057/be.2016.21.

Berthoud, Richard. *The Reform of Supplementary Benefit* (1984).

Bevir, Mark. *New Labour: A Critique* (Abingdon, 2005).

Birmingham Claimants' Union. 'Female Liberation Statement'. *Journal of the National Federation of Claimants Unions* 1 (Aug. 1970), 24.

Black, Amy, and Stephen Brooke. 'The Labour Party, Women, and the Problem of Gender, 1951–1966'. *Journal of British Studies* 36/4 (1997), 419–52. doi:10.1086/386144.

Blackburn, Sheila. 'How Useful are Feminist Theories of the Welfare State?' *Women's History Review* 4/3 (1995), 369–94. doi:10.1080/09612029500200091.

Blackburn, Sheila. *A Fair Day's Wage for a Fair Day's Work? Sweated Labour and the Origins of Minimum Wage Legislation in Britain* (Aldershot, 2007).

Blanchard, Olivier. 'European Unemployment: The Evolution of Facts and Ideas'. *Economic Policy* 21/45 (2006), 6–59. doi:10.1111/j.1468-0327.2006.00153.x.

Blaug, Mark. 'The Myth of the Old Poor Law and the Making of the New'. *Journal of Economic History* 23/2 (1963), 151–184. doi:10.1017/S0022050700103808.

Blaug, Mark. 'The Poor Law Report Reexamined'. *Journal of Economic History* 24/2 (1964), 229–45. doi:10.1017/S0022050700103808.

Blaug, Mark. 'The Fundamental Theorems of Modern Welfare Economics, Historically Contemplated'. *History of Political Economy* 39/2 (2007), 185–207.

Block, Fred, and Margaret Somers. 'In the Shadow of Speenhamland: Social Policy and the Old Poor Law'. *Politics & Society* 31/2 (2003), 283–323. doi:10.1177/0032329203252272.

Blundell, Richard. 'Welfare-to-Work: Which Policies Work and Why?' *Proceedings of The British Academy* 117 (2002), 477–524.

Blundell, Richard. 'Earned Income Tax Credit Policies: Impact and Optimality. The Adam Smith Lecture, 2005'. *Labour Economics* 13/4 (2006), 423–43. doi:10.1016/j.labeco.2006.04.001.

Blundell, Richard, Alan Duncan, Julian McCrae, and Costas Meghir. 'The Labour Market Impact of the Working Families Tax Credit', *Fiscal Studies* 21/1 (2000), 75–104, doi:10.1111/j.1475-5890.2000.tb00581.x.

Blundell, Richard, and Costas Meghir. 'Active Labour Market Policy vs Employment Tax Credits: Lessons from Recent UK Reforms'. *Swedish Economic Policy Review* 8/2 (2002), 13–37.

Blunkett, David. *The Blunkett Tapes: My Life in the Bear Pit* (2006).

Blyth, Mark. 'Structures Do not Come with an Instruction Sheet: Interests, Ideas, and Progress in Political Science'. *Perspectives on Politics* 1/4 (2003), 695–706. doi:10.1017/S1537592703000471.

Bochel, Hugh M. *Parliament and Welfare Policy* (Aldershot, 1992).

Booker, H. S. 'Lady Rhys Williams' Proposals for the Amalgamation of Direct Taxation with Social Insurance'. *Economic Journal* 56/222 (1946), 230–43. doi:10.2307/2225792.

Booth, Alan, and Mark Billings. 'Techno-Nationalism, the Post Office, and the Creation of Britain's National Giro'. In *Technological Innovation in Retail Finance: International Historical Perspectives*, edited by Bernardo Bátiz-Lazo, J. Carles Maixé-Altés, and Paul Thomes (Abingdon, 2011), 155–72.

Boyer, George. *An Economic History of the English Poor Law, 1750–1850* (Cambridge, 1990).

Boyer, George R., and Robert S. Smith. 'The Development of the Neoclassical Tradition in Labor Economics'. *Industrial and Labor Relations Review* 54/2 (2001), 199–223. doi:10.1177/001979390105400201.

Boyson, Rhodes. *Centre Forward: A Radical Conservative Programme* (1978).

Brewer, Mike, and Liam Wren-Lewis. *Why Did Britain's Households Get Richer? Decomposing UK Household Income Growth between 1968 and 2008–09*. IFS Briefing Note no. 125 (2011).

Bridgen, Paul. 'The One Nation Idea and State Welfare: The Conservatives and Pensions in the 1950s'. *Contemporary British History* 14/3 (2000), 83–104. doi:10.1080/13619460008581595.

Brittan, Samuel. 'How to Reform the Welfare State', *The Observer*, 10 Nov. 1963, 3.

Brittan, Samuel. 'A One Nation Tax System', *Financial Times*, 12 July 1984, 23.

Brittan, Samuel. 'Redistributive Market Liberalism'. In Samuel Brittan, *Essays, Moral, Political and Economic* (Edinburgh, 1998), 22–32.

Brittan, Samuel. Review in Citizen's Income Trust *Newsletter* 2 (2005), 8–9.

Brittan, Samuel, and Barry Riley. 'A People's Stake in North Sea Oil', *Lloyds Bank Review* (Apr. 1978), 1–18.

Brown, C. V., and D. A. Dawson. *Personal Taxation, Incentives and Tax Reform* (1969).

Brown, Gordon. *My Life, our Times* (2017).

Brown, William. 'The Process of Fixing the British National Minimum Wage, 1997–2007'. *British Journal of Industrial Relations* 47/2 (2009), 429–43. doi:10.1111/j.1467-8543.2009.00722.x.

Brown, William. 'The Toxic Politicising of the National Minimum Wage'. *Employee Relations* 39/6 (2017), 785–9. doi:10.1108/ER-04-2017-0072.

Browne, James, and Herwig Immervoll. 'Mechanics of Replacing Benefit Systems with a Basic Income: Comparative Results from a Microsimulation Approach'. *Journal of Economic Inequality* 15/4 (2017), 325–44. doi:10.1007/s10888-017-9366-6.

Bulmer, Martin. 'The British Tradition of Social Administration: Moral Concerns at the Expense of Scientific Rigor'. *Hastings Center Report* 11/2 (1981), 35–42. doi:10.2307/3561073.

Bulpitt, Jim. 'The Discipline of the New Democracy: Mrs Thatcher's Domestic Statecraft'. *Political Studies* 34/1 (1986), 19–39. doi:10.1111/j.1467-9248.1986.tb01870.x.

Burgin, Angus. *The Great Persuasion: Reinventing Free Markets since the Depression* (Cambridge, Mass., 2012).

Butler, Patrick. 'Low-Income Tenants Face "Heat, Eat or Pay Rent" Choices'. *The Guardian* (online edn), 29 Aug. 2018. Accessed 30 Aug. 2018. <https://www.theguardian.com/society/2018/aug/29/low-income-tenants-face-heat-eat-or-pay-rent-choices-study>.

Cairncross, Sir Alec. 'The Heath Government and the British Economy'. In *The Heath Government 1970–74: A Reappraisal*, edited by Stuart Ball and Anthony Seldon (Harlow, 1996), 107–38.

Campbell, Alastair. *The Alastair Campbell Diaries*, vol. 1: *Prelude to Power 1994–1997* (2010).

Campbell, Alastair. *The Alastair Campbell Diaries*, vol. 2: *Power and the People 1997–1999* (2011).

Campbell, Alastair. *The Alastair Campbell Diaries*, vol. 3: *Power & Responsibility 1999–2001* (2011).

Campbell, John. *Edward Heath: A Biography* (1993).

Campbell, John L. 'The State and Fiscal Sociology'. *Annual Review of Sociology* 19/1 (1993), 163–85. doi:10.1146/annurev.so.19.080193.001115.

Caputo, Richard K., ed. *Basic Income Guarantee and Politics: International Experiences and Perspectives on the Viability of Income Guarantee* (Basingstoke, 2012).

Card, David, and Alan B. Krueger. 'Minimum Wages and Employment: A Case Study of the Fast-Food Industry in New Jersey and Pennsylvania'. *American Economic Review* 84/4 (1994), 772–93.

Card, David, and Alan B. Krueger. *Myth and Measurement: The New Economics of the Minimum Wage* (Princeton, 1995).

Carnegie UK. *Exploring the Practicalities of a Basic Income Pilot* (Dunfermline, 2019).

Carson, Carol S. 'The Conference on Research in Income and Wealth: The Early Years'. In *Fifty Years of Economic Measurement: The Jubilee of the Conference on Research in Income and Wealth*, edited by Ernst R. Bendt and Jack E. Triplett (Chicago, 1990), 3–8.

Centre for Analysis of Social Exclusion. *Persistent Poverty and Lifetime Inequality: The Evidence* (1999).

Centre for Social Justice. *Dynamic Benefits: Towards Welfare that Works* (2009).

Chambers, S. P. 'Taxation and Incentives'. *Lloyds Bank Review*, new series no. 8 (Apr. 1948), 1–12.

Chartered Institute of Housing. *Missing the Target: Is Targeted Affordability Funding Doing its Job?* (Coventry, 2018).

Cherrier, Béatrice. 'Remembering Tony Atkinson as the Architect of Modern Public Economics'. The Undercover Historian blog. 2 Jan. 2017. <https://beatricecherrier.wordpress.com/2017/01/02/remembering-tony-atkinson-as-the-architect-of-modern-public-economics/>.

Child Poverty Action Group. 'Family Poverty: Memorandum'. Nov. 1965. Accessed 25 July 2017. <http://www.cpag.org.uk/content/family-poverty-memorandum>.

Child Poverty Action Group and Trades Union Congress, *Reforms to Universal Credit* (2015). Accessed 17 Sept. 2018. <https://www.tuc.org.uk/sites/default/files/ReformstoUniversalCredit_0.pdf>.

Chiplin, Brian. 'Professor Dennis Lees: Industrial Economist who was a Staunch Believer in the Free Market'. *The Independent*, 27 Feb. 2008.

Christopher, Anthony, George Polanyi, Arthur Seldon, and Barbara Shenfield. *Policy for Poverty: The Report of an IEA Study Group* (1970).

Clark, Colin. *Poverty before Politics: A Proposal for a Reverse Income Tax* (1977).

Clasen, Jochen. 'Subsidizing Wages or Supplementing Transfers? The Politics and Ambiguity of in-Work Benefits'. *Social Policy & Administration* early view (2019), doi:10.1111/spol.12488.

Clasen, Jochen, and Daniel Clegg. 'Adapting Labour Market Policy to a Transformed Employment Structure: The Politics of "Triple Integration"'. In *The Politics of the New Welfare State*, edited by Giuliano Bonoli and David Natali (Oxford, 2012), 135–57.

Clegg, Daniel. 'The Demise of Tax Credits'. *Political Quarterly* 86/4 (2015), 493–9. doi:10.1111/1467-923X.12203.

Clinton, David, Michael Yates, and Dharminder Kang. *Integrating Taxes and Benefits?* (1994).

Cobham, David, Christopher Adam, and Ken Mayhew. 'The Economic Record of the 1997–2010 Labour Government: An Assessment'. *Oxford Review of Economic Policy* 29/1 (2013), 1–24. doi:10.1093/oxrep/grt014.

Colander, David, Richard P. F. Holt, and J. Barkley Rosser Jr. 'The Changing Face of Mainstream Economics'. *Review of Political Economy* 16/4 (2004), 485–99.

Cole, Dorothy, and John Utting. *The Economic Circumstances of Old People* (Welwyn, 1962).

Cole, G. D. H. *The Next Ten Years in Social and Economic Policy* (1929).

Cole, G. D. H. *Principles of Economic Planning* (1935).

Collard, David. 'Pigou, Arthur Cecil (1877–1959)'. In *Oxford Dictionary of National Biography*, vol. 44, edited by H. C. G. Matthew and Brian Harrison (Oxford, 2004), 296–9.

Commission on Social Justice. *Social Justice: Strategies for National Renewal. The Report of the Commission on Social Justice* (1994).

Connell, Andrew. *Welfare Policy under New Labour: The Politics of Social Security Reform* (2011).

Conservative Party. *Make Life Better* (1968).

Conservative Party. *For All the People* (1972).

Conservative Party. 'Michael Howard Warns Labour Minimum Wage Fiasco "Could Double Unemployment"' (press release, 22 Apr. 1991).

Conservative Party. *Forward, Together: Our Plan for a Stronger Britain and a More Prosperous Future* (2017).

Conservative Party General Election Manifestos 1900–1997, edited by Iain Dale (2000).

Cook, Robin. *The Point of Departure* (2003).

Cook, S. L. *Can a Social Wage Solve Unemployment?* (Birmingham, 1979).

Corkery, Jim, Jay Forder, Enrico Mercuri, and Dan Svantesson. 'Taxes, the Internet and the Digital Economy'. *Revenue Law Journal* 23/1 (2013), 128–43.

Corlett, Adam, Stephen Clarke, Conor D'Arcy, and John Wood. *The Living Standards Audit 2018* (2018).

Coutts, Ken, Andrew Glyn, and Bob Rowthorn. 'Structural Change under New Labour'. *Cambridge Journal of Economics* 31/6 (2007), 845–61.

Cowburn, Ashley. 'Labour Sets up "Working Group" to Investigate Universal Basic Income, John McDonnell Reveals'. *The Independent*, 5 Feb. 2017. Accessed 23 Mar. 2018. <https://www.independent.co.uk/news/uk/politics/labour-sets-up-working-group-to-investigate-radical-idea-of-basic-income-john-mcdonnell-reveals-a7563566.html>.

Crewe, Ivor, Anthony Fox, and Neil Day, eds. *The British Electorate 1963–1992* (Cambridge, 1995).

Crewe, Ivor, Bo Särlvik, and James Alt, 'The Why and How of the February Voting'. *New Society*, 12 Sept. 1974, 669–72.

Crosland, Anthony. *The Future of Socialism*, 2nd edn (1964).

Crossman, Richard. *The Diaries of a Cabinet Minister*, vol. 1: *Minister of Housing 1964–66* (1975).

Crossman, Richard. *The Diaries of a Cabinet Minister*, vol. 2: *Lord President of the Council and Leader of the House of Commons 1966–68* (1976).

Crouch, Colin. 'Privatised Keynesianism: An Unacknowledged Policy Regime'. *British Journal of Politics and International Relations* 11/3 (2009), 382–99. doi:10.1111/j.1467-856X.2009.00377.x.

Crowcroft, Robert. 'Financial Policy, Coalition and Sir Kingsley Wood, 1940–1'. *Twentieth Century British History* 26/1 (2015), 74–96. doi:10.1093/tcbh/hwu044.

Crowson, N. J. 'Introduction: The Voluntary Sector in 1980s Britain'. *Contemporary British History* 25/4 (2011), 491–8. doi:10.1080/13619462.2011.623861.

Cruddas, Jon, and Tom Kibasi. 'A Universal Basic Mistake', *Prospect* 224 (July 2016), 50–2.

Daunton, Martin. *Trusting Leviathan: The Politics of Taxation in Britain, 1799–1914* (Cambridge, 2001).

Daunton, Martin. *Just Taxes: The Politics of Taxation in Britain, 1914–1979* (Cambridge, 2002).

Davala, Sarath, Renana Jhabvala, Soumya Kapoor Mehta, and Guy Standing. *Basic Income: A Transformative Policy for India* (2015).

Davies, Gareth. *From Opportunity to Entitlement: The Transformation and Decline of Great Society Liberalism* (Lawrence, Kan., 1996).

Davies, Gavyn, et al. *Tax Options for 1992: The Green Budget* (1992). Accessed 28 Feb. 2019. <https://www.ifs.org.uk/comms/comm28.pdf>.

Davies, Will. 'Thoughts on the Sociology of Brexit'. Goldsmiths Political Economy Research Centre blog. 24 June 2016. Accessed 19 July 2018. http://www.perc.org.uk/project_posts/thoughts-on-the-sociology-of-brexit/.

Davis, Abigail, Donald Hirsch, Matt Padley, and Claire Shepherd. *A Minimum Income Standard for the UK, 2008–2018: Continuity and Change* (York, 2018).

Davis, E. H., A. W. Dilnot, and J. A. Kay, 'The Social Security Green Paper', *Fiscal Studies* 6/3 (Aug. 1985), 1–8. doi:10.1111/j.1475-5890.1985.tb00403.x.

Deacon, Alan. 'The Scrounging Controversy: Public Attitudes towards the Unemployed in Contemporary Britain'. *Social and Economic Administration* 12/2 (1978), 120–35. doi:10.1111/j.1467-9515.1978.tb00127.x.

Deacon, Alan. *Perspectives on Welfare: Ideas, Ideologies and Policy Debates* (Buckingham, 2002).

Deacon, Alan, and Jonathan Bradshaw. *Reserved for the Poor: The Means Test in British Social Policy* (Oxford, 1983).

Deacon, Bob. *Global Social Policy in the Making: The Foundations of the Social Protection Floor* (Bristol, 2013).

Deakin, Nicholas, and Richard Parry. *The Treasury and Social Policy: The Contest for Control of Welfare Strategy* (Basingstoke, 2000).

Dean, Hartley. 'The Ethical Deficit of the United Kingdom's Proposed Universal Credit: Pimping the Precariat?' *Political Quarterly* 83/2 (2012), 353–9. doi:10.1111/j.1467-923X.2012.02292.x.

de Jouvenel, Bertrand. *The Ethics of Redistribution* (Cambridge, 1951).

Denman, Andrew, and Mark Garnett. *Keith Joseph* (Chesham, 2001).

Department for Work and Pensions, *Measuring Child Poverty* (2003).

Department of Employment and Productivity. *A National Minimum Wage: An Inquiry* (1969).

Department of Health and Social Security. *Social Assistance: A Review of the Supplementary Benefits Scheme in Great Britain* (1978).

de Roo, Alexander. 'Basic Income Initiatives in the European Parliament'. *BIRG Bulletin* 7 (1988), 27.

de Roo, Alexander. 'Citizen's Income too Radical for the European Parliament'. *BIRG Bulletin* 15 (1992), 19–20.

de Wispelaere, Jurgen. 'The Struggle for Strategy: On the Politics of the Basic Income Proposal'. *Politics* 36/2 (2016), 131–41. doi:10.1111/1467-9256.12102.

de Wispelaere, Jurgen. 'Basic Income in our Time: Improving Political Prospects through Policy Learning?' *Journal of Social Policy* 45/4 (2016), 617–34. doi:10.1017/S0047279416000039.

de Wispelaere, Jurgen, and Lindsay Stirton. 'The Case against Participation Income—Political, not Merely Administrative'. *Political Quarterly* 89/2 (2018), 262–7. doi:10.1111/1467-923X.12513.

Dickens, Richard. 'Child Poverty in Britain: Past Lessons and Future Prospects'. *National Institute Economic Review* 218 (2011), R7–R19. doi:10.1177/002795011121800102.

Dickens, Richard, and Alan Manning. 'Has the National Minimum Wage Reduced UK Wage Inequality?' *Journal of the Royal Statistical Society* Series A, 167/4 (2004), 613–26. doi:10.1111/j.1467-985X.2004.ael2.x.

Dillon, Sara. 'Tax Avoidance, Revenue Starvation, and the Age of the Multinational Corporation'. *The International Lawyer* 50/2 (2017), 275–327.

Dilnot, A. W., J. A. Kay, and C. N. Morris, *The Reform of Social Security* (Oxford, 1984).

Dilnot, Andrew. 'A New Sense of Security'. *The Guardian*, 4 May 1994, A12.

Dilnot, Andrew, and Steven Webb. 'The 1988 Social Security Reforms'. *Fiscal Studies* 9/3 (Aug. 1988), 26–53. doi:10.1111/j.1475-5890.1988.tb00324.x.

Dodds, Elliott. 'The Welfare State'. *The Fortnightly* (Sept. 1949), 172–8.

Dodds, Elliott. 'Liberty and Welfare'. In *The Unservile State: Essays in Liberty and Welfare*, edited by George Watson (1957), 13–26.

Dolowitz, David. *Learning from America: Policy Transfer and the Development of the British Workfare State* (Brighton, 1998).

Donnison, David. 'Research for Policy'. *Minerva* 10/4 (1972), 519–36.

Donnison, David. *The Politics of Poverty* (Oxford, 1982).

Donnison, David. 'Is Citizen's Income Still a Serious Option?' *Citizen's Income Bulletin* 25 (1998), 27.

Douglas, Mary. *Purity and Danger: An Analysis of the Concepts of Pollution and Taboo* (New York, 1966).

Drakeford, Mark. *Social Movements and their Supporters: The Green Shirts in England* (Basingstoke, 1997).

Drèze, Jean, and Amartya Sen. *Hunger and Public Action* (Oxford, 1989).

Duncan, Colin. *Low Pay—Its Causes, and the Post-War Trade Union Response* (Chichester, 1981).

Duncan Smith, Iain. 'We've Brought Fairness Back to Welfare'. *Sunday Telegraph*, 30 Dec. 2012. Accessed 23 July 2018. <https://www.telegraph.co.uk/news/politics/9772131/Iain-Duncan-Smith-weve-brought-back-fairness-to-welfare.html>.

Dutton, David. 'On the Brink of Oblivion: The Post-War Crisis of British Liberalism'. *Canadian Journal of History* 27/3 (1992), 425–50. doi:10.3138/cjh.27.3.425.

East London Claimants' Union. *A Guaranteed Minimum Income: A Socialist Strategy for Social Security* (1980).

Economic Dependency Working Group. *Dynamic Benefits: Towards Welfare that Works* (2009).

Edgerton, David. *The Rise and Fall of the British Nation: A Twentieth-Century History* (2018).

Ellison, Nick. 'The Conservative Party and the "Big Society"'. In *Social Policy Review 23: Analysis and Debate in Social Policy, 2011*, edited by Chris Holden, Majella Kilkey, and Gaby Ramia (Bristol, 2011), 45–62.

Elming, William, Carl Emmerson, Paul Johnson, and David Phillips. *An Assessment of the Potential Compensation Provided by the New 'National Living Wage' for the Personal Tax and Benefit Measures Announced for Implementation in the Current Parliament*. IFS Briefing Note 175 (2015).

Esping-Andersen, Gøsta. *The Three Worlds of Welfare Capitalism* (Cambridge, 1990).

Evans, Geoffrey, and James Tilley. *The New Politics of Class: The Political Exclusion of the British Working Class* (Oxford, 2017).

Evans, Tanya. 'Stopping the Poor Getting Poorer: The Establishment and Professionalization of Poverty NGOs, 1945–95'. In *NGOs in Contemporary Britain: Non-State Actors in*

Society and Politics since 1945, edited by Nick Crowson, Matthew Hilton, and James McKay (Basingstoke, 2009), 147–63.

Fabian Society. *Narrowing the Gap: The Final Report of the Fabian Commission on Life Chances and Child Poverty* (2006).

Falk, Gene. 'The Earned Income Tax Credit: An Overview'. Congressional Research Service report RL31768, 22 Oct. 2014. Accessed 19 July 2018. <https://fas.org/sgp/crs/misc/RL31768.pdf>.

Farrell, Henry, and John Quiggin. 'Consensus, Dissensus, and Economic Ideas: Economic Crisis and the Rise and Fall of Keynesianism'. *International Studies Quarterly* 61/2 (2017), 269–83. doi:10.1093/isq/sqx010.

Favretto, Ilaria. '"Wilsonism" Reconsidered: Labour Party Revisionism, 1952–64'. *Contemporary British History* 14/4 (2000), 54–80. doi:10.1080/13619460008581603.

Fawcett, Helen. 'Jack Jones, the Social Contract and Social Policy 1970–4'. In *Welfare Policy in Britain: The Road from 1945*, edited by Helen Fawcett and Rodney Lowe (Basingstoke, 1999), 158–83.

Federation of Claimants Unions. *Women and Social Security*, rev. edn (1982).

Feinstein, Charles. 'Structural Change in the Developed Countries in the Twentieth Century'. *Oxford Review of Economic Policy* 15/4 (1999), 35–55. doi:10.1093/oxrep/15.4.35.

Ferguson, James. *Give a Man a Fish: Reflections on the New Politics of Distribution* (Durham, NC, 2015).

Fielding, Steven. 'What Did "The People" Want? The Meaning of the 1945 General Election'. *Historical Journal* 35/3 (1992), 623–39. doi:10.1017/S0018246X00026005.

Figart, Deborah M., Ellen Mutari, and Marilyn Power. *Living Wages, Equal Wages: Gender and Labor Market Policies in the United States* (2002).

Finch, David, and Laura Gardiner. *Back in Credit? Universal Credit after Budget 2018* (2018).

Fleetwood, Steve. 'Reflections upon Neoclassical Labour Economics'. In *What is Neoclassical Economics? Debating the Origins, Meaning and Significance*, edited by Jamie Morgan (Abingdon, 2016), 273–310.

Fleischacker, Samuel. *A Short History of Distributive Justice* (Cambridge, Mass., 2004).

Fontaine, Philippe. 'Blood, Politics, and Social Science: Richard Titmuss and the Institute of Economic Affairs, 1957–73'. *Isis* 93/3 (2002), 401–34, doi:10.1086/374061.

Fowler, Norman. *Ministers Decide* (1991).

Freud, David. *Reducing Dependency, Increasing Opportunity: Options for the Future of Welfare to Work* (2007).

Friedman, Milton. *Capitalism and Freedom* (Chicago, 1962).

Friedman, Milton, and Rose Friedman. *Two Lucky People: Memoirs* (Chicago, 1998).

Gamble, Andrew. *The Spectre at the Feast: Capitalist Crisis and the Politics of Recession* (Basingstoke, 2009).

Gazeley, Ian. *Poverty in Britain, 1900–1965* (Basingstoke, 2003).

Genet, Michel, and Philippe van Parijs. 'Eurogrant'. *BIRG Bulletin* 15 (1992), 4–7.

George, Vic, and Paul Wilding. *Ideology and Social Welfare* (1976).

Glennerster, Howard. *Tibor Barna: The Redistributive Impact of Taxes and Social Policies in the UK: 1937–2005*. CASE Paper 115 (2006).

Glennerster, Howard. 'LSE's Contributions to the Economics of Social Policy'. In *The Palgrave Companion to LSE Economics*, edited by Robert A. Cord (Basingstoke, 2018), 145–64.

Goes, Eunice. *The Labour Party under Ed Miliband: Trying but Failing to Renew Social Democracy* (Manchester, 2016).

Goldman, Peter. 'Preface'. In *The Future of the Welfare State: Seven Oxford Lectures*, Conservative Political Centre (1958), 7–10.

Gordon, David. 'The Scientific Measurement of Poverty: Recent Theoretical Advances'. In *Researching Poverty*, edited by Jonathan Bradshaw and Roy Sainsbury (Aldershot, 2000), 37–58.

Gorz, André. *Farewell to the Working Class: An Essay on Post-Industrial Socialism*, trans. Michael Sonenscher (1982).

Gorz, André. *Paths to Paradise: On the Liberation from Work* (1985).

Gough, Ian. 'Basic Income: A Powerful Tax Engine Pulling a Tiny Cart'. In *It's Basic Income: The Global Debate*, edited by Amy Downes and Stewart Lansley (Bristol, 2018), 101–102.

Gould, Philip. *The Unfinished Revolution: How the Modernisers Saved the Labour Party* (1998).

Gould, Tony, and Joe Kenyon. *Stories from the Dole Queue* (1972).

Graham, Andrew. 'Thomas Balogh (1905–85)'. *Contemporary Record* 6/1 (1992), 194–207. doi:10.1080/13619469208581204.

Gray, Ann. 'Resisting Economic Conscription'. *Capital & Class* 12/1 (1988), 119–46. doi:10.1177/030981688803400109.

Gray, Paul, and Nicholas Timmins. *Reforming Working-Age Social Security: Lessons for Policy Makers* (2018).

Green, A. Romney. 'The Tax Curve'. *Economic Journal* 50/200 (1940), 469–74. doi:10.2307/2226206.

Green, A. Romney. 'Social Reconstruction by Redistribution of Incomes'. *Economic Journal* 52/205 (1942), 37–44. doi:10.2307/2225699.

Green Party. *For the Common Good: General Election Manifesto 2015* (2015).

Gregg, Paul. 'The Potential and Limits of Predistribution in the UK: Tackling Inequality and Poverty'. In *The Predistribution Agenda: Tackling Inequality and Supporting Sustainable Growth*, edited by Claudia Chwalisz and Patrick Diamond (2015), 79–92.

Gregg, Paul, Susan Harkness, and Stephen Machin. *Child Development and Family Income* (York, 1999).

Gregg, Paul, Alex Hurrell, and Matthew Whittaker. *Creditworthy: Assessing the Impact of Tax Credits in the Last Decade and Considering What This Means for Universal Credit* (2012).

Griggs, Julia, Andrew Hammond, and Robert Walker. 'Activation for All: Welfare Reform in the United Kingdom, 1995–2009'. In *Activation or Workfare? Governance and the Neo-Liberal Convergence*, edited by Ivar Lodemel and Amilcar Moreira (Oxford, 2014), 73–100.

Grimond, Joseph. *The Liberal Future* (1959).

Grimshaw, Damian, Caroline Lloyd, and Chris Warhurst. 'Low-Wage Work in the United Kingdom: Employment Practices, Institutional Effects, and Policy Responses'. In *Low-Wage Work in the United Kingdom*, edited by Caroline Lloyd, Geoff Mason, and Ken Mayhew (New York, 2008).

Grover, Chris. *Social Security and Wage Poverty: Historical and Policy Aspects of Supplementing Wages in Britain and Beyond* (Basingstoke, 2016).

Guinan, Joe, and Martin O'Neill. 'The Institutional Turn: Labour's New Political Economy'. *Renewal* 26/2 (2018), 5–16.

Hacker, Jacob. 'The Institutional Foundations of Middle-Class Democracy'. In *Priorities for a New Political Economy: Memos to the Left*, Policy Network (2011), 33–7.

Hacker, Jacob. 'Foreword: The Promise of Predistribution'. In *The Predistribution Agenda: Tackling Inequality and Supporting Sustainable Growth*, edited by Claudia Chwalisz and Patrick Diamond (2015), xxi–xxx.

Hacker, Jacob, and Paul Pierson. 'Winner-Take-All Politics: Public Policy, Political Organization, and the Precipitous Rise of Top Incomes in the United States'. *Politics & Society* 38/2 (2010), 152–204. doi:10.1177/0032329210365042.

Haddon, Catherine. 'Making Policy in Opposition: The Commission on Social Justice, 1992–1994'. Institute for Government report, Dec. 2012. <https://www.instituteforgovernment.org.uk/publications/making-policy-opposition-commission-social-justice-1992-1994>.

Hall, Christopher. 'The Future of Basic Income in Great Britain'. In *Basic Income. Proceedings of the First International Conference on Basic Income, Louvain-La-Neuve, Belgium, 4–6 September 1986* (Antwerp, 1986), edited by Anne G. Miller, 309–13.

Hall, Peter, and David Soskice, eds. *Varieties of Capitalism: The Institutional Foundations of Comparative Advantage* (Oxford, 2001).

Hall, Suzanne, Katrina Leary, and Helen Greevy. *Public Attitudes to Poverty* (York, 2014).

Halsey, A. H. *A History of Sociology in Britain: Science, Literature, and Society* (Oxford, 2004).

Hamlin, Alan. 'What Political Philosophy Should Learn from Economics about Taxation'. In *Taxation: Philosophical Perspectives*, edited by Martin O'Neill and Shepley Orr (Oxford, 2018), 18–36.

Hampton, Jameel. *Disability and the Welfare State in Britain: Changes in Perception and Policy 1948–79* (Bristol, 2016).

Handy, Charles. *The Future of Work: A Guide to a Changing Society* (Oxford, 1984).

Handy, Charles. *Myself and Other More Important Matters* (2006).

Hanlon, Joseph, Armando Barrientos, and David Hulme. *Just Give Money to the Poor: The Development Revolution from the Global South* (Sterling, Va, 2010).

Harris, José. 'Some Aspects of Social Policy in Britain During the Second World War'. In *The Emergence of the Welfare State in Britain and Germany, 1850–1950*, edited by W. J. Mommsen (1981), 247–62.

Harris, José. 'Political Thought and the Welfare State 1870–1940: An Intellectual Framework for British Social Policy'. *Past and Present* 135 (1992), 116–41. <https://www.jstor.org/stable/650972>.

Harris, José. 'Beveridge's Social and Political Thought'. In *Beveridge and Social Security: An International Retrospective*, edited by John Hills, John Ditch, and Howard Glennerster (Oxford, 1994), 23–36.

Harris, José. *William Beveridge: A Biography*, 2nd edn (Oxford, 1997).

Harris, José. 'From Poor Law to Welfare State? A European Perspective'. In *The Political Economy of British Historical Experience, 1688–1914*, edited by Donald Winch and Patrick K. O'Brien (Oxford, 2002), 409–37.

Harrison, Royden. 'Bertrand Russell: From Liberalism to Socialism?' *Russell* 6/1 (1986), 5–38.

Harrod, Roy. 'The Outlook for 1949'. *World Review*, Jan. 1949, 15–19.

Harrop, Andrew. *For Us All: Redesigning Social Security for the 2020s* (2016).

Hay, Colin. *The Failure of Anglo-Liberal Capitalism* (Basingstoke, 2013).

Hayek, Friedrich. *The Road to Serfdom* (1944).

Hayhoe, Barney. *Must the Children Suffer?* (1968).

Haynes, A. T., and R. J. Kirton. *Income Tax in Relation to Social Security* (1943).

Hayton, Richard, and Libby McEnhill. 'Rhetoric and Morality—How the Coalition Justifies Welfare Policy'. In *Rhetoric in British Politics and Society*, edited by Judi Atkins, Alan Finlayson, James Martin, and Nick Turnbull (Basingstoke, 2014), 101–15.

Hemerijck, Anton. 'Prospects for Basic Income in an Age of Inactivity?' In *Basic Income on the Agenda: Policy Objectives and Political Chances*, edited by Robert van der Veen and Loek Groot (Amsterdam, 2000), 137–54.

Hemerijck, Anton. *Changing Welfare States* (Oxford, 2013).

Hennock, E. P. 'The Measurement of Urban Poverty: From the Metropolis to the Nation, 1880–1920'. *Economic History Review* 40/2 (1987), 208–27. doi:10.1111/j.1468-0289.1987.tb00426.x.

Hevenstone, Debra. *The American Myth of Markets in Social Policy: Ideological Roots of Inequality* (Basingstoke, 2015).

Hewitt, Patricia. 'Social Justice in a Global Economy?' In *Citizenship Today: The Contemporary Relevance of T. H. Marshall*, edited by Martin Bulmer and Anthony M. Rees (1996), 249–68.

Hewitt, Patricia, and Philip Gould. 'Learning from Success—Labour and Clinton's New Democrats'. *Renewal* 1/1 (Jan. 1993), 45–51.

Hick, Rod, and Alba Lanau. 'Moving in and out of In-Work Poverty in the UK: An Analysis of Transitions, Trajectories and Trigger Events'. *Journal of Social Policy* 47/4 (2018), 661–82. doi:10.1017/S0047279418000028.

Hicks, J. R. *The Theory of Wages* (1932).

Hills, John. *Ends and Means: The Future Roles of Social Housing in England* (2007).

Hills, John. *Good Times, Bad Times: The Welfare Myth of Them and Us*, rev. edn (Bristol, 2017).

Hills, John, Howard Glennerster, and Julian Le Grand. *Investigating Welfare: Final Report of the ESRC Welfare Research Programme*. Welfare State Programme Discussion Paper WSP/92 (1993).

Hirsch, Donald. 'Contemporary UK Wage Floors and the Calculation of a Living Wage'. *Employee Relations* 39/6 (2017), 815–24. doi:10.1108/ER-03-2017-0048.

Hirsch, Donald. 'The "Living Wage" and Low Income: Can Adequate Pay Contribute to Adequate Family Living Standards?' *Critical Social Policy* 38/2 (2017), 367–86. doi:10.1177/0261018317729469.

Hirschman, Daniel, and Elizabeth Popp Berman. 'Do Economists Make Policies? On the Political Effects of Economics'. *Socio-Economic Review* 12/4 (2014), 779–811. doi:10.1093/ser/mwu017.

Hirst, Paul. *Associative Democracy: New Forms of Economic and Social Governance* (Cambridge, Mass., 1994).

HM Treasury. *The Modernisation of Britain's Tax and Benefit System—Number Two. Work Incentives. A Report by Martin Taylor* (1998).

HM Treasury. *The Modernisation of Britain's Tax and Benefit System—Number Six. Tackling Poverty and Making Work Pay—Tax Credits for the 21st Century* (2000).

HM Treasury. *Child Poverty Review* (2004).

HM Treasury, Department for Children, Schools and Families, and Department for Work and Pensions, *Ending Child Poverty: Mapping the Route to 2020* (2010).

Hodson, Dermot, and Deborah Mabbett. 'UK Economic Policy and the Global Financial Crisis: Paradigm Lost?' *Journal of Common Market Studies* 47/5 (2009), 1041–61. doi:10.1111/j.1468-5965.2009.02034.x.

Hood, Christopher, and Ruth Dixon. *A Government That Worked Better and Cost Less? Evaluating Three Decades of Reform and Change in UK Central Government* (Oxford, 2015).

Hood, Christopher, and Rozana Himaz. *A Century of Fiscal Squeeze Politics: 100 Years of Austerity, Politics, and Bureaucracy in Britain* (Oxford, 2017).

Hopkin, Jonathan, and Kate Alexander Shaw. 'Organized Combat or Structural Advantage? The Politics of Inequality and the Winner-Take-All Economy in the United Kingdom'. *Politics & Society* 44/3 (2016), 345–71. doi:10.1177/0032329216655316.

Hotz, V. Joseph, and John Karl Scholz. 'The Earned Income Tax Credit'. In *Means-Tested Transfer Programs in the United States*, edited by Robert A. Moffitt (Chicago, 2003), 141–97.

Houghton, Douglas. *Paying for the Social Services* (1967).

Howard, Michael W. 'Basic Income and Migration Policy: A Moral Dilemma?' *Basic Income Studies* 1/1 (2006). doi:10.2202/1932-0183.1001.

Howarth, Angus. 'Scottish Tories want "Unaffordable" Basic Income Pilots Scrapped'. *The Scotsman*, 27 June 2018. Accessed 2 Aug. 2018. <https://www.scotsman.com/news/scottish-tories-want-unaffordable-basic-income-pilots-scrapped-1-4760913>.

Howarth, Catherine, and Peter Kenway. *Why Worry any More about the Low Paid?* (2004).

Howell, Chris. *Trade Unions and the State: The Construction of Industrial Relations Institutions in Britain, 1890–2000* (Princeton, 2005).

Howell, Ralph. *Why Work? A Challenge to the Chancellor* (1976).

Hudson, John, and Neil Lunt, with Charlotte Hamilton. 'Nostalgia Narratives? Pejorative Attitudes to Welfare in Historical Perspective: Survey Evidence from Beveridge to the British Social Attitudes Survey'. *Journal of Poverty and Social Justice* 24/3 (2016), 227–43. doi:10.1332/175982716X14721954315002.

Institute for Fiscal Studies. 'Cost of Cutting Child Poverty Rises as Families Fall Further below Poverty Line' (press release, 18 Feb. 2009).

Institute of Economic Affairs. *Choice in Welfare* (1963).

Ironside, Philip. *The Social and Political Thought of Bertrand Russell: The Development of an Aristocratic Liberalism* (Cambridge, 1996).

Iversen, Torben. 'Economic Shocks and Varieties of Government Responses'. In *Varieties of Capitalism: The Institutional Foundations of Comparative Advantage*, edited by Peter Hall and David Soskice (Oxford, 2001), 278–304.

Iversen, Torben, and David Soskice. 'Electoral Institutions and the Politics of Coalitions: Why Some Democracies Redistribute More than Others'. *American Political Science Review* 100/2 (2006), 165–81. doi:10.1017/S0003055406062083.

Jackman, Richard. 'Richard Layard (1934–)'. In *The Palgrave Companion to LSE Economics*, edited by Robert A. Cord (Basingstoke, 2018), 743–63.

Jackson, Ben. *Equality and the British Left: A Study in Progressive Political Thought, 1900–1964* (Manchester, 2007).

Jackson, Ben. 'At the Origins of Neo-Liberalism: The Free Economy and the Strong State, 1930–1947'. *Historical Journal* 53/1 (2010), 129–51. doi:10.1017/S0018246X09990392.

Jackson, Ben. 'An Ideology of Class: Neo-Liberalism and the Trade Unions, *c.*1930–79'. In *Classes, Cultures, and Politics: Essays on British History for Ross McKibbin*, edited by Clare V. J. Griffiths, James J. Nott, and William Whyte (Oxford, 2011), 263–81.

James, Selma. *Women, the Unions and Work, or, What is not to be Done* (1972).

Jay, Douglas. *The Socialist Case* (1937).

Jenkins, Stephen P. 'Anthony B. Atkinson (1944–)'. In *The Palgrave Companion to Cambridge Economics*, vol. 2, edited by Robert A. Cord (Basingstoke, 2017), 1151–74.

Jenson, Jane. 'A New Politics for the Social Investment Perspective: Objectives, Instruments, and Areas of Intervention in Welfare Regimes'. In *The Politics of the New Welfare State*, edited by Giuliano Bonoli and David Natali (Oxford, 2012), 21–44.

Jessop, Bob. 'From Thatcherism to New Labour: Neo-Liberalism, Workfarism, and Labour Market Regulation'. In *The Political Economy of European Employment: European*

Integration and the Transnationalization of the (Un)employment Question, edited by Henk Overbeek (2003), 137–53.

Johnson, Carol, and Fran Tonkiss. 'The Third Influence: The Blair Government and Australian Labor'. *Policy & Politics* 30/1 (2002), 5–18. doi:10.1332/0305573022501539.

Jones, Harriet. 'New Tricks for an Old Dog? The Conservatives and Social Policy, 1951–55'. In *Contemporary British History 1931–61: Politics and the Limits of Policy*, edited by Anthony Gorst, Lewis Johnman, and W. Scott Lucas (1991), 33–43.

Jones, Jack. 'Wages and Social Security'. *New Statesman*, 7 Jan. 1972, 7.

Jones, Peter. 'Swing, Speenhamland and Rural Social Relations: The "Moral Economy" of the English Crowd in the Nineteenth Century'. *Social History* 32/3 (2007), 271–90. doi:10.1080/03071020701425304.

Jones, Tudor. '"Reluctant" or Liberal Collectivists? The Social Liberalism of Keynes and Beveridge, 1922–1945'. *Journal of Liberal History* 78 (Spring 2013), 32–41.

Jordan, Bill. Paupers*: The Making of the New Claiming Class* (1973).

Joseph Rowntree Foundation. *UK Poverty 2017* (York, 2017).

Kaletsky, Anatole. 'Why the Treasury Must Now be Brought to Heel'. *The Times*, 18 July 1996, 27.

Katz, Michael B. *The Undeserving Poor: America's Enduring Confrontation with Poverty*, 2nd edn (New York, 2013).

Kay, J. A. 'Tax Reform in Context: A Strategy for the 1990s'. *Fiscal Studies* 7/4 (Nov. 1986), 1–17. doi:10.1111/j.1475-5890.1986.tb00526.x.

Kay, J. A. 'Research and Policy: The IFS Experience'. *Policy Studies* 9/3 (1989), 20–6. doi:10.1080/01442878908423522.

Kay, John. 'Staking a Moral Claim'. *New Statesman*, 11 Oct. 1996, 18–20.

Kay, John. *The Truth about Markets: Why Some Nations Are Rich but Most Remain Poor* (2003).

Kay, John. 'The Left is Still Searching for a Practical Philosophy'. *Financial Times*, 5 May 2010, 13.

Kelsey, Tom. *An Unexpected Cut: Revisiting the Diamond Commission and Assessing Inequality in Post-War Britain* (2018).

Kemp, Peter. 'The Reform of Housing Benefit', *Social Policy & Administration* 21/2 (1987), 171–86. doi:10.1111/j.1467-9515.1987.tb00272.x.

Kentish Town Claimants' Union. *S.S. Times* (Spring 1972).

Keynes, John Maynard. 'The Question of High Wages'. *Political Quarterly* 1/1 (1930), 110–24. doi:10.1111/j.1467-923X.1930.tb01472.x.

Keynes, John Maynard. 'Economic Possibilities for our Grandchildren'. In *Essays in Persuasion* (1931), 358–73.

Keynes, John Maynard. *The General Theory of Employment Interest and Money* (1936).

Keynes, John Maynard. *How to Pay for the War: A Radical Plan for the Chancellor* (1940).

King, Anthony, and Ivor Crewe. *The Blunders of our Governments*, rev. paperback edn (2014).

King, Desmond. *Actively Seeking Work? The Politics of Unemployment and Welfare Reform in the United States and Great Britain* (Chicago, 1995).

King, Desmond, and Mark Wickham-Jones. 'Bridging the Atlantic: The Democratic (Party) Origins of Welfare to Work', in *New Labour, New Welfare State? The 'Third Way' in British Social Policy*, edited by Martin Powell (Bristol, 1999), 257–80.

Kingdon, John. *Agendas, Alternatives and Public Policies*, 2nd edn (New York, 1995).

Labour Party. *Report of the Nineteenth Annual Conference. Southport, 1919* (1919).

Labour Party. *Report of the Twentieth Annual Conference. Scarborough, 1920* (1920).

Labour Party. *Report of the Twenty-First Annual Conference. Brighton, 1921* (1921).

Labour Party. *The Welfare State* (1952).

Labour Party. *A Better Deal for Families: Delivered by Labour—Opposed by the Tories* (1999).

Labour Party. *For the Many not the Few: The Labour Party Manifesto 2017* (2017).

Labour Party General Election Manifestos, 1900–1997, edited by Iain Dale (2000).

Lange, Oskar. 'On the Economic Theory of Socialism: Part I'. *The Review of Economic Studies* 4/1 (1936), 53–71. doi:10.2307/2967660.

Lansley, Stewart, Duncan McCann, and Steve Schifferes. *Remodelling Capitalism: How Social Wealth Funds Could Transform Britain* (2018).

Lavery, Scott. 'The Legitimation of Post-Crisis Capitalism in the United Kingdom: Real Wage Decline, Finance-Led Growth and the State'. *New Political Economy*, 23/1 (2018), 27–45. doi:10.1080/13563467.2017.1321627.

Lavery, Scott. *British Capitalism after the Crisis* (Basingstoke, 2019).

Lawson, Kayte, Graeme Cooke, and Nick Pearce. *The Condition of Britain: Strategies for National Renewal* (2014).

Layard, Richard. *Unemployment in Britain: Causes and Cures* (1981).

Layard, Richard. *More Jobs, Less Inflation: The Case for a Counter-Inflation Tax* (1982).

Layard, Richard, Stephen Nickell, and Richard Jackman. *Unemployment: Macroeconomic Performance and the Labour Market* (Oxford, 1991).

Layard, Richard, David Piachaud, and Mark Stewart. *The Causes of Poverty. Royal Commission on the Distribution of Income and Wealth Background Paper No. 5* (1978).

Lee, Anthony, and John Hills, eds. *New Cycles of Disadvantage: Report of a Conference Organised by CASE on Behalf of ESRC for HM Treasury* (1998).

Lees, D. S. 'Poor Families and Fiscal Reform'. *Lloyds Bank Review*, Oct. 1967, 1–15.

Le Grand, Julian. *The Strategy of Equality: Redistribution and the Social Services* (1982).

Lenkowsky, Leslie. *Politics, Economics, and Welfare Reform: The Failure of the Negative Income Tax in Britain and the United States* (Lanham, NY, 1986).

Lerner, Abba. *The Economics of Control: Principles of Welfare Economics* (1944).

Levine-Clark, Marjorie. *Unemployment, Welfare, and Masculine Citizenship: 'So Much Honest Poverty' in Britain, 1870–1930* (Basingstoke, 2015).

Lewis, Jane. *The Politics of Motherhood: Child and Maternal Welfare in England, 1900–1939* (1980).

Lewis, Jane. 'Models of Equality for Women: The Case of State Support for Children in Twentieth-Century Britain'. In *Maternity and Gender Policies: Women and the Rise of the European Welfare States, 1880s–1950s*, edited by Gisela Bock and Pat Thane (1991), 73–92.

Lewis, Jane. 'Gender and the Development of Welfare Regimes'. *Journal of European Social Policy* 2/3 (1992), 159–73. doi:10.1177/095892879200200301.

Liberal Democrats, *Freedom from Poverty, Opportunity for All* (2007).

Liberal Party. *Family Allowances and Social Security: Lady Rhys-Williams' Scheme. With the Report of a Liberal Committee thereon* (1944).

Liberal Party, *Reform of Income Tax and Social Security Payments* (1950).

Liebman, Jeffrey. *Lessons about Tax-Benefit Integration from the US Earned Income Tax Credit Experience* (York, 1997).

Lindert, Peter H. *Growing Public: Social Spending and Economic Growth since the Eighteenth Century*, 2 vols (Cambridge, 2004).

Lindley, Joanne, and Stephen Machin. 'Wage Inequality in the Labour Years'. *Oxford Review of Economic Policy* 29/1 (2013), 165–77. doi:10.1093/oxrep/grt009.

Lister, Ruth. 'Coming off the Fence on Universal Basic Income'. In *It's Basic Income: The Global Debate*, edited by Amy Downes and Stewart Lansley (Bristol, 2018), 54–7.
Little, Adrian. *The Political Thought of André Gorz* (Abingdon, 1996).
Little, Adrian. *Post-Industrial Socialism: Towards a New Politics of Welfare* (1998).
Lowe, Rodney. 'The Rediscovery of Poverty and the Creation of the Child Poverty Action Group, 1962–68'. *Contemporary Record* 9/3 (1995), 602–11. doi:10.1080/13619469508581356.
Lowe, Rodney. 'The Replanning of the Welfare State, 1957–1964'. In *The Conservatives and British Society, 1880–1990*, edited by Martin Francis and Ina Zweiniger-Bargielowska (Cardiff, 1996), 255–73.
Lowe, Rodney. 'The Social Policy of the Heath Government'. In *The Heath Government 1970–74: A Reappraisal*, edited by Stuart Ball and Anthony Seldon (Harlow, 1996), 191–214.
Lowe, Rodney. *The Welfare State in Britain since 1945*, 3rd edn (Basingstoke, 2005).
Lowe, Rodney, and Paul Nicholson. 'The Formation of the Child Poverty Action Group'. *Contemporary Record* 9/3 (1995), 612–37. doi:10.1080/13619469508581357.
McBride, Damian. *Power Trip: A Decade of Policy, Plots and Spin* (2013).
McFarland, Kate. 'UK's Largest Trade Union Endorses Basic Income'. BIEN. 11 July 2016. Accessed 2 Aug. 2018. <https://basicincome.org/news/2016/07/uks-largest-trade-union-endorses-basic-income/>.
McGuinness, Feargal, and Jennifer Brown. 'Child Poverty'. House of Commons Library Briefing Note CDP-0256. 15 Dec. 2016.
Machin, Stephen. 'Childhood Disadvantage and Intergenerational Transmissions of Economic Status'. In Centre for Analysis of Social Exclusion, *Persistent Poverty and Lifetime Inequality: The Evidence* (1999), 17–21.
MacInnes, Tom, Hannah Aldridge, Sabrina Bushe, Peter Kenway, and Adam Tinson. *Monitoring Poverty and Social Exclusion 2013* (York, 2013).
McIvor, Arthur. *Working Lives: Work in Britain since 1945* (2013).
McKay, Ailsa. *'Welfare to Work' or a Welfare System that Works? Arguing for a Citizens Basic Income in a New Scotland* (Edinburgh, 2013).
Macnicol, John. *The Movement for Family Allowances, 1918–45: A Study in Social Policy Development* (1980).
Macnicol, John. *Neoliberalising Old Age* (Cambridge, 2015).
Malpass, Peter. *Reshaping Housing Policy: Subsidies, Rents and Residualisation* (1990).
Malpass, Peter. *Housing and the Welfare State: The Development of Housing Policy in Britain* (Basingstoke, 2005).
Mandle, Jon. *Rawls' A Theory of Justice: An Introduction* (Cambridge, 2009).
Marshall, Alfred. *Principles of Economics* [1890], 8th edn (1920).
Marshall, Alfred. 'Preliminary Statement and Evidence before the Royal Commission on the Aged Poor' [1893]. In *Official Papers of Alfred Marshall*, edited by J. M. Keynes (1926), 197–262.
Marshall, T. H. 'Citizenship and Social Class'. In T. H. Marshall, *Citizenship and Social Class and Other Essays* (Cambridge, 1950), 1–85.
Martin, Cathie Jo, and Duane Swank. *The Political Construction of Business Interests: Coordination, Growth, and Equality* (New York, 2012).
Martinelli, Luke, and Nick Pearce. 'Basic Income in the UK: Assessing Prospects for Reform in an Age of Austerity'. *Social Policy and Society* 18/2 (2019), 265–75. doi: 10.1017/S147474641800026X
Mason, Paul. *Postcapitalism: A Guide to our Future* (2015).

Meade, J. E. 'Outline of Economic Policy for a Labour Government' [1935]. In *The Collected Papers of James Meade*, vol. 1, ed. Susan Howson and Donald Moggridge (1988), 33–78.

Meade, J. E. *Planning and the Price Mechanism: The Liberal-Socialist Solution* (1948).

Meade, J. E. *Efficiency, Equality and the Ownership of Property* (1964).

Meade, J. E. *The Intelligent Radical's Guide to Economic Policy: The Mixed Economy* (1975).

Meade, J. E. *The Structure and Reform of Direct Taxation. Report of a Committee Chaired by Professor J. E. Meade* (1978).

Meade, J. E. 'A New Keynesian Approach to Full Employment'. *Nationaløkonomisk Tidsskrift* 131/3 (1983), 299–316.

Meade, J. E. *Agathotopia: The Economics of Partnership* (Aberdeen, 1989).

Meade, J. E. *The Building of the New Europe: National Diversity Versus Continental Uniformity* (Edinburgh, 1991).

Meade, J. E. *Fifteen Propositions concerning the Building of an Equitable, Full-Employment, Non-Inflationary, Free-Enterprise Economy* (1993).

Meltzer, Allan H., and Scott F. Richard. 'A Rational Theory of the Size of Government'. *Journal of Political Economy* 89/5 (1981), 914–27. doi:10.1086/261013.

Meredith, Stephen. *Labours Old and New: The Parliamentary Right of the British Labour Party 1970–79 and the Roots of New Labour* (Manchester, 2008).

Mesher, John. 'The 1980 Social Security Legislation: The Great Welfare State Chainsaw Massacre?' *British Journal of Law and Society* 8 (1981), 119–27.

Middlemas, Keith. *Politics in Industrial Society: The Experience of the British System since 1911* (1979).

Middleton, Roger. *Charlatans or Saviours? Economists and the British Economy from Marshall to Meade* (1998).

Miliband, Ed. 'The Inequality Problem'. *London Review of Books*, 4 Feb. 2016, 19–20.

Mill, John Stuart. *Principles of Political Economy* (1848). Reprinted in *Collected Works of John Stuart Mill*, vol. 2, edited by J. M. Robson (1965).

Millar, Jane. 'Making Work Pay, Making Tax Credits Work: An Assessment with Specific Reference to Lone-Parent Employment'. *International Social Security Review* 61/2 (2008), 21–38. doi:10.1111/j.1468-246X.2008.00308.x.

Millar, Jane, and Fran Bennett. 'Universal Credit: Assumptions, Contradictions and Virtual Reality'. *Social Policy and Society* 16/2 (2017), 169–82. doi:10.1017/S1474746416000154.

Miller, Anne G., ed. *Basic Income. Proceedings of the First International Conference on Basic Income, Louvain-La-Neuve, Belgium, 4–6 September 1986* (Antwerp, 1986).

Miller, Annie. *A Basic Income Handbook* (Edinburgh, 2017).

Miller, Dale E. 'Mill's "Socialism"'. *Politics, Philosophy & Economics* 2/2 (2003), 213–38. doi:10.1177/1470594X03002002004.

Millward, Gareth. 'Social Security Policy and the Early Disability Movement—Expertise, Disability, and the Government, 1965–77'. *Twentieth Century British History* 26/2 (2015), 274–97. doi:10.1093/tcbh/hwu048.

Milner, E. Mabel, and Dennis Milner, *Scheme for a State Bonus: A Rational Method of Solving the Social Problem* (Darlington, 1918).

Minford, Patrick. 'The Poverty Trap after the Fowler Reviews'. In *Improving Incentives for the Low-Paid*, edited by Alex Bowen and Ken Mayhew (Basingstoke, 1990), 121–38.

Minford, Patrick, with David Davies, Michael Peel, and Alison Sprague. *Unemployment: Cause and Cure* (Oxford, 1983).

Ministry of Pensions and National Insurance. *Financial and Other Circumstances of Retirement Pensioners* (1966).

Ministry of Social Security. *Circumstances of Families* (1967).
Minutes of Evidence Taken before the Royal Commission on the Taxation of Profits and Income (1953).
Mitchell, Austin. *Calendar Boy* (Barnsley, 2014).
Mitchell, Peter. 'Sick Sheep, Fit Goats'. Letter, *BIRG Bulletin* 3 (1985), 17.
Mitchell, William, and Joan Muysken. *Full Employment Abandoned: Shifting Sands and Policy Failures* (Cheltenham, 2008).
Montgomerie, Tim. *Whatever Happened to Compassionate Conservatism?* (2004).
Moore, Charles. *Margaret Thatcher: The Authorized Biography*, vol. 1: *Not for Turning* (2013).
Moran, Michael. 'The Rise of the Regulatory State in Britain'. *Parliamentary Affairs* 54/1 (2001), 19–34. doi:10.1093/pa/54.1.19.
Morgan, Jamie, ed. *What is Neoclassical Economics? Debating the Origins, Meaning and Significance* (Abingdon, 2016).
Morgan, Janet, ed. *The Backbench Diaries of Richard Crossman* (1981).
Morgan, Kenneth O. *Labour in Power 1945–1951* (Oxford, 1984).
Morris, Peter W. G., and George H. Hough. *The Anatomy of Major Projects: A Study of the Reality of Project Management* (Chichester, 1987).
Moyn, Samuel. *Not Enough: Human Rights in an Unequal World* (Cambridge, Mass., 2018).
Mullin, Chris. *A View from the Foothills* (2009).
Mumford, Enid. Values, *Technology and Work* (The Hague, 1981).
Murie, Alan. 'The Housing Legacy of Thatcherism'. In *The Legacy of Thatcherism: Assessing and Exploring Thatcherite Social and Economic Policies*, edited by Stephen Farrall and Colin Hay (Oxford, 2014), 143–66.
Murray, Charles. *The Emerging British Underclass* (1990).
Musgrave, Richard A. *The Theory of Public Finance: A Study in Public Economy* (New York, 1959).
Myles, John, and Paul Pierson. 'Friedman's Revenge: The Reform of "Liberal" Welfare States in Canada and the United States'. *Politics & Society* 25/4 (1997), 443–72. doi:10.1177/0032329297025004004.
National Association of Citizens Advice Bureaux. *Work in Progress: CAB Clients' Experiences of Working Families' Tax Credit* (2001).
'National Federation of Claimants Unions'. *Journal of the National Federation of Claimants Unions* 1 (Aug. 1970).
New Society Open Group. *Social Reform in a Centrifugal Society* (1969).
'New Times', *Marxism Today*, Oct. 1988, 3.
Nicoll, William. 'Williams, Dame Juliet Evangeline Rhys (1898–1964)'. In *Oxford Dictionary of National Biography*, vol. 59, edited by H. C. G. Matthew and Brian Harrison (Oxford, 2004), 254–5.
Norman, Peter. 'The Poor Cousin of Poverty Fighters'. *Financial Times*, 25 June 1991, 16.
Nozick, Robert. *Anarchy, State, and Utopia* (New York, 1974).
O'Brien, J. Patrick, and Dennis O. Olson. 'The Alaska Permanent Fund and Dividend Distribution Program'. *BIRG Bulletin* 12 (1991), 3–6.
O'Connor, Alice. *Poverty Knowledge: Social Science, Social Policy, and the Poor in Twentieth-Century U.S. History* (Princeton, 2001).
O'Connor, James. *The Fiscal Crisis of the State* (New York, 1973).
OECD (Organisation for Economic Co-operation and Development). *Divided We Stand: Why Inequality Keeps Rising* (Paris, 2011).

Offer, Avner. 'The Market Turn: From Social Democracy to Market Liberalism'. *Economic History Review* 70/4 (2017), 1051–71. doi:10.1111/ehr.12537.

Office for Budget Responsibility. *Fiscal Sustainability Report, July 2018* (2018).

O'Hara, Glen. *From Dreams to Disillusionment: Economic and Social Planning in 1960s Britain* (Basingstoke, 2007).

O'Kelly, Rory. 'Why Social Dividends are not the Answer'. *Policy Studies* 5/2 (1984), 24–30. doi:10.1080/01442878408423415.

O'Neill, Martin. 'Survey Article: Philosophy and Public Policy after Piketty'. *Journal of Political Philosophy* 25/3 (2017), 343–75. doi:10.1111/jopp.12129.

Oude Nijhuis, Dennie. 'Low Pay, Wage Relativities, and Labour's First Attempt to Introduce a Statutory National Minimum Wage in the United Kingdom'. *Journal of Policy History* 28/1 (2016), 81–104. doi:10.1017/S089803061500038X.

Page, Robert M. *Clear Blue Water? The Conservative Party and the Welfare State since 1940* (Bristol, 2015).

Paine, Thomas. *Agrarian Justice* (1797). Reprinted in *The Writings of Thomas Paine*, vol. 3, edited by Moncure Daniel Conway (New York, 1894), 322–44.

Painter, Anthony, Jake Thorold, and Jamie Cooke. *Pathways to Universal Basic Income: The Case for a Universal Basic Opportunity Fund* (2018).

Painter, Anthony, and Chris Thoung. *Creative Citizen, Creative State: The Principled and Pragmatic Case for a Universal Basic Income* (2015).

Parker, Hermione. *Goodbye Beveridge?* (1980).

Parker, Hermione. *The Moral Hazard of Social Benefits: A Study of the Impact of Social Benefits and Income Tax on Incentives to Work* (1982).

Parker, Hermione. 'Editorial'. *BIRG Bulletin* 5 (1986), 1.

Parker, Hermione. 'Are Basic Incomes Feasible?' *BIRG Bulletin* 7 (1988), 5–7.

Parker, Hermione. 'The Tax and Benefit Systems, and their Effects on People with Low Earnings Potential'. In *Improving Incentives for the Low-Paid*, edited by Alex Bowen and Ken Mayhew (Basingstoke, 1990), 73–119.

Parker, Hermione, ed. *Basic Income and the Labour Market* (1991).

Parker, Hermione. *Taxes, Benefits and Family Life: The Seven Deadly Traps* (1995).

Patrick, Ruth. *For Whose Benefit? The Everyday Realities of Welfare Reform* (Bristol, 2017).

Peacock, Alan. 'Welfare Philosophies and Welfare Finance'. In *The State and Social Welfare*, edited by Thomas and Dorothy Wilson (1991), 37–54.

Peacock, Alan. *Anxious to Do Good: Learning to be an Economist the Hard Way* (Exeter, 2010).

Peacock, Alan, and George Peden. 'Merging National Insurance Contributions and Income Tax: The Lessons of History'. *Economic Affairs* 34/1 (2014), 2–13. doi:10.1111/ecaf.12050.

Peacock, Alan T. *The Economics of National Insurance* (Edinburgh, 1952).

Peacock, Alan T. 'Welfare in a Liberal State'. In *The Unservile State: Essays in Liberty and Welfare*, edited by George Watson (1957), 113–30.

Peacock, Alan T., and P. R. Browning. 'The Social Services in Great Britain and the Redistribution of Income'. In *Income Redistribution and Social Policy*, edited by Alan T. Peacock (1954), 139–77.

Peacock, Alan T., and Jack Wiseman, *The Growth of Public Expenditure in the United Kingdom* (Princeton, 1961).

Peacock, Alan T., and Jack Wiseman. *Education for Democrats* (1964).

Pearce, John H. N. 'The Road to 1944: Antecedents of the PAYE Scheme'. In *Studies in the History of Tax Law*, vol. 5, edited by John Tiley (Oxford, 2011), 193–218.

Pearce, Nick, and Eleanor Taylor. 'Government Spending and Welfare: Changing Attitudes towards the Role of the State'. In *British Social Attitudes: The 30th Report*, edited by Alison Park, Caroline Bryson, Elizabeth Clery, John Curtice, and Miranda Phillips (2013), 33–61.

Peck, Jamie, and Nik Theodore. *Fast Policy: Experimental Statecraft at the Thresholds of Neoliberalism* (Minneapolis, 2015).

Pedersen, Susan. *Family, Dependence, and the Origins of the Welfare State: Britain and France, 1914–1945* (Cambridge, 1993).

PEOPLE. *A Manifesto for Survival* (Coventry, 1974).

Pereira, Anthony W. '*Bolsa Família* and Democracy in Brazil'. *Third World Quarterly* 36/9 (2015), 1682–99. doi:10.1080/01436597.2015.1059730.

Pessoa, João Paulo, and John Van Reenen. 'Decoupling of Wage Growth and Productivity Growth? Myth and Reality'. Report to the Resolution Foundation Commission on Living Standards, 29 Jan. 2012. Accessed 13 Dec. 2017, <http://www.livingstandards.org/wp-content/uploads/2012/02/Decoupling-of-wages-and-productivity.pdf>.

Peston, Robert. *Brown's Britain* (2005).

Piachaud, David. 'The SDP's Plan to Top up the Poor'. *New Society*, 11 Nov. 1982, 56.

Pierson, Paul. 'Coping with Permanent Austerity: Welfare State Restructuring in Affluent Democracies'. In *The New Politics of the Welfare State*, edited by Paul Pierson (Oxford, 2001), 410–56.

Pigou, A. C. *Wealth and Welfare* (1912).

Pigou, A. C. *The Economics of Welfare* [1920], 4th edn (1932).

Piketty, Thomas. *Capital in the Twenty-First Century* (Cambridge, Mass., 2014).

Pinker, Robert. 'Social Policy and Social Justice'. *Journal of Social Policy* 3/1 (1974), 1–19. doi:10.1017/S0047279400003457.

Pitts, Frederick Harry, and Ana Cecilia Dinerstein. 'Corbynism's Conveyor Belt of Ideas: Postcapitalism and the Politics of Social Reproduction'. *Capital & Class* 41/3 (2017), 423–34. doi:10.1177/0309816817734487.

Plant, Raymond. 'Citizenship, Employability and the Labour Market'. *Citizen's Income Newsletter* 24 (1997), 2–3.

Polanyi, George and Priscilla. 'Tax Credits: A Reverse Income Tax'. *National Westminster Bank Quarterly Review* (Feb. 1973), 20–34.

Polanyi, Karl. *The Great Transformation: The Political and Economic Origins of our Time* (New York, 1944).

Portes, Jonathan. 'Welfare and Work: Continuity and Change'. *National Institute Economic Review* 221 (2012), F4–F9. doi:10.1177/002795011222100103.

Powell, J. Enoch. 'A Policy of Sewage'. In *The Future of the Welfare State: Seven Oxford Lectures*, Conservative Political Centre (1958), 38–47.

Powell, Martin. 'Introduction'. In *New Labour, New Welfare State? The 'Third Way' in British Social Policy*, edited by Martin Powell (Bristol, 1999), 1–27.

Pressman, Stephen. 'Keynes and Antipoverty Policy'. *Review of Social Economy* 49/3 (1991), 365–82. doi:10.1080/00346769100000031.

Przeworski, Adam, and Michael Wallerstein. 'Structural Dependence of the State on Capital'. *American Political Science Review* 82/1 (1988), 11–29. doi:10.2307/1958056.

Purdy, David. 'Citizenship, Basic Income and the State'. *New Left Review* I/208 (1994), 30–48.

Putnam, Robert D. *The Beliefs of Politicians: Ideology, Conflict, and Democracy in Britain and Italy* (New Haven, 1973).

Radice, Giles. *Southern Discomfort* (1992).

Raison, Timothy. *Tories and the Welfare State: A History of Conservative Social Policy since the Second World War* (Basingstoke, 1990).
Ramsden, John. *The Age of Churchill and Eden, 1940–1957* (1995).
Ravallion, Martin. *The Economics of Poverty: History, Measurement, and Policy* (Oxford, 2016).
Raven, Susan. 'Which Way Forward? Susan Raven Talks to Sir Gordon Borrie'. *Citizen's Income Newsletter* 17 (Jan. 1994), 13–14.
Raven, Susan. 'Obituary: Hermione Parker'. *Citizen's Income Trust Newsletter* 3 (2007).
Rawls, John. *A Theory of Justice* (Cambridge, Mass., 1971).
Redmond, Gerry, Holly Sutherland, and Moira Wilson. *The Arithmetic of Tax and Social Security Reform: A User's Guide to Microsimulation Methods and Analysis* (Cambridge, 1998).
Reed, Howard. *Plan B+1: Rebuilding Britain and a Good Society* (2012).
Reed, Howard, and Stewart Lansley. *How to Boost the Wage Share* (2013).
Reed, Howard, and Stewart Lansley. *Universal Basic Income: An Idea Whose Time Has Come?* (2016).
Renwick, Chris. *Bread for All: The Origins of the Welfare State* (2017).
Resolution Foundation. *More than a Minimum. The Resolution Foundation Review of the Future of the National Minimum Wage: The Final Report* (2014).
Rhodes, Martin. 'Desperately Seeking a Solution: Social Democracy, Thatcherism, and the "Third Way" in British Welfare'. In *Recasting European Welfare States*, edited by Maurizio Ferrera and Martin Rhodes (2000), 161–86.
Rhys-Williams, Sir Brandon. *The New Social Contract* (1968).
Rhys-Williams, Juliet. *Something to Look Forward To* (1943).
Rhys-Williams, Juliet. *Income Tax Reform. Outline of Lady Rhys-Williams's Proposals* (1949).
Richard, Ivor. 'The Programme before Us'. *Socialist Commentary* (June 1966), 11–13.
Richards, Peter G. 'The Recent History of Local Fiscal Reform'. In *The Reform of Local Government Finance*, edited by S. J. Bailey and R. Paddison (1988), 25–41.
Richards, Steve. *Whatever it Takes: The Real Story of Gordon Brown and New Labour* (2010).
Ricketts, Martin, and Edward Shoesmith. *British Economic Opinion: A Survey of a Thousand Economists* (1990).
Rieger, Bernhard. 'Making Britain Work Again: Unemployment and the Remaking of British Social Policy in the Eighties', *English Historical Review* 133/562 (2018), 634–66. doi:10.1093/ehr/cey087.
Roberts, Keith. *Automation, Unemployment and the Distribution of Income* (Maastricht, 1982).
Robertson, James. *The Sane Alternative: A Choice of Futures*, rev. edn (Ironbridge, 1983).
Rogan, Tim. *The Moral Economists: R. H. Tawney, Karl Polanyi, E. P. Thompson, and the Critique of Capitalism* (Princeton, 2017).
Röpke, Wilhelm. *Civitas Humana: A Humane Order of Society*, English edn (1948).
Rose, Hilary. 'Up against the Welfare State: The Claimant Unions'. *Socialist Register* 10 (1973), 179–203.
Rowntree, B. Seebohm, 'Poverty and the Beveridge Plan'. *The Fortnightly* (Feb. 1943).
Rowntree, B. Seebohm, and G. R. Lavers. *Poverty and the Welfare State: A Third Social Survey of York Dealing only with Economic Questions* (1951).
Royal Commission on the Distribution of Income and Wealth. *Selected Evidence Submitted to the Royal Commission for Report No. 6: Lower Incomes* (1978).
Russell, Bertrand. *Roads to Freedom* (1918).

Russell, Bertrand. 'In Praise of Idleness'. *Harper's Monthly Magazine* (Oct. 1932), 552–9.
Ryan, Alan. *Bertrand Russell: A Political Life* (1988).
Sabbagh, Dan. 'John McDonnell Urges Scrapping "Iniquitous" Universal Credit'. *The Guardian* (online edn), 7 Oct. 2018. Accessed 18 Jan. 2019. <https://www.theguardian.com/society/2018/oct/07/john-mcdonnell-says-universal-credit-needs-to-get-scrapped-benefits>.
Sage, Daniel. 'The Quiet Revolution? The Labour Party and Welfare Conditionality'. *Political Quarterly* 90/1 (2019), 99–106. doi:10.1111/1467-923X.12606.
Sainsbury, Roy, and Kate Stanley. 'One for All: Active Welfare and the Single Working-Age Benefit'. In *It's All about You: Citizen-Centred Welfare*, edited by Jim Bennett and Graeme Cooke (2007), 43–56.
Sandmo, Agnar. 'The Principal Problem in Political Economy: Income Distribution in the History of Economic Thought'. In *Handbook of Income Distribution*, vol. 2, edited by Anthony B. Atkinson and François Bourguignon (Amsterdam, 2015), 3–65.
Sandmo, Agnar. 'Tony Atkinson 1944–2017: A Lifetime Commitment to the Study of Inequality'. *European Journal of the History of Economic Thought* 24 (2017), 612–23. doi:10.1080/09672567.2017.1307628.
Savage, Michael, and Chaminda Jayanetti. 'Revealed: Universal Credit Sends Rent Arrears Soaring'. *The Observer*, 17 Sept. 2017. Accessed 9 Jan. 2017. <https://www.theguardian.com/society/2017/sep/16/universal-credit-rent-arrears-soar>.
Schmidt, Vivien A. 'Taking Ideas and Discourse Seriously: Explaining Change through Discursive Institutionalism as the Fourth "New Institutionalism"'. *European Political Science Review* 2/1 (2010), 1–25. doi:10.1017/S175577390999021X.
Schumpeter, Joseph. 'The Crisis of the Tax State' [1918]. In *Joseph Schumpeter: The Economics and Sociology of Capitalism*, edited by Richard Swedberg (Princeton, 1991), 99–140.
Scott, Gill, and Gerry Mooney. 'Poverty and Social Justice in the Devolved Scotland: Neoliberalism Meets Social Democracy?' *Social Policy and Society* 8/3 (2009), 379–89. doi:10.1017/S1474746409004916.
Seawright, David. *The British Conservative Party and One Nation Politics* (2010).
Seldon, Arthur. *Pensions in a Free Society* (1957).
Seldon, Arthur. 'Beveridge: 20 Years after'. *New Society*, 14 Feb. 1963, 9–12.
Seldon, Arthur. 'Why not Top up the Poor Man's Pay?' *Daily Telegraph*, 22 Feb. 1971, 12.
Seldon, Arthur, and Hamish Gray. *Universal or Selective Social Benefits* (1967).
Sellers, Paul John. 'The UK Living Wage: A Trade Union Perspective'. *Employee Relations* 39/6 (2017), 790–9. doi:10.1108/ER-04-2017-0095.
Sewill, Brendon. 'A View from the Inside: In Place of Strikes', in Ralph Harris and Brendon Sewill, *British Economic Policy 1970–74: Two Views* (1975), 27–64.
Sewill, Hilary. *AUNTIE* (1966).
Sheard, Sally. *The Passionate Economist: How Brian Abel-Smith Shaped Global Health and Social Welfare* (Bristol, 2014).
Shepherd, Robert. *Iain Macleod: A Biography* (1994).
Shepherd, Robert. *Enoch Powell: A Biography* (1997).
Sheppard, David. 'The Poverty that Imprisons the Spirit'. *The Listener* (19 Apr. 1984), 8–12.
Skidelsky, Robert. *Keynes: The Return of the Master* (2009).
Skinner, Quentin. 'Meaning and Understanding in the History of Ideas'. *History and Theory* 8/1 (1969), 3–53. doi:10.2307/2504188.
Sloman, Peter. *The Liberal Party and the Economy, 1929–1964* (Oxford, 2015).

Sloman, Peter. 'Universal Basic Income in British Politics: From a "Vagabond's Wage" to a Global Debate'. *Journal of Social Policy* 47/3 (2018), 625–42. doi:10.1017/S0047279417000800.

Sloman, Peter. 'Redistribution in an Age of Neoliberalism: Market Economics, "Poverty Knowledge", and the Growth of Working-Age Benefits in Britain, *c*.1979–2010', *Political Studies* early view (2018). doi:10.1177/0032321718800495.

Smith, Adam. *An Inquiry into the Nature and Causes of the Wealth of Nations*, 5th edn [1789], ed. Edwin Cannan (1904).

Soboul, Albert. *Précis d'histoire de la Révolution Française* (Paris, 1962).

Social Justice Policy Group. *Breakdown Britain: Interim Report on the State of the Nation* (2006).

Solow, Robert. 'Introduction'. In *Low-Wage Work in the United Kingdom*, edited by Caroline Lloyd, Geoff Mason, and Ken Mayhew (New York, 2008), 1–14.

Spence, Thomas. *The Constitution of Spensonia* (1803). Reprinted in *The Political Works of Thomas Spence*, edited by H. T. Dickinson (Newcastle, 1982), 104–18.

Spicker, Paul. 'Definitions of Poverty: Twelve Clusters of Meaning'. In *Poverty: An International Glossary*, 2nd edn, edited by Paul Spicker, Sonia Alvarez Leguizamón, and David Gordon (2006), 229–43.

Srnicek, Nick, and Alex Williams. *Inventing the Future: Postcapitalism and a World without Work* (2015).

Stabile, Donald. *The Living Wage: Lessons from the History of Economic Thought* (Cheltenham, 2008).

Standing, Guy. 'An Alternative to Wage-Capping'. Letter, *BIRG Bulletin* 4 (1985), 19.

Standing, Guy. 'How Cash Transfers Promote the Case for Basic Income'. *Basic Income Studies* 3/1 (2008). doi:10.2202/1932-0183.1106.

Standing, Guy. *The Precariat: The New Dangerous Class* (2011).

Standing, Guy. *Basic Income: And How We Can Make it Happen* (2017).

Steensland, Brian. *The Failed Welfare Revolution: America's Struggle over Guaranteed Income Policy* (Princeton, 2008).

Stewart, Mark. 'The Employment Effects of the National Minimum Wage'. *Economic Journal* 114/494 (2004), C110–C116. doi:10.1111/j.0013-0133.2003.00200.x.

Stewart, Mark B. 'Low Pay, No Pay Dynamics'. In Centre for Analysis of Social Exclusion, *Persistent Poverty and Lifetime Inequality: The Evidence* (1999), 71–6.

Stigler, George J. 'The Economics of Minimum Wage Legislation'. *American Economic Review* 36/3 (1946), 358–65. <https://www.jstor.org/stable/1801842>.

Stiglitz, Joseph E. *Rewriting the Rules of the American Economy: An Agenda for Growth and Shared Prosperity* (New York, 2015).

Stoller, Sarah. 'Forging a Politics of Care: Theorizing Household Work in the British Women's Liberation Movement'. *History Workshop Journal* 85 (2018), 95–119. doi:10.1093/hwj/dbx063.

Stone, Jon. 'SNP Conference Backs Universal Basic Income for Independent Scotland'. *The Independent*, 15 Mar. 2016. Accessed 2 Aug. 2018. <https://www.independent.co.uk/news/uk/politics/universal-basic-income-snp-scotland-independent-conference-vote-a6931846.html>.

Stuart, Mark. *John Smith: A Life* (2005).

Sutcliffe-Braithwaite, Florence. 'Neoliberalism and Morality in the Making of Thatcherite Social Policy'. *Historical Journal* 55/2 (2012), 497–520. doi:10.1017/S0018246X12000118.

Sutherland, Holly, and Francesco Figari. 'EUROMOD: The European Union Tax-Benefit Microsimulation Model'. *International Journal of Microsimulation* 6/1 (2013), 4–26.

Swank, Duane. 'Taxing Choices: International Competition, Domestic Institutions and the Transformation of Corporate Tax Policy'. *Journal of European Public Policy* 23/4 (2016), 571–603. doi:10.1080/13501763.2015.1053511.

Taverne, Dick. 'Looking Back'. *Fiscal Studies* 4/3 (Nov. 1983), 1–6. doi:10.1111/j.1475-5890.1983.tb00366.x.

Taverne, Dick. *Against the Tide: Politics and Beyond. A Memoir* (2014).

Tawney, R. H. *Equality* (1931).

Thane, Pat, and Ruth Davidson, eds. *The Child Poverty Action Group in the 1990s and 2000s: Witness Seminar* (2016).

Thatcher, Margaret. *The Downing Street Years* (1993).

Thompson, Helen. 'The Thatcherite Economic Legacy'. In *The Legacy of Thatcherism: Assessing and Exploring Thatcherite Social and Economic Policies*, edited by Stephen Farrall and Colin Hay (Oxford, 2014), 33–68.

Thompson, Noel. *Political Economy and the Labour Party: The Economics of Democratic Socialism, 1884–2005*, 2nd edn (2006).

Thornton, Stephen. *Richard Crossman and the Welfare State: Pioneer of Welfare Provision and Labour Politics in Post-War Britain* (2009).

Timmins, Nicholas. *Universal Credit: From Disaster to Recovery?* (2016).

Timmins, Nicholas. *The Five Giants: A Biography of the Welfare State*, 3rd edn (2017).

Tinson, Adam, Carla Ayrton, Karen Barker, Theo Barry Born, Hannah Aldridge, and Peter Kenway. *Monitoring Poverty and Social Exclusion 2016* (York, 2016).

Titmuss, Richard M. 'The Social Division of Welfare: Some Reflections on the Search for Equity'. In Richard M. Titmuss, *Essays on 'the Welfare State'* (1958), 34–55.

Titmuss, Richard M. *Income Distribution and Social Change: A Study in Criticism* (1962).

Titmuss, Richard M. *Commitment to Welfare* (1968).

Tomlinson, Daniel. *You're Hired! Lessons for President Trump from a Comparison of Living Standards and Inequality in the US and the UK* (2017).

Tomlinson, Jim. *The Labour Governments 1964–1970*, vol. 3: *Economic Policy* (Manchester, 2004).

Tomlinson, Jim. 'De-Industrialization not Decline: A New Meta-Narrative for Post-War British History'. *Twentieth Century British History* 27/1 (2016), 76–99. doi:10.1093/tcbh/hwv030.

Tomlinson, Jim. 'Distributional Politics: The Search for Equality in Britain since the First World War'. In *The Contradictions of Capital in the Twenty-First Century: The Piketty Opportunity*, edited by Pat Hudson and Keith Tribe (Newcastle-upon-Tyne, 2016), 167–91.

Tomlinson, Jim. *Managing the Economy, Managing the People: Narratives of Economic Life in Britain from Beveridge to Brexit* (Oxford, 2017).

Tondani, Davide. 'Universal Basic Income and Negative Income Tax: Two Different Ways of Thinking Redistribution'. *The Journal of Socio-Economics* 38/2 (2009), 246–55.

Torry, Malcolm. *Money for Everyone: Why We Need a Citizen's Income* (Bristol, 2013).

Torry, Malcolm. *An Update, a Correction, and an Extension, of an Evaluation of an Illustrative Citizen's Basic Income Scheme*. Addendum to EUROMOD Working Paper 12/17 (Colchester, 2018).

Torry, Malcolm. 'History and the Contemporary Debate in the UK'. In *It's Basic Income: The Global Debate*, edited by Amy Downes and Stewart Lansley (Bristol, 2018), 123–7.

Tory Reform Group. *Tax Credit Report* (1979).

Townsend, Peter. 'The Difficulties of Negative Income Tax'. In *Social Services for All? Eleven Fabian Essays*. Fabian Society (1968), 106–11.

Townsend, Peter. *Poverty in the United Kingdom* (1979).

Toye, Richard. '"The Gentleman in Whitehall" Reconsidered: The Evolution of Douglas Jay's Views on Economic Planning and Consumer Choice, 1937–47'. *Labour History Review* 67/2 (2002), 187–204. doi:10.3828/lhr.67.2.187.

Toynbee, Polly, and David Walker. 'Social Policy and Inequality'. In *New Labour, Old Labour: The Wilson and Callaghan Governments, 1974–79*, edited by Anthony Seldon and Kevin Hickson (Abingdon, 2004), 105–22.

Tuck, Penelope, Dominic de Cogan, and John Snape. 'A Tale of the Merger between the Inland Revenue and HM Customs & Excise'. Forthcoming in *Studies in the History of Tax Law*, vol. 9, edited by Peter Harris and Dominic de Cogan (Oxford, 2019).

University of York. 'Development of the "Single Working Age Benefit" and Impact on Welfare Reform' (impact case study, submission to REF2014). Accessed 14 Dec. 2017. <https://www.york.ac.uk/spsw/research/research-impact/single-working-age-benefit-impact-case-study/>.

van der Veen, Robert, and Philippe van Parijs. 'A Capitalist Road to Communism'. *Theory and Society* 15/5 (1986), 635–55. doi:10.1007/BF00239129.

van Parijs, Philippe 'Why Surfers Should be Fed: The Liberal Case for an Unconditional Basic Income'. *Philosophy and Public Affairs* 20/2 (1991), 101–31. <https://www.jstor.org/stable/2265291>.

van Parijs, Philippe. *Real Freedom for All: What (if Anything) Can Justify Capitalism?* (Oxford, 1995).

van Parijs, Philippe, and Yannick Vanderborght. *Basic Income: A Radical Proposal for a Free Society and a Sane Economy* (Cambridge, Mass., 2017).

van Trier, Walter. *Every One a King: An Investigation into the Meaning and Significance of the Debate on Basic Incomes with Special Reference to Three Episodes from the British Inter-War Experience* (Leuven, 1995).

Veit-Wilson, John. 'Paradigms of Poverty: A Rehabilitation of B. S. Rowntree'. *Journal of Social Policy* 15/1 (1986), 69–99. doi:10.1017/S0047279400023114.

Veit-Wilson, John. 'Muddle or Mendacity? The Beveridge Committee and the Poverty Line'. *Journal of Social Policy* 21/3 (1992), 269–301. doi:10.1017/S0047279400019954.

Veit-Wilson, John. 'Condemned to Deprivation? Beveridge's Responsibility for the Invisibility of Poverty'. In *Beveridge and Social Security: An International Retrospective*, edited by John Hills, John Ditch, and Howard Glennerster (Oxford, 1994), 97–117.

Veit-Wilson, John. 'The National Assistance Board and the "Rediscovery" of Poverty'. In *Welfare Policy in Britain: The Road from 1945*, edited by Helen Fawcett and Rodney Lowe (1999), 116–57.

Veit-Wilson, John. 'The Tax Threshold: Policy, Principles, and Poverty'. *Twentieth Century British History* 10/2 (1999), 218–34. doi:10.1093/tcbh/10.2.218.

Veit-Wilson, John. 'Poverty'. In *International Encyclopaedia of Social Policy*, vol. 1, edited by Tony Fitzpatrick, Huck-ju Kwon, Nick Manning, James Midgley, and Gillian Pascall (Abingdon, 2006), 1036–42.

Vince, Philip. *To Each According: Liberal Tax Credit Proposals* (1979).

Vince, Philip. 'After Sixteen Years in Favour of CI, Britain's Liberal Democrats Do a U-Turn'. *Citizen's Income Bulletin* 20 (1995), 21.

Vives, Jean Luis. *De Subventione Pauperum: Sive de humanis necessitatibus libri II* (Antwerp, 1526).

von Gliszczynski, Moritz, and Lutz Leisering. 'Constructing New Global Models of Social Security: How International Organizations Defined the Field of Social Cash Transfers in the 2000s'. *Journal of Social Policy* 45/2 (2016), 325–43. doi:10.1017/S0047279415000720.

Waldfogel, Jane. *Britain's War on Poverty* (New York, 2010).

Walker, Peter. 'John McDonnell Announces £10 an Hour Living Wage Plan'. *The Guardian* (online edn), 26 Sept. 2016. Accessed 10 Jan. 2018. <https://www.theguardian.com/politics/2016/sep/26/john-mcdonnell-10-an-hour-living-wage-plan-labour-conference>.

Walker, Robert, and Michael Wiseman. 'The Possibility of a British Earned Income Tax Credit'. *Fiscal Studies* 18/4 (1997), 401–25, doi:10.1111/j.1475-5890.1997.tb00271.x.

Walter, Tony. 'What are Basic Incomes?' *BIRG Bulletin* 8 (1988), 3–5.

Waltman, Jerold L. *Minimum Wage Policy in Great Britain and the United States* (New York, 2008), 100–3.

Wass, Sir Douglas. 'Obituary: Sir David Hancock, Civil Servant with Eye for Fiscal Policy'. *Financial Times*, 6 Oct. 2013.

Waters, Tom, 'Personal Tax and Benefit Measures'. Presentation to IFS budget briefing, 30 Oct. 2018, accessed 16 Jan. 2019. <https://www.ifs.org.uk/uploads/budgets/budget2018/tw_budget2018.pdf>.

Watson, George, ed. *The Unservile State: Essays in Liberty and Welfare* (1957).

Waugh, Auberon. 'A Red-Toothed Pioneer'. *The Spectator*, 23 July 1976.

Weaver, Findley. 'Taxation and Redistribution in the United Kingdom'. *The Review of Economics and Statistics* 32 (1950), 201–13. doi:10.2307/2937526.

Webb, Adrian. 'The Abolition of National Assistance: Policy Changes in the Administration of Assistance Benefits'. In *Change, Choice and Conflict in Social Policy*, edited by Phoebe Hall, Hilary Land, Roy Parker and Adrian Webb (1975), 410–71.

Webb, Kate. *Bricks or Benefits? Rebalancing Housing Investment* (2012).

Webster, David. 'Long-Term Unemployment, the Invention of "Hysteresis" and the Misdiagnosis of Structural Unemployment in the UK'. *Cambridge Journal of Economics* 29/6 (2005), 975–95. doi:10.1093/cje/bei082.

Wedderburn, Dorothy. 'The Old and the Poor'. *New Society* (22 July 1965), 7–8.

Weiler, Peter. 'The Rise and Fall of the Conservatives' "Grand Design for Housing", 1951–64'. *Contemporary British History* 14/1 (2000), 122–50.

Welfare Conditionality Project. *Welfare Conditionality Project, 2013–2018: Final Findings Report* (York, 2018).

Wells, William. 'From Restart to the New Deal in the United Kingdom'. In *Labour Market Policies and the Public Employment Service*, OECD (Paris, 2001), 241–62.

Welshman, John. *From Transmitted Deprivation to Social Exclusion: Policy, Poverty and Parenting* (Bristol, 2007).

Westlake, Martin (with Ian St John). *Kinnock: The Biography* (2001).

West London Claimants Union. 'The Claimants Unions'. *Journal of the National Federation of Claimants Unions* 1 (Aug. 1970).

Weston, Trevor, and Philip Ashworth. *Old People in Britain* (1963).

White, Stuart '"Revolutionary Liberalism"? The Philosophy and Politics of Ownership in the Post-War Liberal Party'. *British Politics* 4/2 (2009), 164–87. doi:10.1057/bp.2008.35.

White, Stuart. 'Democratic Equality as a Work-in-Progress'. In *A Companion to Rawls*, edited by Jon Mandle and David A. Reddy (Chichester, 2014), 185–99.

Whiteford, Peter, Michael Mendelson, and Jane Millar. *Timing it Right: Tax Credits and How to Respond to Income Changes* (York, 2003).

Whiting, R. C. 'Income Tax, the Working Class and Party Politics, 1948–52'. *Twentieth Century British History* 8/2 (1997), 194–221. doi:10.1093/tcbh/8.2.194.

Whiting, Richard. *The Labour Party and Taxation: Party Identity and Political Purpose in Twentieth-Century Britain* (Cambridge, 2000).

Widerquist, Karl. *A Critical Analysis of Basic Income Experiments for Researchers, Policy-makers, and Citizens* (Basingstoke, 2018).

Widerquist, Karl, and Michael W. Howard, eds. *Exporting the Alaska Model: Adapting the Permanent Fund Dividend for Reform around the World* (New York, 2012).

Wiles, Peter. 'Property and Equality'. In *The Unservile State: Essays in Liberty and Welfare*, edited by George Watson (1957), 88–109.

Willetts, David, and Nicholas Hillman. *Tax Credits: Do They Add Up?* (2002).

Williams, A. Susan. *Women and Childbirth in the Twentieth Century: A History of the National Birthday Trust Fund 1928–93* (Stroud, 1997).

Wills, Jane, and Brian Linneker. 'In-Work Poverty and the Living Wage in the United Kingdom: A Geographical Perspective'. *Transactions of the Institute of British Geographers* 39/2 (2014), 182–94. doi:10.1111/tran.12020.

Winch, Donald. *Wealth and Life: Essays in the Intellectual History of Political Economy in Britain, 1848–1914* (Cambridge, 2009).

Wincott, Daniel. 'Paradoxes of New Labour Social Policy: Towards Universal Child Care in Europe's "Most Liberal" Welfare Regime?' *Social Politics* 13/2 (2006), 286–312. doi:10.1093/sp/jxj011.

Wincott, Daniel. 'The (Golden) Age of the Welfare State: Interrogating a Conventional Wisdom'. *Public Administration* 91/4 (2013), 806–22. doi:10.1111/j.1467-9299.2012.02067.x.

Wincott, Daniel. 'Original and Imitated or Elusive and Limited? Towards a Genealogy of the Welfare State Idea in Britain'. In *Analysing Social Policy Concepts and Languages: Comparative and Transnational Perspectives*, edited by Daniel Béland and Klaus Petersen (Bristol, 2014), 127–41.

Women's Budget Group. 'New Research Shows Universal Credit Failing the "Just about Managing": With Women and BME Households Hardest Hit' (press release, 16 Nov. 2017). Accessed 24 July 2018. <https://wbg.org.uk/wp-content/uploads/2017/11/pre-budget-press-release-nov-2017-15-11.pdf>.

Wood, Stewart. 'Labour Market Regimes under Threat? Sources of Continuity in Germany, Britain and Sweden'. In *The New Politics of the Welfare State*, edited by Paul Pierson (Oxford, 2001), 368–409.

Woods, Dorian R. *Family Policy in Transformation: US and UK Policies* (Basingstoke, 2012).

Wootton, Barbara. 'Record of the Labour Government in the Social Services'. *Political Quarterly* 20/2 (1949), 101–12. doi:10.1111/j.1467-923X.1949.tb00611.x.

Wootton, Barbara 'The Labour Party and Social Services'. *Political Quarterly* 24/1 (1953), 55–67. doi:10.1111/j.1467-923X.1953.tb00248.x.

Wright, Erik Olin. 'Why Something Like Socialism is Necessary for the Transition to Something Like Communism'. *Theory and Society* 15/5 (1986), 657–72. doi:10.1007/BF00239130.

Wrigley, Chris. 'Industrial Relations'. In *Work and Pay in Twentieth-Century Britain*, edited by Nicholas Crafts, Ian Gazeley, and Andrew Newell (Oxford, 2007), 203–24.

Yamamori, Toru. 'A Feminist Way to Basic Income: Claimants Unions and Women's Liberation Movements in 1970s Britain'. *Basic Income Studies* 9/1–2 (2014), 1–24. doi:10.1515/bis-2014-0019.

Young, Charlie. *Realising Basic Income Experiments in the UK: A Typology and Toolkit of Basic Income Design and Delivery* (2018).

Ziegler, Rafael, and Bill Jordan. 'The Trade Unions, Tax-Benefit Reform and Basic Income: Stumbling towards a Policy?' *Citizen's Income Newsletter* 3 (2001), 2–4.

Zweiniger-Bargielowska, Ina. 'Rationing, Austerity, and the Conservative Party Recovery after 1945'. *Historical Journal* 37/1 (1994), 173–97. doi:10.1017/S0018246X00014758.
Zweiniger-Bargielowska, Ina. *Austerity in Britain: Rationing, Controls, and Consumption, 1939–1955* (Oxford, 2000).

Unpublished papers and dissertations

Balls, Edward, Lawrence F. Katz, and Lawrence H. Summers. 'Britain Divided: Hysteresis and the Regional Dimension of Britain's Unemployment Problem' (unpublished working paper, 1991).
Dent, Anna. 'From Utopia to Implementation: How Basic Income Has Progressed from Radical Idea to Legitimate Policy Solution. An Exploratory Study' (MSc dissertation, University of Bristol, 2017).
Forget, Evelyn. 'The Basic Income Path to a Healthier Society' (paper delivered at BIEN Congress, University of Tampere, 24–26 Aug. 2018).
Jones, Harriet. 'The Conservative Party and the Welfare State, 1942–1955' (PhD thesis, University of London, 1992).
Martinelli, Luke. 'A Basic Income Trilemma: Inadequate, Unaffordable—or not Worth the Bother?' (paper delivered at BIEN Congress, University of Tampere, 24–26 Aug. 2018).
Millward, Gareth. 'Invalid Definitions, Invalid Responses: Disability and the Welfare State, 1965–1995' (PhD thesis, London School of Hygiene and Tropical Medicine, 2014).
Rhys-Williams, Sir Brandon. 'Economic and Monetary Union: New Approaches'. Working document for European Parliament Committee on Economic and Monetary Affairs, PE 41.975 (1975).
Römer, Felix. 'Inequality Statistics and Knowledge Production under Thatcher' (paper delivered at the Contemporary British History Seminar, Institute of Historical Research, 3 Oct. 2018).
Velez Osorio, Veronica, and Romy Siegert. 'European Trade Union Positions towards Universal Basic Income' (paper delivered at BIEN Congress, University of Tampere, 24–26 Aug. 2018).
Zamora, Daniel. 'An Intellectual History of the Universal Basic Income: How a Fringe Idea Went Global (1962–1972)' (paper delivered at the History and Economics Seminar, University of Cambridge, 6 Feb. 2018).

Speeches and public statements

Blair, Tony. Leader's Speech, Labour Party conference, 4 Oct. 1994. Accessed 2 Mar. 2017. <http://www.britishpoliticalspeech.org/speech-archive.htm?speech=200>.
Blair, Tony. Speech at Toynbee Hall, London, 18 Mar. 1999.
Lawson, Nigel. 'The British Experiment'. Mais Lecture at City University Business School, 18 June 1984. Accessed 16 Jan. 2019. <http://www.margaretthatcher.org/document/109504>.
Miliband, Ed. Speech to Inland Revenue Senior Managers' Conference, 5 July 2001.
Osborne, George. Summer Budget Speech, 8 July 2015. Accessed 23 July 2018. <https://www.gov.uk/government/speeches/chancellor-george-osbornes-summer-budget-2015-speech>.

Thatcher, Margaret. Speech to Dartford Conservative Association AGM, 31 Mar. 1949. Reported in *Dartford Chronicle*, 8 Apr. 1949. Accessed 16 Jan. 2019. <http://www.margaretthatcher.org/document/100822>.

Thatcher, Margaret. Speech to Greater London Young Conservatives (Iain Macleod Memorial Lecture), 4 July 1977. Accessed 16 Jan. 2019. <http://www.margaretthatcher.org/document/103411>.

Statistics and data series

Department for Work and Pensions. Benefit Expenditure and Caseload Tables 2018. Accessed 18 Jan. 2019. <www.gov.uk/government/publications/benefit-expenditure-and-caseload-tables-2018>.

Department for Work and Pensions, 'Benefit Sanctions Statistics to January 2018'. 15 May 2018. Accessed 24 July 2018. <https://www.gov.uk/government/statistics/benefit-sanctions-statistics-to-january-2018>.

The Guardian. 'UK Public Spending since 1963'. 19 Mar. 2013. Accessed 28 Feb. 2019. <https://www.theguardian.com/news/datablog/2010/apr/25/uk-public-spending-1963#data>.

HM Revenue and Customs. 'Child and Working Tax Credits Statistics: Finalised Annual Awards, 2009–2010'. May 2011. Accessed 19 July 2018. <http://webarchive.nationalarchives.gov.uk/20121112124508/http://www.hmrc.gov.uk/stats/personal-tax-credits/cwtc-final-awards-may11.pdf>.

HM Revenue and Customs. 'Child and Working Tax Credits Statistics: Finalised Annual Awards. Geographical Analyses, 2009/10'. 2011. Accessed 3 Oct. 2017. <http://webarchive.nationalarchives.gov.uk/20121106034103/http://www.hmrc.gov.uk/stats/personal-tax-credits/cwtc-geog-final-awards-may11.xls>.

HM Revenue and Customs. 'Tax Structures and Parameters. TA1. Income Tax Personal Allowances and Reliefs, 1948–49 to 1972–72'. Accessed 28 July 2017. <http://webarchive.nationalarchives.gov.uk/20060214102705/http://www.hmrc.gov.uk/stats/tax_structure/00ap_a1a_2.htm>.

Institute for Fiscal Studies. 'Fiscal Facts: Social Security Spending'. 29 Sept. 2015. Accessed 28 Feb. 2019. <https://www.ifs.org.uk/tools_and_resources/fiscal_facts/public_spending_survey/social_security>.

Institute for Fiscal Studies. 'Fiscal Facts: Income Support and Supplementary Benefit Rates'. Accessed 28 July 2017. <https://www.ifs.org.uk/ff/is.xls>.

Low Pay Commission. 'Low Pay Commission Report Data Tables'. 22 Nov. 2017. Accessed 9 Jan. 2018. <https://www.gov.uk/government/uploads/system/uploads/attachment_data/file/661518/All_data_2017_Report.xlsx>.

Low Pay Commission. 'Low Pay Commission 2018 Report Data'. 27 Nov. 2018. Accessed 9 Jan. 2019. <https://assets.publishing.service.gov.uk/government/uploads/system/uploads/attachment_data/file/759273/LPC_2018_Report_data.xlsx>.

Office for Budget Responsibility, 'July 2011 Fiscal Sustainability Report—Main Report Charts and Tables'. 13 July 2011. Accessed 12 Dec. 2017. <http://budgetresponsibility.org.uk/download/july-2011-fiscal-sustainability-report-main-report-charts-and-tables>.

Office for Budget Responsibility. 'Public Finances Databank'. 22 Nov. 2017. Accessed 12 Dec. 2017. <http://budgetresponsibility.org.uk/download/public-finances-databank/>.

Office for National Statistics. 'Middle Income Households, 1977–2010/11'. 18 Mar. 2013. Accessed 13 Dec. 2017. <http://webarchive.nationalarchives.gov.uk/20160107031032/http://www.ons.gov.uk/ons/dcp171776_303386.pdf>.

Office for National Statistics. 'The Effect of Taxes and Benefits on Household Income: Historical Datasets'. 20 June 2018. Accessed 27 Feb. 2019. <https://www.ons.gov.uk/peoplepopulationandcommunity/personalandhouseholdfinances/incomeandwealth/datasets/theeffectsoftaxesandbenefitsonhouseholdincomehistoricaldatasets>.

Office for National Statistics. 'The Effects of Taxes and Benefits on Household Income, Disposable Income Estimate: 2018'. 26 Feb. 2019. Accessed 27 Feb. 2019. <https://www.ons.gov.uk/peoplepopulationandcommunity/personalandhouseholdfinances/incomeandwealth/datasets/householddisposableincomeandinequality>.

RSA/Populus Universal Basic Income Survey. 27–29 July 2018. Accessed 3 Aug. 2018. <https://www.thersa.org/globalassets/pdfs/reports/rsa-populus-basic-income-polling.pdf>.

Webster, David. 'Benefit Sanctions Statistics: Universal Credit, JSA, ESA, and Income Support: February 2018'. 20 Mar. 2018. Accessed 24 July 2018. <https://suwn.files.wordpress.com/2018/03/18-02-sanctions-stats-briefing-d-webster-20-mar-2018.pdf>.

Interviews

George Aylett, 27 July 2018
Barb Jacobson, 3 Apr. 2017
Bill Jordan, 2 Aug. 2017
Stewart Lansley, 6 Aug. 2018
Ruth Lister (Baroness Lister of Burtersett), 18 July 2018
Annie Miller, 17 Apr. 2018
Tony Orhnial, 12 Oct. 2016
Anthony Painter, 28 Sept. 2017
Brendon Sewill, 14 Sept. 2016
Holly Sutherland, 6 Dec. 2018
Malcolm Torry, 30 Mar. 2017
Bill Wells, 13 Dec. 2018

Index

Note: Figures and boxes are indicated by an italic '*f*' and '*b*', respectively, following the page number.

For the benefit of digital users, indexed terms that span two pages (e.g., 52–53) may, on occasion, appear on only one of those pages.

The manufacturer's authorised representative in the EU for product safety is Oxford University Press España S.A. of el Parque Empresarial San Fernando de Henares, Avenida de Castilla, 2 – 28830 Madrid (www.oup.es/en or product.safety@oup.com). OUP España S.A. also acts as importer into Spain of products made by the manufacturer.

www.ingramcontent.com/pod-product-compliance
Lightning Source LLC
LaVergne TN
LVHW011914200926
848484LV00002B/624
9780198813262